APPROACHES TO SCHOOL MANAGEMENT

APPROACHES TO SCHOOL MANAGEMENT

A Reader

edited by
Tony Bush, Ron Glatter, Jane Goodey,
and Colin Riches

at the Open University

Harper & Row, Publishers
London
in association with the Open University Press

Harper & Row Ltd
28 Tavistock Street
London WC2E 7PN

British Library Cataloguing in Publication Data

Approaches to school management. – (Open University.
    Set books) – (Harper education series).
    1. School management and organization – Addresses,
    essays, lectures
    I. Bush, Tony   II. Series
    658′.91′371008   LB2805

    ISBN 0-06-318167-3
    ISBN 0-06-318168-1 Pbk

Typeset 10 on 12pt. VIP Plantin
by Inforum Ltd, Portsmouth
Printed and bound in Great Britain
at The Pitman Press, Bath

CONTENTS

PREFACE

This reader comprises a collection of papers published in connection with the Open University course E323, entitled 'Management and the School', which examines the concepts of educational management in the light of actual management situations and decision-making processes in schools.

Because this reader is only one part of a total learning package, it does not claim to offer a complete picture of the issues with which it deals. The editors have attempted, nevertheless, to make it as 'free-standing' as possible.

This reader is one part of an Open University integrated teaching system and the selection is therefore related to other material available to students. It is designed to evoke the critical understanding of students. Opinions expressed in it are not necessarily those of the course team or of the university.

It is not necessary to become an undergraduate of the Open University in order to take the course of which this reader is part. Further information about the course associated with this book may be obtained by writing to: The Admissions Office, The Open University, P.O. Box 48, Walton Hall, Milton Keynes, MK7 6AB.

INTRODUCTION

Management in the education service is increasingly recognized as a vital ingredient in enabling the teaching and learning process to thrive. The pupil-teacher relationship, so central to the success of our educational institutions, can be truly effective only within a sound framework. Good management is an essential precondition for that framework. This is true of central government, of the local education authorities, and of institutions of higher education. Recognition has been given to the need for effective management in these spheres increasingly within the last decade. More recently the need for good management in our schools has begun to be acknowledged. It is the aim of this reader, and the course which it serves, to heighten the level of awareness of the importance of good management within our schools. There are a number of developments which appear significant for school management in the early 1980s and which might be thought likely to dominate the educational scene throughout the decade. In the first place, the 1980s is destined to be a decade of decline for the education service, unparalleled by anything since compulsory education was first introduced. Demographic projections, based on birth figures already known, show that the number of clients of education will fall significantly during this period. The decline will be most marked in the secondary schools.

The effects of these adverse demographic trends will be exacerbated by the effects of economic stagnation or decline. Spending on the education service may well fall in proportion to student numbers and certainly the scope for protecting schools, colleges, and universities from the worst effects of falling numbers is reduced by the weakness of the British economy.

A further problem is the decline in public confidence in educational institutions. Parents, employers, and public representatives at national and local levels increasingly feel that schools especially are failing to achieve what they expect from an educational system. The fact that these expectations are diverse, conflicting, and subject to change does not protect the service from the implications of declining confidence in educational institutions. On the contrary, reduced confidence serves to reinforce the effects of demographic and economic trends. Those with the power to protect and nurture the education service can be expected to exercise that power only if they are satisfied with the products of our institutions. This in turn requires that schools should become more open and responsive to opinions expressed outside the profession instead of clinging too closely to views expressed within it.

The implications of these adverse trends for our schools are of real significance. Effective management within schools is essential if pupils and teachers alike are to be protected from the worst ravages of decline. Curriculum planning and development, desirable enough during periods of expansion, becomes fundamental as pupil and teacher numbers decline. The core curriculum and subject options have to reflect both what is basic to pupil development and also what is realistic in terms of declining staff numbers. Likewise, in-service training, always valuable to the personal development of teachers, could become vital to the well-being of schools. The only way to retain a second language, separate sciences, and some middle and upper school options may be by expanding the competence of existing staff. Specialist staff may not be replaced as pupil numbers fall.

The human relations implications of decline also serve to stretch the management skills of heads and senior staff. Teachers, and particularly junior staff, are likely to find teaching a much less congenial career in the 1980s than it was in the 1970s and 1960s. They will be able to specialize less and may find that they have fewer 'free' periods as schools strive to maintain curriculum cover with fewer staff. Above all, promotion opportunities are declining as fewer posts are advertised and above-scale points are reduced. This may well result in able young teachers remaining subordinate for many years to less able but somewhat older staff, who gained promotion in what now appear to be the 'golden' years. Frustration and reduced effectiveness are inevitable if managers fail to appreciate the problems and prepare staff accordingly.

Perhaps enough has been said to support the view that effective management in schools is central to the health and well-being of our educational system. Yet, teachers in schools have appeared until recently to have little interest in management studies. The editors believe that this reflects the nature of the material too often presented in the name of education management. Much of management theory emanates from the USA and most management studies have been based on industrial contexts. This industry-based approach to management has since been deemed 'general' management and considered applicable to all management contexts. This view has been prevalent in management departments in many British polytechnics and colleges, including those in which two of the editors have worked. That these 'general' management courses have failed to attract teachers has been attributed by some to their lack of interest in management. We consider that this apparent uninterest may be due to the failure of most management courses to recognize the very special nature of the educational context.

Schools and other educational institutions do differ sharply from industrial plants. The major differences are probably the following:

1 School objectives are much less easy to define than industrial objectives. There are no clear-cut educational equivalents to such major private sector objectives as profit maximization, output maximization, increased market share, or product diversification. Schools look rather to such vague-sounding but nevertheless important objectives as developing the personal capacity of individuals and preparation of pupils for the world of work or the next stage of education.

2 The 'raw material' of schools is human, consisting of children and adolescents. Young people cannot be processed, programmed, or manipulated as can iron ore, computer software, or crude oil. The 'production' process is built on personal relationships with all the idiosyncracy and unpredictability that implies.

3 The managers and most staff in schools are from a common professional background with shared values, training, and experience. Schools cannot be managed in the same way as factories or offices. Professionalism entitles teachers to a measure of autonomy in their key task, the teaching and learning process. It determines also that decision-making in schools cannot be organized simply on a hierar-

chical basis. Schools, more than most other organizations, have to take account of the opinions of staff before decisions are reached if they are to be implemented in an effective way.

4   The output of schools cannot be measured or evaluated in the same way as industrial output. Examination results contribute to the evaluation process at secondary level but they cannot tell the whole story and are not relevant at all in primary schools. Rather the physical, mental, and emotional development of children is the essence of the task and success or failure has to be evaluated against these vital but elusive criteria.

These differences between schools and other organizations go a long way towards explaining the limited interest shown by teachers in general management courses. They simply fail to see what it means for them. Yet, as we have sought to demonstrate, management is potentially of considerable significance for schools in the 1980s, *provided* it is based firmly on the school context. This reader, and the course it serves, is geared primarily to examining aspects of management in British schools. The articles selected largely support the view that a management course for people concerned with schools must relate to schools and their staffs and clients first and foremost.

The reader has been organized into sections which reflect different aspects within the field of school management. An important criterion for inclusion is that most articles should be set reading for the course which the reader accompanies. Another factor is the desirability of maintaining some balance between different parts of the field. The major test employed by the editors, though, is that the articles should be perceived as relevant to school management by teachers and others concerned with the education service.

Section I, 'Education Management: Overviews', consists of articles by two leading academics in this field. Baron introduces readers to many of the major sources in the field of educational administration and management, while Glatter discusses the relationship between education management and educational policy and administration. These pieces should be invaluable to readers who wish to extend their reading beyond the present volume.

Section II, 'The School and Its Environment', deals with the boundary role of the school and particularly with its autonomy and accountability in the context of the local and wider social, economic, and political environment. Pateman examines the relationship between possible forms of accountability and different social values, such as response to parental preferences and the requirements of society, which they reflect. The extract from Bacon's book draws our attention to the effects of schools in Sheffield being largely answerable to a decentralized and democratic governing body in the shape of the 'new and board system' made up of a predominantly lay group of people when the schools and the board system had to establish a new pattern of social relationships in a new situation of participation. Two extracts from a book by Becher and his colleagues deal with the accountability of the school. The authors use evidence from empirical work to develop a conceptual framework for the school's pattern of accountabilities.

Section III, 'The School as an Organization', is the major theoretical component of the reader. Landers and Myers give a very useful guide to the development of organizational and management theory. Their article deals with the different theoretical strands in a fairly conventional manner. Ideally it should be read in conjunction with Hoyle's innovatory unit in the E323 course, entitled 'The Process of Management'. T. Barr Greenfield (writing in 1974) expounds his views on how the phenomenological perspective calls into question the whole notion of conceptually distinguishing organizations from the actions, feelings, and purposes of people. Subsequent papers by Greenfield and his respondents have become more sophisticated but have not added much to the argument. Handy, in one of the few articles not based directly on educational evidence, looks at some of the intricacies of group decision-making, increasingly important in the school context. Rutter and his colleagues demonstrate the significance of the individual school to a variety of educational outcomes and point to certain organizational variables which influence these outcomes. The article by Conway reports on the relationship between the power of headteachers and the participation of subordinate teachers based on another empirical study of a limited sample of English schools. Heads in this survey appear to retain power when favours can be given or withheld, and to support participatory management where teachers are not interested in involvement or where only minimal resources are involved. Packwood's provocative article examines some of the subtle variations of management relationships in schools. Hughes, in an article based on important empirical work, examines the different demands made in schools by professional and bureaucratic imperatives and points to reasons for their often successful, if sometimes uneasy, alliance.

Section IV, 'Leadership in Schools', looks at aspects of the role of senior managers in schools. Nias analyses the responses of teachers to a variety of leadership styles employed in primary schools. Coulson argues that a less paternal approach is desirable for the primary head. Watts gives a fascinating insight into the highly participative policy-formulation and decision-making patterns employed at Countesthorpe College and analyses his own role as head within the participative framework. Todd and Dennison, in an article based on empirical work in eleven northern secondary schools, examine the changing role of the deputy head.

Section V, 'Management of the Curriculum', examines aspects of academic and pastoral provision in schools. The reading by Weston explores a number of constraints on a balanced curriculum using a detailed empirical examination of the third-year curriculum in secondary schools. She raises questions which have implications for managing the curriculum at all stages of school life. The extract from a paper by HM Inspectorate gives guidelines for timetabling for the compulsory age-groups in secondary schools. Passages from the Auld Report on William Tyndale School illustrate the problems that can occur when planning for curriculum change is inadequate. Best, Jarvis, and Ribbins take a critical look at pastoral care in comprehensive schools, using some of the insights advocated by Greenfield for their research, and this leads them to question what they call the 'conventional wisdom' of pastoral care provision given in prescriptive accounts. Johnson, in an extract based on empirical work in four outer-London boroughs, examines links between secondary schools and the welfare network.

Section VI, 'Management of Staff Development', considers aspects of personnel management in schools with particular reference to teaching staff. It includes Schmuck's presentation of the case for an 'organizational development' approach to school renewal. We then present two important 'semiofficial' documents which have greatly influenced the discussion about, and set plausible guidelines for, the professional development of teachers: the first consultative document on in-service training from the Advisory Committee on the Supply and Training of Teachers (ACSTT), and the same body's booklet on 'Making INSET Work'. We make no apology for including these, even though the climate of the 1980s may prove hostile to implementing any such framework *in toto*. At least they present a set of coherent rationales which could form the basis for policies on staff development at different levels of our system. Finally, there are extracts from March's penetrating discussion of possible content in the training of educational managers.

Section VII, 'The Management of Contraction', considers the implications for school management of falling pupil numbers and economic stagnation. Bush examines some of the problems posed by these twin threats and points to some benefits for schools. Antcliffe, Director of Education for Liverpool, examines the special problems of depopulation, unemployment, and decline in that city. This article provides the background for the case study of a Liverpool comprehensive school, featured in the E323 course. Hunter and Heighway, in an article based on empirical work, look at the impact of falling rolls on middle schools.

The inclusion, or exclusion, of any article from a reader is always a matter of judgement and the editors take full responsibility for those chosen for inclusion here. If this reader serves to disseminate knowledge and develop understanding about school management we shall consider our selection vindicated.

SECTION I

EDUCATION MANAGEMENT: OVERVIEWS

CHAPTER 1.1

RESEARCH IN EDUCATIONAL ADMINISTRATION IN BRITAIN*
GEORGE BARON

During the past decade there has been a substantial increase of research activity in many varied aspects of educational administration. To provide an overview of the whole field is a task which is as impossible to achieve as it is fascinating to engage in. But an overview has to be attempted, if subsequent discussions in this seminar are to be based on a commonly available stock of knowledge. This then will be my first endeavour.

I shall go on to say what I consider to be the main characteristics of the research done up to the present.

Against the background thus established, I shall examine some main areas of debate and controversy.

Finally, I shall set out the various positions which may be taken in approaching research in the hope that in so doing I can throw light on the especial role of the British Educational Administration Society.

The scope and content of research in educational administration

It is not my purpose here to enclose what follows within a carefully delimited definition of educational administration and to set out the relationship between the various emphases on the behavioural, the economic, the managerial, and the political which can already be identified within the field. Nor shall I rehearse the possible contributions of the social science and other disciplines in its further development. These are tasks I have attempted elsewhere and there is a substantial amount of writing seeking to

* Paper given at the seminar on Research in Educational Administration held by the British Educational Administration Society, University of Birmingham, March 1979.

clarify the significance of the terms 'administration' and 'management'.[1]

In this chapter I shall extend my consideration to all, or at least most, of the themes and topics which appear in references to educational administration. Such references are scattered in a number of sources. These include books and articles dealing with general educational theory or with specific themes such as curriculum development or the education of the handicapped, lists of theses and dissertations, and reports of complete work or of work in progress compiled by research foundations and funding bodies.[2] In addition there is a growing amount of factual survey material collected by professional associations, unions, and voluntary associations.[3]

In so far as there is any systematic ordering of this material it is in topic form, as in the Howell[4] and Coulson[5] bibliographies, rather than in terms of subject disciplines or research methodologies. I propose to adopt a broad classification which will reveal the main themes under which recent and current researches can be grouped. In no sense, of course, can my treatment be exhaustive and no doubt opinions will differ about my choice of examples to illustrate my argument.

Leadership[6] and the internal organization of schools and other educational institutions

The first theme with which I wish to deal is that of leadership in the school or college, and in particular the role of the head or principal. It is within the individual institution that educational and administrative considerations are most closely interwoven and it is within the role of the head or principal that their relationship can be at its most sensitive. The form of providing agencies at national, federal, regional, or local level may be highly diverse, as may be also the nature of the relationships between teachers, officials, students, parents, and community, but leadership within the institution and its internal organization are the channels through which other elements in the process must express themselves in pedagogical terms. That this is generally realized is shown, I would argue, by the place occupied by the study of the principalship in North American literature and by the attention now being given to the training of principals in countries as far apart, in terms of geography and culture, as Sweden and Singapore.

In this country we have made a beginning, but only a beginning, in studies of the position of the head. Hughes[7] has drawn on role theory to relate the professional and administrative aspects of the head's task and Cohen[8] has examined heads' views of their role as modified by the nature and size of their schools. There is also a study of the development and selection of secondary school headteachers by Bispham[9] and the analysis by Bernbaum[10] of a national sample of secondary school heads in terms of their social origins, experience, values, and guiding ideas. The position of the deputy head in the secondary school has been studied by Burnham[11] and this study was followed by an examination of the influence of school size on the deputy head's role by McIntyre[12] and by another of the deputy head in the primary school by Coulson.[13] It is surprising, in view of the substantial amount of discursive and prescriptive writing on the theme of the head,[14] that, apart from the studies named and a few others, it has attracted relatively little attention from researchers. The neglect of the headteacher position in the infant and the junior school is particularly marked.

Studies in school organization are also sparse. Here again there is much discussion and accounts of current practice, but little in the way of major research save that contained in a series of studies conducted by the National Foundation for Educational Research.[15] But there is a wide-ranging survey by Halsall[16] which also includes North American material and the highly distinctive study by Richardson[17] of interrelationships within a single school. The handbook by Lyons[18] differs from others of similar purpose by being based on empirical studies and points the way to the translation of research findings into practical terms.

Closely related to the study of school organization viewed in terms of structure and roles is the growing and important area of the administration of the curriculum. Curriculum studies have, in recent years, come to constitute a major field in their own right and increasingly they are extending their range, as indeed they must, to take into account the political and administrative context. A pioneer study is that by Marten Shipman,[19] *Inside a Curriculum Project,* which gives a microcosmic view of curriculum change in a small group of schools. Also falling within the territory of educational administration as well as of curriculum studies is *The Dissemination of Curriculum Development,* by Ruddock and Kelly.[20] It is in this context too that I would place the ongoing work at the University of Bristol School of Education described by Bolam in his paper at this seminar.

Both general school organization and the administration of the curriculum in particular are now, of course, being greatly influenced by the wave of interest in evaluation and the related concern with accountability. The Assessment of Performance Unit[21] signalled a new interest in government circles in monitoring the work of the schools and in developing, through research, sophisticated techniques and tests to make this possible. Last summer a substantial programme in studies in accountability in education was announced by the Social Science Research Council. This programme is making grants totalling £200,000 available to encourage studies seeking to clarify such concepts as democracy, professional responsibility, and parental rights; to promote legal studies in the powers and rights of the various agencies and groups concerned with the provision of education; and to make possible studies in policy formation and implementation.[22]

The further itemization of research areas could, if space permitted, be extended to embrace such distinctive fields as special education, adult education, and the education of the young worker. In all of these, the translation of policy into administrative action is attracting increasing attention.

Government of educational institutions

A clearly defined area of research has emerged, as a result of the increased interest in the government of schools, further education institutions, and universitites. The first study to emerge in the schools field was my own, with D.A. Howell, which resulted from my somewhat idiosyncratic concern with the (at the time) neglected existence of school governing and managing bodies coinciding, by happy chance, with the pending reform of local government.[23] It is unfortunate that a similar research survey has not been carried out into developments in the government of further education institutions since the Weaver Report. There is, however, a well-designed study being made of the school councils set up in Scotland following the Local Government (Scotland) Act, 1973.[24] This is an interesting and important exercise which traces in detail the action taken in every region in Scotland in response to legislation and government action. There is every reason for a study on similar lines to be made in England and Wales in respect to whatever changes result from the forthcoming Education Act.[25] Research on a countrywide basis could then be followed by case studies of individual authorities, of the kind presented by Bacon[26] in his detailed examination of school government in Sheffield and its decade of reform. It is interesting to note that a study has been made of school councils in Australia[27] and that a major project is under way in Canada to examine public involvement in educational decision-making at all levels.[28]

In view of the significance attached to local education authorities in England and Wales and to the regional authorities in Scotland the amount of work done on their internal structures and their activities is disappointing. In the United States and Canada there are a very large number of studies of school boards and of their functions and membership. Here the field is only just being opened up, through such studies as that by David[29] on local education officers as an occupational group; by Greenhalgh and Booth[30] on local education officers as an occupational group; and by Bolam[31] and others on the functions of local education authority advisory services. Individual local education authorities were studied some years ago by Peschek and Brand,[32] who dealt with Reading and West Ham; Leicester has been the subject of research theses by both Brand[33] and Mander;[34] and there is a historical account by Gosden and Sharp[35] of the superseded West Riding local education authority. A more general and very well-informed study of politics and policy-making in local education authorities is provided by Jennings,[36] an American student of local politics in England, and there is the substantial and closely researched examination of the local allocation of resources by Byrne.[37] Resources and particularly their allocation is also the subject of a major project being carried out in the University of Sussex.[38] There is need for further comparative studies across a substantial number of authorities of both pre-Maud and post-Maud committee structures, officer roles, and community relations. Equally needed are studies comparing English and Welsh authorities and Scottish authorities. The advantage, for research purposes, of having two major and distinctive systems of educational administration in England and Wales on the one hand and Scotland on the other continues to be unrecognized.[39]

In the main, energies devoted to the studies of local education authorities have been directed to the reorganization of secondary education, of which the most scholarly is that by Saran.[40] This topic features largely in several of the studies already mentioned and is a popular theme for theses and dissertations.[41]

A new factor in the situation, as far as local education authorities are concerned, is that the need for research or at least for scrutinizing some aspects of present practice is being felt by education officers themselves. Thus the Society of Education Officers has published a study, *Management in the Education Service*,[42] which looks at programme structures and objectives and resource allocation and management in four authorities. The society also commissioned a short-term empirical investigation of the reactions of chief education officers to the coming of corporate management.[43]

Research studies of how the Department of Education and Science and the Scottish Education Department are structured, staffed, and shaped to meet new needs have not been undertaken, although there is a substantial amount of report material which has been brought together for governmental purposes.[44] Still less can it be said that research as such has been carried out into the present-day inspectorate in either country although, as in the case of the departments, there is a substantial literature of analysis and comment.[45]

Teacher and other associations

Beginnings have been made in the study of teacher associations which, together with the departments and the local authorities and their associations, constitute the main framework within which educational policies and their execution are determined. Manzer opened up this area in his *Teachers and Politics*[46] and this study was followed by those of Roy[47] and Coates,[48] whilst Kogan[49] has carried out a far-ranging analysis of the major interest groups involved in the decision-making process at both national and local levels. The field is a tempting one, with such topics to be explored as the changing roles of the local authority associations, the consequences for the teacher unions of TUC affiliation, and the rising power of unions of which nonteaching staff are members. There is certainly need for studies of strikes and other forms of industrial action by teachers, both because of their significance in delimiting many areas of administrative action and as elements in the wider arena of industrial relations.

More generally, the greatly increased weight of legislation (e.g., the Health and Safety at Work Act, 1974; the Contracts of Employment Act, 1972; the Employment Protection Act, 1975; the Sex Discrimination Act, 1975; the Race Relations Act, 1976) have already revealed far-reaching implications for education. Furthermore, complaints against local education authorities can now be investigated by a Commissioner for Local Administration (Ombudsman). A new factor is a European presence in the shape of the European Court of Human Rights which has shown interest in the use of corporal punishment in our schools and in the teaching of the mother tongue to immigrants. In short, the whole area of the law relating to education needs to be systematically explored and studied in terms of the consequences of recent trends for our administrative structures and practices.

Education in its wider social and administrative settings

The relationship between school and community has long been one which has lent itself to exhortation and general discussion. Specific areas have attracted political controversy, notably social class influences on education and education in deprived areas. Studies, too, have been made of the problems of immigrants and other minority groups.[50] It is work in these areas which demonstrates the difficulty of defining what is to be classified as 'administrative' for my purpose here. Researches into the causes of educational deprivation and handicap are clearly of great general interest for those concerned with fashioning policy and giving it expression in administrative action; but a line has to be drawn somewhere between such studies and those which direct themselves at least in part to the specifically administrative role. A beginning has been made in the examination of the school welfare service by Macmillan,[51] but otherwise there seem to be no research studies made of the various groups of nonteaching staff in the education service whose numbers and importance have increased so greatly in recent years.

Research into the administration of higher and further education

In higher and further education there has been, certainly since the publication of the Robbins Report, with its substantial research appendices, a constant flow of descriptive, analytical, expository, and polemical writing and also extensive statistical surveys of student numbers, qualifications gained, and financial costs. An appreciable amount of this effort has gone into the examination of major policy decisions (such as that which led to the introduction of the 'binary' system) or of social class influences on student recruitment. For some ten years much work was done by the Higher Education Research Unit of the London School of Economics,[52] which was particularly concerned with problems of higher education and highly qualified manpower and which extended its range to the education system as a whole in some of its published studies.[53]

To identify writing in this field bearing on the administrative as distinct from the economic or statistical aspects of higher and further education is a difficult task. But studies with a substantial administrative content include that on university government by Moodie and Eustace,[54] the work of Burgess and Pratt on colleges of technology and the polytechnics,[55] and the edited collection of papers by Lomax on the education of teachers.[56] These and other studies utilize research findings from a wide range of sources, including the weighty appendices of the Robbins, Franks, and Murray Reports,[57] and the statistics emanating from government departments, the University Grants Committee, and other agencies. They also draw on a considerable amount of comment, criticism, and minor research reported in such journals as the *Times Educational Supplement* and the *New Universities Quarterly*. A major piece of work, now being brought up to date by its author, is Berdahl's study of the University Grants Committee.[58] Other research studies are Taylor's study of teacher education[59] and Howell's examination of the coming of the B.Ed. degree.[60] Studies for higher degrees range over a wide field. Several deal with the economics of higher education and particularly with its cost-effectiveness.[61] Others deal with resource allocation[62] and with issues of structure and government.[63]

Operational research at school system level[64]

Any survey of developing areas of research in educational administration would be incomplete without mention being made of the detailed statistical studies essential for the maintenance and improvement of large school systems. Such studies, in some form or another, are carried out by government departments and local education authorities, and also by the Schools Council and examination boards. In more specific form they are found in the context of the Local Government Operational Research Unit[65] which has, since its inception in 1965, made studies in pupil population forecasting, in school transport costs, and in computer-assisted timetabling.

The Inner London Education Authority has its own Research and Statistics Group which has made quantitative studies of school population projections and sixth-form patterns, truancy and nonattendance, and of the construction and use of priority indices of the in-service training and of the induction of probationary teachers.[66] Somewhat similar studies are being carried out in other local education authorities.[67]

Management development

Finally, I think that we should bring very much to the forefront of our minds the major thrust in educational administration at the present time. This is the effort being made to improve management effectiveness and to do this by staff development programmes which include carefully constructed courses built up from case studies and field experiences, and exercises based on the needs of individual course members. By its nature much of the exploratory work being done in polytechnics, in some local education authority centres and others such as the Further Education Staff College, does not easily fit into the accepted categories of academic research. Yet, because it is advancing into unknown and problematic territories, in which the guidelines of established disciplines and methodologies are soon found inadequate, it can constitute research of a high order. It depends upon intensive and exacting study of actual management situations in local education authorities, schools, and colleges, the laborious compiling of records, and the utilization of whatever is of use from the social and mathematical sciences. Glatter[68] has given an account of work of this kind in connection with a programme financed by the Calouste Gulbenkian Foundation and, with Piper, subsequently described the Staff Development in Universities Programme, financed by the University Grants Committee. There has, as yet, been no comprehensive presentation of the developmental work done in this area in the several polytechnics and other institutions which run their own or CNAA-validated programmes. There have, however, been a number of dissertations, one of which, by Bernard Baron,[69] has recently been published.

Characteristics of research in educational administration

1   Educational administration, as a field of research, has very ill-defined boundaries. It can be taken to embrace planning, economics, and the politics of education; and also substantive areas such as the administration of the curriculum or the recruitment and supply of teachers. But central to it, at least in the North American context, is the study of the behaviour of those who carry out administrative functions. Only isolated studies in this area (among them, those of Richardson, Shipman, and Tipton,[70] throwing light on individual and group motivations) have so far appeared in Britain. In the main, attention has been directed away from the dynamics of interpersonal and intergroup relationships towards the structure and functioning of institutions, resource allocation and use, and policy-making and its implementation.

2   There has been little funding of research in educational administration from governmental or other sources, but there is increasing attention being paid to *how* research findings in curriculum development or educational

technology are to be put into practice. Projects in such areas are thus tending to produce spin-offs for educational administration. In addition, inquiry into policy-making at national level has been encouraged by critical comment by the OECD[71] and at local level by the after-effects of local government reorganization. But there has so far been no massive and continued research effort on the scale made possible by the Kellogg Foundation grants in the United States and Canada.[72] Save in the case of studies by the National Foundation for Educational Research and, for a time, some studies of the Higher Education Research Unit of the London School of Economics, each project has stood in isolation and has operated through *ad hoc* teams recruited from young graduates in the social sciences, teachers on secondment, retired heads, or education officers. Indeed, most of the published research dealing specifically with educational administration has been the result of individual part-time work by graduate students in teaching or administrative posts or by junior academic staff. Under present conditions, such men and women, although virtually our only source of research expertise, have little prospect of being able to carry out further and more advanced work.

3   Factors determining the choice of research topics are varied. Governmentally funded research tends to be supportive of projects which can help in throwing light on immediate and urgent problems such as those associated with comprehensive secondary education and with resource use, evaluative processes, and 'accountability'. And generally, and this is true of the National Foundation for Educational Research and the Scottish Council for Research in Education as well as the independent foundations, interest centres on pedagogical rather than on administrative issues. For this reason we owe a debt to visitors from North America (such as Manzer, Berdahl and Jennings), Australia, and elsewhere, who can take a broader view of our concerns and whose interests lie in policy-analysis and the working of our institutions.

4   Despite what has been argued so far, there are positive aspects of the present situation. There is a quickening of interest in the Department of Education and Science and in the Scottish Education Department in research designed to improve practice, an interest which, as has been seen, extends to local education authorities also. The old reliance on custom and use has been replaced by a willingness to accept that research should be able to contribute to better decision-making and administrative action in educa-

tion just as it contributes to improvement in other activities of modern life. But there is very genuine uncertainty concerning what research can actually achieve, in which areas rare resources should be deployed, and by what means research findings can be translated into practice.

Problem areas

Rather than attempt to answer directly the questions just raised, I think it may be helpful in structuring discussion to concentrate attention on debates in which we each individually have to take up positions. These I would characterize as the academic/practitioner debate, the theory/practice debate, the systems theory/phenomenology debate, and the relationship of educational administration to the social science disciplines.

The academic/practitioner debate

The conflict between academic and practitioner arises from each party necessarily inhabiting a different universe. As the researcher develops his approach to his problem, no matter how 'practical' its orientation, he draws on material and ideas from outside the immediate situation to help him in his analysis and his explanations. By so doing he distances himself from the administrator who, when subsequently reading the research report, is alienated by what appears to be irrelevant and extraneous material: furthermore, from his experience he brings to his reading a multitude of questions stimulated by the research but not answered by it. Discussing this conflict, Taylor writes:

> The roots of the problem lie in the fact that the knowledge about education that is possessed by all the people who are labelled teachers, administrators, inspectors, researchers and so forth, is to a large and increasing extent *role specific knowledge*.[73]

This kind of conflict is not between different kinds of people, or even between different types of mind: it is a situational conflict, which occurs even if the researcher is an experienced administrator and the reader a career academic concerned with a practical problem which is the subject of the research. Moreover, we each have, or may have as individuals, two or more types of role-specific knowledge: for example, that which follows from being a practising teacher, that which follows from being a student of curriculum development, and that which follows from being a parent whose children are facing school-leaving examinations. Conflict of this kind cannot be resolved, although awareness of its nature may enable it to be contained and lived with.

Other problems arise which can be avoided by greater competence or goodwill on the part of those concerned. Shipman, in his capacity as a research worker with the Inner London Education Authority, wrote:

> From within local government the research enterprise based in academia seems to deliver the wrong goods, at the wrong time, without an invoice. It also produces conclusions about education that are subject to gross misinterpretations. The net harmful impact arises from the combination of failure to help in the solution of practical problems, of the promotion of dubious theoretical notions and in the recommendations whose implementations are beyond the dreams of even optimistic administrators.[74]

In reply to this, the comment by Brian Simon on the role of educational research in general is apposite:

> The real issue is whether scientists are to operate as scientists, educationists as educationists, researchers as researchers; or whether all are to become service personnel, waiting cap in hand for orders in response to which appropriate methods will be sorted out to produce acceptable results or conclusions.[75]

The tension is further increased, of course, when it is a governmental or public body which is the funding agency. The argument put forward some years ago by Lord Rothschild[76] takes the hard line that the funding agency says what it wants and the researcher works within a defined brief. Against this, there is the broader view that research in the social sciences necessarily draws on concepts and knowledge of which the sponsors are not aware and which modify the content of the problem as work progresses.[77]

It is, I think, helpful that the Department of Education and Science is now clarifying its position, by expressing its concern with policy-related research, by identifying specific topics within agreed areas, and by seeking early reconciliation between the interests of the parties involved.[78] Such a stand makes possible a parallel clarification of positions by those primarily concerned with research and not directly concerned with policy matters. It is here that the Social Science Research Council has a major role to play and it is to be hoped that this seminar will assist it in establishing the place of educational administration within the total field of educational research.

The theory/practice debate

To what extent should research in educational administration, whether serving the purposes of the practitioner or the academic, seek to be theory-based? This is the first question which confronts the nonsocial scientist who encounters for the first time the highly organized teaching and research programmes of American, Canadian, and Australian universities. There the place of 'theory' in educational administration is accepted, though its content and its uses and abuses are vigorously debated: here there is still, in so many quarters, a contemptuous dismissing of any study going beyond the collection of opinions and facts.

In a recent book Rosamund Thomas has boldly contrasted the American and British approaches to administrative studies. She argues that, in Britain,

> doctrines [of administration] remained essentially a philosophy and not a theory of administration, embodying description, subjective attitudes and explanations rather than rigorous, systematic analysis.[79]

On the other hand, she argues, in the United States respect for the expert in administration has led to more attention being paid to academics and more attempts being made to theorize, with the result that administration has advanced 'from miscellaneous description to an integrated body of knowledge'.[80]

The absence of native-born theory in this country and of anything approaching 'an integrated body of knowledge' explains the fascination felt for the work of North American theoreticians as a source for conceptual frameworks into which schemes of research can be neatly fitted. This has dangers, if it results in our limiting topics to those which can be so treated, or in our setting out, once a problem has been identified, to unearth a theory to give it academic respectability. Certainly, the understanding of the researcher should be fortified by a thorough critical acquaintance with reading in the works of the major theoreticians in his field. But it would be unfortunate if it came to be a convention that each piece of work must be related to a specific theory or theories. Moreover, as Hughes[81] has pointed out, research studies describing and analysing current administrative practice do not necessarily require highly sophisticated theoretical underpinnings to be of value.

There is a way of reducing unproductive conflict and of avoiding the reification of theory as being an entity or entities having some kind of existence independent of the world of real events. Glaser and Strauss[82] advocate the notion of *grounded theory*, by which they mean the gradual generation and testing of explanatory concepts as a piece of research proceeds. The emphasis is on theorizing rather than on theory. Their approach means, of course, that the researcher is not only knowledgeable about existing theories but that he has a capacity for theorizing. It follows that the training or self-education of the researcher needs to be broad and diffuse: the aim of his reading of theory is to nourish his powers to perceive and to relate, rather than to lead him to work within the confines of the formulated perspectives of others.

The systems theory/phenomenology debate

To some extent the issue I have just attempted to present has bearing on the far-reaching debate which followed Greenfield's paper in the 1974 International Intervisitation Programme. This debate has been conducted with warmth by many better fitted than myself. I refer to it because it bears so intimately on the uses of theory. One charge made against Greenfield's paper is that he has failed to provide a viable alternative paradigm to that provided by systems theory; another is that he has not shown how research can emerge from a phenomenological perspective. Both charges seem to me to sidestep his argument because implicitly, if not explicitly, 'research' and 'paradigm', in their taken-for-granted meanings, are within the world of systems theory and the positivist approach. To me, Greenfield's paper made its impact not so much because it put forward a 'phenomenological perspective' as an alternative to 'systems theory', but rather because it was a first frontal attack on the latter and particularly on the 'emphasis which much of social science places upon quantification, more complex mathematical models, and bigger number crunchers in the shape of better and faster computers'.[84] This explains, to me at least, why Greenfield incurred the wrath of the 'establishment' of research in educational administration within which, at Stanford, Chicago, and Alberta, hypothesis-formulation has been a prevailing orthodoxy; it also explains the welcome accorded to his argument in Britain by academics uneasy with the formidable research apparatus of the North Americans and reluctant to acknowledge its achievements, and by practitioners happy to seize on any vindication of intuitive judgement.

Educational administration and the social sciences

Some years ago, in my contribution to *Educational Administration and the Social Sciences*,[85] I sought to show how the latter could contribute to our field of study. My thinking was very much influenced by my contacts with American and Canadian scholars and with the work of Professor William Walker in Australia; and it was motivated by the *political* need to legitimate the study of educational administration in the university world in this country. Certainly, at the University of London Institute of Education, educational studies were and are regarded largely as the philosophy of education, the sociology of education, the economics of education, and the psychology of education. Difficulty then arises in arguing the case for *fields* of study, such as curriculum development, comparative education, and educational administration: in this context it is necessary and appropriate to stress the contribution of the 'disciplines'. I do not wish to quarrel with the position I then took up, although I think I would now incorporate within it the idea of 'squeezing' the disciplines, which Glatter took over from Richard Snyder.[86] But, when it comes to *research* in educational administration, I am much more aware than I was before of the problems which arise when subject specialists are recruited into the field after their primary allegiance has been established. I think that Brian Simon (in the paper already quoted) expresses my concern more adequately than I could myself in a passage relating to general research in education. He writes:

> The study of education has manifestly suffered from subordination to disparate modes of approach and methodologies deriving from fields quite other than education which have simply been transferred into the educational sphere and which, once there, have tended to maintain their distinctive languages and approaches, or pursue their own ends.

Later, he argues that:

> If he [the researcher] starts from the position established in a particular discipline with corresponding norms of its own, the research is likely to be primarily directed to adding to the capital of that discipline. Conducted by methods evolved within its confines it may well have a direct connection with education only insofar as use has been made in the given way of educational materials.[87]

In Britain, because of our high degree of specialization in university studies and the strength of the allegiance of the scholar to his initial discipline, the dangers Simon suggests are very real. But I see no justification for throwing up the barricades, even if that were possible. On the contrary, we need to seek to enlarge the field of endeavour so that all can play their part, no matter what their earlier academic affiliations. If this can be done, it may be possible to resolve some of the issues which I have put before you in this chapter.

Research for understanding, research for policy development, research into administrative structure and process, evaluative research

What are the various positions from which we can view research? I can identify four, but others may no doubt occur to members of this seminar and readers of this chapter.

1   Research for understanding

This, I suppose, is the position of the historian, who is concerned with explaining the past in terms comprehensible to the present. It is also the position of the anthopologist, concerned to explain in terms of his own culture the practices of primitive peoples. The results of such labours may be of use to the politician, the administrator, or the professional worker, but this is not their main purpose. The audience for research of this kind is composed of those with similar or closely related interests, able to cope with highly technical and esoteric language.

2   Policy-related research

I am indebted to Brian Kay for this term, which he uses for research promoting 'the formulation of national policies on a more secure foundation of knowledge, and of monitoring and evaluating the implementation of such policies'.[88] Such research requires specialized knowledge combined with a readiness to work within the frameworks established by political and administrative practicalities. Much work on resource allocation falls within this category.

Policy-related research may precede and help in policy-formulation or it may monitor the working out of policies already being put into operation. In either case it is expensive, it is likely to take time, and it requires considerable adjustment of attitudes and working habits by both the academics and the administrators involved. Its immediate audience is relatively small, since by design it is directed at the limited numbers concerned with policy-making at national or local level.

3   Research into administrative structure and process

In putting forward this category I am very much aware of the difficulty of distinguishing usefully between 'policy' and 'administration'. But it seems to me to be essential to give identity to that vast area of research concerned with the performance of administrative functions and roles, whether these be in relation to running a school, a college, a department, or a supporting service; or with the setting up and maintenance of structures for governing institutions and regulating their relationships with their environments.

This is the area in which I would argue that the maximum effort should be made at the present time; and it is also the area in which all members of the Society are concerned in one way or another.

4   Evaluative research

Evaluation is necessarily a part of any research project. But what I have in mind here is research which is able to stand outside the world of the policy-maker and the administrator and view their intentions and their activities from a variety of political, social, and cultural standpoints. It seems to me a main vehicle for research of this kind should be comparative studies, in which scholars and administrators from elsewhere would share in substantial projects in this country. A network of Commonwealth and European agencies exists to foster such exploration and we have our own affiliations with the Commonwealth Council for Educational Administration and the European Forum.

I have spent a little time in presenting these very tentative categories of research for consideration because I feel that it is important for this seminar to consider what should be its focus for the future activities and indeed for the efforts of the British Educational Administration Society in the research field. Clearly, we are interested and supportive of all four categories; indeed interest in the one presupposes at least some measure of involvement with the others, since they are interrelated. My own conclusion, however, is that we should at this time pay particular attention to that which I have termed 'research into administrative structure and process'. It is in this area that most of the problems which beset those responsible for the conduct of our educational institutions and those with similar responsibilities in other countries lie. It is also a major aim of this Society to advance the *practice* of educational administration.

Notes and references

1. I am referring here to two of my earlier papers, 'The Study of Educational Administration in England', in Baron, George and Taylor, William (eds) *Educational Administration and the Social Sciences*, Athlone Press, 1969, and 'Approaches to Educational Administration as a Field of Study, Research and Application', in Hughes, Meredydd (ed) *Administering Education: International Challenge*, Athlone Press, 1974. For a lucid discussion of the distinctions which may be drawn between 'administration' and 'management' see Open University Course 321, *Management in Education*, Unit 1, *Management in Education – Dissimilar or Congruent?* Open University Press, 1976.
2. See Association of Special Libraries and Information Bureaux (ASLIB): *Index to theses accepted for higher degrees in the universities of Great Britain and Ireland* (published annually); Department of Education and Science, List 1 *Current Educational Research Projects supported by the Department*, 1978, and List VII *Research Projects supported financially by the Department which have been completed*, 1978; National Foundation for Educational Research in the United Kingdom, *Register of Educational Research in the United Kingdom*, Vol 1, 1973–1976, Vol 2, 1976–1977; Social Science Research Council, *Research* supported by the Council, 1978; and Cave, Cyril and Maddison, Pamela, *A survey of recent research in special education*, NFER Publishing Co., 1978.
3. Notably in the journals and publications of the Advisory Centre for Education, the Educational Institute of Scotland, the National Association of Governors and Managers, the National Association of Schoolmasters/Union of Women Teachers, the National Association of Teachers in Further and Higher Education, and, latterly, the Society of Education Officers.
4. Howell, D.A., *A Bibliography of Educational Administration in the United Kingdom*, NFER Publishing Co., 1978.
5. Coulson, Alan A., *School Administration and Management: a select annotated bibliography*, Flag Publications, Hull, 1975.
6. The term 'leadership' may, in this context, jar on the sensitive British ear, but it is widely used in the literature in Europe as well as in the United States, Canada, Australia, and elsewhere.
7. Hughes, M.G., *The role of the secondary head*, Ph.D. thesis, University of Wales, 1972.
8. Cohen, L., *Conceptions of headteachers concerning their role*, Ph.D. thesis, University of Keele, 1970.
9. Bispham, G.R., *Development and selection of secondary school headteachers*, University of Leicester, 1975.
10. Bernbaum, G., 'Headmasters and schools: some preliminary findings', *Sociological Review*, 1973, and 'The role of the head', in Peters, R.S. *The Role of*

the Head, Routledge & Kegan Paul, 1976.

11. Burnham, Peter S., 'The Deputy Head', chapter XII in Allen, Bryan (ed) *Headship in the 1970s*, Blackwell, 1968.

12. McIntyre, W., *Size of School as a Factor in the Role of the Deputy Head*, M.Sc. thesis, University of Bradford, 1972.

13. Coulson, A.A., *The Deputy Head in the Primary School: Conceptions of Heads and Deputy Heads*, M.Ed. thesis, University of Hull, 1974.

14. For example, Edmonds, E.L., *The First Headship*, Blackwell, 1968; Barry, F.H. and Tye, F., *Running a School*, Temple Smith, 1972.

15. In particular the two reports (ed T.G. Monks) of the NFER Comprehensive Education Project, *Comprehensive Education in England and Wales: a survey of schools and their organization*, 1968, and *Comprehensive Education in Action*, 1970, both published by the NFER.

16. Halsall, Elizabeth, *The Comprehensive School: guidelines for the reorganisation of secondary education*, Pergamon Press, 1973.

17. Richardson, Elizabeth, *The Teacher, the School and the Task of Management*, Heinemann, 1973.

18. Lyons, Geoffrey, *Heads' Tasks: A Handbook of Secondary Administration*, NFER Publishing Co, 1976.

19. Shipman, Marten, *Inside a Curriculum Project: a case study in the process of curriculum change*, Methuen, 1974.

20. Ruddock, Jean and Kelly, Peter, *The Dissemination of Curriculum Development*, NFER Publishing Co, 1976.

21. The work of the unit is briefly described in *Assessing the Performance of Pupils*, DES Report on Education, Number 93, August, 1978.

22. SSRC press release, *Accountability in Education*, 30 June, 1978.

23. See Royal Commission on Local Government in England: Research Studies No 6: *School Management and Government*, HMSO, 1968, and Baron, G. and Howell, D.A., *The Government and Management of Schools*, Athlone Press, 1974.

24. This study, supported by a grant from the Scottish Education Department, is being carried out in the Department of Education, University of Glasgow. An interim report has been published, *Foundation Facts about Scottish School Councils*, 1977.

25. The omens are favourable, as the department has already made a substantial grant to the Open University for the preparation of a course for school governors and to carry out research into the ways in which the course is used and its effectiveness.

26. Bacon, William, *Public Accountability and the Schooling System: a sociology of school board democracy*, Harper & Row, 1978.

27. Fitzgerald, R.T., et al., *Participation in Schools? Five Case Studies*, Australian Council for Educational Research, 1976.

28. This project is being carried out by the Canadian Education Association and is particularly concerned with public involvement in decision-making at school level. No reports are yet available.

29. David, Miriam, *Reform, Reaction and Resources: the Three Rs of Educational*

Planning, NFER Publishing Co, 1977.
30. Greenhalgh, V.C., *Local educational administrators, 1870–1974: the emergence and growth of a profession*, Ph.D. thesis, Leeds, 1974, and Booth, H., *The chief education officer in English education, 1870–1968*, M.Ed. thesis Manchester, 1971.
31. Bolam, R., Smith, G., and Canter, H., *Local Education Authority Advisers and Educational Innovation*, University of Bristol School of Education, 1976.
32. Peschek, David and Brand, J., *Politics and Policies in Secondary Education*, London School of Economics, 1966.
33. Brand, J., *The Implementation of the 1944 Act in Leicester: a case study in administrative relationships*, Ph.D. thesis, London, 1962.
34. Mander, J.A.H., *Freedom and constraint in a local education authority*, Ph.D. thesis, University of Leicester, 1975.
35. Gosden, P.H.J.H. and Sharp, P.R., *The Development of an Education Authority*, Ph.D. thesis, University of Leicester, 1975.
36. Jennings, Robert E., *Education and Politics: policy-making in local education authorities*, Batsford, 1977.
37. Byrne, Eileen M., *Planning and Educational Inequality: a study of the rationale of resource allocation*, NFER Publishing Co., 1974. See also Open University Course E321, *Management in Education* Unit 16, *The Rationale of Resource Allocation*.
38. This project, which is under the direction of Professor Eric Briault, was set up 'to examine the curriculum and associated management problems and to set out the options open to local education authorities and secondary schools'.
39. But the way has been cleared for such comparative studies by the stimulating *Patterns of Education in the British Isles*, by Robert Bell and Nigel Grant, Allen and Unwin, 1977.
40. Saran, Rene, *Policy-Making in Secondary Education: a case study*, Oxford University Press, 1973.
41. For example, Wilkie, J., *The reorganisation of secondary education in the county of Sutherland following the publication of SED circular No. 600*, M. Litt. thesis, University of Aberdeen, 1974; Marsh, C.A.A., *The reorganisation of education in the County of Worcestershire, with special reference to 9–13 middle schools*, M.Ed. thesis, University of Birmingham, 1972; White, P.T., *The reorganisation of secondary school education in Bath and Southampton*, M.Phil. thesis, University of Southampton, 1975.
42. Society of Education Officers, *Management in the Education Service: Challenge and Response*. Published by the society, n.d.
43. Winter, G.A., *The position of the education service following local government reorganisation*, Society of Education Officers, 1977.
44. As, for example, in the Tenth Report from the Expenditure Committee, Session 1975–1976, *Policy-Making in the Department of Education and Science*, HMSO, 1976.
45. As, for example, in the Report from the Select Committee on Education and Science 1967–1968, Part I, Her Majesty's Inspectorate (England and Wales), HMSO, 1968. It should be noted that no attempt has been made in this paper to

bring within its scope the growing number of historical studies of educational policy and administration (although some examples have been cited: Greenhalgh and Booth, Gosden and Sharp). Such studies have become increasingly attractive to historians with the coming of easier access to the twentieth-century file material of government departments and local authorities. A major study is *Education in the Second World War: a study in policy and administration*, Methuen, 1976.

46. Manzer, R.A., *Teachers and Politics: the role of the National Union of Teachers in the making of national education policy in England and Wales since 1944*, Manchester University Press, 1970. This is a much abbreviated version of a Harvard Ph.D. thesis for which the field work was done in this country. Unfortunately, chapters of the original thesis showing how Manzer relates his empirical data to Beer-Eckstein interest-group theory are not included in the book.

47. Roy, W.R., *The Teachers' Union: aspects of the policy and organisation of the National Union of Teachers*, Schoolmaster Publishing Co., 1968.

48. Coates, R.D., *Teachers' Unions and Interest Group Politics: a study in the behaviour of organised teachers in England and Wales*, Cambridge University Press, 1972.

49. Kogan, Maurice, *Educational Policy-Making: a study of interest groups in Parliament*, 1975.

50. E.g., Townsend, H.E.R., *Immigrant Pupils in England: the L.E.A. Response*, NFER Publishing Co., 1971, and Townsend, H.E.R. and Brittan, E.M., *Organisation in Multiracial Schools*, NFER Publishing Co., 1972.

51. Macmillan, Keith, *Education Welfare: strategy and structure*, Longman, 1977.

52. The Higher Education Research Unit was set up in 1964 and continued until 1974. Its successor was the Centre for the Economics of Education, which gave way in 1977 to the Centre for Labour Economics.

53. For example, Peacock, Alan, Glennerster, Howard, and Lavers, Robert, *Educational Finance: its sources and uses in the United Kingdom*, and Blackstone, Tessa, *A Fair Start: The Provision of Pre-School Education*, Penguin, 1971.

54. Moodie, Graeme C. and Eustace, Rowland, *Power and Authority in British Universities*, Allen & Unwin, 1974.

55. Burgess, Tyrrell and Pratt, John, *Policy and Practice: the colleges of advanced technology*, Penguin, 1970, and Pratt, John and Burgess, Tyrrell, *Polytechnics: a report*, Pitman, 1974.

56. Lomax, D.E. (ed), *The Education of Teachers in Britain*, Wiley, 1973.

57. Committee on Higher Education, *Report* (Robbins Report), Cmnd 2154, HMSO, 1963; Commission of Inquiry (Franks Report).

58. Berdahl, Robert O., *British Universities and the State*, Cambridge University Press, 1959.

59. Taylor, William, *Society and the Education of Teachers*, Faber, 1969.

60. Howell, D.A., *The introduction of the Bachelor of Education degree: a case study in British university decision-making*, Ph.D. thesis, University of London, 1976.

61. Gifford-Gifford, M.B., *An analysis of the cost functions of university departments*, M.Phil. thesis, University of London, 1974; Verry, D.W., *Cost and production functions in higher education*, Ph.D. thesis, University of London, 1974; and

Cook, W.R., *Incentives to economic efficiency in universities: an investigation of the problem of using budgetary devolution to academic units within a university as a means of encouraging the most economic use of resources*, Ph.D. thesis, University of Bradford, 1975.

62. Dasey, R.M., *Staff allocation and the organisation of university teaching*, M.Sc. thesis, University of Bradford, 1972; and Legg, K.L.C., *Simple mathematical modelling of staff and resource requirements in university-type institutions*, Ph.D. thesis, University of Loughborough. See also paper by Derek W. Birch and John R. Calvert, 'A Review of Academic Staffing Formulae', in *Educational Administration Bulletin*, Vol 3, No 1, autumn, 1974, and their 'Performance indicators in higher education: a comparative study' in the same journal, Vol 6, No 2, winter 1977–1978.

63. Ebutt, K., *A study of academic boards in institutions of higher education in the light of Rex's conflict theory*, M.Phil. thesis, University of London, 1976; and Marsden, J.J., *An assessment of some of the effects of Circular 7/70* on technical college administration, University of Wales, 1975.

64. An early account of some of the applications of operational research to educational administration is given by C.L. Myers in chapter 9 of Baron and Taylor (op. cit.).

65. LGORU Information Bulletin, 1977–1978, gives brief summaries of the reports of these studies.

66. Inner London Education Authority Research Report, No 1 (1976) and Report No 2 (n.d.).

67. Studies recently reported to the National Foundation for Educational Research for inclusion in its *Register of Educational Research and Development* include the forecasting of pupil populations (Cheshire County Council Research and Information Department), and the development of a 'central computer for each school, summarizing all the essential information such as accommodation, pupil numbers, teaching and nonteaching establishments' (Hampshire County Council Education Department).

68. Glatter, Ron, *Management Development for the Education Profession*, Harrap, 1972; and Piper, David Warren and Glatter, Ron, *The Changing University: a report on the staff development in universities programme*, 1972–1974, NFER Publishing Co., 1977.

69. Baron, Bernard, *The Managerial Approach to Tertiary Education: a critical analysis*, University of London Institute of Education, 1978. Unpublished London dissertations include: Clarke, D.B., *Staff Development in the Four Essex Area Technical Colleges*, 1976; Gould, Rosemary M., *The Development of Senior Teachers for Management: the study of a six week course held by the Inner London Education Authority*, 1975; and Sherratt, B.W., *The Effectiveness of Multi-Purpose Teachers' Centres in terms of their In-Service Function*, 1976.

70. Tipton, Beryl F.A., *Conflict and Change in a Technical College*, Hutchinson Educational, 1973.

71. OECD, *Reviews of National Policies for Education: Educational Development Strategy in England and Wales*, 1975.

72. During the ten years from 1955 the Kellogg Foundation made available six

million dollars for projects designed to improve school administration; substantial grants were also made available in Canada from 1952 to 1956.

73. Taylor, William (ed), *Research Perspectives in Education*, Routledge & Kegan Paul, 1973; chapter 8, *Knowledge and Research* (by William Taylor), p. 194.
74. Shipman, Marten, 'Research and Local Government', in *Research Intelligence*, Vol 2, No 2, 1976, p. 14.
75. Simon, Brian, 'Educational Research: Which Way?', in *Research Intelligence*, Vol 4, No 1, 1978, p. 2.
76. *A Framework for Government Research and Development*, Cmnd 4814, HMSO, 1971.
77. Two recent papers discuss this area in some depth. They are 'Government and research policy' by Martin Davies, in Jones, Kathleen (ed), *The Year Book of Social Policy in Britain 1975*, Routledge & Kegan Paul, 1976, and 'The relationship between researchers and policy-makers' by Olive Stevenson and Michael J. Hill, in *Social Security Research*, papers presented at a DHSS Seminar on 7–9 April, 1976, HMSO, 1977.
78. Kay, Brian W., 'The DES and Educational Research', in *Research Intelligence*, Vol 4, No 1, 1978, p. 8.
79. Thomas, Rosamund, *The British Philosophy of Administration, A comparison of British and American ideas, 1900–1939*, Longmans, 1978, p. 29.
80. ibid. p. 30.
81. Hughes, Meredydd, 'Critical Issues in the Preparation of Educational Administrators in Britain', paper presented at the Fourth International Intervisitation Program on Educational Administration, Vancouver, Canada, 1978.
82. Glaser, Barney G., and Strauss, Anselm L., *The Discovery of Grounded Theory: strategies for qualitative research*, Weidenfeld and Nicolson, 1968.
83. Greenfield, T. Barr, 'Theory about Organisations: a new perspective and its implications for schools', chapter 5 in Hughes, Meredydd (ed), *Administering Education: International Challenge*, Athlone Press, 1975.
84. ibid. p. 86.
85. Baron and Taylor, op. cit.
86. Glatter, op. cit., pp. 48–49, 68.
87. Simon, op. cit., p. 4.
88. Kay, op. cit., p. 8

CHAPTER 1.2

EDUCATIONAL 'POLICY' AND 'MANAGEMENT': ONE FIELD OR TWO?*
RON GLATTER

My brief for this chapter was to defend educational management as a 'proper' subject of study within the broader field of educational administration. To begin to do this, I must traverse again ground which I have partly covered elsewhere (Glatter, 1979a; 1979b).

As a field of study and research, educational administration draws on several disciplines in the social sciences. Moreover, as Baron's (1979) survey of research in the subject over its short life in Britain makes clear, its area of application has been similarly broad, covering both system and institutional levels. By contrast, over its much longer history in North America, it has focused predominantly on organizational studies relating chiefly to schools, though in recent years there has been increased interest and activity in 'policy research' (Culbertson, 1978). This close correspondence of educational administration in America with school organization studies is obviously connected with the fact that for many years university departments there have been training grounds for senior school and school district personnel. Yet the term 'management' has only come into use in very recent years, and even then partly, one suspects, as a result of influence from British developments.

I shall argue shortly that our own more inclusive view of the subject must be preserved, and is especially appropriate to the nature of our system. But first I want to suggest that we in Britain stumbled on the use of the term 'educational management' almost by accident, because of the growth of the subject in Britain at a time when there was increasing interest, training, and research in management in other parts of the public sector and in the private

* *Educational Analysis* 1.2, 1979 (ed. G. Fowler), Falmer Press

sector. What we were actually doing was no different in essence from what in America was called 'educational administration', namely research and teaching focused on the internal organization of schools and other educational institutions, drawing upon concepts and frameworks developed in a number of social science disciplines. British 'education management' was that part of our broader conception of 'educational administration' which dealt primarily with the functioning of the institutions. We were always concerned to set such work firmly in the context of British national and local policy-making, and indeed sometimes came under fire for allegedly taking too parochially British a stance, in contrast for example to work in America and Australia, some of which seemed to us too 'context free' in its view of the generalizability of theory and findings about the ways in which educational institutions function.

Policy and management: how distinctive?

Very recently in Britain there have been suggestions that there is a separate area of 'policy' or 'political' studies in education which is distinct not simply in terms of the focus of its interest but conceptually as well. It is possible also to detect the implication that such studies are academically superior to, or more respectable than, organization or management studies in education. In what follows, I shall examine and challenge this distinction.

The work which is being given the label 'policy' appears to me to comprise:

> the relationships of power, influence and control between the various bodies and groups of participants within the educational system, and the way in which these relationships affect the policy process in the many areas of policy with which education is concerned. The term 'areas of policy' here would include both policy relating to particular stages of education, such as higher education or pre-schooling, and also policy relating to particular categories of client, such as the handicapped or the adult illiterate. (Glatter, 1979b, paragraph 5.2)

By contrast, what have come to be known as management studies are concerned with:

> the internal operation of educational institutions, and also with their relationships with their environments, that is, the communities in which they are set, and with the governing structures to which they are formally responsible. (Glatter, 1979b, paragraph 5.3)

This simple dichotomy seems currently to be a convenient one. When academic work in educational administration began in Britain in the mid-1960s, the small number of people involved in it inevitably had to cover the full spectrum (at least in their teaching), all the way from so-called 'policy' to so-called 'management'. Growth, as always, has brought special-ization, and, not surprisingly, the primary focus of some has tended to be on the government of education, while that of others has been upon the institutions: the macro and the micro.

It would be highly misleading, however, if this distinction of convenience were taken to imply a genuine conceptual dichotomy, leading to two separate and discrete areas of study and teaching. In the first place, the source disciplines which we draw upon all have a clear contribution to make at both governmental and institutional levels, though perhaps in different degrees (for example, economics may be less relevant at micro than at macro level). The conceptual tools which are applicable at one level are basically those which are applicable at the other.

The policy continuum

The practical significance of this point can be illustrated by considering the notions of 'policy-making' and 'politics'. Much recent research, particu-larly that on the fate of educational innovations, has drawn attention to the gross discrepancies often encountered between policies as formulated at macro level and as implemented at micro (Dalin, 1973, 1978; Whiteside, 1978). As Tomlinson (1978) writes, in a short but stimulating piece, the lesson of these findings is that

> we need an approach to education, whether changing or continuing as before but facing social and economic change, which is based on a more realistic view of people working in organisations, which recognises men's ability to respond to situations and to alter them in ways which carry significance for those concerned.

He goes on to plead for educational thinking and change to be made 'a connected continuum – not a dichotomy of "policy-makers" and "opera-tives" '.

Like other institutions, educational institutions are up to their necks in policy-making and politics (Morgan, 1979) and if the term 'policy studies' has any meaning at all it must apply to them no less than to the levels above them. The politics of educational institutions are particularly evident in a diffused educational system such as that of England and Wales, with such a high premium placed on institutional autonomy. If politics are concerned with value-setting, then they are likely to be especially significant in a situation in which, as Kogan notes, each one of the heads of 30,000 educational institutions 'is allowed to develop organizational and educational styles of his own. . . . This system of delegated authority carries with it a corresponding power system which enables values to be stored at points sufficiently distant from and impervious to central government or other mechanisms by which society is governed' (Kogan, 1975, p. 56). However, it is clear that even in highly centralized systems such as those of Sweden and Norway the relationship between macro and micro levels is a difficult one, and that the educational practices adopted at school level are often at variance with those propounded by central policy-makers (Lauglo, 1977).

The wider significance of concepts more usually associated with the macro level was strongly emphasized by Mackenzie (1967). He devoted more than one-third of his massive survey *Politics and Social Science* to a long section entitled 'Politics without States' in which he discussed *inter alia* politics in communities, organizations, and small groups. He justified this large allocation of space in these terms:

> It is not wrong to say that 'political science is about states', to define states ostensively, and to leave it at that. But it is difficult to rest content with this position. . . . Both political scientists and plain men feel that what they meet in the politics of the state turns up again in the politics of the club, the office, the army unit and even the family. What generates political interest in all this range of institutions is that we think we can feel politics in them, and that we cannot describe them adequately without using political concepts. (Mackenzie, 1967, p. 156)

Is management 'narrow'?

If a major ground for the attempt to set up a policy/management dichotomy based on a disparaging view of management studies is that the latter have been too 'narrow' in their academic base, then, as the above quote makes clear, this has been because of an inadequate conception of the subject rather than because there is a fundamental distinction to be made between the forms of analysis appropriate to the two areas. A common view, for instance, is that policy studies concerned with the macro level are about educational and social values and philosophies, whereas management/organizational studies are merely concerned with techniques, often derived from industrial and commercial settings and largely divorced from considerations of the educational purposes which should underpin the actions of professional educators.

It is this limited conception of education management studies which Taylor (1976) seems to have had in mind when he wrote about the dangers of managerial approaches to the running of schools. It is probably true that, in the early 1970s when these studies were beginning in this country, they were overinfluenced by noneducational models and were somewhat mesmerized by techniques, many of which had been developed elsewhere. Very few of the techniques widely discussed at the time (such as planning-programming-budgeting systems, management by objectives, and critical path analysis) have been implemented on any scale in British education. Interestingly, the techniques which have gained a substantial degree of acceptance and application are those, such as curriculum and staff deployment analyses (Davies, 1969), which were developed *within* education and relate closely to the specific teaching and managerial context of educational institutions.

More generally, it seems to me that there is now a much greater awareness of the need to examine 'the political, occupational and technical characteristics of the types of organisations' within which it is proposed that particular techniques might be applied (Glatter, 1972, p. 47). It seems, too, that as the scale of research into educational institutions has grown, so we have passed through the phase of overreliance on generalized models. It is interesting, in this connection, that the Americans are also presently concerned about the need to base theory more firmly 'upon leadership and management practice in *educational* organisations. While scholarship on administration in non-education organisations has been and can continue to be suggestive, its results provide a weak and insufficient base for building theories of management and leadership in education' (Culbertson, 1978, p. 21). It is also apparent that general management studies are moving away from a narrowly technical and consensual approach. A recent survey, for instance (Handy, 1976), is much concerned with the analysis of concepts such as politics, power, influence, and conflict in relation to organizations.

The increasing use of phenomenological as distinct from (or in conjunction with) systems perspectives in educational administration research (Best, Jarvis, and Ribbins, 1979) should help to ensure that such research is more closely related to the perceptions and understandings of those who are actually members of educational institutions, thus reducing the temptation to rely on general models. More use of models of bargaining, exchange, and coalitions (March, 1974; Shaw, 1975) would also help in this direction.

The return of 'school climate'

So far, I have been arguing against the creation of a dichotomy of macro- and micro-level studies in educational administration on the ground that studies at each level should employ a similar broad range of analytical tools, in recognition of the fact that policy processes, as well as the factors which impinge upon them, have much in common at the two levels. This does not by itself constitute a sufficient justification for a unified field. The other main point I would want to stress is that the separation is difficult if not impossible to make in empirical terms. It is as difficult to conceive of institutional studies which do not have substantial policy implications as of the reverse. To take an apparently extreme example, Richardson's (1973) case study of a single school raised fundamental questions about a major policy issue – the academic/pastoral distinction in the Burnham salary structure – by probing the consequences of the present policy in the case study school for pupils, for teachers' careers, and for institutional politics and conflicts.

Two current preoccupations of many researchers in educational administration, accountability and falling rolls, must clearly be examined in terms both of institutional management and national and local policy, and these dimensions of the problems are not separate but interact strongly with one another. The same can be said of many other topics (Glatter, 1979a).

In one respect, it is strange that this debate should be initiated at this particular time, for not only has the research on educational innovations referred to earlier drawn attention to the power of those at institutional level to modify or frustrate the aims of the policy-makers, but the recent, well-publicized research of Rutter et al. (1979) has resurrected the half-buried concept of school climate or ethos (Halpin, 1966) – in other words, the qualities of the school as a social organization. In the authors' view, their findings demonstrate a clear connection between decisions taken within the school and pupil outcomes. In their conclusion, they place their findings in context in terms which are highly relevant to our present discussion.

> Schools constitute just one element in a complex set of ecological interactions, and are shaped and constrained by a variety of societal factors outside their immediate control. . . . The pattern of connections is complex. It is nevertheless clear that within this network, schools have a considerable degree of

choice in how they are organised, and that teachers have a similar choice in their decisions on how to respond to the children they teach. Our results suggest that these decisions on how to respond are likely to affect the chances of the children improving in their behaviour and attainments.

It is not argued that schools are the *most* important influence on children's progress, and we agree with Bernstein (1970) that education cannot compensate for the inequities of society. Nevertheless, we do suggest that schools constitute one major area of influence, and one which is susceptible to change. (Rutter et al., 1979, pp. 181–182)

As a result of their work, the authors call for further research into management and leadership styles, planned change in schools, and the relationship between school policies and classroom teaching practices. The central puzzle became this:

How was it that twelve schools set up to undertake the same task with children from much the same geographical area came to develop such different styles? Doubtless, part of the answer lies in the history of the schools and in a variety of external factors outside their control. In addition, however, the schools' expressed philosophies and chosen ways of working were important. (Rutter et al., 1979, p. 203)

This central puzzle is well recognized by policy-makers, teachers, and parents alike. It provides the *raison d'être* for those studies within the broad field of educational administration which are focused on the internal organization and external relationships of educational institutions (not simply schools) and which, for want of a more satisfactory label, are frequently covered by the term 'education management'.

The development of capability

Many would accept that no clear-cut separation between macro and micro, between something 'up there' called educational policy and something 'down here' (or there) called educational management, is tenable, and certainly that it is fruitless to study one in isolation from the other. Yet I have been invited to present the case here for education management studies conceived as at least partly distinct from politics/policy studies. Up to now, I have been emphasizing the similarity of macro and micro studies in terms of their conceptual roots, and their interdependence in terms of the real world; I have also implicitly been referring to research and scholarship rather than teaching and training. If we turn to the latter, there may well be a significant point about the *purpose* of training in education management which has led to the distinction, however artificial, being made.

The last decade has seen a rapid growth in courses which are most frequently classified as 'education management': they are usually taken by those in, or aspiring to, senior positions of responsibility in educational institutions or authorities. They normally cover both macro- and micro-level concerns, recognizing that the relationship between governmental and institutional policy-making is a highly interactive one. Nor are they (generally) narrowly focused on management techniques: hardly anyone concerned with such work believes that running, say, an educational institution is simply a technical process. But – and this is what may be disturbing the purists – neither are these courses concerned with purveying knowledge for its own sake. They must, in my view, be concerned with developing the capability of their 'students' in initiating and managing educational activities. Their job is to promote 'learning to some purpose' (Nuttgens, 1978) beyond a purely academic one.

The ways of doing this will be various. At one level, developing *understanding*, say, of how organizations work, or of the many dimensions of a particular socio-educational policy issue, will contribute to such capability. I recall asking an Australian lecturer in educational administration, who saw his teaching task solely in terms of developing understanding, what he hoped to achieve with his practitioner students. He thought for a while, then said, 'To make them more alert, I suppose.' That seemed to me a perfectly valid, if limited, objective as part of the overall aim of developing capability.

Barnett (1979, p. 118) defines 'capability' in simple commonsense terms: 'an ability successfully to tackle the practical situations of life. This also means possessing the specialized skills and knowledge necessary successfully to tackle the operational problems of a particular professional sphere.' This must be our aim in education management courses, both because it is obviously and naturally our students' aim when coming onto the courses, and because it can be the only rationale for our providing such courses at all.

I believe this involves going beyond developing understanding into the domains of method and skill development. 'What is important is not a particular fact or even a particular ordered collection of facts, but *method*. It is method rather than information which gives mastery . . .' (Burgess, 1979, p. 152). *How* we go about formulating problems and testing and implementing solutions to them in education is a fundamental question of the quality of our methods: it is a question which applies equally at macro and micro levels, and is no less important than our value orientations to educational and social issues. The nature of the service which we as *clients* of the educational system receive is as much affected by the quality of methods and skills which have been deployed as by the way in which policy differences have been resolved, and obviously these two elements interact with one another.

Is such an approach narrow, illiberal, purely technical? Only if methods and skills are developed in isolation from consideration of values, purposes, and policies. Herein lies the danger of the putative policy/management dichotomy. If there were two distinctive forms of training provision as proposed by Taylor (1976, pp. 48–49), one labelled 'educational administration', a long, broadly based liberal education, sometimes seeming to lack 'relevance', and the other labelled 'education management', 'specific and narrowly conceived', then the separation would be confirmed. The first form would be heavily knowledge-based, unconcerned with developing capability, and probably available only to a few. The second would be concerned with methods divorced from purposes and therefore either 'useless, or illiberal in its consequences, or both' (Taylor, 1976, p. 48). I would argue that it is the proposed formal separation of purposes and methods which is illiberal, rather than education management studies *per se*.

Learnable talents and skills

We understand well how to provide a broadly based liberal education: we have had centuries of experience in doing so. But we scarcely understand at all how to harness this experience to providing an education which also develops methods and skills and hence promotes capability; so we tend (in many fields) to fall back on providing a lopsided education based on the accumulation of knowledge rather than the development of capability, and court disappointment in our students, the sense that what has been offered is worthy in its own terms but does not really satisfy expectations. We have become expert at rationalizing this lopsidedness, for instance by implying that the expectations were not legitimate, that academic institutions cannot or should not be in the business of developing capability.

In the field of educational administration, one powerful attempt to rebut this thesis, and to suggest some skills and methods which universities (for example) might seek to develop, has been made by March (1974). His basic stance is closely in line with what has been argued above:

The graceful wisdom of an educated person is not enough. An administrator needs to be competent both in the fundamental skills of administration and in the basic technology of the institution he administers; and universities need to provide education in those competences if they are able to do so efficiently. Administration is a job, and it calls for talents. Some of those talents are learnable. (March, 1974, pp. 23–24)

He nevertheless recognizes that academic institutions could not develop all the qualities which might be relevant to a capable educational administrator. They have a distinctive area of competence – the domain of the intellect: their advantage for the training of educational administrators 'is in providing the research basis for intelligence and in teaching the intellective skills of management' (p. 28). He goes on to suggest five 'critical skills of analysis' which universities could in his view develop, and examines each in some detail. They are: the management of expertise, the management of coalitions, the management of ambiguity, the management of time, and the management of information. In each case he shows that there exists relevant scholarly and research work to support training, though in some cases it is rather slight and in all cases it needs to be extended. At least the items in the list have the virtues that they are all 'relevant, appropriate to the things managers do, consistent with the kinds of organizations in which they do them, and intellectually demanding' (p. 28).

The point about such a list is not that it is comprehensive (it is not), nor that it is indisputable (it is not), but that it is illustrative of an approach and a method which takes the development of capability as its aim and a given situation rather than a body of knowledge as its starting-point. It is clear that the research and development base to support such an approach needs to be strengthened substantially. Such an approach is no easy option: it requires rigorous thought and penetrating analysis, as well as creativity and imagination, and the terrain is not clearly marked out. It will be a still more difficult path to follow if it is subject to the undeserved charge of intellectual inferiority.

I have argued that the attempt to create two separate and distinct fields of study of educational 'policy' and 'management' is unjustified both conceptually and empirically. I speculated that this attempt is possibly related to the perceived connection between institutional studies in educational administration and the development of competence and capability in those working within educational institutions and authorities. It may therefore represent a further manifestation of our strong tendency in Britain over more than a century to devalue 'the culture which is concerned with doing, making and organizing' (Nuttgens, 1979, p. 143; also Barnett, 1979), and which may well lie at the roots of many of our current economic and social problems. The debate about the place of institutional management studies in educational administration appears therefore really to be part of a wider debate about the purposes and direction of education in Britain. If the decisive shift in our aims towards education for capability, which is sorely needed, is not secured in relation to the education of our present and future educational leaders, there seems little chance that it will be effected elsewhere.

References

Barnett, C., 1979, 'Technology, Education and Industrial and Economic Strength', *Royal Society of Arts Journal*, 127.5271 (February).

Baron, G., 1979, 'Research in Educational Aministration in Britain', *Educational Administration*, 8.1, (autumn). (Reprinted in this volume.)

Bernstein, B., 1970, 'Education cannot compensate for society', *New Society*, 387.

Best, R., Jarvis, C., and Ribbins, P., 1979, 'Pastoral Care in the Comprehensive School: a discussion', *Educational Administration*, 8.1, (autumn).

Burgess, T., 1979, 'New Ways to Learn', *Royal Society of Arts Journal*, 127.5271, (February).

Culbertson, J., 1978, 'Educational Administration: where we are and where we are going', presented at 4th International Intervisitation Program in Educational Administration, Vancouver, (Mimeographed).

Dalin, P., 1973, *Case Studies in Educational Innovation IV: Strategies for Innovation in Education*, Paris, OECD.

Dalin, P., 1978, *Limits to Educational Change*, London, Macmillan.

Davies, T., 1969, *School Organisation*, London, Pergamon.

Glatter, R., 1972, *Management Development for the Education Profession*, London, Harrap (now distributed by NFER Publishing Co., Windsor).

Glatter, R., 1979a 'Future Directions in the Professional Development of Educational Administrators', in McHugh, R. (ed) *Educational Administration: Approaches to Professional Development*, Proceedings of the 7th Annual Conference of the British Educational Administration Society, Bristol, Further Education Staff College.

Glatter, R., 1979b, *Influence or Control? A Review of the Course*, Unit 16 of Open University Course E222, Milton Keynes, Open University Press.

Halpin, A., 1966, *Theory and Research in Administration*, London, Macmillan.

Handy, C., 1976, *Understanding Organisations*, Harmondsworth, Penguin.

Kogan, M., 1975, *Educational Policy Making: a Study of Interest Groups and Parliament*, London, Allen & Unwin.

Lauglo, J., 1977, 'Educational change and aspects of bureaucratic organisation: The Scandinavian school reforms', in Glatter, R. (ed), *Control of the Curriculum: Issues and Trends in Britain and Europe,* Proceedings of the 5th Annual Conference of the British Educational Administration Society, London, University of London Institute of Education.

MacKenzie, W., 1967, *Politics and Social Science,* Harmondsworth, Penguin.

March, J., 1974, 'Analytical Skills and the University Training of Educational Administrators', *Journal of Educational Administration,* 12.1, (May).

Morgan, C., 1979, *The Schools (5–16) Part 1,* Unit 10 of Open University Course E222, Milton Keynes, Open University Press.

Nuttgens, P., 1978, 'Learning to Some Purpose', *Higher Education Review,* (summer).

Nuttgens, P., 1979, Chairman's remarks on p. 131 of *Royal Society of Arts Journal,* 127.5271, (February).

Richardson, E., 1973, *The Teacher, the School and the Task of Management,* London, Heinemann.

Rutter, M. et al., 1979, *Fifteen Thousand Hours: Secondary Schools and their Effects on Children,* London, Open Books.

Shaw, K., 1975, 'Negotiating curriculum change in a College of Education', in Reid, W. and Walker, D. (eds), *Case Studies in Curriculum Change: Great Britain and the United States,* London, Routledge & Kegan Paul.

Taylor, W., 1976, 'The head as manager: some criticisms', in Peters, R. (ed) *The Role of the Head,* London, Routledge & Kegan Paul.

Tomlinson, J., 1978, 'Edging forward', in *Education,* (30 June).

Whiteside, T., 1978, *The Sociology of Educational Innovation,* London, Methuen.

SECTION II

THE SCHOOL AND ITS ENVIRONMENT

CHAPTER 2.1

ACCOUNTABILITY, VALUES, AND SCHOOLING*
TREVOR PATEMAN[1]

In this chapter I argue that preferences among different possible forms of accountability in education relate to and serve different orderings of socially available values. I distinguish five such values and for simplicity treat each as if it was the only value governing the choice of accountability procedures. On this basis, I try to show what procedures will be preferred, why, and with what consequences. Though my discussion is not, I hope, unreal, I do not discuss combinations of accountability procedures in relation to combinations of values (which is how we find things in the real world), for I wish to emphasize the distinctive nature of each value and of its possible translations into forms of accountability.

The five values I distinguish are these: schooling (which I use interchangeably with 'education' for the purposes of this chapter) should (a) respond to parental preferences; (b) use public resources efficiently; (c) allow teachers professional freedom; (d) meet the requirements of society; and (e) satisfy children's needs.

As for *accountability*, this is a concept distinct from that of *responsibility*, as Mary Warnock has urged in a different context[2] where she distinguishes the accountability of an institution to another institution, with legal or quasi-legal authority over it, from the responsibility which an institution may owe or feel it owes to those it affects, but where those affected do not, directly, exercise authority over it. In the real world, the accountability which an institution owes fuses insensibly with the responsibilities which it feels, and this should be kept in mind in reading this chapter, which

* *Accountability In Education*, Becher, Tony and Maclure, Stuart (eds), NFER, 1978, pp. 61–94.

concentrates on the accountability end of the spectrum.

Parental choice

> In the exercise and performance of all powers and duties conferred and imposed on them by this Act the Secretary of State and Local Education Authorities shall have regard to the general principle that, so far as is compatible with the provision of efficient instruction and the avoidance of unreasonable public expenditure, pupils are to be educated in accordance with the wishes of their parents. (1944 Education Act, Section 76)

In the present context, I take 'parental choice' to mean that parents should be able, collectively or individually, to determine the general character of the education which their children receive in maintained schools in relation to curriculum, method of teaching, discipline, etc. On this interpretation of 'parental choice' there are no existing institutions in the public sector of education which provide for the direct translation of parental wishes into educational practice, subject even to the constraints specified in the 1944 act as quoted above. Yet it is plainly possible to create mechanisms, such as voucher systems or the democratic election of school boards (an expression I use to avoid the cumbersome 'managers or governors'), which would give parents considerably more power than they have at present to translate whatever wishes they have into reality. Voucher systems and democratically elected school boards are possible mechanisms for making schools accountable to parents for whatever parents wished schools to render them account. We do not have the mechanisms because we reject parental choice as an overriding or even an important value, and this is simply a consequence of a history in which the claim of market mechanisms or democratic procedures to govern central areas of our existence has been rejected. Instead the state has successfully developed extensive activities which take place outside the marketplace, and the state has developed as a representative government: Parliament has conceded much to what nineteenth-century liberals called the 'numerical principle', but it has not conceded it dominance. Our practice remains faithful to the aspirations of John Stuart Mill's *Representative Government*, not Rousseau's *Social Contract*. And where nineteenth-century liberalism perfected the case for representative government, twentieth-century social democracy has entrenched the case for extensive state activity, the 'mixed economy'. Both together made provision of education a central part of the state's activity. The private education ghetto reflects the relegation of market principles to a secondary role in education, and the purely token representation of parents on school boards, as also the auxiliary functions of parent-teacher associations (as fund-raisers, etc.), indicates that recognition of the numerical principle is only a concession.

If parents were successfully to assert that schools should be accountable to them, through the obvious mechanisms I have indicated, they would have to throw overboard the inherited cultural-ideological baggage alluded to in the previous paragraph. That would involve them in arguments at least one of which seems particularly relevant to my discussion.

In our practice in relation to the government of education, there is still embodied a theory which may well seem culturally outdated, even offensive when put in the terms in which it was developed in the nineteenth century, and employed explicitly for much of the present century. That theory held that if education was to have – as it should – a progressive, civilizing function, as opposed to a nonprogressive, merely socializing one, then power to determine its contents and forms must rest with those who had reached the higher eminences of the achieved level of culture, not those still engaged on the fatiguing climb, or happily encamped at the bottom. Since most parents are at the bottom, it follows that educational power cannot rest in their hands, unless it can be shown that they are best able to see the summits, know how to get their children there, and want to do so.

Now the general break-up of faith in progress and in the existence of nonrelative values makes this position impossible any longer to rationalize, which leads those whose practice still commits them to the old theory either to silence or to purely verbal substitutions, such as the replacement of the nineteenth century's 'civilizing purposes' with our positivistic 'socializing functions', which will not, however, do the job required.

For those with no faith in 'progress' and 'absolute values' it is easy to justify market and democratic forms of educational accountability, since they no longer recognize the existence of summits which they have yet to climb. For those who retain the faith, it is difficult but not impossible to believe in parent power, as Rhodes Boyson has shown. He takes the view that parents, though not themselves representatives of the higher culture out of which further progress will come, are qualified and eager to recognize those who do stand high (though not *very* high) above them and able to detect the false prophets among the true.[3] In this way, he is able to combine a belief in market accountability with adherence to traditional values.

Boyson's way of reconciling belief in the traditional values with parental power will, of course, be unacceptable and unnecessary to those who take their stand with twentieth-century relativism, and my general feeling is that the long-term factor working to push up parental choice on any list of educational values is the breakdown of the old hegemonic value system, and its replacement with patterns of preference which are perceived as merely personal and subjective.[4]

But commitment to value relativism is not a sufficient condition of a belief in parental power, any more than it is a necessary condition. A relativist can dispute the assumption, which has tacitly been made, that parental wishes or choices are or would be original or nonderivative – that is, in some sense *genuine*. Just as Schumpeter argues that the political values held by citizens are outputs from the political system, not inputs to it,[5] so parental preferences could be argued to be creatures not creators of a system. To privilege parental preferences would then merely represent a confirmation of the power of those institutions or constellations of influence which had created those preferences in the first place, and a relativist could consistently give that as a reason for refusing to take parental preferences at face value. (The believer in progress is most likely to find in parental preferences a demand that their own educational experience be repeated on their children, a demand which – to use a favourite Victorian expression – would reduce society to a state of 'Chinese stationariness'.)

So both the believer in progress and the relativist can find arguments to bring for and against claims for according parental choice a high place among the values education is supposed to serve. There are other possible arguments, and two other negative ones deserve mention here. First, a sociologically minded critic would point out that democratic values are rarely realized in class- and status-divided societies, even where the necessary legal mechanisms exist, and this because of variations in political participation rates. So if we had elected school boards, they might well be legally representative yet not at all socially or politically representative. And if we had direct democratic government of schools, through parents' meetings, they would not be representative either. In other words, formally democratic procedures can create or leave unrepresented minorities, and even majorities, just as much as existing systems for the appointment of school boards.[6] Second, a logically minded critic would use Arrow's general possibility theorem[7] to show how even a voucher mechanism could not consistently represent parental choice where more than two choices are available.

These are not decisive criticisms: they serve only to indicate some of the dimensions along which we might argue about the weight to be accorded to the value of parental choice, and hence of accountability to parents.

Efficient use of public resources

Education, like any other public service, is answerable to the society which it serves and which pays for it. (*Education in Schools, A consultative document,* para 1.5)[8]

To measure the efficiency of resource allocation requires a prior specification of performance or output objectives. This is as true for schooling as for soap powder. In an educational system where determination of objectives was effectively delegated to individual schools, the assessment of efficiency had to be correspondingly individualized. In British educational practice this is where, so it seems to me, the inspectorate fitted in; for it was able to offer assessments of efficiency which took into account a school's own specification of its objectives. Theoretically, an unholy row might be going on about the aims of a school, but the national or local inspectorate could remain above it, confining itself to study of and advice about the means-end relationship. There are elements of this in the relation which the ILEA inspectorate had to William Tyndale Junior School.[9] In general, like exhibits in a horticultural show, schools were judged good or bad of their kind, but not all of them were expected to be apples.

This is an oversimplified account, and a number of modifications are required to approximate it to reality. Notably, there were fewer actual differences than the system theoretically permitted since there existed mechanisms, formal and informal, through which schools were made much more alike: appointments policies; managerial and parent pressure tending in a common direction; the occasional open bust-up; and, notably, public examinations.[10] Yet I want to argue that the oversimplified picture was useful to both teachers and inspectors, since it justified a practice with which both were reasonably satisfied. This can be seen if we look at a phenomenon which seems anomalous if it was indeed the case that inspectors were mainly concerned with the subjective and qualitative[11] judgement of efficiency in relation to individualized systems of ends.

That phenomenon is, or was, the absence of explicit, written-down policies, objectives, targets, or plans in most schools. If schools were autonomous and valued their autonomy as a means of creating difference, would they not have stressed this in written formulations? Is their lack of explicitness compatible with the thesis being argued? The answer to these questions can be made by employing distinctions drawn by Weber:[12] schools had goals, but they were expressed in *traditional* terms (ritual, routine, implicit understandings) rather than *rational-legal* ones (aims, objectives, rules, regulations). No doubt this was connected with the actual existence of an educational consensus, the breakdown of which Rhodes Boyson laments.[13] Now this traditional mode of operation increased the power of both teachers and inspectors. In the case of teachers, it made it difficult for them to be held to account by parents or managers with whom it was possible, if desired, to pursue a 'catch us if you can' game. In the case of inspectors, it required of them a hermeneutic understanding of the schools, the efficiency of which they were assessing. They could not do their job with a standard inventory, but had to engage in the kind of interpretation at which only insiders can be really adept. I suggest that this put them at a distance from their political masters, at both local and national level. That we still have Her Majesty's Inspectors, not DES Inspectors, may be symbolic of this. Education, like medicine and the law, had its mysteries to which teachers and inspectors were privy, and parents and politicians were not. Politicians were dependent on their inspectors to interpret to them these mysteries, the secret garden. There was no question of their barging in on something they could not fully understand, even when the value in question was such an eminently rational one as efficiency.

This is now changing: as *Education in Schools* puts it, 'Growing recognition of the need for schools to demonstrate their accountability to the society which they serve requires a coherent and soundly based means of assessment for the educational system as a whole, for schools, and for individual pupils' (para 3.3). Now I suggest that this change, ironically enough, has been made possible by the 'legitimation crisis', to use Jürgen Habermas' expression,[14] in which some teachers' own acceptance of the traditional curriculum and values has crumbled, and in which the traditions have been challenged to justify and rationalize themselves. This has permitted the politicians to intervene legitimately and on an equal footing, something those same teachers never desired.[15] For the breakdown of a traditional consensus constitutes not only a sort of desacralization, but also reequalizes rights to contribute to argument. There are no longer self-evident specialists. In other words, when the priests have doubts, then is the layman free to make his intervention again, of which history affords numerous examples.

Congregationalism is analogous to demands for parent power, and where in the seventeenth century demands were heard for the cashiering of kings, now it is for the cashiering of teachers. In the present conjuncture politicians have emerged principally as flag carriers for the fourth value in my initial list (i.e., 'meeting the requirements' of society) and so I shall have something to say about them when I discuss that.

In summary, efficiency as a value would have been less important if there had been no traditionally expressed consensus, and the inspectorate had derived its importance from its ability to assess efficiency against unwritten standards. Efficiency was the only value for which politicians felt able to demand accountability. Inspectors have consequently enjoyed considerable independence, and schools have felt more accountable to them, perhaps, than to anyone else. In this way, schools have been held accountable to inspectors.

It is consistent with and indeed part of this analysis that the role of the national and local inspectorates has become increasingly advisory. For if it can be ruled out that schools are wilfully inefficient or hopelessly incompetent, then by definition they are committed to being efficient, and must rationally be willing to accept advice on improving their efficiency, advice which the inspectorate has been able to offer.[16]

The professional freedom of teachers

The type of freedom claimed by teachers is professional freedom. Just as the doctor claims the freedom to treat the patient according to his own best judgement, formed in relation to available knowledge, technology, and resources, so the teacher claims the freedom to teach the pupil. In both medicine and teaching, as in science, recognized hierarchies of knowledge and status define who is best qualified to decide in case of conflict over what constitutes the appropriate course of action.[17]

This notion of professional freedom is acceptable so long as the ends or different ends being pursued are not generally contested, and can coexist, if diverse, without creating a pressing awareness of incompatibility. If there was no consensus on the meaning of *health* and *cure*, then doctors would not be able to make the claims to professional freedom which they do. The same applies to teachers. More strongly, once the ends are agreed it is rational to institutionalize professional freedom, for that is only to grant what is due to expertise, and professionals are simply experts in the means required to achieve given ends.[18] In the consensual situation, the extent to which, for example, a school board can hold teachers or a school to account for its performance is strictly limited, since by definition its members are not expert and can at best only claim to be able to identify cases of gross incompetence, gross inefficiency, and plain corruption – and even here they may well feel constrained to rely on the advice of the headteacher or an inspector.[19]

As for accountability, where the value of professional freedom thrives the notion and practice of intraprofessional accountability will thrive too, though the fact that teaching has never achieved this to the degree that law and medicine have indicates that neither consensus nor professionalism have been so strongly developed in teaching as in these other occupations.

When the ends of education cease to be consensual, and differences can no longer peaceably coexist, becoming territories to defend or attack, the claim to professional freedom logically collapses. For in such a situation there is no longer a neutral professional practice dealing in expertly assessible means.

The contrast which is being made here will appear oversimplified, though, just as teachers have an interest in exaggerating their professionalism, so in a crisis of values, politicians and parents have an interest in painting the consequences for professionalism more bleakly than is really warranted. In practice, means and ends are not so sharply distinguished as I have painted them: 'ends' are rarely simple matters of subjective preference, and 'means' are rarely neutral techniques. Even in a crisis situation, teachers can claim some special competence: they can claim to know something about what ends it is possible to pursue within the school system; they can point out that the miracles expected of them do not come cheap; and they can claim to understand something about the relation of secondary ends (e.g., teaching basic skills) to primary ends (e.g., meeting the child's needs). Most importantly, a good part of current dispute concerns not conflicting ends, but whether means alleged to be effective in reaching agreed ends are actually so, a dispute which could be eminently scientific.[20]

Nonetheless, the collapse of agreed values – the legitimation crisis again – has put teachers on the spot, and put 'professional freedom' in danger of being relegated to the fourth division of values. It is not surprising, therefore, to find teachers actively suggesting new forms of accountability which are effectively proposals for more effective and responsive forms of intraprofessional accountability than have hitherto been used, though there are plainly limits beyond which they cannot go. Thus, at the time I write this, politicians are putting the question of getting rid of dud teachers on the agenda (*Education in Schools*, paras. 6.36–6.39) – something teachers could scarcely do themselves.

In this context, we can appreciate proposals like Margaret Maden's[21] for CNAA-style validation of school plans which would be drawn up internally by each school showing targets, curricula, teaching methods, resources, etc., and arguing out the relations conceived to exist among the elements of the plan. This is a particularly interesting idea, and the borrowing of an approach from higher education strikes me as significant. For it ties the disputed idea of teacher control to the still consensual value of academic freedom. This is legitimate, since teachers are plainly involved to some degree in the same line of business as academics – the transmission of knowledge, over the production and dissemination of which it would be irrational to introduce formalized administrative and political controls, since that would require of politicians and administrators that they know better than those who are defined as those who know best.[22] But the proposal's weakness is that it takes no account of the important fact that schooling is universal and compulsory, whereas higher education is selective and voluntary. Is it really enough for one group of professionals to certificate another group of professionals to practise their skills on children who have little or no say in whether they wish those skills to be exercised on them, and whose parents have as little say, too? Furthermore, schooling is not only about the transmission of knowledge, but also about the civilizing, socializing, or controlling of a new generation. Could a CNAA-style panel successfully legitimize a claim to deal authoritatively with the nonintellectual aspects of schooling, such as discipline regulations?

In reality, such proposals as Margaret Maden's seem to have come too late. Traditional forms of intraprofessional accountability have ceased to satisfy, and critics will not be satisfied with more rigorous versions of the old mechanisms. This is partly a dissatisfaction specific to teaching, but partly belongs to a more general movement of distrust of autonomous professional groups, including lawyers and doctors. Individuals do their own conveyancing and defend themselves in court cases; the women's movement has developed a critique of doctors and started alternative forms of medical practice. As these examples should make clear, these criticisms cannot always be associated with traditional right-wing and left-wing political positions: some of them hark back to traditional self-help doctrines; all of them dissent from the social democrat's confidence in the state. Of course, there are critics whose positions are typically right- or left-wing, especially in relation to schooling. Thus, on the one hand, we have those who argue that teachers have abandoned their own previous good standards, to which the rest of us allegedly remain attached. On the other hand, it is argued that teachers retain a typical professional attachment to barbaric practices no longer acceptable to lay people, such as their retention of corporal punishment, uniform,[23] and curricula which stereotype children into traditional sex roles.

In conclusion, this section has relied on fairly intuitive notions of 'professional freedom'. I suggest that a useful research project would concern itself in analysing and differentiating varieties of professional freedom, the sorts of arguments which can be advanced for each of them, and the kinds of accountability procedures which would put them out of existence.

Social needs

> Whether or not it is found that standards have remained constant, risen or fallen over some past period is less important than whether the standards which are being achieved today correspond as nearly as possible to society's needs. (DES Guidelines for the regional conferences of the Great Debate)[24]

> The speech [by the Prime Minister at Ruskin College, October 1976] was made against a background of strongly critical comment in the Press and elsewhere on education and educational standards. Children's standards of performance in their school work were said to have declined. The curriculum, it was argued, paid too little attention to the basic skills of reading, writing and arithmetic, and was overloaded with fringe subjects. Teachers lacked adequate professional skills, and did not know how to discipline children or instil in them concern for hard work or good manners. Underlying all this was the feeling that the educational system was out of touch with the fundamental need of Britain to survive economically in a highly competitive world through the efficiency of its industry and commerce. (*Education in Schools*, para. 1.2)

The interpretation of 'social needs' is no more, and probably much less, consensual than the interpretation of the other educational values we have considered. For in practice its meaning is not established by argument, but by the authoritative definition of the state. The epigraph to this section from *Education in Schools* illustrates this splendidly: education has been criticized for all sorts of reasons, apparently from numerous different standpoints. The Green Paper disabuses us: all along, you know, you have *really* been feeling 'that the educational system was out of touch with the fundamental need of Britain to survive economically'. And this is not just a persuasive definition in the philosophical sense,[25] but an authoritative one, for it is a definition on which government intends to act and has the ability to act.

In the nineteenth century the state defined society's needs primarily as a need for *citizens*. As everyone knows, universal compulsory education was introduced after the second great Reform Act of 1867. Its citizen-forming purpose was immortalized by Sir Robert Lowe: 'Educate your Masters'.[26] Today the definition has radically altered and society's needs are defined principally as a need for *workers*, a concern largely absent from nineteenth-century political debate.

For the purpose of this chapter there is no need to document the emphasis being placed on education as a preparation for working life; one has only to read *Education in Schools*. Parents plainly regard education as the principal determinant of job prospects; politicians have sought to make it so – here they again differ from their predecessors;[27] employers complain about the failure of schools to produce workers competent in the required skills. However, the volume of and stress placed on these positions should not lead us into assuming that each party is making a correct judgement.

For instance, while parents are more or less right, individually, in thinking that if their children achieve higher standards in core subjects then their job prospects will be improved, collectively this does not hold, for a fallacy of composition is involved in the transition from individual to universal case. If job opportunities are relatively fixed in number and distribution and determined by the semiautonomous and slow development of the economic system (and leaving aside policy-created unemployment), then if all children achieve higher standards all that can happen is that either employers raise job qualifications all round (as in the USA)[28] or they resort to non-meritocratic selection criteria (jobs for the boys).

Again, individual employers may be right in protesting the lack of skill displayed by school-leavers, but it can also be true that overall there is a secular trend towards a deskilling of work, job requirements becoming increasingly polarized between very high- and very low-skill jobs. Roy Edgley summarizes some of the evidence which points this way in a recent paper.[29] Even if it is not the case that work is being deskilled, a belief that it is may be involved in pupil perception of the world of work. For there do exist 'reluctant learners' who justify their opposition to school in terms of the pointlessness of learning what they are taught. Habermas categorizes such phenomena as belonging to a general 'motivation crisis',[30] pretty obviously connected to phases of economic crisis and which in Britain's case are chronic rather than acute, with the dole queue the certain destination of a proportion of school-leavers. Youth unemployment may be small percentage-wise, but it has a ripple-effect impact on morale. It is all very well for *Education in Schools* to list as an aim of education 'to help children to appreciate how the nation earns and maintains its standard of living and properly to esteem the essential role of industry and commerce in this process' (para. 1.19, v), but this is not a lesson anyone can teach young people who think that they are destined not for industry and commerce but unemployment, or even for what were called, when I worked in the Youth Employment Service, 'dead-end jobs', to the elimination of which we looked forward. Some school-leavers might have to put up with such jobs; we did not consider it our business to make them esteem them. But that was a dozen years ago.

Rhodes Boyson seems to me entirely wrong in denying the existence of a motivation crisis among pupils, other than one brought about by the schools themselves. He has to take this position since he also takes the view that parents have not changed, but only the schools. *Education in Schools* also makes light of the 'lack of motivation and unco-operative attitudes displayed by some pupils' (para. 2.16), but these seem to me of quite fundamental importance. Partly, we do not adequately understand them; partly, we are reluctant to face up to them, since we realize that their resolution (as opposed to their repression) may lead us outside the range of policies we are prepared to consider – a range which threatens to get more, not less, restricted.[31]

Unfortunately, I must leave such issues aside, and return to the current advancement of 'society's needs' as a value to be served by schooling, for this emphasis explains many of the most important new forms of accountability being canvassed, such as a government-defined core curriculum and government-administered national testing or monitoring in specified subjects at various ages.[32] Some of the connections are fairly obvious. A government can no more have an active manpower policy without predictive knowledge of and ability to influence the qualifications which school-leavers will have, than it can have a rational teacher-training policy without a registry of births. If the analogy serves to raise a grim smile, it may also introduce some remarks on the possible limitations of accountability procedures designed to permit the implementation of labour market policies (although these procedures are not designed for this purpose alone).

My first and central question is this: are we witnessing an overestimation of the possibilities of central planning? My second question is: is an extension of political and administrative power, through the activation of existing legal rights (*Education in Schools*, para. 1.14, iii), being proposed in response not to a crisis of administrative rationality, but to a crisis in belief (legitimation) and motivation which cannot be solved by administrative means?

My answers to the two questions are interconnected. Habermas uses the expression 'rationality crisis' to refer to the systematic failure of an administrative system to produce the required quantity and quality of rational decisions.[33] He has in mind, for example, the apparent inability of governments to translate the theoretically simple Keynesian stabilizing strategies into effective economic management policies. Not only have grandiose national plans had to be abandoned, but even more limited, expert-formulated wage and price policies have had to be ditched in favour of *ad hoc* coercion, political bargains, compromises, and understandings.[34] Habermas' explanation is partly in terms of the inherent limitations of administrative rationality as such; partly in terms of the workings of uncontrolled forces outside the power of individual governments (such as the level of oil prices); and partly in terms of the political resistances which supposedly neutral, technocratic policies create, and which administrative procedures are unable to process.

This general argument of Habermas seems to me relevant to the appraisal of the kinds of national educational planning-through-accountability mechanisms which are being proposed. For these are also vulnerable both to the impact of autonomous economic and social developments which they cannot control (such as crisis-enforced educational cutbacks in which the Assessment of Performance Unit may be an early victim) and to political resistances: the day that the Secretary of State puts on the agenda the question of getting rid of incompetent teachers, the General Secretary of the National Union of Teachers warns her that she is 'entering a minefield'.[35]

Political resistances will be that much stronger to the degree that the government is reacting, not to failures, internally or externally recognized, of its own administrative system, but to a crisis of belief and motivation arising independently of actions by the administration. Now it seems to me that the government *is* reacting to such an external crisis, and is advancing the value 'social needs', to be pursued through core curricula and national monitoring, as a means of resolving that crisis. I suggest that this underestimates the actual autonomy and rationality of the belief and motivation crisis, and cannot possibly resolve it, though it may suppress it. Maladjustment, truancy, vandalism, and radical educational innovations (which are often only reactive crisis-avoidance adaptations) will not go away because government enforces a core curriculum and national monitoring of standards in the interests of British industry, or for any other motive. If there really is a deep-seated crisis of motivation and belief, the effect of the political and administrative measures being proposed may only be to increase conflict at the classroom chalk face; and to deepen antagonisms between teachers, government and parents, and within the teaching profession itself. In the crudest terms, the list of aims which *Education in Schools* hopes that 'the majority of people would probably agree with' (para. 1.19) may just not be consensual enough for the most relevant groups – parents, teachers, and pupils. To return to the analogy with British economic policy, governments are prone to launch policies on the assumption that they are broadly supported (and they may even have reason to suppose this from opinion polls and the like). But then trouble develops, the government calls on us to stand up and be counted – and we all remain sitting down. I am not saying that governments should avoid political battles; far from it. I am saying that governments seem to be naïve about the extent of agreement which they can achieve or enforce by administrative means. Nor do government systems learn rapidly from mistakes, so that the tragedies of history have plenty of opportunity to return as farce.

The above discussion leaves aside the larger question of whether in principle administrative systems can meet the increased demands which are now likely to be placed upon them. Yet this is relevant too; I do not know enough about organization theory to enter into this; I only know of arguments to show that the bounds of possible administrative rationality are quite limited.[36] Fortunately, it is the task of other contributors to consider whether the road to hell is paved with good intentions, and I do not enter into the topic here.

Children's needs

The schools available for an area shall not be deemed to be sufficient unless they are sufficient in number, character, and equipment to afford for all pupils opportunities for education offering such variety of instruction and training as may be desirable in view of their different ages, and aptitudes, and of the different periods for which they may be expected to remain at school, including instruction and training appropriate to their respective needs. (1944 Education Act, section 8 (i))

Where society's needs are stressed in the epigraphs to the previous section, the 1944 act quoted immediately above is committed to the value of the needs of the individual child, which is an expression of a traditional, liberal regard for the individual as the end which policy must serve, not the means to the furtherance of some other policy goal. This regard endured in official educational thinking at least up until the Robbins Report and the endorsement of its proposal to gear the expansion of higher education to student demand for it rather than to manpower needs. In this section I want to consider, and reassert, the value that education should satisfy or meet children's needs.

Of course, the interpretation which is given to 'children's needs' is disputed and, perhaps, essentially contested.[37] But I do not think that the concept is necessarily useless for purposes of rational argument or social scientific research. It need not be a nonoperational, merely 'boo-hooray' expression. In the first part of this section, I shall seek to give 'a child's needs' an interpretation which is at the same time plausible and operational, and then go on to argue for a further development of the concept. I shall use this differentiated concept both to defend parts of the present school curriculum which *Education in Schools* passes over with indifference, and to suggest lines of social scientific research which could result in the identification of areas of unmet human needs (to meet which the curriculum could possibly be adapted) as well as to evaluate areas of the existing curriculum. I think that the approach I adopt offers a way of treating children as human beings, without being either subjective, unrealistic, or sentimental. In short, I am looking for a way of interpreting 'children's needs' which puts this value in a form where it can be served by policy-related research. In conclusion, I consider the relation of this value to forms of accountability.

My first task, then, is to give an interpretation to 'children's needs'. The first point to note is the way in which the word 'need' applies to both intermediate and final needs, as is illustrated in the following hypothetical interchange:

a: John needs a holiday
b: Why does he need a holiday?
a: Because he's been ill

b: Why is that a reason for saying he needs a holiday?
a: Because a holiday will restore his health
b: Why is that a reason?
a: Because we all have a need for health
b: Why?
a: We just do

The need for a holiday is what I call an intermediate need; the need for health is a final need. Now, while the intermediate needs which any individual has depend on peculiarities of himself and his circumstances, and so vary infinitely from person to person, the final needs which we recognize are rather restricted in number. In argument, we rarely have to refer to the final needs, since the specification of an intermediate need will usually indicate to what final need it could be related. Thus, the statement 'He needs a meal' would not normally produce a series of challenges which we could eventually stop by referring to the need for survival. But it could do so, and it could meet those challenges.

On the other hand, a statement about an intermediate need could be challenged not because the questioner had doubts about the final need to which it related, but because he considered that there were other or better ways of meeting the final need than those envisaged by the initial speaker.

This discussion could be extended at length, but in its present form it provides just about enough for a discussion of children's needs. What are the final needs of children? It seems to me there are at least eight which we would all recognize: children have a need to be able to survive; to get or stay healthy; to be able to work with application; to enjoy themselves; to have a sense of their own worth; to be able to relate to others; to understand the world in which they live; and to be able to participate in its major institutions.[38] It is possible to reduce some of these needs to others; the need for health could be said to be served by having a sense of one's own worth; the need to be able to work and the need to enjoy oneself are not unrelated. But I shall not pursue that possibility. Likewise, I won't break down these final needs into more precisely specified ones. Nor will I sharply distinguish the child's present and future needs.

But there is one point I should like to take up, namely, the suggestion that these supposedly 'individual' needs are just as much 'social' needs as those discussed in the previous section. It might be said that while some of the needs specified in my list are quasi-anthropological (for instance, the survival need), others are historically conditioned (such as the participation need), but that they could all be put on a more logical and equal footing as expressions of social requirements: there could be no society if no one survived, and society could not function if, for example, no one could 'relate to' anyone else. Why not admit this social determination of needs, and avoid the false dichotomy you set up between needs which society has, and needs which individuals have?

This is an important question which I would answer by saying that as I conceive things not all individual needs are perfectly convertible into functional social needs. Some individual needs, whether anthropological or historically conditioned, stand in tension with social requirements and it is out of that tension that progress may be generated. An education which fails to respect individual needs as a guiding value necessarily becomes a one-dimensional practice which gives no push either to the individual or to the emergence of new social forms. It fails both in an individually civilizing mission and in a socially progressive purpose. Liberal theory is often criticized for polarizing the 'individual' and 'society'; but if there is a contradiction there, it is an incredibly dynamic one, which will hopefully survive the application of an undialectical logic.

Whether this is granted or not, it remains to consider what one can possibly do with a list of needs such as the one I wrote out above. We can clearly use it in argument to show that certain positions simply overlook needs which children have. Thus, should someone say 'Children don't need to learn to sing at school; they are unlikely to become singers', we could reply: 'Children need more than to be able to get jobs; they also need to be able to enjoy themselves, and singing is an activity in which they can learn to enjoy themselves'. Of course, there are other ways of enjoying oneself. Schools provide several enjoyable activities to children, because not all children can enjoy themselves in the same way. The range they provide is, of course, conditioned by cultural tradition; time and resources available; the suitability of an activity to an age-range; and the popularity of different activities. But so long as they provide a *range* of activities in which children can find present and (ideally) future enjoyment, then schools can claim to be meeting children's needs in at least one area.

Should anyone doubt that children have a need to enjoy themselves, or to learn how to enjoy themselves in adult life, it is surely only necessary to point out that doctors' surgeries and mental hospitals are full of people who are unable to enjoy themselves, for reasons which are not obviously connected to their material circumstances.

The argument sketched above is very simplified, but it should indicate that we can argue about children's needs without plunging immediately into the depths of irreconcilable differences of ultimate value. Indeed, I think we could use the concept of 'need' in social scientific research. For example, suppose it is asserted that 'Children need to know the multiplication tables by heart'. When it is put this way we can legitimately ask for a kind of justification which we could not have asked for had it been said, 'I want children to learn the multiplication tables by heart'. Since a need to know the multiplication tables is not final, but intermediate, we can ask why it is thought that children need to know them. Suppose the answer is, 'To prepare them for the world of work', which we can intuitively connect up with our survival needs. In this form the answer is in principle scientific. It can be either true or false that children need to learn the multiplication tables in order to prepare them for the world of work. If this is so, there is the possibility of scientific investigation. A historically minded sociologist might start out in his investigations by noting that prior to the invention of printing, memory skills, comparable to mental arithmetic skills, were much more developed than they are now. People needed them and developed them. Nowadays, the Greek memory method of places[39] has no other use than as a party trick. The sociologist might then ask, does the apparent decline in mental arithmetic skills, if it exists, reflect the fact that it has ceased to be a skill people need? If this has happened, what technological or organizational changes have brought it about? These seem to me genuine questions, though obviously ones to be tackled in a broader perspective than I have indicated. The fact that they can be asked, and that we can hope for a scientific answer does have the consequences that as far as any debate on children's need to learn mental arithmetic goes, there is no need to strike 'traditionalist' or 'progressive' postures. We can do so if we wish but then risk the charge that what interests us is not the needs of children but our own prejudices: 'Children need . . .' really means, 'I want . . .'

An approach which studies needs is complementary to an approach which studies deprivations, for to ask 'Does a child need to learn to x?' is only a way of asking 'Would a child be deprived if he did not learn to x?', for 'deprivation' means inability to satisfy needs (except that it is restricted to inabilities which have social rather than natural origins: I can have a need for health which cannot be satisfied because of an inherited, biological weakness, a situation to which we would not normally refer as 'deprivation').

But as so far developed, my view of needs and deprivations is one-dimensional, since it only allows for the identification of needs by reference to observable deprivations. But just as political scientists have argued that there are nonobservable second and third dimensions of *power*,[40] I want to argue that there are second and third dimensions of deprivation, and of children's needs – dimensions which are very relevant to our understanding both of those needs and of school practice.

In their famous article, 'The Two Faces of Power', Peter Bachrach and Morton Baratz[41] argue that behavioural scientists in studying only the actual exercise of power in overt acts in conflict situations overlook the power of individuals or institutions which resides in the fact that they do not need to exercise power overtly, because they are not challenged. They are not challenged because those who might otherwise enter into conflict with them recognize their possession of superior power, and so abstain from courses of action in which they would be bound to lose. Bachrach and Baratz call this the other face of power, the power of nondecision-making.

How is this relevant to our understanding of children's needs and deprivation?

Consider the following two statements:

A Jill Smith could not get a job of type *a* (which she would have enjoyed/felt worthy in/been able to apply herself to), because the school did not teach her to *x*, which it could have done. Therefore, school has failed to meet her needs.

B Jill Smith has never tried to get a job of type *a* (which she would have enjoyed/felt worthy in/been able to apply herself to), because she knows you have to be able to *x* to get such a job. School did not teach her to *x*, which it could have done. Therefore, school has failed to meet her needs.

In the case of statement A we can *observe* the deprivation someone suffers when they are turned down for the job; this is deprivation in the first dimension. In the case of statement B, we can observe nothing. Jill Smith may appear contented. But just as power can be said to be exercised over people even though they do not contest it, just as much as when they do contest it, so Jill Smith can be said to be deprived, though she may appear satisfied. And statement B is no less scientific than the first, even though we will have to use different research methods to detect the second dimension of deprivation and need then to identify the first dimension. We would have to interview Jill Smith, not look at her unsuccessful job applications – which is to say that research into the second dimension does not require a revolution in research methodology. But it might yield revolutionary findings, for example, about participation and nonparticipation in institutions, since we could certainly research statements of the form:

> C   Jill Smith (a parent) never goes to parent-teacher meetings because she knows you need to be able to speak well in public to have any impact on them. School could have sought to give her the skills and confidence to speak in public, but didn't. Therefore, school failed to meet her needs.

And if the statement was shown to be true, the question would automatically follow: What are we going to do about it?

By definition, a school's failures in the second dimension do not come to light in the way that failures in the first dimension do. They are failures which we must want to bring to light, and which once brought to light will require changes in schools if they are to be remedied. Now an accountability procedure can only hold schools to account for things the importance of which we are already aware. I suggest that one task of social science research is to search for things of which we are not aware, but of which we would hopefully be glad to be aware and willing to do something about. I assign the task to social science, but it should not be overlooked that the achievement frequently belongs to pressure groups. It is the women's movement which has made us aware that Jill Smith suffers second-dimension deprivations.

I turn now to the argument for the existence of a third dimension of deprivation, by analogy with Steven Lukes' theory of a third dimension of power.[42] Lukes argues that individuals or groups can legitimately be said to be oppressed by a structure of power even in cases where they neither contest the structure of power or refrain from contesting it, but are actually unaware of its existence as a structure of power (or consider justifiable what others call their 'oppression' – as in deference politics). This is how Lukes puts it: 'Is it not the supreme and most insidious exercise of power to prevent people, to whatever degree, from having grievances, by shaping their perceptions, cognitions and preferences in such a way that they accept their role in the existing order of things, either because they can see or imagine no alternative to it, or because they see it as natural and unchangeable, or because they value it as divinely ordained and beneficial?'[43] Of course, it is difficult to formulate and research testable propositions about such a third dimension of the exercise of power, but Lukes concludes after discussing the question (pp. 50–55) that 'A pessimistic attitude towards the possibility of such an analysis is unjustified' (p. 56). And Habermas, who develops a similar idea to that of Lukes in his *Legitimation Crisis* (pp. 111–117) using the concept of 'suppressed interest' (p. 117), is able to list four 'empirical indicators of suppressed interests' (p. 116) and concludes by expressing the view that the approach he has sketched enjoys 'some hope of success' (p. 117). Debate on the viability of the approach favoured by Lukes is spreading rapidly across the pages of *The British Journal of Political Science* and *Sociology*. Rather than summarize that debate, I enter directly into the question of third-dimension deprivation in relation to children's needs.

Let us return to Jill Smith and statement c above, reformulating it in the way which would be required for it to indicate a third dimension of deprivation. We could write:

D It has never occurred to Jill Smith (a parent) to go to parent-teacher meetings, because she never thinks of things like that as meant for her. School could have opened up to her the possibility of perceiving participation in society's institutions as a need or as a means to satisfying her needs but did not. Therefore, school failed to meet her needs.

This is an extremely cumbersome statement, but it can be linked to very familiar ideas which form part of our educational and political tradition. Notably, we distinguish between people who don't do something, because they have considered doing it and rejected it, and people who don't do something, because they have never considered it. And when we think of education, one of the things which has always been emphasized is the rightness of opening up possibilities to children in such a way that they have the choice in later life of pursuing *or* declining to pursue them. This differs both from an approach which introduces activities as the sort-of-thing-you-will-do-regardless, and the approach which leaves things out so-that-you-don't-do-them-whatever. John Stuart Mill speaks in opposition to the first approach when, in his inaugural address at the University of St. Andrew's, he says that religion should be taught not as something which has been chosen for people but as something they will have to choose for themselves.[44] The second approach has coloured much of our thinking about sex education and is just as illiberal.

Yet over broad ranges of school activity the underlying justification is precisely this idea of opening up possibilities to children, in order that now or later they can choose whether and how to incorporate into their own lives the activities opened up. As I shall indicate below, it can't and doesn't always work out as we would like, but there is no satisfactory alternative to it as a way of realizing an aspiration not to confine the individual with invisible threads. For while there is no doubt an element of fiction in a teacher's conceptualization of children as separate individuals with specific needs, this does create a space for the child to develop and exercise autonomy which is restricted or eliminated in approaches which see the child as a mere bearer of an intelligence quotient or class position. Undoubtedly, children 'have' IQs and 'belong' to classes, but if the perception of these elements exhausts the teacher's preceptions of his pupils, then the child is limited from the outset. Either he will be offered no more than is appropriate to his IQ, or else he will be taught that which in virtue of his position it is believed he ought to know, and no more. Very simply, there is in liberal theory an idea of the individual person as someone who can play an active part in shaping his own culture, which indicates an educational practice responsive to such activity. To what extent practice institutionalizes such conceptions is another question, which I cannot pursue here.

To return to statement D, however cumbersome this is, it does seem to indicate the direction in which we could hope to make talk of a third dimension of deprivation scientific. We can entertain some hope of identifying things which people never do because they have never thought of doing them, and we can envisage explaining them by referring to possibilities which have never been opened up to people. In connection with the current debate on education, I think we are in danger of overlooking just how valuable that is. Even a traditionalist like Rhodes Boyson narrows his attention to deprivation in the first dimension; *Education in Schools* goes as far as the second dimension; but the awareness we were beginning to have of the third dimension seems in danger of being foreclosed.

One possible explanation of a wariness to approach the third dimension is that it does involve us in facing up to awkward issues, and may even commit us to taking up positions which it has become fashionable to reject. For, firstly, the idea of opening up possibilities is associated with what is now dismissed as 'cultural élitism', unacceptable in a relativist culture where all modes of socialization are equal; and, secondly, the experience of possibilities cannot be separated from the experience of disappointment which we shy away from. I want briefly to consider these two lines of criticism, for they seem to me to be double-edged.

The critic of cultural élitism would, I think, say that the idea of 'opening up possibilities' to children has meant and continues to mean, in practice, the attempt to get working-class children to take to middle-class culture. No wonder we have reluctant learners when all we try to do is impose our own peculiar version of the good, the true, and the beautiful on everyone else! I certainly used to think like that at school: I was fascinated by Agatha Christie, Edgar Wallace, and John Steinbeck, but could not abide Shakespeare. In the school of my dreams, Shakespeare would have gone and Steinbeck would have ruled. But what happens when Steinbeck, or to put it more sharply, Mickey Spillane or Manchester United Football Club rule? It is one thing, as a pedagogic method, to start from where the children are at; it is another thing to stop there. One is more likely to stop at the latest craze manufactured by the entertainment industry than at any other destination; nor is one likely to discover anything which might be called 'working-class culture'. For if by that is meant the sort of culture with which social and labour historians are concerned, then it is something which just as much as 'middle-class culture' has to be discovered and consciously learnt. Chap book, ballad and broad-sheet literature are no closer to children's experience than Shakespeare, nor is the matchgirls' strike more real than the Crimean War – and that is why it is important to introduce children to all the different worlds which these examples instantiate. This is quite different from a simple 'responsiveness' to children's expressed interests and definitions of relevance, a responsiveness which can have radical intentions but end up educating children for their station. So while I take to heart some of the critique of middle-class cultural imperialism, I want to try to retain this idea of 'opening up possibilities'. Otherwise, I think we will only increase whatever third-dimension unmet deprivations exist.

This is relevant to the question of 'disappointment'. Disappointment is an inseparable consequence of opening up possibilities, yet it has become unacceptable to disappoint children. In effect, this is on a par with preferring people to be content but ignorant, a position denounced right through our radical tradition, in Oscar Wilde's *Soul of Man under Socialism* and George Orwell's *1984*, for instance. The resistance to disappointing children stems, I think, from failure to distinguish two sources of disappointment, from one of which it is absurd to shelter us, the other of which has to be combatted, not covered up.

First, disappointment arises from everyone's discovery at some time or other that certain things are outside his abilities, or beyond the amount of effort he is willing to devote to them, but which he would have to contribute to achieve success. I would have liked to learn to play the recorder at primary school but somehow, and unlike everyone else, I could not get the hang of it and ended up hiding my lack of skill as I moved my fingers up and down, not blowing at all. This first sort of disappointment is a lesson we all learn about something or other, and it does us no service to shelter us from it.

Second, disappointment arises from discovering that some things are beyond our reach because we lack the money, backing, connections, or facilities to grasp them. In this case, a formal equality of opportunity is like inviting guests to a banquet in the knowledge that they cannot afford to attend, as Tawney puts it in *Equality*. This second source of disappointment is of overwhelming practical importance and remains something to be contested, not covered up by sheltering children from it in making no demands on them that they might be unable to meet. I think we should make those changes in society which would make it possible for all children to benefit from educational possibilities, not restrict education to a core curriculum (or equally a child-centred course)[45] which anyone can be got through, even if dad is unemployed, mum drinks, and elder brother beats you.

If there is a third dimension of deprivation, is it important? In our desire to tackle deprivations in the first and second dimensions, could we increase deprivations in the third dimension? I want to approach these questions in a rather naïve manner, but one which, I hope, can be turned to good account.

I begin, then, by asking myself three questions about my own schooling. First, what possibilities and opportunities do I think it opened up to me from which I have subsequently benefited? Second, what opportunities did it offer which I couldn't cope with, ignored, or have now more or less forgotten all about? Third, what opportunities did it not offer, which I now think I could have benefited from? Anyone could produce answers to these questions; they don't have scientific value, but they may be indicators for argument and research.

To begin with, I am able to say that my schooling played a part in teaching me to sing, dance, take an interest in nature, speak up in public, write adequate English, as well, of course, as making it possible for me to go on being educated past compulsory school age. Second, I am aware of not having learnt to swim, understand physical scientific procedures, or play the recorder, though the opportunities were there, and others were able to take advantage of them. Third, I do wish I had had the benefit of proper health education, including sex education. I imagine I would have benefited from a more cooperative working atmosphere and from a less sexist curriculum and environment than a boys' grammar school offered.

Despite the fact that our own perceptions of our schooling are highly problematic this list does indicate one thing, I hope, and that is the *breadth* of schooling which is required actually to go any way towards meeting children's needs – awareness of which fact seems absent from, or even rejected in, current debate. Thus *Education in Schools*, in listing the aims of the schools (para. 1.19), makes no mention of *any* aims which might justify what schools presently do in teaching children to develop, use, and enjoy their bodies (P.E., health education, etc.), or in learning to cope with adolescence, independence, and parenthood (sex education, domestic science, etc.). All we have are the aims to 'instil respect for moral values, for other people and for oneself, and tolerance of other races, religions, and ways of life' (aim ii) and to, 'teach children about human achievement and aspirations in the arts and sciences, in religion and in the search for a more just social order' (aim vii), neither of which can sound very promising to the P.E. or housecraft teacher. It is still so intellectualist, moralizing (in the bad sense), and limited in its view of human needs and potentialities. *Education in Schools* does not seem to have been written by people who have any appreciation of the world in which people need to work; have to cook; or enjoy singing, swimming, or sewing.

In terms of an investigation of a third dimension, the social scientist might use the politician's and the administrator's insensitivity to some obvious children's, or more generally human, needs as an indicator that within the area of those needs or associated with them are needs which are scarcely recognized, and scarcely met, though evidence can be produced to show that such needs do exist and are important.

Consider, for example, the question of our health. We seem to recognize the existence of a need here and apparently try to meet it. But are our expectations in fact much lower than the need itself justifies? The critical social scientist might compare, on the one hand, the existing knowledge which we have that the general level of health of the population is much lower than it need be as a result of wrong diet; growing consumption of alcohol; high consumption of tobacco; and unhealthy working conditions; with, on the other hand, the rock-bottom importance given to health education. In *Education in Schools* it cannot compete for attention with Welsh in the curriculum of the schools in Wales, which rates six paragraphs.[46] There is no health education lobby with any political clout, but that does not mean, once we allow for a third dimension of need and deprivation, that there are no unmet needs as far as our health is concerned. What I am suggesting is that one of the research tasks of social scientists is to gather and interpret data relevant to questions about needs and deprivations in all three dimensions, not just the first two. From what I have said, I conclude that schools may have developed greater sensitivity to the range of children's needs than parents or politicians, and that that has become a weakness when it should be a strength. The danger at the moment is that we increase the number of unmet needs unnecessarily, and with results we shall later have cause to regret.

But now I face a difficulty. How does all this relate to accountability? On the one hand, I think that schools should be held accountable for meeting children's needs. On the other hand, parents and politicians and administrators seem determined to think of the functions of schooling in the narrowest instrumental terms. The most active and organized parents quite reasonably want their own children to get on and are apparently prepared to sacrifice the all-round development of all children to that end; after the comprehensive will come the crammer school. National politicians bear the weight of a permanent economic crisis on their backs and inevitably dream sweetly of transforming us into a nation of technicians producing transistors for Taiwan. (What sort of schools do they have there, I wonder?) The two together are capable of squeezing children into a *Hard Times* mould. So we are left with teachers, social scientists, and the children themselves. These lack either the ability or the right to enforce accountability to themselves. But they can and will try to modify the plans of parents or politicians. I hope they do so. Otherwise we risk moving to a state of affairs in which children will never see a recorder, let alone learn to play one.

June/July 1977

Postcript

In a comment on the above, Michael Eraut pointed out that schooling is expected to serve a value which cannot be assimilated to any in my list, a value which he calls 'generational control'. By this he means that schools are expected to ensure that children behave as children are expected to behave in relation to adults, in terms of manners, politeness, deference, etc. Acceptance of this value by schools explains their insistence on such things as school uniform, and a great deal of popular criticism of schools is concerned with their failure to secure an acceptable level of generational control.

I agree that such a value exists, and I overlooked it because it seems to me illegitimate. However, it is socially legitimate and is therefore required in any explanation of what schools do. I take the view that schools are able to do much less towards meeting children's needs than otherwise they might be able to achieve, just because they also have to secure acceptable inter-generational control. This does not come across in my chapter, which paints schooling in its most favourable aspects and is misleading in so far as it suggests that schooling can and does do a great deal for children; it does not, and one of the reasons for this is that it has to control the children assigned to it.

Too optimistic about schools, I have been too negative about parents. For from the way in which parents behave in an exclusionary system we cannot infer how they would behave in a participatory system. (Consider how people can express anger that criminals 'get away with it' when interviewed by pollsters, but prove quite reluctant to convict when converted into jurors.) It was the genius of John Stuart Mill to realize that participation civilizes people – less tendentiously, that it broadens their outlook in forcing on them awareness of conflicting imperatives.

In a low-growth economy, conflicting imperatives of special importance seem to me to exist between individual demands on the educational system and social requirements. For example, individuals may demand socially expensive higher education, though the economic system is unable to make use of their qualifications. Fairness to the rest of society may demand that opportunities for higher education be restricted, or else made available in diluted form as a consumer good to the whole population. Only in a participatory system is there any hope of reconciling such conflicts in a mutually acceptable way.

Notes

1. I had the benefit of discussion with Tony Becher, Judy Keiner, Heather Lyons before putting pen to paper. Tony Becher, Maurice Kogan, and Ian Lister made written comments on the draft version of this chapter. None of these people, who were so generous with their time, necessarily agrees with my

arguments; none of them has read the final version.

2. In relation to broadcasting. See *Report of the Committee on the Future of Broadcasting* (Chairman: Lord Annan), Cmnd 6753, HMSO 1977, para 4.11.

3. Boyson, Rhodes, *The Crisis in Education*, Woburn Press, London, 1975. The question of how a relatively uninstructed person distinguishes false from true prophets is an important preoccupation of both French and English political theory in the eighteenth and nineteenth centuries. For France, see Robert Darnton, *Mesmerism and the End of the Enlightenment in France*, Harvard University Press, Cambridge, Mass., 1968, especially the extract from a paper by Condorcet, pp. 189–192. For England, see Sir George Cornewall Lewis, *An Essay on the Influence of Authority in Matters of Opinion*, John Parker, London, 1849. I discuss the question at length in my M. Phil. thesis, *How is Political Knowledge Possible?* (University of Sussex, 1978).

4. Central to Boyson's argument is the claim that parents have not changed, and from this follows the necessity of denying that children have changed. In his view, it is only schools which are different, see, e.g., p. 13 of his book, op. cit.

5. Schumpeter, Joseph, *Capitalism, Socialism and Democracy*, 3rd edition, George Allen and Unwin, London, 1950, pp. 250–283, reprinted in Anthony Quinton (ed), *Political Philosophy*, Oxford University Press, 1967.

6. In the case of William Tyndale School, the extent to which managers of a school can be socially unrepresentative can be gathered from Robin Auld, *William Tyndale Junior and Infants Schools Public Inquiry*, ILEA, London, 1976. The evidence there, interpreted in the light of more general knowledge of developments in inner-London, seems to confirm the analysis of Barry Hindess, *The Decline of Working Class Politics*, MacGibbon and Kee, London, 1971.

7. Arrow, Kenneth, *Social Choice and Individual Values*, 3rd edition, Yale University Press, New Haven, 1963. Arrow rediscovered and generalized an inherent limitation of voting (aggregation) procedures, which had first been pointed out by Condorcet in his little-read *Essai sur l'application de l'analyse à la probabilité des decisions rendues à la pluralité des voix*, Imprimerie Royale, Paris, 1785, and periodically rediscovered ever since. Roughly, if there are more than two choices, no voting mechansim can be devised which consistently represents voters' preferences; it will sometimes produce less preferred to more preferred results. This is usually called the 'paradox of voting'. See Arrow, especially pp. 59–60.

8. Cmnd 6869, HMSO, London, 1977, hereinafter referred to as *Education in Schools*.

9. See Auld, op. cit. and Terry Ellis et al., *William Tyndale, The Teachers' Story*, Writers and Readers Publishing Cooperative, London, 1976.

10. See the account of the functioning of the 11+ in Boyson, op. cit., p. 57.

11. *Education in Schools*, op. cit., para 3.6.

12. Weber, Max, *The Theory of Social and Economic Organization*, Free Press, Glencoe, 1964.

13. Boyson, op. cit., p. 141.

14. Habermas, Jürgen, *Legitimation Crisis*, Heinemann, London, 1976.

15. Compare Boyson: 'The malaise in schools in Britain has followed from a

breakdown in accepted curriculum and traditional values. There was little concern about either political control or parental choice so long as there was an 'understood' curriculum which was followed by every school. Schools may have differed in efficiency but their common values of curriculum were broadly acceptable. The present disillusionment of parents arises from their resentment that their children's education now depends on the lottery of the school to which they are directed. Standards decline because both measurement and comparisons are impossible when aims and curriculum become widely divergent. These problems can be solved only by making schools again accountable to some authority outside them. The necessary sanction is either a nationally enforced curriculum or parental choice or a combination of both' (p. 141).

16. On the role of the inspectorate, see the interesting letter from Val Arnold-Foster and Sarah Wood, of CASE, in *The Guardian*, 21 June, 1977.

17. On the theory of this in relation to science, see Ziman, J.D., *Public Knowledge, An Essay Concerning the Social Dimension of Science*, Cambridge University Press, 1968. In practice, hierarchies often put obstacles in the way of the progress of knowledge, though not so systematically as to halt it.

18. This seemed obvious to early social scientists who embraced what we should now call social engineering approaches to policy-formation and administration, since they were confident that scientific knowledge could be secured about both ends and means. Condorcet, Comte, and Saint-Simon fit this bill, though Condorcet has more democratic spirit than the others: see Baker, Keith M., 'Scientism, Elitism and Liberalism: The Case of Condorcet', in *Studies on Voltaire and the Eighteenth Century*, Vol LV, Geneva, 1967, pp. 129–165; and more generally, Bramson, Leon, *The Political Context of Sociology*, Princeton University Press, 1961.

19. The Auld Report, op. cit., is instructive in this connection. See, for example, paras 346–351 (pp. 109–111).

20. Often it is scientific, which is not to say it is without shortcomings, such as biases in the research design. But all science is open to misuse, and this is what will happen to educational research in a crisis situation, especially where its shortcomings match social prejudices. See the reception of Neville Bennett's *Teaching Styles and Pupil Progress*, Open Books, London, 1976.

21. Reported in the *Times Educational Supplement*, 18 March, 1977.

22. Marx takes great pleasure using this argument in his 'Comments on the latest Prussian censorship instruction', in Easton, Lloyd D. and Guddat, Kurt H., *Writings of the Young Marx on Philosophy and Society*, Doubleday, New York, 1967, pp. 67–92.

23. To intrude a personal concern, I do think that the commitment given in *Education in Schools* to discriminate 'in favour of children who are underprivileged for whatever reason' (para 1.13) ought to be followed by legislation outlawing compulsory school uniform or by large increases in school clothing grants. For whatever the intentions, schools which impose school uniform requirements discriminate *against* 'underprivileged' children, as the Child Poverty Action Group has argued.

24. Quoted in the *Times Educational Supplement*, 11 February, 1977, p. 3.

25. Stevenson, Charles, 'Persuasive Definitions', in *Mind*, 1938.
26. Quoted in Gregg, Pauline, *A Social and Economic History of Britain, 1760–1963*, 4th edition, Harrap, London, 1964, p. 247. G.M. Trevelyan observes, 'It was characteristic of the two nations that whereas the German people already enjoyed good schools but not self-government, the rulers of England only felt compelled to 'educate their masters' when the working-men were in full possession of the franchise. It was felt that for so important a purpose as voting for Parliament, if for nothing else, it was good that a man should be able to read' (*British History in the Nineteenth Century and After, 1782–1919*, new edition, Longmans, Green and Co, London, 1937, p. 353).
27. See the further quotations from Sir Robert Lowe in Gregg, op. cit., p. 508.
28. See Berg, Ivar, *Education and Jobs, The Great Training Robbery*, Penguin Books, Harmondsworth, 1973.
29. Edgley, Roy, 'Education for Industry', in *Educational Research*, November, 1977.
30. Habermas, op. cit., especially chapter 7.
31. In the period that I am writing this, ILEA has cut off its grant to White Lion Free School, which has had to be rescued by the National Association for Mental Health.
32. *Education in Schools*, para. 3.6, refers to the work of the Assessment of Performance Unit and says that it is concentrating at present on the development of tests suitable for national monitoring in English language, mathematics, and science. The emphasis is revealing. The original intention of the APU was to assess six areas of curriculum; the verbal, mathematical, scientific, ethical, aesthetic, and physical. The last three are taking second place in the APU's work, not just because of the intrinsic difficulties of assessing them but also because of political decisions which have been taken. See the interesting article on the APU by Leonard, Martin, 'Art of the Impossible?', in the *Times Educational Supplement*, 17 June, 1977, p. 19.
33. Habermas, op. cit., especially chapters 4 and 5.
34. Compare the numerous post-mortems on British incomes policy.
35. As reported in *The Daily Telegraph*, 22 July, 1977, p. 6.
36. See, for example, Arrow, Kenneth, *The Limits of Organization*, Norton, New York, 1974.
37. Gallie, W.B., 'Essentially Contested Concepts', in *Proceedings of the Aristotelian Society*, 1955–1956, pp. 167–198. Gallie says, 'there are concepts which are essentially contested, concepts the *proper* use of which inevitably involves endless disputes about their proper uses on the part of their users' (p. 169, my italics).
38. I argue that a need for participation exists in 'The Experience of Politics', *Philosophy and Phenomenological Research*, 1973, pp. 547–560, though I do so in an anthropological rather than historical manner, which is inadequate.
39. There is a fascinating account of this in Yates, Frances, *The Art of Memory*, Routledge & Kegan Paul, London, 1966.
40. The existence of a second dimension of power has been identified and theorized by Bachrach, Peter and Baratz, Morton, 'The Two Faces of Power,' in *American*

Political Science Review, 1962, pp. 947–952, and also in their *Power and Poverty*, Oxford University Press, New York, 1970. The existence of a third dimension of power is argued for in Lukes, Steven, *Power*, Macmillan, London, 1974 (revised edition 1976).

41. op. cit., note 40.
42. op. cit., note 40.
43. Lukes, op. cit., p. 24.
44. Mill, J.S., *Inaugural Address delivered to the University of St. Andrew's, 1 February 1867*. Longmans, Green and Co., London, 1897.
45. See Sharp, Rachel and Green, Anthony, *Education and Social Control, A Study in Progressive Primary Education*, Routledge & Kegan Paul, London, 1975. They show how the definition of children as 'having problems' easily turns into the denial of opportunity to those who have been defined as unable to benefit from it.
46. I feel free to make this comparison, having elsewhere done my bit on behalf of a Welsh nationalist cause (in *Television and the February 1974 General Election*, British Film Institute, London, 1974).

CHAPTER 2.2

HEADTEACHERS AND SCHOOL GOVERNORS*
WILLIAM BACON

Introduction

My readers will perhaps find it not surprising to learn that at first many Sheffield headteachers were extremely worried about their authorities' proposals to break with their long-centralized traditions of administration and establish individual and representative boards for each of its schools. This disquiet was perhaps partly due to a natural conservatism, and partly due to the uncertainty associated with negotiating a new set of social relationships with an unknown and predominantly lay group of people. One Sheffield headteacher expressed the views of many of his colleagues when he told me:

> I was against it at first. The city had managed for many years with its primary schools being run by the schools subcommittee of the education committee, and I saw no need to change it. Indeed, I was anxious about the authority's proposals since I had heard so many nasty stories from colleagues in other parts of the country about governors trying to interfere with the curriculum and the proper professional concerns of teachers.

Potential loss of freedom

A number of headteachers took the view that the new board system posed a serious threat to their traditional personal autonomy, while a few simply saw the new participatory system as a public and formal confirmation of a subtle policy which sought to undermine their traditional 'leadership role',

* *Public Accountability and the School System: A Sociology of School Board Democracy*, William Bacon, Harper & Row Ltd, 1978, chapter 4, pp. 73–99.

and transform it into that of a chief executive directly responsible to a powerful representative body. Some headteachers told me how much they had worried about the details included in the articles of the new boards and, in particular, the legal requirement that 'there shall be full consultation at all times between the headteacher and the Chairman of governors', and the direction that 'all major changes in the school shall be reported to the governors'.

This was mainly because they thought that these kinds of legalistic stipulations might not only limit their general effectiveness as leaders, and stimulate a general 'looking-over-the-shoulder mentality', but would also increase their administrative burdens and make for indecisiveness in their day-to-day reactions to the crisis situations typically confronting a modern headteacher. One head made this very clear when he said,

> I was not terribly enthusiastic about the new boards. I saw them as a further bureaucratic assignment which my superiors had decided to load on me. I took the view that I had better accept the inevitable and that if it was what my masters wanted, then it was my duty to do my best to make it work in the long-term interests of the school.

However, perhaps the one feature of the new board system giving the greatest general concern to Sheffield's headteachers was the formal requirement that the managers were 'through the agency of the headteacher to have general direction of the conduct and curriculum of the school', and that they were to receive at their meetings 'the report of the headteacher on the organisation, curriculum, expenditure and activities of the school'.

Many headteachers were initially worried that well-meaning but mis-informed lay managers might use these powers to interfere too closely in what they saw as their proper professional concerns. One headteacher made this explicit when he said,

> There was always a danger that governors or managers might tread over the delicate line, which separates their functions from those of the headteacher, who is responsible for the internal organization of the school. There was always the danger that boards would tend to get at cross-purposes with their heads, and try to interfere in the curriculum and other matters which were properly a professional concern.

This initial reaction was not simply a case of professional conservatism; rather many headteachers were worried that the new boards might tend to seriously limit the progress of some of the most innovatory curriculum developments taking place in their schools. They felt it might be difficult to convince a predominantly lay board, which was unfamiliar with the complexities of modern educational policy, of the merits in, or desirability of, introducing new developments into their schools. There were, of course, many good practical reasons for their disquiet, for some of the most radical innovations in English education in the last thirty years have been introduced in the primary sector, where in the main headteachers have not been fettered by the presence of effective lay managing bodies or a suffocatingly close supervision from their local authority inspectorate. Largely, as a result of this freedom, they have often been able to carry through some quite fundamental innovations in their schools' curricula and teaching methods. Consequently, it was hardly surprising that some Sheffield headteachers were worried that under the new participatory board system they might lose their effectiveness as the powerful, innovatory leaders of a professional team, and become little more than chief executive officers accountable to generally conservative lay boards, who were unfamiliar with the detailed day-to-day problems of their schools, or the latest trends in educational research and development. One headmaster of a large comprehensive school expressed this anxiety most cogently when he told me,

> There is very little the governors can do to help me as far as the internal organization and curriculum of this school is concerned. They can't possibly know better than the professional who is working at the coal face. If some lay person tells me what to do without giving me the wherewithall to do it, I'll tell him to shut up. Lay boards don't tell doctors what to do, they respect his professional competence, the same is true of teachers. Of course I don't mind lay governors discussing educational issues, but they mustn't try and subvert the professional's judgement on these matters.

The strains of the headteacher's role

However, this initial response to the new board system was not simply a reflection of the headteachers' perhaps quite natural desire for the maximum amount of freedom and flexibility in their working situations; it also had deeper roots and must also be looked at in terms of their structural positions within Sheffield's school system. In spite of their official designation, I soon found out that most headteachers I met rarely had the time or opportunity to develop a substantial teaching programme; rather most of them performed an essentially managerial function and were concerned with the effective deployment of their school's human and physical resources. They were largely responsible for the overall organization of their school, the allocation of its financial resources, the appointment of staff, the admission and exclusion of its pupils, and the general nature of its educational provision. They were also, largely because of their dominant position, able to exert a considerable influence on the daily lives of their teachers and through them upon their pupils and the wider community. They were not only largely responsible for the initial selection and appointment of their staff, but were also in a key position to award, or to withhold, promotional opportunities from them. In the same way, they could direct them into congenial or uncongenial teaching situations, and ultimately, since they were invariably approached for references, were in an unrivalled position to influence their future career prospects.

However, I soon found that although headteachers enjoyed wide powers, their unique position as what at times appeared to be quasi-baronial figures in their own independent fiefdoms also generated its own peculiar set of problems. In the first place, simply because most schools are not organized as democratic institutions, but possess an essentially hierarchic line-management structure, then it was extremely difficult for a series of balanced social relationships to develop between the headteacher, who after all stands at the apex of an institutional power structure, and the remainder of the staff. Most headteachers occupied a strategic position where they were able to mobilize so many sanctions against people and policies they found undesirable, and so much patronage in support of those they found acceptable, that it became virtually impossible for their subordinate staff to engage in an open and free dialogue with them. The structural imperatives of these basically asymmetrical series of social relationships were perhaps unconsciously reflected in the everyday language of the staffroom. In Sheffield, as typically occurs in the rest of England, teachers customarily referred to their headteachers using such concepts as, 'the benevolent dictator', 'a liberal autocrat', the 'old man', or more simply the 'boss', or the 'gaffer'. These labels were not only used as slightly ironical terms of praise, but also reflected, perhaps unwittingly, the basic social if not geographic space separating the head from the remainder of his staff.

In the second place, I also found that many headteachers in Sheffield also suffered from all of those traditional psychological discomforts and anxieties which are classically associated with people occupying what is perhaps best labelled as 'the man in the middle role' in society. They were not simply administrators primarily responsible for the effective deployment of their schools' staff and physical resources, but at the same time, and largely because of the centralized traditions of the Sheffield school system, they were also forced to assume a quasi-political role in the community. Thus they were typically 'caught between' and at times 'torn between' conflicting demands from local pressure groups, their teachers, pupils, parents, and local authority advisory staff. They not only had to balance all of these conflicting interests, but at the same time had to act as general advocates of their school, and seek to maintain good relationships with all allied institutions and interests in the surrounding community.

Finally, what is perhaps best seen as a series of interrelated structural and cultural developments has tended to increase the magnitude of all these problems in the last twenty years. In simple structural terms, the increasingly elaborate nature of the division of educational labour within schools, the increasing employment of graduates and subject specialists, and the growth in the size of all educative institutions has simply meant that the modern headteacher must develop new skills in, and spend most of his time performing, what may be seen as essentially managerial and coordinative tasks. At the same time, wider cultural changes have led both those who exercise power and those who are subject to it to question the legitimacy of many traditional structures of authority. Largely as a result of these complex developments, many of the headteachers I spoke to in Sheffield appeared to be suffering from a severe identity crisis in the sense that they were no longer the 'inner-directed', morally righteous, autocratic figures who were so overtly conscious of their educative mission; rather they tended to be 'other-directed', mild-mannered, often diffident men, who were explicitly conscious of their power, but were at the same time uncertain as to how to use it wisely. These people often told me that they found their isolated, but peculiarly visible 'man in the middle' situation particularly distressing, since it subjected them to so many different, and often competing, interests and value systems. Some parents, teachers, and pupils expected them to display traditional qualities of leadership, and to uphold what were once seen as widely accepted community values; others were more critical of what they saw as the autocratic role of headteachers and their own marginal or subordinate position within the educational decision-making process.

Headteachers and elected representatives

In short then, largely as a result of all the pressures generated by this difficult working situation, it was not surprising to find that many Sheffield headteachers were worried about their authorities' proposals to introduce into the city what was at the time one of the most fully democratized school board systems in the country. Thus, although, as we have already seen, the proposal to include elected parents' representatives on school boards was receiving widespread political support by the late 1960s, many headteachers were not altogether convinced of the utility of this measure. They continued to worry that these elections would be dominated by the articulate 'pushing' middle-class parent who might support policies which were not in the long-term interests of all their children, and might also utilize their position to interfere in what they saw as matters of proper professional rather than lay concern, such as streaming, reading schemes, and examination strategies.

However, if some headteachers, particularly those who had traditionally followed a policy of discouraging a too active parental involvement in their schools, were worried about parental representation on governing bodies, they tended to feel even more threatened by the proposals for teacher representation. This was seen at the time to be a radical departure which might have considerable repercussions upon the existing power structure within schools. Under the new board system, teachers were not only to be given representation on the body which considered the appointment of the head and deputy headteacher but, perhaps more vital as far as the day-to-day life of the school was concerned, could examine and critically discuss 'the headteacher's proposals for head of department and other above-scale posts within the establishment approved by the authority' and recommend candidates for 'any posts carrying allowances above the basic scale which are to be filled by promotion inside the school'.

This general concern about the impact of the Sheffield reforms upon the internal power structure and status hierarchy of the school system was obviously highlighted by the decision to include representatives of the nonteaching staff – school secretaries, caretakers, dinner ladies, cooks, and cleaners – on their school's governing body. Their presence on the new Sheffield boards was of course in part an official recognition of the importance of the work of a group which has always done the least prestigious work in schools. However, it was also in some ways a gentle reminder to headteachers that, although these people have often been regarded as marginal to central educational tasks, they were in fact extremely important people who were not only very influential in the informal life of the school, but who, unlike most teaching staff, also lived locally and thus represented an excellent means of maintaining communication with the surrounding community. Nonetheless, whatever the merits of Sheffield's decision to include representatives from the nonteaching staff on school boards, their formal presence and potential involvement in discussion on such key issues as school policy, the curriculum, financial allocation, and staff appointments and promotions made headteachers apprehensive. This was not only because their presence threatened to upset their school's traditional status hierarchy, but also because it might possibly lead nonteaching staff to ask fundamental questions about their present marginal role, or the utility of the social barriers separating them, and their work, from that of the professional teaching staff.

In short, I found that, although the Sheffield reforms were not introduced in the teeth of bitter opposition, local headteachers tended to take a generally cautious attitude to these changes. This concern sprang quite naturally from their own peculiarly isolated but pivotal position within the school system. They were worried that the new boards might not only diminish their authority, but also lead to a gradual weakening of their managerial role and their capacity to act both as educational innovators and leaders of an effectively integrated team of professional workers.

The headteachers' responses to the new board system

Although many headteachers had misgivings about the wisdom of the Sheffield reforms in general, and the inclusion of parents, staff, and non-teaching representatives on their school boards in particular, I soon found that their own experiences of the day-to-day workings of the new system over the last five years have gradually convinced most of them of the merits of their authority's initiative. They found that their new boards have tended to strengthen their managerial prerogative and have not only been a means of making contact with groups previously unfamiliar with the school, but have also acted as generally supportive bodies tending to protect them from some of the worst tensions associated with their peculiarly isolated 'man in the middle' position. An early official appraisal of the work of the new board system also reflected this changing mood; it reported that many headteachers were speaking enthusiastically about the ways in which their schools had benefited from the new boards as these bodies were drawing together groups of 'knowledgeable people' who really cared about education and were keen to serve their local schools. It also records that headteachers pointed out how valuable the new participatory system had been in 'tapping new sources of public service', and in attracting the 'splendid assortment of educational talent and zeal, local and city wide', which had been drawn in to help their schools.[1]

These initial and official impressions were reinforced by my own work in Sheffield. A number of heads, particularly those working in comprehensive schools in the middle-class suburban areas of the city, also told me how much they had come to value their governing bodies as insulating devices, protecting them from the buffets of local political controversy. This was mainly because as heads of large comprehensive schools they had, perhaps inevitably, found themselves much more closely involved in the local political process than was ever the case when pupils either went to grammar or secondary modern schools, and when most people pragmatically accepted the inevitability, if not the legitimacy, of a selective secondary educational system. In Sheffield in the mid-1970s many parents not only had strong views about the merits of comprehensive education in general, but also about streaming, examination policies, and discipline. One head made this quite clear when he said,

> I feel much more of a political figure as a head of a comprehensive school than I ever did when I was in charge of a grammar school. People in this locality of course did not all agree with the comprehensive idea, they assumed that this was going to be a 'rough school' since it was to be nonselective, and they were determined to take a close interest in our activities and make certain that their children did not suffer. Moreover, I am in a neighbourhood school now, my parents are no longer scattered all over the city, they live locally, and it is much easier for them to keep a 'close eye' on their children's progress in this school. I feel as a head that I am much more visible, and liable to be challenged about my policies than was ever the case in my old grammar school days.

It was perhaps quite natural that in this kind of volatile social situation headteachers had learnt to attach more importance to their governing boards than was traditionally the case. From their point of view, these lay bodies could not only offer effective moral support for the policies of their schools, but were also able to act as effective filtering devices which could direct local criticism into the appropriate consultative channels. This process consequently lessened the probability of a situation of conflict developing between the headteacher and the leaders of factions within his school's local community or catchment area.

Many headteachers also told me how much they appreciated the ways in which the new board system had allowed them to establish new links with people and interest groups who were not encapsulated within the educational system for most of their working life, but who, perhaps because they were working in a variety of industrial and commercial situations, held points of view perhaps more typical of lay feeling generally. Consequently, they had soon found that their governing bodies provided them with an excellent sounding board through which they could judge the potential public support for, or opposition to, any policy they were planning to introduce into their school. The head of a small comprehensive school in the north of the city made this testing function quite explicit when he said, 'I find my governors a great help, they are a windtunnel I can use for experiments with my new designs. I think gosh!! if there are no reactions from them, then the idea must be fairly acceptable and I'll try it on in school.'

Nonetheless, while most headteachers saw their governors as basically helpful and supportive groups of people, a few of them still retained a predilection for Sheffield's older centralized system of administrative control. This was partly because they took the view that the assessment of priorities in education was purely a matter for the expert, partly because they thought a predominantly lay board could not serve any useful purpose in what they saw was a purely professional matter – the education of children – and partly because they were worried that the most vociferous and influential boards would secure the largest slices of the city's resources for their own schools.

Headteachers and new board members

However, apart from this critical minority of generally older people, most headteachers tended to value the new board system, and few continued to see the boards in terms of a real or potential threat to their authority. They had come to learn that their school boards were in the main generally supportive bodies, which not only helped them to maintain their own positions as managerial innovators, but which also made them less vulnerable to uninformed or radical criticism of their schools' policies.

Largely as a result of this situation, most newly appointed board members told me that they not only tended to look towards their headteachers for advice, but also found their headteachers helpful in initiating them into the duties and responsibilities associated with their office. This impression was also clearly supported by the survey data. As we can see from the table on page 82, the majority of people who replied to the following question:

Which people were most helpful when you first became a manager or governor?

reported that their headteacher had either solely, or in conjunction with the clerk or chairman, played a great part in helping them to settle into their new office.

Of course in the first stages of the introduction of the new system, some headteachers were inexperienced in the work of school boards and the chairman, clerk, or another person with previous experience of this work might also take the initiative and help the newcomer. In some cases, all members were new to the school board system and all helped each other; in other places, the clerk, or a local politician, had a fairly clear idea of the authorities' aims and took a leading role in initiating newcomers into the responsibilities of their office. However, as the system has gradually settled down and as people have gained experience of this type of work, then the influence of the headteacher has naturally grown, for they are usually one of the longest-serving members of the board and many new members, particularly the 'short-service' parental representatives, tend to depend upon them for an introduction to the nature of their responsibilities and duties.

The growth of affective social relationships

This natural tendency for new board members to rely upon their headteachers for guidance was reinforced by their own generally positive attitude towards the local educational service. These sentiments were articulated very clearly within the survey data and, in particular, in the pattern of replies I received to the question,

Why did you want to become a school governor/manager?

Apart from headteachers who were ex-officio members of boards and consequently had little choice in this matter, and teachers who generally said they wanted to represent their professional interests and be involved in

The people most helpful to new board members

	Primary schools	Second-dary schools	Special schools	Total
	N=262	N=54	N=28	N=344
	%	%	%	%
The chairman	11	11	4	10
The headteacher	51	43	71	52
The clerk	11	4	8	9
A fellow member	7	10	—	7
The head and clerk	3	—	—	2
The chairman and clerk	1	—	—	1
The chairman and head	4	6	4	4
Everybody	6	9	4	7
No answer	6	17	9	8
	100%	100%	100%	100%

their school's policy-making and administrative affairs, most people tended to give very general and sometimes exceptionally vague answers to this question. They obviously mentioned their interest in children and educational affairs, but apart from these fairly diffuse observations their main motivation was the desire to help, and serve, the teachers and children in their local school. Most of their replies tended to confirm many of the intuitive feelings of those who had fought to introduce a new system into Sheffield. A substantial reservoir of interest and latent goodwill for schools existed in the community at large, and the reforms had done much to mobilize these resources into the service of education. However, most people found it extremely difficult to articulate these sentiments in a precisely formulated series of statements; rather they characteristically gave such general and vague replies as, 'I wanted to serve the school and its community'; 'I wanted to take part in the life of the community and have some small say in matters.'

People had not sought this office because they had a personal axe to grind, or any definitive ideas about how their school or its teachers should conduct their affairs; rather most of them subscribed to what might best be called an ethic of community service and simply wanted to become involved with, and help in whatever way was possible, the work of their local school. This generally diffuse, if at the same time constructive and supportive, series of sentiments was expressed in a variety of different ways and included 13 percent who simply expressed some kind or form of general interest in education, 11 percent who reported an interest in community affairs, 16 percent who simply wanted to help their local school, 11 percent who felt an innate concern as parents for the education and future of their children, and 16 percent who simply said they were interested in the welfare and well-being of children. In contrast, only a few people gave passive replies and indicated they had originally been reluctant to take up this work, had simply become a manager or governor because someone had persuaded them to do so, or had been nominated without their knowledge. The greatest number of these 'reluctant draftees' were found amongst nonteaching staff and this may be because many of these people, after occupying a relatively subordinate position within the school system for most of their lives, needed a great deal of sympathetic encouragement by either a local councillor or their headteacher before they were willing to stand for this office.

In general, as one might reasonably expect, the balance of emphasis within this widely diffused concern for education and community service tended to vary between different types of board members. The majority of parental representatives reported seeking office because of their quite natural interest in the current welfare and future well-being of their children. One respondent, Mrs. Smith, was fairly typical when she said, 'I wanted to participate in the organization and administration of the school in which my children are to be educated.'[2] Another parent, Mrs. Brown, recorded similar sentiments: 'I am very interested in the well-being of mine and other children and thought this the best way of showing my interest.'

In contrast, while many coopted board members also mentioned these parental concerns, a far higher proportion mentioned their interest in becoming more actively involved in local community affairs. The Reverend Bailey, an Anglican priest, made this distinction quite clear when he said, 'As the local vicar I wanted to act as a bridge between the school and the community.' Another coopted governor, police constable Clark, expressed a similar point of view: 'I am the local area constable and wanted to take a greater part in the activities of the community in which I live and work.'

Many of the people appointed to represent the education committee on school boards also had strong local interests and had often been involved in the 'rough and tumble' of local parish pump politics for many years. Mr. Green was a fairly typical member of this group. He told me, 'I was appointed by the local authority in recognition of my twenty years political work in this area, and because of my desire to help in some way the young element growing up in changing surroundings.'

Some of these political appointees were not only long experienced in local politics, but were also very sophisticated advocates in participatory forms of democracy, as the following statement by one Labour Party activist and school governor made quite clear:

> The community should accept part of the responsibility for the problems and trials of running a school, as well as simply enjoying the benefits. The teachers don't want to operate in isolation, they need to have positive feedback from people in noneducational streams of life in order to assess the viability and success of their work.

Nonetheless, although many of the governors appointed by the local authority had strong local interests, this was not always the case, and this group also contained many people who not only lived further afield, but who, because of their professional, business, or political activities, were able to bring to their school a different series of perspectives on educational affairs and a wide range of expert advice and cosmopolitan skills which often neatly complemented the interests of the local members. Mrs. Smith was fairly typical when she said, 'As a Principal Lecturer at the local College of Education I wished to be more closely involved in school work, and also to make available to my school such expertise as I have.' Mr. Jenkins brought his school a different but no less relevant type of experience: 'I was on the Education Committee until May 1973 and I wanted to maintain my contact with parents, staff, and children, and also give them the benefit of all my knowledge.'

Largely as a result of this generally positive attitude to education, most new governors tended to seek and, in the main, were successful in establishing strong affective relationships with their headteachers. This was not simply a personal impression but also emerged quite clearly from the survey data. Thus, as we can see from the following table, only a very few governors indicated that any discordance or open conflict had developed between themselves and their headteachers, while in contrast most reported

Relationships with headteachers

	Primary schools	Second-ary schools	Special schools	Total
	N=244	N=52	N=27	N=323
	%	%	%	%
Exceedingly friendly	58	52	56	57
Friendly	36	40	37	37
Neither friendly nor unfriendly	3	8	7	4
Unfriendly	1	—	—	1
No answer	2	—	—	1
Total	100%	100%	100%	100%

the development of strongly sympathetic and supportive bonds. No less than 57 percent of the sample reported they had 'exceedingly friendly relationships' with their headteachers; another 37 percent said they were just friendly; and only a minority, most of whom were recently appointed to their office, indicated that their relationships had not, as yet, passed beyond the formal stage.

The development of these generally harmonious relationships was also greatly facilitated by the attitude of most headteachers. Although, as we have already seen, some of them were initially wary of their authority's proposals for reform, they also made great efforts to generate good relationships with members of their school boards, and in many cases, even before a member attended his first board meeting, he was invited to visit the head, discuss the problems facing the school, and receive a conducted tour of its buildings and surrounding playing fields.

However, these initial encounter sessions were not simply a means of cultivating goodwill; they also witnessed the beginnings of a subtle process which slowly incorporated the newcomer into the power structure of the local school system. Although this course of induction might take many forms, and vary with the needs of individual schools and social situations, it might typically have been achieved in the manner of the following scenario.

This account does not attempt to portray what happened to any specific governor in any specific Sheffield school; rather it is best thought of as an ideal construction which, drawing on the accounts I received from many governors, attempts to highlight some of the social processes which typically occur when a newcomer is first appointed to a school board.

A scenario of the incorporation process

The newly appointed board member is invited to the school and offered tea and biscuits in the headteacher's study. During the course of the meeting the headteacher remains sitting behind his large executive-type desk, but offers his guest a low but comfortable chair facing him. The discussion appears, at least on the surface, to proceed in a friendly and informal manner. The visitor probably talks about his own schooldays, his present work and leisure activities, and his interest in the welfare of children. The headteacher naturally tends to respond with his own anecdotal references, and also attempts to explain what he is trying to achieve in his school and the problems he is facing in pursuing these aims. At times the flow of conversation between them may be broken into, as the school secretary or a senior teacher finds it necessary to consult the head on some pressing administrative matter.

However, although this initial meeting is conducted in a friendly and informal manner, it is also a quite critical meeting for the future career of the newly appointed governor. This is because the first meeting with the 'freshman' gives the headteacher an excellent opportunity to sound out his interests and political views and to assess whether or not he is likely to offer any potential threat to his own long-term policies. If he suspects the latter is the case, then this apparently informal chat provides him with a good means of initiating his visitor into what he considers to be the appropariate role definitions for his new office.

This task of steering the new board member into what the headmaster may himself define as 'positive' or 'constructive' channels may be accomplished in a number of different ways. In the first place, the process of conversion may be facilitated by the very structure of the interview situation itself. The dominating physical presence of the headteacher, his strategic occupation of the desk of office, and the many urgent but nonetheless deferential requests for help which seem to put into his study, are all not only manifest indications of his power, but also tend to subtly convey the message that the new board member must be careful not inadvertently to place fresh burdens on the shoulders of this kindly but obviously over-worked professional, who is unstintingly dedicating his life to the service of young children. In the second place, these initial meetings often tend to give the new board member the impression that the task of administering a school and directing its future development is a peculiarly complex matter which is best left to the appropriate professional manager, and in this way some of the most enthusiastic newcomers are effectively discouraged from taking too active an interest in the educational aims and objectives of their school. This is not of course to suggest that many headteachers don't encourage new board members to express their views; rather it is to note that these formal statements of intent are often followed by the subtle implicit, or explicit, rider that 'education is also a professional matter' and they would be wise to listen to the voice of experience.

Finally, the reeducation of the potentially dissident newcomer may be effectively accomplished by the ritual of the guided tour of the school. In the course of this perambulation his attention is constantly drawn to the pressing physical and financial needs of the school's fabric and equipment, its leaky roof, poor toilets, splintered floors, and crowded classrooms. The visitor is not only rapidly taught the lesson that education is a badly neglected service, and its teachers are devotedly labouring against impossible odds, but he also soon learns that he will be most useful in his new public role if he seeks to help and not criticize these worthy people.

Ironically, although the newcomer's attention is at all stages in this induction process drawn to the question of means, he is also reminded in many subtle ways that he is not expected, except in the most general terms, to ask questions about the ends of education. He soon learns that if he takes too close an interest in his school's curriculum, examination policy, or internal structure and administration, this approach is not only likely to be viewed with disapproval by the headteacher, but also by many of his fellow board members. This is mainly because most long-established governors,

Should board meetings be open or closed?

	Primary	Secondary	Special
	N=262	N=54	N=28
	%	%	%
Yes (open)	16	8	10
No (closed)	82	92	90
No answer	2	—	—

particularly those who are coopted or appointed by the local authority, have already developed strong affective links with their headteachers, and may dismiss the freshman's initiative as a personally malicious and vindictive attack on the integrity of someone who is simply trying to do his best for children.

It is hardly surprising that most lay people experiencing this form of initiation are highly receptive to the role expectations of their headteachers, and in most cases tend to accept without question the legitimacy of the part he wishes them to play in the new board system.

This conversion of the hesitant but potentially critical outsider into the confident and helpful board member is of course greatly facilitated by the very secrecy of school board meetings. Partly because of the confidential nature of some of their work, partly because of their critical, if opaque, role in the school system, most governors' meetings are held in private and, as we can see from the table on page 87, most people take the view that this is a natural and desirable state of affairs.

Thus, only a partial and, at best, highly stereotyped account of their activities is ever circulated to the school staff or general public. As a result of this secrecy, few people have the opportunity to familiarize themselves with the policy of school boards or the ways in which they conduct their business. Consequently, when the newly appointed or elected member attends his first meeting, he finds he is entering a strange new world. He is likely to be unfamiliar both with the issues which are under discussion, and, unless he is an experienced committee man, with the peculiar admin-politico style in which the new board conducts its business. He is also probably very dependent upon and, as we have already seen, usually looks towards his headteacher, clerk, or chairman for advice and information about the past experiences and present work of his board, the status and interests of fellow members, and the policies being pursued by the school. In short, he finds himself in a social situation where he is forced to 'learn on the job', and where most of the teaching is done by the headmaster, chairman, and clerk, with of course additional support from fellow governors and managers who, in their turn, have all been subjected to much the same kind of socialization process.

Role education and school boards

Although the above scenario is baldly sketched and capable of extensive refinement, it does help us to understand a little more fully why Sheffield governors tended to behave in the ways they did. At the same time, their general willingness to learn how they could best 'fit themselves neatly' into the established routine of their school board, their general acceptance of the commonplace assumption that 'I'll be able to pick it up as I go along', had a number of less obvious long-term implications for the local school system. In the first place, it meant that most people who serve on these important public bodies have accepted a form of education for themselves which is generally regarded as anachronistic, and which is gradually being phased out of much of the remainder of the educational system. This is because learning on the job is essentially a craft form of activity, which may have a certain utility in a slowly changing world, but which is less appropriate to the dynamic technologically based society of the late twentieth century. It tends to be both time-consuming and unsystematic, and, in the case of school boards, by the time most representative members such as parents have learnt enough knowledge to be effective, it is time for them to leave the board and be replaced by yet another freshman.

In the second place, learning on the job tends, like most other craft-orientated forms of education, to be a static form of learning. It only tends to familiarize the student with the status quo, and rarely encourages him to be imaginative and to seek alternatives to long-established practices and procedures. In the case of the school board, this usually means that the initiate simply learns the role definitions which the headteacher, clerk, or chairman think are appropriate for him to learn, and, unless he is a very unusual personality, or is politically sophisticated, he is unlikely to play a vigorous or independent role, but rather will generally support established conventions, policies, and their associated power élites.

This type of education is of course a cumulative process and is greatly facilitated by the strongly affective relationships which tend to develop between board members, and which may simply be the product of long familiarity, a common interest in the school, a common allegiance to an ethic of service, or some collective experience of a challenging or critical situation. Consequently, as we can see from the table on page 90, most respondents in the survey reported that they had developed 'close cooperative relationships' with all or most of their fellow board members and only 2 percent suggested that a discordant element had entered into their relationship.

The work of school boards

Largely as a result of the combined effect of all these very subtle social processes, most governors tended to generally accept their headteacher's

Relationships with fellow board members

	Primary	Second-ary	Special	Total
	N=262	N=54	N=28	N=344
	%	%	%	%
Close cooperation with all or most	72	46	60	65
Easy with some, difficult with others	9	15	5	10
Fairly formal	12	26	28	16
Discordant	1	—	—	2
No answer	6	13	7	7
	100%	100%	100%	100%

view of what were their appropriate roles, and duties, within the school system. Moreover, on most boards, fresh arrivals generally tried to fit themselves into what they found was a pleasant and harmonious situation. One comprehensive headteacher described this intricate process of social negotiation and role definition very succinctly when he said,

> I was a bit worried about my new board at first, they were completely unknown to me, and they contained people who were very critical of nonselective schools. However, after the initial trial period, the system is shaking down well and there is a pretty clear understanding between us now about each other's position in the general scheme of things.

Another headteacher said the same thing in a different way when he told me, 'I think our governors have settled down well now, they know what to do, and not to raise unpleasant issues of personality.'

Although this type of 'clear understanding' was not, as we have seen, usually negotiated between two sets of equal partners, but tended to be mediated very much on the head's own terms, it did also mean that the latter's initial worry that their new governors might concern themselves too closely with 'professional matters' had not occurred in practice. In general, most Sheffield boards have been reluctant to use their powers under the articles which direct them to 'receive the report of the headteacher on the organisation, curriculum, expenditure and activities of the school, and through the agency of the headteacher have general direction of the conduct and curriculum of the school'; and they have been unwilling to discuss, except in the most general of terms when the headteacher gives his report, their school's curriculum, teaching methods, internal organization, or financial affairs. They have, in the main, accepted the legitimacy of the view that these issues are the appropriate professional concern of the headteacher and his staff, and that it is improper for them to interfere too closely in this area of their school's affairs. The primacy of this general assumption that the headteacher should be left to get on with his job of leading and running his school largely explains why boards seemed to spend so little of their time examining or discussing what are after all not only some of the most important, but also some of the most fascinating, aspects of the life of a school.

This general unwillingness to become too closely involved in what have traditionally been defined as professional matters was not simply a personal impression, but was also reflected quite sharply in the replies to a series of questions which examined the frequency with which governors discussed their school's curriculum, financial allocation, rules, teaching methods, or educational research in general. Consequently, as we can see from the table on page 92, few board members reported discussing these quite critical matters on a regular basis; rather, most of them tended to spend the bulk of their time discussing routine administrative matters and maintenance and development problems.

This is not of course to imply that Sheffield's governors were unconcerned about education; indeed, as we have already seen, most of them were appointed to, or elected to, their school boards because of their manifest interest in the educational problems of young children. Moreover, only a few people in the survey (16 percent) saw their main task as simply that of looking after the 'proper maintenance of the fabric of their school', and most of them (86 percent) said they thought they ought to discuss the educational aims and objectives their schools were pursuing. However, in spite of these general sentiments, in practice most governors were hesitant to raise these wider policy-related issues and spent much of their time discussing the aims, ends, and methods associated with the educational process taking place within their school. It seems probable that this reluctance was, in part, a reflection of their wish to avoid giving offence to their headteachers and thereby breaking the strongly affective bonds which have grown up between board members, and was in part due to their evident wish to avoid becoming involved too deeply in what they had been taught to believe were truly professional matters.

Frequency of discussion of five key educational issues

	The curri- culum	School rules	Finance	Teaching methods	Educa- tional research
	N=344 %	N=344 %	N=344 %	N=344 %	N=344 %
Regularly (three or more times a year)	11	3	34	6	9
Frequently (twice a year)	20	10	25	10	17
Infrequently (once a year)	37	37	30	25	30
Never	26	44	6	52	32
No answer	6	6	5	7	12

The headteacher's report

This diffidence was particularly evident in the way in which most school boards tended to deal with their headteacher's report. This item was of course in theory, if not always in practice, one of the most important points of their meeting, and was the occasion when the headteacher gave a formal account of his stewardship and when governors fulfilled their overt function of taking responsibility for the 'general direction of the conduct and curriculum of the school'. However, it was not simply the formal occasion when they could familiarize themselves with the policies, problems, and achievements of their school, and in turn communicate them to the local community; it was also an excellent opportunity for them to ask critical questions and provide the professional teacher with the layman's often salutary, if sometimes illuminating, point of view.

Unfortunately, the evidence suggested that in practice most school boards did not always match up to this theoretical ideal; their headteacher's report was often placed towards the end of the agenda and was often given and listened to in a somewhat perfunctory manner. This was hardly surprising, for a number of headteachers simply appeared to treat these occasions as a formality, and used the report to record routine administrative matters and display the positive, if not the negative, side of their school's activities and achievements during the past term. Although, for the sake of confidentiality, the following composite example is based upon several different reports, it is not untypical of this type of eulogistic exercise.

Easton School

Headmaster's report for the governors' meeting to be held on Friday, 11 October at 7.00 pm.

1 *Staff Changes* – The following staff have taken up their appointment at the beginning of this term:

    Mr. Hunt (Rural Science)

    Mrs. Smith (History)

2 The external examination results were very good. The percentage of G.C.E. passes was 85%. There were 76 Grade 1 passes in C.S.E.

3 Repairs have been completed to the school roof and work on the new bicycle sheds is near completion.

4 The school participated in a Sponsored Walk organized by the Variety Club of Great Britain, on Sunday, September 29, and raised nearly £200.00 for charity.

5 The school play *Hamlet* was well received by the audience on two nights. The involvement of Staff in the cast appeared to give added interest. Mr. Casey is to be congratulated on his first production for the school.

6. The following visits have been organized during the present term:

    The Abbeydale Industrial Hamlet (1/11/77)

    International Rugby Match, Twickenham (2/12/77)

    The Sheffield Police Stables (10/11/77)

    The Women's International Hockey Match, Wembley (31/10/77)

7 A Parents' Evening has been arranged for Tuesday 10/12/77 for pupils who entered school this term.

8 Canon Smith has kindly allowed us, as in previous years, to hold the Annual Carol Service in the local church..

9 I wish to ask the governors to confirm the allocation of the five occasional days for 1977/78 as follows:

    Monday and Tuesday – 20/21 February 1978

    Wednesday, Thursday, Friday – 25/26/27 October 1978

10 I enclose a brief account of school policy with regard to A-level choice.

Of course not all headteachers were content to simply give this type of bland and ritualistic account of their school's achievements in the last term. A number also recognized that this occasion could be usefully exploited as a means of galvanizing their governors into action on their school's behalf, and consequently their reports tended to concentrate on the more tangible and remedial aspects of the maintenance, building, or accommodation problems they were struggling with. However, although these initiations often sparked off a great deal of discussion and activity to solve these difficulties, it was only rarely that headteachers extended their reports into the field of education proper, and made a determined effort to inform their boards about such items as books, equipment, examination policy, streaming, and so on. They were generally reluctant to introduce these topics and raise issues which would not only invariably stimulate a lengthy discussion about the long-term aims and interests of their school, but would also inevitably serve to educate their board members, and make them more sophisticated advocates of their school's educational policies in the surrounding community.

Paradoxically, even in those relatively rare social situations where headteachers were manifestly attempting to initiate a general discussion on their school's educational aims and policies, most governors were reluctant to respond and become too closely involved in this debate. This was mainly because most of them tended to take the view that their headteacher was a friendly, but authoritative, person who was successfully coping with a complex and extremely arduous job. Consequently, they were willing to discuss day-to-day administrative details but were generally reluctant to raise critical or fundamental questions of principle.

The reasons for what might at first glance seem this strangely deferential attitude are of course most complex, but might be explained in part in terms of the subtle incorporation processes I have already outlined in this chapter, partly because of a general reluctance, particularly by many working-class people, to become involved in a bitter and potentially divisive demarcation dispute, and partly in terms of the dominant social composition of so many managing or governing boards. A large proportion of board members were professional people who had, in the main, learnt to accept that one must fully respect the competence and professional integrity of one's fellow workers, lest they in turn question your own authority.

Largely as a result of this situation, most school boards were not only reluctant to discuss their school's policies or aims, except of course in the most general terms, but also naturally tended to be ill informed about key areas of local educational policy. This was a generally unfortunate situation and meant that, in many cases, governors had been remarkably ineffective either in representing the views, interests, and sentiments of local groups, or in making sure their school's policy did not become too isolated from the interests and values of its surrounding society. At the same time, their headteacher's reluctance to discuss the curriculum also meant that most governors were often quite ignorant about the details of their school's internal organization or long-term policy. Although this neglect may in the short term be quite a comfortable tactical situation for the headteacher, it also meant that in the long term his board was hampered from effectively playing its full 'advocacy role' in representing the interests of his school, either in the surrounding community or in the wider society.

Conclusions: new styles of democratic leadership

However, although most school boards were tactfully discouraged from taking too active an interest in the curriculum or internal affairs of their school, this is not to imply that they played a marginal role in the Sheffield school system. Their presence not only tended to strengthen the authority of the headteacher, but also encouraged him to develop a new, more flexible style of democratic leadership, and these factors helped him to cope quite successfully with many of the difficult problems which always emerge in times when the issue of 'who controls our schools?' is again troubling the public conscience.

Before the Sheffield reforms of 1971, the extremely centralized tradition of school government management left each headteacher in a peculiarly isolated and visible position, and he was extremely vulnerable to the criticism which inevitably starts to emerge when a society raises fundamental questions about the justice of the system of social and political domination built into its present school system. Consequently, if a serious dispute broke out between a headteacher and his staff, parents, or pupils over such contentious issues as discipline, school uniforms, examination policy, or selection processes, then the headteacher was usually faced with the task of trying to resolve the conflict himself, or, if it became very serious, involving his local inspectorate and the city's education committee.

The new individual participatory board system not only tends to lessen the risk of this abrasive confrontation developing but, if it does occur, allows the headteacher to respond to the challenge on a local basis and in a more flexible manner. This is partly because the elected representatives of some of his potential critics – parents, teachers, auxiliary staff, and community groups – are all present on his school board and he is thus able to learn of and respond to their legitimate criticism at an early, and not at a later and potentially more explosive, stage of its development. It is also partly because the very presence of so many representatives of different and in theory potentially conflicting interest groups on his school board inevitably leads to their public identification with, if not acquiescence in, the policies of the school. It makes it more difficult for a critical group of students, teachers, or parents to challenge the headteacher on the emotive, if populist, grounds that he is an authoritarian leader and they, as groups of clients, workers, or inmates, are not consulted or even represented within the formal structure of the local school system.

Moreover, if in spite of all these insulating precautions, a serious local dispute does lead people to challenge their school's policies and the authority of its headteacher, then, under the new Sheffield system, the latter is able to respond in a much more flexible and adroit manner than was possible under the old centralized form of control. He is no longer faced with the personal tensions of his isolated 'man in the middle' position, but can initially discuss the matter with his chairman and other senior members of his school board and may then look towards a full meeting of his governors for advice and support in finding a specific and locally acceptable solution to the crisis. This approach not only has the advantage that the situation is a less personally stressful experience for the headteacher concerned, but also means that the final decisions resolving the dispute will be taken by a collective lay body and, as a result, the authority avoids potentially damaging personal clashes with his local opponents.

It appears then that the new board system has enabled the headteacher to adopt a new, more flexible response to the problems of his school and community and at the same time has facilitated the development of a new, less brittle type of control, which in the long term promises to strengthen the present managerial prerogative within the school system. Despite some of their initial worries about the creation of individual school boards, most headteachers have found that in practice their governors have not attempted to challenge their authority or undermine their power, but have largely accepted the roles chosen for them. Consequently, most headmasters generally tend to see their governors as kindly, knowledgeable, and mainly professional people, who are invariably enthusiastic about the educational cause, are willing to lend their moral authority to the policies being developed by their school, but who don't usually wish to take too close an interest in its internal affairs or curriculum. One headmaster made this general attitude very explicit when he told me,

> I see my governors as advocates of this school. They are all terribly busy people and usually only come in on formal occasions. They simply don't have the time to spend visiting every week, but I don't think this matters since they know the school is running well and that I can rely upon their support in a crisis.

Notes and references

1. Report to Sheffield Schools Subcommittee, 11 January, 1972.
2. In order to respect the confidentiality of my respondents all names given are fictional.

CHAPTER 2.3

ACCOUNTABILITY AND EDUCATION*
J. Barton, T. Becher, T. Canning, E. Eraut, and J. Knight

Concepts

Public confidence

Educational accountability can be seen as a means of maintaining or improving the level of public confidence in the education system. Widespread unease or distrust gives rise to strong demands for accountability; conversely, a service which is generally well regarded is spared from such demands. But whether or not the political climate happens to be favourable at any given time, the need for appropriate safeguards remains constant. Accountability – in common with accident insurance, or fire precautions, or safety procedures at work – does not depend for its justification on the actuality of disaster, even though it is in moments of crisis that its importance may be most clearly established.

Any sound policy for accountability in the middle years of schooling must depend on an awareness of the particular values and perspectives of the key interest groups concerned.

But there is another, perhaps equally important, consideration to bear in mind: namely the inherent logic of accountability itself. It is to this issue that we must now turn. We shall be concerned with two main distinctions: the first, between problem-solving and maintenance; and the second, between informal, formal, mandatory, and constitutional mechanisms.

* Accountability in the Middle Years of Schooling: An Analysis of Policy Options, Part II of the final report of the East Sussex and University of Sussex research project. The whole of this final report to the SSRC is available from the National Lending Library.

Problem-solving and maintenance

In practice, no sharp distinction can be made between judging an organization in terms of how it responds when things go wrong and evaluating it in terms of the overall quality of its normal operations. However, for the purposes of analytic clarity and administrative effectiveness, it is useful to separate the maintenance of standards from the methods of coping with specific problems.

Most education authorities have developed a variety of procedures for responding when things seem to be going amiss with individual pupils, teachers, or schools. Most forms of trouble-shooting tend to be dealt with through professional rather than public channels. Thus, parental complaints which cannot be satisfactorily resolved by the head are for the most part passed on by the school or referred by the parent to the area office; and any subsequent discussion is normally conducted in private between the office and the school. The alternative mechanism of appeal to the managers is very rarely used. Similarly, any suggestion that a given teacher is performing below an acceptable standard is in the first instance taken up by the advisers. If the complaint seems justified, they will often go to considerable lengths in the provision of remedial support before dismissal or transfer procedures are contemplated. Such support is deliberately (and understandably) inconspicuous in style, and would not normally be notified even to members of the education committee. Again, if a particular school is thought to be functioning badly, extensive investigation by advisers, and appropriate follow-up action at officer level, will in many cases avert public disclosure – unless, that is, the problem happens first to be taken up by the press.

Localized difficulties are thus typically regarded as internal to the system, and as calling in the first instance for a confidential and professional response. There is nothing reprehensible about the concern to keep such matters from the public view for as long as is reasonably possible. Indeed, to bring them immediately into the open could serve only to undermine the confidence of parents and teachers alike. Many issues are better decided out of court by skilled and knowledgeable judgement than submitted to trial by inadequately informed opinion.

We did however find it difficult to see why the very existence of such professional channels of accountability should be regarded as a confidential matter. No attempt seems to be made to apprise parents of the extensive network of procedures which can be called upon within the education service to investigate apparent anomalies and to rectify established defects. It is one thing for a parent to know – and few would demand it – precisely what has transpired between a head and teacher, or an officer and a head, in following up a particular grievance. It is quite another for the same parent to know – and only sensible for the authority to make it known to the parent – what the general procedures are for dealing with such grievances, and that these procedures have been properly employed, and any necessary action taken, in the case in question.

The procedures set up to resolve problems constitute one important aspect of accountability, but by their very nature they only deal with specific local issues. In order to respond to more general issues (for example, the teaching of primary science throughout an authority), and to reassure the public about overall educational standards, different kinds of procedure are needed. If these are to function effectively, they must not depend – as problem-solving techniques do – on being triggered off by *ad hoc* departures from normal practice. On the contrary, they must seek to identify more closely what *is* regarded as normal professional practice, and to investigate whether such established norms are of sufficient quality to merit the confidence of society at large.

Where grievances are often best settled in private, it might be supposed that standards are best certified in public. The matter is not, however, as simple as that, since questions of personal confidentiality and professional discretion can arise in this context as readily as they can in the process of following up anomalies. Much will depend on the particular approach adopted in evaluation and the particular aspect of the education service which is being evaluated.

We shall later review the argument, commonly advanced, that test results taken at their face value can be misleading. We merely need to make the point that fuller interpretation of raw statistics may involve the disclosure that certain children have serious difficulties at home, or may be complicated by a legitimate professional disagreement about curricular emphasis or content. It cannot therefore be taken for granted that the publication of test results is necessarily an appropriate response to questions about standards. Similarly, it is likely to be unproductive for an authority to insist on making public the results of a school inspection. In most cases where defects are identified there will be recommendations for consequent action. It would merely undermine morale to draw attention to the defects before a chance has been given to put the recommendations into operation.

But again, even in potentially sensitive areas of this kind, it can be argued that the exercise of established procedures is a legitimate matter for public knowledge, allowing that the particular results of such procedures are not. It can hardly damage public confidence to know that standardized tests are routinely administered on a county-wide basis at particular stages in the educational process; that each school's average scores are carefully scrutinized by advisers against the overall norms; and that any significant aberrations are followed up with the head concerned. Such information would not necessarily give rise to a demand for the analysis and subsequent discussion to be carried out in public view. A similar argument could reasonably apply to the conduct of in-service programmes to raise overall professional standards. Our inquiries have produced no evidence that the autonomy and confidentiality which is inherent in the notion of a professional service is being called widely into question. It appears, on the contrary, that the public in general, and parents in particular, are unaware of the mechanisms by which standards are kept under review by schools and LEAs. Rather than being secretive about such professional review procedures, the education service might well strengthen its credibility by regarding their operation as a proper aspect of its own accountability – and hence as deserving to be made generally known.

We have been concerned up to this point with procedures which are normally confidential. But there are other procedures relevant to the maintenance of standards which must of their nature be conducted in public rather than in private. For example, an education committee may consider it necessary or desirable to notify its constituency about changes in the aggregate level of pupils' measured performance between one point in time and another – as the Department of Education and Science is now seeking to do on a national basis through its Assessment of Performance Unit. This end can only be achieved by making the overall data available for general scrutiny. In a comparable way, a head may want to inform parents more fully about standards of performance in his school by encouraging them to see a particular class in action or to look at samples of work children have produced, or he may seek to earn their confidence by providing them with a reasonably detailed statement about the school's educational aims and curricular policies. Again, such a purpose demands the detailed disclosure of first-hand information, rather than a general description of how certain internal procedures are carried out.

So far, our emphasis has been on the contrast between monitoring departures from normal practice and ensuring that normal practice is itself up to standard. Within the latter category, we have identified some procedures which are professionally based (but whose availability may deserve to be publicly disclosed) and others which necessarily allow public access to relevant data. But as we have already acknowledged, these analytic and administrative distinctions should not obscure the fact that tackling unexpected problems is very closely connected to certifying standards of normal practice.

The connection can be brought out by considering the nature of public confidence in the education service. If at any particular time there is a high degree of trust invested in the teachers as a profession and a high regard for the standards achieved by their pupils, then both may be undermined by a run of well-publicized disasters involving only a small handful of schools. That is to say, the achievement of a satisfactory level of general performance is no substitute for an adequate set of mechanisms to cope with anomalies and unpredictable events. Conversely, an authority which has developed a sound and effective set of trouble-shooting procedures can thereby build up a bank of credit which will enhance its general image and cast a favourable light on the overall competence of its schools.

The credibility of any routine monitoring process will depend on its ability not only to identify potential problems but also to resolve them at a sufficiently early stage to minimize any contamination of the rest of the system. Just as the occurrence of a particular crisis is likely to give rise to reforms in the way overall standards are safeguarded, so the safeguards themselves cannot be maintained without effective procedures for dealing with any deficiencies which they bring to light. Public trust has to be won by anticipating problems which are foreseeable, by rapidly identifying those which are not, and by dealing resolutely with both.

Informal, formal, mandatory, and constitutional procedures

In the previous section, we argued that the means both to anticipate potential and to follow up actual departures from acceptable standards are vital elements in accountability, and are closely connected one with another. Both, however, become pointless without the possibility of effective remedial action. It is this aspect – the ways in which problem-solving and maintenance may lead on to positive intervention – which underpins the further analytic distinctions we now need to draw.

Most of the heads and teachers we interviewed acknowledged their obligation to give some account to parents of what the school was doing and why, but at the same time doubted the right of parents to take issue with these accounts, and thus to question the teachers' professional decisions. This viewpoint represents accountability in the weak sense of being answerable for, or willing to render an account of, one's activities, without any question of an independent audit, let alone any possibility of ensuing action if the account is contested or found unsatisfactory.

In practice, most of the transactions between teachers and parents are of this informal kind. Responsiveness to one's professional clientele is indeed the bedrock on which more systematic accounting procedures must be built. Any programme of public accountability – of maintaining confidence by the application of recognized routines for monitoring standards and solving problems – would be hopelessly precarious in the absence of any mutual sense of trust. But while this is a necessary ingredient in any comprehensive approach, it is not a sufficient one. By its very nature, it depends on personal and local circumstance; it is private and particularized, usually self-initiated by a head or a teacher, and liable to appear arbitrary and *ad hoc*. It can and must carry conviction for those directly concerned, but it is incapable of generalization to the public at large.

So in addition to the variety of informal ways in which schools are prepared to encourage parents' involvement and respond to their concerns, many heads consider it necessary to go further by promoting certain aspects of professional practice into established school policy – for example, casual parental help in schools can be structured by drawing up rotas of helpers and even involving parents in some training. Such formalization of procedures avoids the obvious limits of informal answerability, but may also run the risk of depersonalizing some practices and removing the element of individual commitment which is their main strength.

A similar distinction can also be noted at the level of the LEA. In response to mounting political demands for greater accountability, some authorities no longer feel able to devolve all policy decisions on this matter to their individual heads. The members of the education committee, being themselves directly accountable to their electors, may justifiably decide that certain practices which are already widely observed among their schools should become enshrined into authority-wide policy. This introduction of what we may call mandatory accountability, demanding the compliance of all schools rather than merely encouraging the cooperation of a significant number, has its attendant liabilities and assets. It too may diminish the sense of direct involvement which comes from spontaneity of choice, and may make less ready allowance for important local and personal variables. However, by achieving general as against particular application, mandatory procedures are – in political terms – more credible than informal ones, and tend to make a more immediate impact on those lay audiences not as closely involved with the schools as are many parents, managers, or members.

We may note two further contrasts between informal accountability procedures on the one side and formal mandatory exercises on the other. First, the distinction can be applied to interprofessional relationships as well as to those between professionals and laymen. Thus, as we have already noted, some heads adopt an informal approach to the monitoring of standards in their schools, while others explicitly invite all their teachers to provide a periodic account of what they are doing. Similarly, in many aspects of their work the advisers will be concerned to make informal and individualistic appraisals of schools and teachers; in others, where they are required to make a standard type of assessment, or to carry out an official review, the process of judgement becomes – as appropriate to a mandatory exercise – detached and impersonal.

Second, although formal and mandatory accountability both admit the possibility of external audit – generalized policies being open to scrutiny in a way that particular actions are not – they both, in common with their informal counterpart, stop short of specifying the sequel to any judgement that is reached. This is not to deny that in practice rewards may be given for excellence or remedies sought for inadequacy. It is merely to point out that any such rewards or remedies are themselves informally determined. They are seen as an implicit consequence of one's actions, rather than as an integral and explicit element of what it is to be called to account for them. Arguably, to lose public or professional reputation is the most powerful sanction which underlies such forms of accountability, and to gain or maintain it the most convincing incentive.

But there is another type of procedure, perhaps best described as constitutional, which invokes a level of authority and demands a degree of consequential action beyond those we have so far considered. It is based firmly on the relationship between employing authorities and employees, rather than on that between senior and junior colleagues or between professionals and clients. Here, a practice which might otherwise have remained at the informal, formal, or mandatory level is in fact incorporated into the political contract between the education authority and the electorate. Not only does it acquire the force of statute, but – as with other elements of the legislative framework – it must necessarily allow for relevant appeal procedures against alleged deficiencies, and spell out an agreed range of consequential penalties, compensations, or commendations.

Constitutional forms of accountability enjoy certain clear advantages. They are the natural and obvious means by which the members of an authority can establish their own accountability to the electorate. The expenditure of substantial sums of public money is held to be justifiable if it can be shown that standards of efficiency are carefully and systematically safeguarded, that poor performance is firmly rooted out, and high expectations rigorously maintained. A councillor who can say, 'In my authority not only do we require all schools to do thus-and-thus, but we also take such-and-such steps to make certain that they do it,' is in a stronger position than one who has to persuade his constituents that most heads are receptive to informed advice or instruction from county hall, and that, in so far as they are not, their professional autonomy must deserve unquestioning support.

But just as there are losses as well as gains in promoting an informal procedure to formal status at the school level, so too the elevation from mandatory to constitutional rank at the authority level must be counted a mixed blessing. There is inevitably an element of the symbolic in any statutory procedure, which may consequently ascribe a higher value to going through the right motions than to having a conviction in what one is doing. Moreover, the ritualism embodied in legislative policies often seems to carry a punitive overtone.

A programme of accountability which rested solely on constitutional measures would thus be likely in the end to defeat its own object – to reduce standards by undermining teachers' morale rather than to enhance them by building up professional self-esteem. Given that each of the four categories we have identified have their particular strengths and weaknesses, it would seem prudent for those designing overall policy to think in terms of a mixed economy of informal, formal, mandatory, and constitutional procedures.

It should be noted, in concluding this analysis, that one and the same activity may well fall within a number of different categories, depending on the context in which it is carried out. To illustrate the point, a particular head may allow teachers individually to decide what to report to parents at interviews on children's progress: in such a case interviews would constitute an exercise of informal accountability. Another head might insist on written reports being issued at specified times, and perhaps in some standardized form, by every teacher: this would clearly be an instance of formal accountability. Or to take the matter to a mandatory stage, an LEA might require all its schools to adopt this practice: indeed, it might go further in the direction of constitutionalizing such policy by instructing advisers to ensure that it is properly carried out, and by specifying a complaints procedure for parents not satisfied with the reliability of the resulting information.

Incentives and sanctions

We noted in the preceding section that both mandatory and constitutional procedures can be reinforced in practice by a system of penalties and/or rewards. In mandatory procedures, the consequential actions are implicit; in constitutional procedures they are by definition public and explicit.

Very few clear-cut instances can be found of constitutional accountability in the contemporary education system of England and Wales; that is not the usual way things are done. The cane exists, though rarely used, but it is kept tactfully in the cupboard rather than hung on the wall for all to see. Because of this convention of reticence, and the rarity of the need to breach it, it is not always easy to call to mind the range of incentives and sanctions which may be invoked to lend greater credence to demands for accountability.

If no such incentives or sanctions existed, the category of constitutional accountability would remain no more than an empty abstraction; mandatory procedures would rest at the level of commandments whose credibility depended on a general willingness to observe them. It is therefore a necessary part of our argument to provide examples of generally recognized prizes and penalties attendant on an individual's or institution's being held to account.

Taking the case of the individual first, we may note various possible forms of incentive for the diligent pursuit of standards and the satisfactory achievement of accounting procedures related to them. The most obvious, perhaps, are conditional candidatures for promotion ('a teacher will not be eligible for appointment to a headship unless . . .') and salary increments linked to the attainment of particular performance targets (the now notorious policy of 'payment by results' provides an instance in history). But one could also point to current practices in other systems than our own, which include the award of an honorific title (e.g., 'Master Teacher', as in some US school districts), the conferment of special privileges (e.g., shorter working hours, as awarded to particular categories of teacher in some Continental countries), or the bestowal of public accolade (which became a favoured practice in Maoist China).

The most prevalent forms of sanction against the individual are suspension or dismissal. Others are generated by the direct inversion of possible rewards. Although demotion seems a sanction peculiar to the armed forces, a positive embargo on promotion ('no teacher may be appointed head who fails satisfactorily to . . .') is more readily imaginable. If titles and privileges can be awarded, they can also in principle be taken away again; and public rebuke is a familiar enough counterpart to public praise.

A somewhat different set of possible rewards and penalties might be applied to institutions. A common form of institutional recognition is the special entitlement to carry out certain prestigious functions (only universities, to take one case in point, are entitled to award their own degrees). Related to this, the promise of promotion to privileged status is a strong incentive to raise standards. It would also seem possible, if unlikely, for a bonus to be offered in the form of a special addition to funds or facilities for schools whose general level of performance notably exceeded expectation.

On the other side of this coin, it should be observed that the sanction of total closure has been used in recent memory to emphasize the accountability of a particular school for its overall educational standards. Again, as with individuals, where entitlements exist they can be taken away, and demotion of status could in principle form a counterpart to its promotion.

In the nature of things, to talk of retribution is never polite and not often productive, and even the contemplation of bonuses is only pleasurable to those who expect to receive them. Enough ground has perhaps already been covered, in this brief discussion, to establish the point needing to be made: that if and when the occasion demands, there are indeed mechanisms which can be invoked to lend clout to otherwise inconsequential demands for accountability. It should not need saying – though for safety's sake we shall say it nonetheless – that we are not ourselves to be taken as commending the use of any such mechanisms as we have described. Our own views of them are not to the point; our task here as elsewhere has been one of analysis, not advocacy.

Some gaps in the framework

It seems appropriate, by way of a brief final comment on our exploration of the concept of accountability, to hold ourselves answerable for certain

notable omissions in the range of possibilities we have taken into consideration. It may be remarked – quite correctly – that we have failed to make any
mention of those procedures for generating public trust which rest on
professionality alone, and that we have similarly overlooked approaches
which depend solely on the sovereignty of the consumer.

As far as professionality is concerned, there are undeniable instances in
which internal monitoring by one's professional peers is regarded as an
acceptable substitute for formal accountability to one's superiors or one's
employers. For example, the medical fraternity are entrusted with the
responsibility to operate their own monitoring and disciplinary procedures,
rather than having to commit matters of professional discretion to external
lay scrutiny.

However, the right of any group in society to set its own norms is never
readily granted, and the case that teachers should be privileged to do so has
not yet been argued with much conviction. There is no unified professional
body entitled to grant or remove the licence to practice, and no strong
consensus on acceptable norms of procedure. Our own inquiry underlined
the reluctance of many teachers and heads to entrust judgements about their
competence to colleagues of equal standing in other schools. (This issue of
mutual certification is clearly distinguishable from that of internal monitoring by advisers, who must be seen in their inspectorial role as superior
members of a hierarchy, acting on behalf of the relevant public authorities.)
Accordingly, we have not considered it appropriate to give any detailed
consideration to policy options based exclusively on the principle of professional responsibility, as opposed to those based on the doctrine of accountability to independent auditors.

Approaches which rest on an appeal to concepts of consumerism are, we
would argue, rightly disqualified on the grounds that they sidestep the
issue. They take two main forms, both peripheral to the education system as
currently administered, and neither involving in any direct way the justification of public trust in its provision. The first involves demystifying and
deprofessionalizing education, so giving the lay public direct access to the
necessary teaching skills. In its extreme form, this approach allows parents
the right to educate their own children or to provide cooperative 'free
schools' untrammelled with the constraints of teacher professionalism;
whether those given such freedom are able to take adequate advantage of it
is another question. However, the argument need not detain us long: given
that it presupposes a dramatic change of political climate and a vast pro-

gramme of constitutional reform, it seems unlikely to be seriously enter-
tained as a policy option in any existing local authority.

The second main form of consumerism regards education as a commodity
rather than a public good, to be purveyed through market mechanisms in
which the choices of individual customers replace the controls exercised by
the elected agencies of society at large. The proposed substitution of the
practices of private schooling for those of public education rests on the
expectation that the individuals and institutions which succeed in building
up a reputation will prosper, and those which lack credibility will fail. But
as against this, it must be noted that the publicly appointed providers of
education would have a much diminished role, in which they would largely
abdicate their statutory responsibilities for the maintenance of standards.
Many teachers would, moreover, contend that the children are the true
clients, and that their best interests are not always served by their parents.
Those we met in the course of the project were concerned that in the kind of
direct democracy engendered by such a process, the more demanding
parents would be atypical of the rest. They were emphatic that to cede a
substantial degree of power to parents could have a seriously damaging
effect on the staff, the school, and its pupils.

It does not seem necessary, in these circumstances, to regard the setting
up of free schools, voucher systems, or other forms of consumer control as
serious policy alternatives to an accountability programme systematically
planned, articulated, and implemented by the education service itself. We
shall therefore move on to our main task, in which we have chosen to mark a
distinction grounded on more firmly practical considerations than the ones
we have so far drawn: namely between those policy options which are
school-based and those which are authority-based.

Conclusions

Aspects of accountability

In earlier parts of our chapter, we have been concerned with reviewing
the armoury of techniques and procedures which schools and LEAs respectively can deploy in the context of accountability. We now turn, in the
concluding stages of our analysis, to a consideration of the different purposes which these techniques and procedures may be called upon to serve.

Three points deserve to be borne in mind by the reader in working through the arguments we shall now rehearse. The first is that accountability can have a positive as well as a negative aspect. It need not be seen simply as a burdensome necessity in meeting external obligations. If properly designed and implemented, an accountability policy can also provide a defence against outside attempts to limit autonomy and the enjoyment of legitimate rights and powers. Such attempts might take the form of political encroachments on freedom, or the unjustified erosion of financial entitlements, as well as campaigns to undermine reputation through the media or to destroy it through libellous gossip.

Second, accountability – as we have come clearly to recognize in the course of our study – is a two-way process. Any LEA, in satisfying its external obligations to maintain proper educational standards, must also see itself as answerable to its teachers and its schools, and must strive actively to sustain its supportive relationships with them.

The third point leads on from these. It is possible to approach accountability as a process of mutual negotiation, in which something is conceded – say, some professional prerogative which contemporary values call into question – and something gained – perhaps a firm declaration of public trust, a renewed guarantee of essential autonomies, or an insurance against future encroachment. Such an approach must call for a gradualist and long-term strategy, based on careful consultation between the authority and its schools. It could be expensive in time and effort, and could risk exasperating public patience. But the alternative, of imposing an apparently cheap, quick, and easy solution, against the wishes of the schools, might in the end prove a hollow victory. It would at best achieve conformity without conviction; at worst it could lead to the general debilitation which now characterizes many school systems in North America.

Six modes of accountability

In the attempt we now make to knit together the diverse strands of our analysis and to give them a coherent shape, we have inevitably had to oversimplify or sharpen a number of familiar distinctions as well as to introduce some new ones of our own. We wish to acknowledge the crudity and occasional artificiality of the barriers which we have found it necessary to erect in marking out the terrain for further exploration. We recognize and welcome the fact that they will be transcended by the subtleties of future political debate.

It is possible to distinguish three facets within the broad meaning of the term accountability: (1) *answerability* to one's clients ('moral accountability'); (2) *responsibility* to oneself and one's colleagues ('professional accountability'); (3) and *accountability* in the strict sense to one's employers or political masters ('contractual accountability').

These distinctions are exemplified in different ways by schools on the one hand and education committees on the other. Schools are primarily answerable to parents, but legally accountable to the LEA (in some circumstances directly, in others via their managers). Education committees are answerable to their schools, but constitutionally accountable to the electorate (either directly, or via their governing council). Both have also to acknowledge certain responsibilites to their own professional consciences and to their peers.

We have earlier remarked that accountability must meet two basic, interconnected demands: (1) the preservation and, where possible, enhancement of overall levels of performance through *maintenance* procedures; (2) the detection and amelioration of individual points of weakness through appropriate *problem-solving* mechanisms.

Taking these two sets of considerations together, we can distinguish six different modes of accounting, as follows:

1 Answerability for maintenance
2 Answerability for problem-solving
3 Responsibility for maintenance
4 Responsibility for problem-solving
5 Strict accountability for maintenance
6 Strict accountability for problem-solving

Between them, these six modes serve to draw attention to the demands which might – in principle if not always in practice – be made on schools and LEAs. We shall accordingly use them as the basis for our subsequent discussion. First, we shall look at the pattern of possible expectation as it relates to schools, taking this to be a matter of legitimate interest also to the education committee and its officers. After that, we shall sketch out the set of requirements for accountability which might be levied on the authority itself.

The elements of school-based accounting

There is a variety of possible ways in which the schools might elect to meet their answerability to parents for the maintenance of standards – the first mode in our list. The parents' awareness of what their children's schools are doing may be promoted through regular communication on individual pupils' progress, or by allowing ready parental access to classrooms and teachers, or by encouraging a general atmosphere of open inquiry. Other forms of provision would include explanations of curricular aims and teaching methods, accounts of overall policy, and reports on general standards of performance.

The second mode concerns the school's potential problem-solving strategies, and especially its means of responding to matters of parental concern. These may include early disclosure of problems – whether affecting individual children or relating to wider issues – where this seems appropriate in averting later crisis, and the prompt acknowledgement and investigation of, and subsequent response to, expressions of parental grievance. All parents have a right to know what the appropriate procedures are within the school if they wish to raise a complaint.

The professional responsibilities which might be exercised by schools in the course of their own internal maintenance – the third mode in our list – could be expected to include the development of good relationships with parents on the one hand and the authority on the other, alongside various forms of domestic monitoring of standards and the regular review of staffing, curricula, and teaching arrangements. Schools may also – in so far as their reputations are interdependent – be called upon to exercise professional responsibility towards one another. Junior and middle schools must, moreover, share responsibility with the infant and secondary schools to which they are linked, for the long-term interests of their pupils.

The fourth mode, relating to internal problem-solving, would include – on the institutional front – being aware of and taking steps to rectify incipient points of weakness, and the vigilant anticipation of potential crisis; and – in relation to individual children – the sensible use of screening procedures (such as pupil records and diagnostic tests) to identify and give remedial help to those at risk.

The fifth mode – strict accountability for maintenance – is concerned with the accountability of each school to its LEA for overall quality of provision. Here, one might note its explicit obligation to observe mandatory and constitutional accounting procedures and to meet centrally agreed specifications. Implicit expectations would include the school's openness to informal visitation by authorized representatives of the authority, its readiness to justify (if reasonably called upon to do so) its curricular goals and methods and its overall policies, and its similar readiness to account for below-average levels of pupil performance.

The sixth and last mode focuses on the ways in which the schools do or should account to the LEA with respect to problem-solving. In this context, they have a clear duty to report on all such grievances or complaints deriving from external sources, and all such internal difficulties, as they are not themselves able to resolve satisfactorily within a reasonable period of time. They would also properly be expected to develop, on their own initiative, appropriate means of anticipating and dealing with such problems as may in fact arise.

These various elements of school-based accounting are summarized in Figure 1. We have not attempted to mark out the distinctions between those items which are universally applicable, those which are common practice, and those at present observed by few schools or none. We have not made any of the subsidiary differentiations between informal and formal, mandatory and constitutional procedures. Nor have we attempted to single out those particular policy options which remain presently available to schools. All such categories are dependent on context: the demarcation lines between them will vary from one time and one place to another. Any reader who wishes to define them for his own purposes will, we hope, have no difficulty in doing so.

The elements of authority-based accounting

It is possible to categorize the different components – both actual and potential – of an authority's programme of accountability in much the same ways as we have just done in relation to a school's. The same list of six modes will serve for this, and we shall examine them in the same order as before.

The first mode, in this setting, concerns an authority's answerability to its schools for the quality of its maintenance activities. Among the possible items under this head, we may note the obligation of an authority to provide each school with the resources appropriate to carry out its essential tasks and to meet the reasonable expectations made of it. The LEA will also have a general responsibility for the quality, morale, and well-being of its professional teaching staff (one particular expression of this might be the institution of systematic forms of personnel development). Authorities may also be expected to support their schools as institutions, both by accrediting (and, where appropriate, publicizing) good practice, and by coming

Figure 1 *Elements of Schools' Accountability*

	Answerability (to parents)	*Responsibility* (to self and peers)	*Strict Accountability* (to LEA direct or via managers)
Maintenance	**1** — Regular communication on individual children's progress (via written reports, etc.) — Accounts of overall policy (via prospectus, etc.) — Explanation of curricular aims and methods — Reports on general standards of performance, academic, and other (via open days, speech days, etc.) — Encouragement of better parental awareness of school's activities and endeavours (via ready access to classrooms and staff, atmosphere of open inquiries, and discussion)	**3** — Domestic monitoring of standards — Regular review of staffing, curricula, and teaching arrangements — Promotion of good relationships with parents (via school social occasions, etc.) — Promotion of good relationships with feeder and receiving (secondary) schools — Promotion of good relationships with managers, advisers, and LEA as a whole	**5** — Observation of mandatory and constitutional procedures — Meeting of centrally agreed specifications — Openness to authorized visitation — Readiness to justify curricular goals and methods and overall policies — Readiness to account for pupil performance standards
Problem-solving	**2** — Notification to all parents of complaints procedures — Prompt acknowledgement and investigation of parental complaints, confirmation of action taken — Early disclosure to parents, where appropriate, of problems (i) relating to individual children (ii) involving wider issues	**4** — Screening of individual children at risk (via internal reporting, pupil records, tests, etc.) — Provision of remedial help to children in need — Awareness of incipient points of weakness — Anticipation of potential crises	**6** — Reporting of unresolved external complaints and grievances — Reporting of unresolved internal difficulties — Development of effective means to deal with problems arising

NB   The entries above are not intended to be comprehensive. They are meant only to indicate possible expectations or demands in each category. They should *not* be taken as indicating policies which are necessarily feasible, desirable, or deserving of priority at the school level.

actively to their defence – in general or in particular – when their overall standards are subjected to demonstrably unjust or unreasonable criticism. Schools, it may be argued, have a natural right to seek an explanation of their authority's policies on accountability.

LEAs are, as our second mode suggests, also answerable to schools in regard to problem-solving. That is to say, they have a moral duty to help schools both to identify potential difficulties and to tackle practical issues for which external support is likely to be necessary or desirable. The former obligation is commonly met through testing programmes designed to pick out areas of weakness or through the various types of diagnostic visitation procedure. Issues serious enough to call for outside help may involve individual children, particular teachers, or the institution as a whole. The forms of response will vary accordingly: they may include intervention by the area office, the temporary presence in the school of advisers, the decision to make extra resources available, or – in the last resort – the transfer or dismissal of staff or even the closure of the school. Furthermore, when a particular complaint registered by a parent or other outside agent (including the press) can be shown to be without basis, the school or teacher concerned may have a right to expect the authority's full backing in contesting it.

An authority's professional responsibility to keep its affairs in good order constitutes the third mode in our list. It is discharged in part by fostering good relationships with its schools and teachers (not to mention its own advisory and administrative staff), and in part by cultivating and enhancing its relationships with the public. Good housekeeping will imply an effective set of procedures for evaluating and reviewing current policy: it can also crucially depend on the ability of officers and members to work together, and the forcefulness of the arguments they are able to muster in their annual bids to council for resources. The demands of mutual responsibility between different authorities, and between local and national administration, could also be included in this general category.

Turning next to internal problem-solving by the LEA – the fourth mode – we reiterate a point made by one of the officers we interviewed during the course of our study. Committee members and their staff, besides responding to problems which have already arisen, or acting on issues which they can identify as likely to arise, are called upon to accommodate rapidly to unforeseen political pressures from outside the educational arena and to devise swift and effective ways of meeting them.

Our fifth mode concerns the accountability of elected members to their constituents for the maintenance of overall standards within the education service. Particular forms of certification include authority-wide testing designed for general monitoring purposes, routine visitation programmes with the same ends in view, and the specification of general aims and curricular policies. An important, but generally neglected, aspect of this form of accountability is the public disclosure of the nature and extent of the maintenance procedures adopted by the authority in respect of its schools.

The final mode – the sixth in our list – draws attention to the authority's obligations to account to the public for the effectiveness of its problem-solving. In this context, its general abilities to predict, handle, and rectify problems come under critical scrutiny. Such problems (whether relating to children, teachers, or schools) fall into two groups: those which arise externally, in relation to a particular grievance, or to some unforeseeable quirk of circumstance; and those which are generated internally, as a result of malfunctioning or maladministration within the system. If either type of issue is inadequately handled, the LEA must ultimately take the blame. Hence the potential importance of making widely known what measures are in fact available to deal with both eventualities. A closely related obligation is to notify the public of the most appropriate forms in which to register possible complaints. Over and above this, the authority will be expected to ensure that any actual complaints are properly acknowledged; that they are carefully investigated, and (where necessary) dealt with; and that the fact that this has been done is duly notified to the original complainant.

In concluding this summary review of the elements of authority-based accountability, we must rehearse the caveats expressed in the previous section on accountability at the level of the individual school. The considerations set out in Figure 2 take no account of time and place – the state of existing practice, or the key policy areas awaiting further consideration. Our concern has been with identifying possible forms of demand for accountability – which we take to be a proper function of policy analysis – rather than with evaluating the significance of those demands in practice – which constitutes a first stage in the formulation of policy proposals as such.

Accountability in the wider policy context

We shall conclude our chapter with a brief consideration of the place of accountability in the overall scheme of things – in the whole policy framework of a school and an authority. One way to approach the question

Figure 2 *Elements of LEA's Accountability*

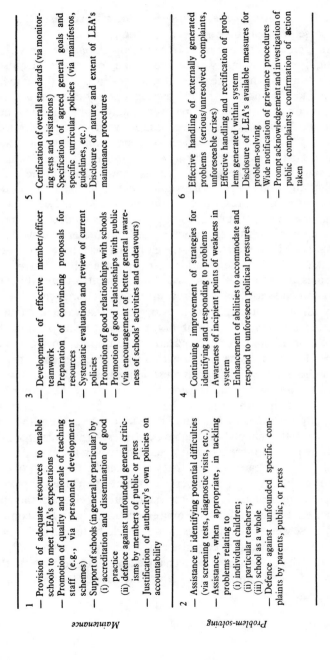

	Answerability (to schools)	*Responsibility* (to self and peers)	*Strict Accountability* (to electorate, direct or via council)

Maintenance	**1**
	– Provision of adequate resources to enable schools to meet LEA's expectations
	– Promotion of quality and morale of teaching staff (e.g., via personnel development schemes)
	– Support of schools (in general or particular) by
	  (i) accreditation and dissemination of good practice
	  (ii) defence against unfounded general criticisms by members of public or press
	– Justification of authority's own policies on accountability
		3
		– Development of effective member/officer teamwork
		– Preparation of convincing proposals for resources
		– Systematic evaluation and review of current policies
		– Promotion of good relationships with schools
		– Promotion of good relationships with public (via encouragement of better general awareness of schools' activities and endeavours)
			5
			– Certification of overall standards (via monitoring tests and visitations)
			– Specification of agreed general goals and specific curricular policies (via manifestos, guidelines, etc.)
			– Disclosure of nature and extent of LEA's maintenance procedures

Problem-solving	**2**
	– Assistance in identifying potential difficulties (via screening tests, diagnostic visits, etc.)
	– Assistance, when appropriate, in tackling problems relating to
	  (i) individual children;
	  (ii) particular teachers;
	  (iii) school as a whole
	– Defence against unfounded specific complaints by parents, public, or press
		4
		– Continuing improvement of strategies for identifying and responding to problems
		– Awareness of incipient points of weakness in system
		– Enhancement of abilities to accommodate and respond to unforeseen political pressures
			6
			– Effective handling of externally generated problems (serious/unresolved complaints, unforeseeable crises)
			– Effective handling and rectification of problems generated within system
			– Disclosure of LEA's available measures for problem-solving
			– Wide notification of grievance procedures
			– Prompt acknowledgement and investigation of public complaints; confirmation of action taken

NB   The entries above are not intended to be comprehensive. They are meant only to indicate possible expectations or demands in each category. They should certainly *not* be taken as indicating policies which are necessarily feasible, desirable, or deserving of priority at the LEA level.

is to reflect on what we, as members of the research team, have learned in the course of our two years' work on the project.

Although we tried not to let our preconceptions influence the course of our inquiries, we certainly had some sketchy notions at the outset of where the investigations might lead us. One of these was that the schools probably held the key to some of the more crucial policy choices, and that school-based accountability procedures were likely to be the focal point of our attention. Another was that accountability would transpire to be closely concerned with the development of good public relations, and that we might need to give particular attention to this aspect. A third was that accountability might begin to emerge as a new heading in the LEA's budget, and that any policy proposals would have to justify their costs alongside competing claims on resources. As our work developed, we found ourselves forced to recognize that we had got each picture out of focus. It was not that we were plainly mistaken in our vision, but rather that we had caught a blurred and slightly distorted image of what was there to be seen. In each case, the reasons – when we hit on them – were instructive.

Schools are undeniably important components in educational accountability, but our hope of building up a policy framework on the 'every-school-for-itself' principle was foredoomed. What we at first failed to realize was that, in terms of accountability, the ruling principle must be that 'no school is an island'. Public reputation presupposes interdependence, not independence – the one school with a bad name contaminates the ninety-nine with a good. So while each must do the best it can in its own cause, the collective interest must in the end be protected by the authority (which is there to guard it) rather than by the schools (who are there to serve it). That is why our report has turned out to be as much about the authority's options as it is about the schools' – though we did not start out with that expectation.

As our many interviews and discussions over the past two years have shown, it is also clearly the case that the successful discharge of accountability must involve the education service in more open dialogue, more vigorous publicity, a more conscious promotion of public relations, than has been its practice in the past. But to equate accountability with communication skills, as we were at first inclined to do, would be to overlook a host of other activities which we now recognize as relevant to our theme. They are those activities which concern the internal well-being of the system: the identification and amelioration of problems, the proper exercise of professional responsibilities, the efforts at self-appraisal, the enhancement of existing skills, and many others we have touched on in the course of our report. In the long term, these may turn out to be more important than mere improvements in the techniques of presentation, persuasion, and pacification, for they can have a catalytic effect in the regeneration of morale and self-respect, and hence in winning the respect of others. The best way of all of earning the public confidence is the most direct: namely to be clearly seen as doing a good job. Again, therefore, while we have no wish to repudiate our initial concern with improved communications with parents and others, our explorations have taken us a long way beyond that point.

At one stage in our thinking, we toyed with the idea of presenting some kind of cost-benefit exercise which could match accountability against other areas of policy. We felt that our analysis would be incomplete if we were not able to present some rationale, however sketchy, to enable the authority to decide whether it wished to commit new resources in this area, and if so what scale of commitment it might sensibly make. We soon came to realize that the task was self-defeating. The elements of accountability are so diverse, multifarious, and pervasive that there is simply no way of separating them out and displaying them as a separate entry in an inventory of tasks or commitments, whether at the level of the authority or at that of the school. Accountability, far from being – as our initial preconception had it – an element among others in the system, is an important aspect of the way the system itself works.

Very few of the activities with which this report has been concerned – take school prospectuses, pupil records, county-wide testing schemes, or formal inspection – were the product of William Tyndale or Mr. Callaghan's Ruskin speech. They were there – albeit undisclosed, unnoticed, and unnamed – long before accountability became the political fashion; and they will doubtless long survive it. What that fashion has done is to call for a more explicit framework of expectations – summarized in Figures 1 and 2 – a framework which may clarify priorities and show the interconnections between activities hitherto separately conceived.

The time may come when accountability becomes a major influence on policy decisions. If so, it may perhaps serve not only to encourage the critical review of existing policies but also to identify the new initiatives which may be needed in response to changes in external circumstance. Such speculation, however, lies at the margins of our present understanding. All we can now say with confidence is that our initial presupposition was mistaken. Accountability – to revive a once much-quoted catchphrase – is not so much a programme, more a way of life.

SECTION III

THE SCHOOL AS AN ORGANIZATION

CHAPTER 3.1

ORGANIZATIONAL AND ADMINISTRATIVE THEORY*

Thomas Landers and Judith Myers

The development of management thought

The Industrial Revolution and the new managerial role

The Industrial Revolution marked the beginnings of the professionalization of management. For centuries, goods had been produced by independent manufacturers in their homes or small shops. But the Industrial Revolution, nurtured by the invention of power-driven machinery and by the use of more modern means of transportation, brought workers together as employees in factories. England was the first nation to develop an industrial commercial society. During the development of these industrial enterprises, the coordination of men and materials emerged as a problem. The efficient operation of commercial enterprises that involved great numbers of people presented a new challenge, and at first, military organizational patterns were copied.

With the foundation of scientific thought already laid in the seventeenth and eighteenth centuries by Bacon, Petty, Locke, Newton, and others, and the idea of the division of management and labour having been raised by early writers such as Sir James Stewart (1767) and Adam Smith (1776), thoughtful industrialists were developing managerial techniques. One such pioneer was Richard Arkwright, who put manufacturing operations under one roof and who developed techniques for the coordination of men, money, materials, and machines in large-scale production. He was also a pioneer in continuous production, plant-site planning, coordination, and division of labour.

* *Essentials of School Management*, W.B. Saunders Company, 1977, pp. 365–393.

During this period, other writers contributed to the rise of managerial science. Carl von Clauswitz (1780–1831), a Prussian general, proposed that decisions should be based on scientific analysis rather than on intuition. Charles Babbage, the English mathematician, was the first to propose (*On the Economy of Machinery and Manufacture*, 1832) that certain principles of organization must exist that will apply to every type of human enterprise that involves the coordination of people and resources to achieve a shared goal.

Americans, like Europeans, were struggling with the new types of organizations created by the Industrial Revolution. The latter part of the nineteenth century saw the westward movement and the creation of vast new markets, the abolition of slave labour, the growth of the railroads, and the expansion of industry.

One of the most significant events of this period was the introduction of the first joint-stock company in 1862. The result was the creation of financial resources with almost unlimited potential and organizations of a size and scope heretofore unimagined. The separation of capital and management would also lead to the rise of salaried professional noncapitalist managers who would have to be trained and produced in large numbers.

Many influential people demanded more scientific management methods. Among these was the president of Yale and Towne Manufacturing Company, Henry R. Towne, who pled for recognition of a science of management with its own literature, journals and associations. The movement for formal education in management was begun in 1881, when Joseph Wharton gave $100,000 to the University of Pennsylvania to establish the first school to train managers. By 1911, thirty schools had been established, and management was becoming a recognized area of academic study. It was out of this milieu that the scientific management movement began.

The scientific management movement

The term 'scientific management' has no precise definition. It was first used by Supreme Court Justice Louis Brandeis in 1910, to refer to modern management techniques during an Interstate Commerce Commission hearing. Frederick W. Taylor used the term in the title of his book, *The Principles of Scientific Management*, first published in 1911.[1] Generally, the term connotes the process of approaching the various aspects of organizations in the manner and spirit of a scientist, using scientific tools such as research, measurement, and analysis.

Although he rejected the distinction, Frederick W. Taylor is recognized as the 'father' of the scientific management movement. Taylor, a mechanical engineer, plant manager, consultant, and writer, made many contributions to the advancement of management as a science.[2] An example of Taylor's scientific approach to management was his experiment at Bethlehem Steel with the handling of pig iron. Taylor examined the process by which workmen lifted the iron from a pile, carried it up a plank, and loaded it in a railroad car. At the beginning of his study, Taylor noted that the average amount of pig iron loaded was twelve and one-half long tons per man per day. Armed with a stopwatch, Taylor analysed and determined optimum movement, pace and rest periods. He increased the average from twelve and one-half long tons per man per day to forty-seven and one-half, using monetary rewards to motivate the workmen to adopt his procedure and increase their productivity.

Another example was Taylor's study of the shovelling of minerals such as rice coal and iron ore. When he began his study, workmen were using their own shovels of varying sizes and were working in their own way. By scientifically analysing the process, Taylor determined optimum shovel size, optimum shovel load, and efficient shovelling techniques. He induced the company to furnish shovels appropriate for the different materials; by training the men and by supervising the work, Taylor achieved remarkable results. The number of men required to do one particular task was reduced from 600 to 140. The average number of tons shovelled per man per day increased from sixteen to fifty-nine. He reduced shovelling costs from 7.2 cents per ton to 3.3 cents per ton. Wages were increased from $1.15 to $1.88.

Taylor's 30,000 experiments with the metal-cutting process over a period of twenty-six years resulted in the development of high speed steel-cutting machinery and the establishment of optimum speeds and feed-rates for various machines. The scientific analysis of the processes and tasks performed by workmen, resulting in increased productivity, was one of Taylor's greatest contributions. He conducted thousands of experiments to support theories such as the piecework approach to production – rewarding increased individual output with increased pay.

The many contributions of Frederick W. Taylor include:

1 The exception principle: all recurring decisions should be routinized and delegated; the manager should deal only with the exceptions.
2 The concepts of specialization and standardization.
3 The professionalization of the management function, resulting in the

movement of work from the floor level to the management level.

4 Time standards (a time analysis of each well-defined job).
5 Mathematical models for production.
6 Economic lot size.
7 The differential piece-rate system.

Taylor's ideas and practices spread rapidly and, after 1903, he devoted most of his time to writing and lecturing and presenting papers.

Frank and Lilian Gilbreth[3] were also outstanding figures in the scientific management movement, with their development of the concept of *motion study*. In analysing the hand and body motions used in certain tasks, they developed optimum movements and machinery for increasing production, while minimizing the effort involved.

Henry L. Gantt, a contemporary and protégé of Taylor, made many contributions to the movement. In his experiments, he often achieved a doubling of production. In 1922, his *Gantt Chart*, a progress chart for the internal management of manufacturing and production control, was called 'the most notable contribution to the art of management made in this generation'.[4] Gantt also emphasized Taylor's idea that the training of workers is the responsibility of management.

Another significant aspect of the scientific management movement was the introduction of *industrial psychology*. Harvard psychology professor Hugo Munsterberg, who popularized psychology, first introduced its applications to industry. The early aims of industrial psychology, as conceived by Munsterberg, were to help identify which individuals were best fitted for a particular kind of work, to determine what psychological conditions created the greatest output, and to produce the influences on the human mind that achieved the results desired by management. Early applications of psychology to industry were oriented toward management's purposes rather than toward the worker's well-being. Interest in human relations and morale was to come as part of a later movement.

Widespread academic recognition of the accomplishments of Taylor and his contemporaries in the scientific management movement resulted from the first scientific management conference in the United States, organized by Harlowe Stafford Person, dean of the Tuck School at Dartmouth.

The impact of the scientific management movement on the development of management thought is immeasurable. Taylor and his contemporaries advocated: (1) inquisitiveness, (2) replacement of rule-of-thumb methods with scientific determination of each element in a worker's job, (3) cooperation between management and labour to accomplish work, in accordance with scientific methods, and (4) more equal division of responsibilities between managers and workers, with managers planning and organizing the work.

The scientific management movement, however, concentrated on repetitive muscular tasks and was concerned primarily with problems on the operational level. It has been criticized because of its failure to deal with higher levels of management, such as planning, decision-making, and problem-solving. March and Simon described scientific management as 'physiological organization theory'. The host of 'efficiency experts' who invaded industry with their stopwatches during the twenties and thirties often tended to ignore the human factors and, therefore, generated hostility towards the movement. The movement also emphasized a very simplistic means of motivation, i.e., monetary rewards. It reflected assumptions about human behaviour that would later be referred to by Douglas McGregor as 'Theory X'. When considering the deficiencies of the scientific management movement, however, one must remember the nature of the times out of which it grew, and its contribution to the American industrial growth.

The universal principles movement

During the latter part of the nineteenth century and well into the twentieth century, there developed, concurrently with the scientific management movement, another school of thought, sometimes called the 'universal principles movement', or the 'process' or 'functions' school. Some writers group together the ideas of this movement with the scientific management movement and call it the 'functional school of thought'. In spite of an overlap in certain areas, there is a distinction between the two movements. While Taylor's ideas developed from the operations level and ignored the larger top-level issues, the concepts of the universal principles movement developed from the top levels. Practising managers were looking for common principles that characterized successful management, and most of the writers of the movement were already active managers. The most prominent was Henri Fayol, a French engineer and managing director of the S.A. Commentry-Fourchambault mining firm. Fayol sought to develop a set of universal principles that could be taught. He published these principles, in France, in a book called *Administration Industrielle et Generale*. This 1916 work was later published in an English edition in 1929.[5]

Fayol contended that management was an activity common to all human undertakings – at home, in business, or in government – and that every enterprise involved certain management processes, such as planning, organizing, commanding, coordinating, and controlling. Fayol's contributions were: (1) applying the concepts of management, a separate body of knowledge, to all forms of group activity; (2) developing the first comprehensive set of principles that could apply to any endeavor; (3) giving impetus to the concept of teaching the skills of management, e.g., the development of management curricula in colleges and universities.

Fayol developed the following fourteen universal principles:

1 Division of work (specialization belongs to the natural order)
2 Authority and responsibility (responsibility is a corollary with authority)
3 Discipline (discipline is what leaders make it)
4 Unity of command (no person should have two bosses)
5 Unity of direction (one head and one plan for a group of activities having the same objectives)
6 Subordination of individual interest to the general interest
7 Remuneration (fair, rewarding of effort, reasonable)
8 Centralization (centralization belongs to the natural order)
9 Scalar chain of command
10 Order (a place for everyone and everyone in his place)
11 Equity (results from kindness and justice)
12 Stability (of tenure of personnel)
13 Initiative (great source of strength for business)
14 *Esprit de corps* (union is strength).[6]

Over the years, many writers identified hundreds of principles, perhaps the most familiar being: (1) Fayol's concept of *unity of command* – no member of an organization should report to more than one superior; (2) *span of control* – the optimum number of subordinates reporting to the same superior should be from five to eight; (3) Taylor's *exception principle* – the concept of delegated decision-making, i.e., the development of policy for recurring problems, with the superior dealing only with the exceptions; and (4) *the scalar principle* – the concept of a hierarchy of superior-subordinate relationships, with an emphasis on authority and well-defined responsibilities.

Urwick's universal principles of organization

In 1943, Lyndall Urwick first analysed the principles of Fayol, Taylor, and other writers and then synthesized them into the following list:

1 *Principle of the objective:* each part and subdivision of the organization should be the expression of a definite purpose, in harmony with the objective of the undertaking.
2 *Principle of authority and responsibility:* responsibility for the execution of work must be accompanied with the authority to control and direct the means of doing the work.
3 *Principle of ultimate authority:* the responsibility of a higher authority for the acts of surbordinates is absolute.
4 *Principle of assignment of duties:* the duties of every person in an organization should be confined as far as possible to performing a single leading function.
5 *Principle of definition:* the duties, authority, responsibility, and relations of everyone in the organizational structure should be clearly and completely defined in writing.
6 *Principle of homogeneity:* an organization, to be efficient and to operate without friction, should be so designed that only duties and activities that are similar or are directly related are combined for execution by a particular individual or by a particular group.
7 *Principle of organization effectiveness:* the final test of an industrial organization is how smooth and frictionless is its operation.

He further adds:

· Organization should determine the selection of personnel rather than personnel determining the nature of the organization.
· A member does not, by delegation, divest himself of responsibility.
· Two members should not delegate responsibility to the same member.
· The number of stages of delegation of responsibility should be as few as practicable.
· Responsibilities should be defined by identifying and then grouping the elements of administration.
· Responsibilities delegated and reserved must be mutually exclusive.
· A particular responsibility is better performed by one member than by two or more.

> Whereas organizational principle is a science, the practice of organization is an art.[7]

These universal principles have dominated organizational thinking and management training for many years. They characterize the traditional structural pattern known as the *formal organization*.

The formal organization

There are three types of formal organizational patterns:

1 The line organization
2 The line and staff organization
3 The functional organization

An example of the simple *line* organization, which is rarely used except in very small organizations, may be seen in Figure 3. It is characterized by direct lines of authority, with no staff, advisory, or auxiliary officers.

The *line and staff* organizational pattern is more common. It is basically the same as the line organizational pattern, but it does have advisory or staff positions that *are not* links in the chain of command. In the simplified organization chart shown in Figure 4, solid lines denote the chain of command, lighter lines the staff relationships. There are many advantages to the line and staff organizational pattern – clear-cut divisions of authority and responsibility, great stability, and ease in maintaining discipline. It is based on planned specialization, and, especially for very large organizations, it provides a means of orderly administration, communication, continuity, and control.

Most large school systems employ the *functional* organizational pattern which is the line and staff pattern with variations. This pattern differs from the line and staff pattern in that functional specialists (or line officers) at lower levels report primarily or partly to staff specialists in higher levels, rather than reporting to the next level line officer. There is a tendency in the functional organization to deemphasize line positions, and problems sometimes emerge because of the complexity of the interaction variables and frequent role ambiguity or overlap. An example of a functional organizational pattern may be seen in Figure 5. A formal organization that has many hierarchical levels is commonly referred to as a *tall* organization. A formal organization with few vertical levels, but wider spans of control, is referred

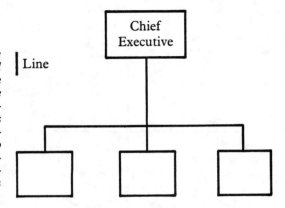

Figure 3 *A simple line organization chart. The bold lines show the authority of the chief executive over three coequal subordinate line officers. There are no staff positions in a pure line organization pattern. Adapted from Theo Haiman,* Professional Management: Theory and Practice *(New York: Houghton Mifflin Co., 1962), p. 198.*

to as a *flat* organization.

According to Haynes and Massie, formal organizations rest on the following assumptions:

1 Members of an organization are unable to work out relations among their positions without thorough guidance and planning.
2 Some members are aggressive and trespass on the domain of others unless clear boundaries are drawn. This arouses hostility which may reduce the effectiveness of the undertaking.
3 Some members are reluctant to assume responsibilities unless assigned a definite task.
4 Members generally prefer the security of a definite task to the freedom of a vaguely defined one.
5 Delineation of clear-cut responsibilities offers incentive by providing a more exact basis for evaluation.
6 It is possible to predict in advance the responsibilities that will be required in the future.
7 Members are prone to conflict and if this conflict is permitted to arise it takes its toll in personal energy and productivity.
8 Justice is more certain if the enterprise is organized on an objective, impersonal basis.[8]

These assumptions (which obviously are not all valid today for all types of groups) grew out of an earlier era, and many of them have been attacked by

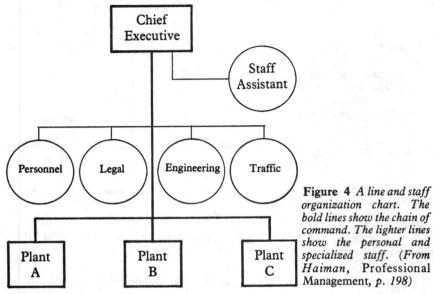

Figure 4 *A line and staff organization chart. The bold lines show the chain of command. The lighter lines show the personal and specialized staff. (From Haiman,* Professional Management, *p. 198)*

behavioural scientists. The formal organization pattern in its traditional form has many weaknesses, when strictly applied to some modern enterprises. It has been accused of being too mechanistic, with the emphasis on orderly structure rather than on people. It has also been criticized for its rigidity, for its potential for impeding information communication, and for stifling creativity. The inadequacies of the traditional formal organization and the long-accepted universal principles are particularly evident in modern enterprises involving highly educated employees and professional personnel. In recent years, much research, thought, and experimentation have been devoted to developing other organizational patterns. It is now obvious that some types of enterprises with different personnel constituencies may operate more effectively with other types of organizational patterns. A large number of business and industrial concerns have abandoned many of the traditional universal principles. School systems, in particular, have been experimenting with alternative patterns. Even in those school systems which have retained a formal organizational structure, the trend has been away from high 'position-power', and toward participative decision-making, using a team-approach in setting objectives and task-accomplishments.

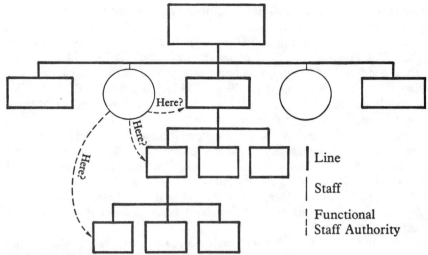

Figure 5 *Functional staff authority. This organization pattern is common in complex organizations. An example in a large school system would be the authority exercised by the central office media staff over media personnel and services at all levels. (From Haiman,* Professional Management, *p. 223)*

The universal principles of management movement and the scientific management movement (which developed concurrently) are often consolidated and categorized under the term 'classical school of management thought'. The two movements still have great influence on the practice of modern management. Most contributors to the literature of these schools, however, focused on task, process, and structure rather than on people. Neither movement has produced management theories, in the current sense of the term. The student who wishes to pursue reading in this area would do well to read the works of Peter F. Drucker,[9] an influential contemporary classicist noted for his innovative ideas such as the 'challenge and response' approach, the MBO concept, and his popularization of the decentralization idea.

The human relations movement

During the 1930s a reaction developed to Taylor's scientific management movement and to the impersonality of the formal organization. Criticisms were expressed in the works of several researchers and writers who were concerned with the human factors in organizations. The human relations movement brought behavioural scientists into the management field; its literature is more experimental and analytical than theoretical.

The most influential figures in the human relations movement were Elton Mayo,[10] a Harvard professor of psychology, and F.J. Roethlisberger.[11] Mayo and Roethlisberger are probably best known for research at Western Electric's Hawthorne plant in the late 1920s and the early 1930s. The research was based on the hypothesis that improved working conditions would improve human productivity.

Mayo tended to be a social philosopher who reached broad conclusions about industrial civilizations. He contended that industrialization and specialization had resulted in the psychological deterioration of the individual. He felt that there was a need to restore small spontaneous groups and a need for face-to-face interaction. He expressed concern about the dehumanization of the large industrial organizations of a technological society.

Roethlisberger, his colleague, believed that human behaviour is complex, each situation is unique, and problems should be dealt with individually. He is credited for developing the *case method* for the study of management. This approach to the study of management maintains that one should study and learn from actual specific cases. The human relationists differed from the later behavioural science theorists in that human relationists proceeded from facts to generalizations, whereas the theorists proceeded from generalizations to facts.

The human relations movement has had great impact on management practice. It made management aware of workers as human beings, rather than as cogs in the machinery. Chester Barnard made a significant contribution by leading industrial executives to recognize the importance of the human being in the psycho-social industrial setting.[12] Out of this movement grew many reforms of business and industry and an increasing concern for employee morale and well-being. Organizations began to implement participatory decision-making, suggestion systems, and management training in human relations.

Just as the scientific management movement spawned its latter-day 'efficiency experts', the human relations movement spawned a plethora of 'human relations experts'. In both cases, the popularizers of the ideas of the founders often incurred unfavourable reactions because of the superficiality of their understanding of the original basic concepts involved. In many cases, human relations programmes were implemented as techniques for manipulating people, instead of for bringing management to an understanding of human nature and creating desirable changes in the organization.

McGregor's Theories X and Y

Douglas McGregor made a significant contribution to the human relations movement by suggesting that the underlying assumptions about human beings must be changed. McGregor lists certain assumptions about human behaviour that he believes are held by management traditionally. These he calls 'Theory X':

1 The average person has an inherent dislike for work and will avoid it if he can.
2 Because of this human characteristic of dislike of work, most people must be coerced, controlled, directed, and threatened with punishment to get them to put forth adequate effort toward the achievement of organization objectives.
3 The average person prefers to be directed, wishes to avoid responsibility, has relatively little ambition, and wants security above all.[13]

McGregor believes that enlightened management should embrace an opposing list of assumptions, which he calls 'Theory Y':

1 The expenditure of physical and mental effort in work is as natural as play or rest.
2 Man will exercise self-direction and self-control in the service of objectives to which he is committed.
3 Commitment to objectives is a function of the rewards associated with achievement.
4 The average person learns, under proper conditions, not only to accept, but to seek responsibility.
5 The capacity to exercise a relatively high degree of imagination, ingenuity, and creativity in the solution of organizational problems is widely, not narrowly, distributed in the population.[14]

McGregor's 'Theory Y' is congruent with Abraham Maslow's 'hierarchy of human needs'. Maslow contends that man is a wanting animal – as soon as one of his needs is satisfied, another appears in its place and that these needs are organized in a series of levels, according to their importance in the hierarchy. Beginning with the lowest level needs, they are: (1) *physiological needs* – the need to satisfy hunger, the need for rest, shelter, and protection; (2) *safety needs* – the need for protection against danger, threat, or deprivation; (3) *social needs* – the need to belong, to be accepted, to give and be receiving of friendship; (4) *ego needs* – the need for esteem, status, recognition, and appreciation of one's self, and the need for respect from one's associates; and (5) *self-fulfillment needs* – the need for self-actualization, continued self-development, and the opportunity to be creative.[15]

The human relations movement rejects earlier simplistic approaches to motivation at the lower levels of human needs. It states that the management of an organization should be concerned with the *whole* person and should recognize the complex aspects of human motivation and satisfaction.

Both McGregor's 'Theory Y' and Maslow's hierarchy have been criticized because of (1) the lack of empirical data to validate them, (2) their extreme humanistic bias,[16] and (3) their limitations in accounting for all situational variables.

The behavioural science movement

The maturation of the behavioural sciences as disciplines has generated widespread and rapidly increasing research activity in management; therefore, it is useful to classify it as a separate movement of management thought. Modern behavioural scientists look for answers to questions about human groups, complex organizations, human relations within these organizations, morale, motivation, communication, productivity, power, authority, administrative effectiveness, and leader behaviour. In the literature, one finds many conflicting data and diverse disciplinary and philosophical biases. But an encouraging fact is that there is evidence, in some areas, of a confluence of thought that is based on empirical data. From the behavioural science movement arose efforts to develop behavioural theories of management (which will be discussed later in the chapter).

The influence of early management thought on educational organizations

There was very little similarity between the problems and objectives of small schools or school systems and those of business and industry. Before educational administration became professionalized, the 'headteacher' view of the administrator prevailed. However, as urban school systems grew larger and more complex during the early part of the twentieth century, large school systems adopted the formal organization pattern – the line and staff organization – and employed the universal principles (discussed earlier in this chapter).

The concept of teaching administrative skills was also introduced, and formal training programmes for educational administrators developed. The 'process' approach to educational administration, based on the processes identified by Henri Fayol and his successors, was also introduced into administration courses, and educational administrators began to recognize the universality of management processes.

More recently, there has been extensive borrowing from management in the areas of human relations, personnel administration, quantitative approaches to decision-making, school business administration, and systems approaches to administration.

Several factors can be cited as marking the beginning of interest in theory on the part of academics in educational administration. One of these was the establishment of the National Conference for Professors of Educational Administration (NCPEA) in 1947. The formation of this group facilitated a more rapid dissemination of ideas that have increasingly infiltrated the educational literature from the social sciences and management literature. Another significant factor was the Kellogg Foundation's funding of the Cooperative Programme in Education Administration (CPEA) in 1950. This programme provided financial support for research, as well as bringing professors in educational administration and social scientists together. The third significant force in generating interest in administrative theory in education has been the University Council for Educational Administration (UCEA), which was established in 1956.

In the 1950s and 1960s, the first literature on the subject of educational administration theory came into use. Early significant publications included: *The Use of Theory in Educational Administration*, by Coladarci and Getsils in 1955; *Studies in School Administration: A Report of the CPEA*, which was published by AASA; the NCPEA-sponsored *Administrative Behaviour in Education*, edited by Campbell and Gregg; Andrew Halpin's anthology, *Administrative Theory in Education* (1958) and his *Theory and Research in Administration* (1966). Griffiths and Campbell were writers who also stirred interest in the movement. It was during this period that some of the professors of educational administration first recognized that the research and theory being produced by the behavioural sciences were pertinent to education administration. Gradually, courses in educational administrative theory were added to the curricula of administrator-training programmes in major universities throughout the United States. Subsequently, scholars in educational administration have contributed to the research and theoretical literature in educational administrative theory.

The development of organization theory

There is some overlap between organizational and administrative theory, and integrative models have been developed from the two theories. A distinction can be made, however; organizational theory (the older area of inquiry) has been primarily the domain of the sociologists, beginning with Max Weber's theory of bureaucracy.

Max Weber's theory of bureaucracy

Max Weber, a pioneer German sociologist, defines bureaucracy as 'an administrative system adapted to the needs of large and complex organizations that deal with large numbers of clients'.[17] Basic elements of his ideal bureaucracy included: (1) fixed and official jurisdictional areas, regularly ordered by rules, policies, regulations, and bylaws; (2) principles of hierarchy and levels of graded authority that ensure a firmly ordered system of supervision and subordination, in which those people in higher offices supervise those in lower ones; (3) administration based upon written documents; (4) administration run by full-time, trained officials; and (5) administration planned according to stable and comprehensive general policies. The term *bureaucracy* may hold a negative connotation for many modern Americans. One can appreciate, however, the advantages of Weber's concept when it is perceived in the context of a Europe that has been governed for centuries (often whimsically and incompetently) by monarchial systems. Weber contrasted three types of organizations in existence in his contemporary milieu:

1 *Traditional organizations.* The right to occupy positions of power or authority is inherited or handed down from generation to generation. The spirit of traditional authority is captured in the phrase, 'the king is dead – long live the king'.
2 *Charismatic organizations.* This type of organization, according to Weber, is headed by a single leader to whom everyone owes loyalty and

allegiance by force of the leader's personality.

3 *Bureaucracies*. This type of organizational structure described by Weber is designed specifically to make maximum use of administrative specialists who possess a high level of expertise. Positions in this system are created on a functional basis and office-holders are recruited to fill them on the basis of their technical competence to do the work required in those positions. Authority in this system is based on the supremacy of laws. This concept of legal authority is epitomized in the phrase, 'a government of laws, not man'.[18]

Weber's principles are reflected in democratic governmental organizations that employ civil service systems and in the formal organization patterns dominant in the commercial and educational sectors. His ideal organization has a hierarchy of authority, a division of labour, technically competent participants, procedural devices for work situations, rules governing members' actions, limited authority of office (authority is vested in the office, not the individual), differential rewards by office, administration that is separate from ownership, emphasis on written communications, and discipline.

Weber holds that these characteristics, which are typical of bureaucracy, are capable of obtaining the highest degree of efficiency. In precision, speed, lack of equivocation, knowledge of the documentary records, continuity, sense of discretion, uniformity of operations, system of subordination, and reduction of friction, he contends that bureaucracy surpasses all other forms of administration. His bureaucracy has a built-in attribute of calculability of predictability that is central to his theory. By this he means that the decisions made by bureaucrats are predictable, thus supporting a steadiness and stability in the organization. Weber also believes that bureaucracy has a levelling effect on people's social and economic differences. He feels that this type of organization makes economic exploitation of a position, because of rank and prestige, obsolete.

Criticisms of Weber's theory of bureaucracy

The criticisms of Weber's concept of bureaucracy, in many instances, are the same criticisms that have been made of all formal organizations. Many believe that such an organization encourages 'overconformity' and induces 'group think'. Another criticism is that bureaucracy modifies the very personality of bureaucrats so that they become conforming 'organization men'. A potential problem often cited is communications overloading. Another problem common to bureaucracy is goal displacement, i.e., when the adherence to rules becomes an end in itself. It is also possible that the goals and activities of the bureaucracy may become subverted by the goals and interests of outside groups. A criticism that is frequently stated is the inability of the formal organization or bureaucracy to respond to change. There is also the difficulty in developing congruence between the needs of the individual in the organization and the needs of the organization itself.

Trends in modern organization theory

A classic work that represents an attempt to analyse organizations is March and Simons' *Organizations*.[19] The student interested in the study of organizations should read this book, which discusses the development of the study of organizations, the principles of organizations (such as perpendicular coordination, horizontal coordination, leadership, delegation, and authority), and the sixty-six 'propositions' that characterize organizations. March and Simons' sixty-six propositions cannot be called a theory, but rather, they are a list of principles observed through analyses of organizations.

There seems to be a recent trend in organizational theory away from the analytical approach towards a broader view. The tendencies are either to view the organization in its wider social context and environment or to account for the dynamics of its internal related parts.

The different approaches to the study of organizations reflect differing philosophical and disciplinary orientations. One conceptual approach is from the 'systems frame of reference'. It draws on *general systems theory*, which is interdisciplinary, as well as *structural functionalism*, which is rooted in sociology. This approach is based on the assumption of the interrelatedness of all parts of an organization.[20] According to Silverman, the problem with *systems theory of organization* and *structural formalism* is 'their alleged concentration on consensus and order and their apparent incapacity to explain conflict situations'.[21] Other critics of this approach are European sociologists Dahrendorf (1958) and Rex (1961) and the American sociologist Horton (1964). Cohen (1968) stresses that the least convincing aspect of the systems approach lies in its inability to explain change as it arises – not from system needs, but from the interaction of motivated actors.[22] These critics of the systems/functional theories propose an alternative, *conflict model* of social structures, typified by the theoretical work of Krupp (1961).[23]

The controversy between functionalism versus conflict management in organizations is now outdated, however, according to Silverman, who contends that the most fundamental issue is the nature of the social order. Silverman's basis for organization theory-building is 'a view of social reality as socially constructed, socially sustained, and socially changed'.[24]

The literature of the sociologists provides useful insights to the student of organizations. However, any comprehensive theory of organizational effectiveness must include treatment of all the variables, including the behaviour of its members and the technology, structure, and environment of the organization.

Recent research by psychologists has focused on the behaviour of people within organizations.

Human behaviour and organizational change

Group dynamics

In the early 1950s, a great amount of interest was generated concerning interaction among people in small groups – both structured and informal. This work is related to organization theory because, in every society, the group is the agency for developing, accommodating, and realizing goals – personal, group, organizational, and societal.

By definition, a group is 'a number of persons who communicate with one another, often over a span of time, and who are few enough so that each person can communicate with all the others, not through other people, but face to face'.[25] Elton Reeves adds to the definition of group the concept of 'two or more persons with common objectives'.[26] Other definitions cite characteristics of the group as including status and role relationships, and common values and norms. According to Lewin, a group, as an entity, 'has definite properties of its own'.[27] Reeves contends that groups are 'capable of becoming neurotic or even psychotic'.[28]

Numerous studies have been made of small groups concerning their patterns of formal and informal interaction, informal and formal organization, power differentials between leader and members, group cohesiveness, group norms, and peer pressure. (In addition to Homans, the student should read the works of Bradford et al.,[29] Bennis and his associates,[30] and Miles.[31]) Various group-training techniques, such as 'sensitivity training' or 'T-groups', have grown out of this movement. The concepts and training techniques of the group dynamics movement have been widely used in change models and in *organizational development* (OD), a process growing popular with educational as well as management consultants. However, the efficacy of 'sensitivity training' is not universally accepted. Its use as a training device for managers has been severely attacked by Odiorne[32] and strongly defended by Argyris.[33]

The OD approach employed by a number of current practitioners seems, in the opinion of some, to emphasize human relations and group process but neglects measurable outcomes. There is ongoing research on OD, however, in the behavioural sciences and in education. (The student should read further in the existing literature and expect increasing experimentation with and utilization of OD theory in school organizations.[34])

Lewin's force field theory

Many organization change models have been influenced by the significant theoretical work of psychologist Kurt Lewin. Lewin's *force field theory*[35] is based on his work in (1) field theory (analysis of causal relationships and attendant values, needs, and desires); (2) life space (the psychological environment as it exists for the group or the individual); and (3) variables of life space (behaviour, function, person, environment).

He developed a technique called 'force field analysis', which is a method for diagnosing causal relationships in life space. Interrelationships within the life space are symbolized by a formula that shows behaviour as a function of both the person and his environment:

$$B = F(PE)$$

Lewin's theory identifies two forces in the environment:

1   *driving forces* – those forces pushing in a given direction, and
2   *restraining forces* – those forces tending to resist or decrease the driving forces.

The *driving forces* are those which tend to initiate, promote, and sustain change. When these forces are equal, a *state of equilibrium* exists. Since groups tend toward equilibrium, the process of change involves either increasing the *driving forces* or reducing the *restraining forces* in order to move the point of equilibrium – a point that is never permanently fixed.

Lewin identifies three steps involved in moving the point of equilibrium or in achieving change: (1) *unfreezing*, (2) *changing*, and (3) *refreezing*.

Argyris's intervention theory

Organizations that want to change, often use a 'change agent' to help

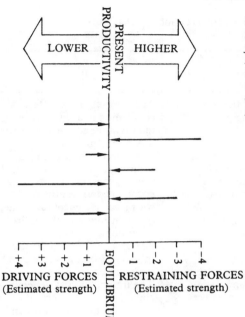

Figure 6 *Lewin's concept of driving forces and restraining forces in equilibrium. From P. Hersey and K.H. Blanchard,* Management of Organizational Behavior *(Englewood Cliffs, N.J.: Prentice-Hall, Inc., 1969), p. 100*

them accomplish their goal. This resource person may be a trained change agent from inside the organization or a skilled consultant brought in from the outside. Both research and experience support the employment of a change agent for this process.

Chris Argyris has devised what might be called a two-style behavioural theory of change-agent effectiveness. Argyris's *intervention theory* is based on 'Theory X' and 'Theory Y' behaviour. He defines this intervention process as 'entering into an ongoing system of relationship, to come between or among persons, groups, or objects for the purpose of helping'.[36] According to him, it is possible to use the skills and knowledge of the behavioural scientist for assisting the client system in implementing change. Argyris believes that the intervener (or interventionist) and the client system exist independently and exercise independent roles. For the interventionist to function successfully as a change agent, it is necessary to examine the interventionist and the client organization, as well as the relationship between them. He believes that technical and human resources of the organization must be utilized in order for organizational change to occur.

Table 1 Interventionist behaviours

Less effective *XA*	More effective *YB*
1. The interventionist takes the most prominent role in defining goals of the programme.	1. The subjects participate in defining, confirming and disconfirming, and modifying or adding goals defined by the interventionist.
2. The interventionist assumes the role of being strictly professional. He cannot be influenced by a client. He maintains the power of expertise.	2. The interventionist realizes that in addition to being a professional, he is a stranger to his clients. Clients are encouraged to test their relationship with him. He encourages clients to question him and the entire programme.
3. The amount of client participation in the project is controlled by the interventionist.	3. The amount of participation is influenced by the subject and the interventionist.
4. The interventionist depends on the client's need to be *cooperative* as a basis for his involvement. He expects people to be used as information-givers.	4. The interventionist depends on the client's need to be *helped* to encourage him to control and define the programme. The client becomes internally involved and feels he is as responsible as the interventionist for the programme's success.
5. If participation is encouraged it tends to be 'skin deep', designed to keep the client happy.	5. Participation is encouraged in terms of instrument design, research methods, and change strategy.
6. The costs and rewards of the change program are defined primarily by the interventionist.	6. The costs and rewards of the change programme are defined by client and interventionist.
7. Feedback to subjects is designed to inform them how much the diagnostician learned.	7. The feedback is designed to unfreeze subjects, as well as to help them develop more effective interpersonal relations and group processes.

The theory reflects Argyris's 'Theory Y' bias. He has developed a list of interventionist behaviours based on 'Theory X' that he refers to as XA behaviours (undesirable) and a list of interventionist behaviours based on 'Theory Y' that he calls YB behaviours (desirable). The characteristics of these two polar positions are described in Table 1. Argyris contends that YB behaviours exercised by the interventionist enable him to help the organization to become more effective in problem-solving, decision-making, and decision-implementation. He also contends that the client should have a decreasing need for the interventionist. The three primary tasks of the change agent, according to Argyris, are: (1) the generation of valid and useful information, (2) free choice, and (3) internal commitment.

Frederick Herzberg's motivation-hygiene theory[37]

Frederick Herzberg is another contemporary psychologist, management theorist, and management consultant who has concentrated his work on the people within the organization rather than on the structure of the organization. His contribution has been in the area of subordinate motivation. Influenced by Maslow and other humanistic psychologists, Herzberg conducted research, from which he developed his theory.

The theory includes two sets of factors that affect the worker. Herzberg calls one set of factors *hygiene factors*. These are factors in the environment that result in job dissatisfaction. The favourable modification of these factors, Herzberg contends, neither increases satisfaction nor generates motivation, but merely either decreases or removes dissatisfaction.

The other set of factors are called *motivators*. They are intrinsically involved in the job itself (roughly corresponding to Maslow's *higher order needs*). His hygiene factors and motivators are shown in Table 2.

Improving hygiene factors can *decrease* dissatisfaction, but cannot improve motivation. Motivation occurs only when *motivators* or *satisfiers* are present. Herzberg approaches change in organizations by a method he calls 'job enrichment'. This is a process of upgrading an individual's responsibility, along with increasing the scope and challenge of his or her work. This

Table 2   Motivation and hygiene factors

Hygiene factors (dissatisfiers) *Environment*	Motivators (satisfiers) *The job itself*
Policies and administration	Achievement
Supervision	Recognition
Working conditions	Challenging work
Interpersonal relations	Increased responsibility
Money, status, security	Growth and development

process helps the individual to self-actualize. Herzberg distinguishes bet-ween *job enrichment* and *job enlargement*, which is merely adding more work (horizontal job-loading) and does not necessarily result in motivation. *Job enrichment* (or vertical job-loading) is characterized by (1) removing or reducing controls, (2) increasing the accountability of individuals, (3) increasing authority in job freedom, and (4) new and more differentiated tasks that should, when possible, match the interests of the individual.

Many psychologists and managers have cautioned against unrealistic expectations when the theory is viewed as universally effective. The motivation-hygiene theory has been praised, however, by many large business and industrial organizations, which have applied it with good results in the improvement of employee morale.

The development of administrative theory

In addition to the research and theory-building that have focused on organizations, their members, and their environments, a large body of literature has developed that focuses on the behaviour of the leader/manager/administrator. For many years, researchers and theorists have sought to identify the causal factors in administrative effectiveness. Much of the early research has been invalidated by later research, so the student will discover many incongruent concepts. A great deal of work narrowly focuses on limited parts of the complex whole. In recent years, however, there has been confluence of thought in certain areas, and efforts to synthesize the various research findings have resulted in progress towards the construction of a viable and comprehensive behavioural theory of administrative effectiveness.

The trait approach

Prior to 1945, most studies of leadership were devoted to identifying traits or qualities of successful leaders. These studies were based on two assumptions.

1   All human beings can be divided into two groups: leaders and followers.
2   Leaders possess certain qualities and traits that followers do not.

Scientists and management theorists have long since abandoned the trait approach in seeking answers to effective leader behaviour. Although some traits are common to some, there has been no agreement on a set of universal traits that characterize all leaders in all situations. At this point in time, more than a thousand different traits have been identified. Stogdill, in his 1948 review of 124 trait studies, concluded that 'a person does not become a leader by virtue of possession of some combination of traits . . .' He also concluded that situational variables evidently influence the leader's behaviour pattern.[38]

The skills approach

There have been other attempts to identify the skills essential to successful administration. Katz, for example, proposes that 'effective administration rests on the three basic developable skills, which we will call *technical, human,* and *conceptual'*.[39] Katz suggests that *technical skill* is 'an understanding of, and a proficiency in, a specific kind of activity, particularly one involving methods, processes, procedures or techniques'. *Human skill* is the ability to work effectively as a group member; *conceptual skill* is defined as the ability to see the enterprise as a whole. Katz's perception of these three skills is certainly not invalid, and it fits into a later model of administrative effectiveness that is more definitive and more comprehensive. Efforts in educational administration to identify 'competencies' have been useful but, as yet, have not produced a viable theory.

Style theories and models

The first use made of multiple leadership behaviour pattern descriptions was by Lewin, Lippitt, and White, in an experimental study during 1939. They classified leadership styles as *autocratic, laissez-faire,* and *democratic*.[40] More than forty style models with many differing (and often conflicting) features have since been developed. The number of styles per model vary from two to eight.

Two factors in leader behaviour – a significant consensus

One of the most significant milestones in the development of administrative theory was the extensive research at Ohio State University during the late 1940s and early 1950s under the direction of Carroll Shartle. These studies, published in a series of monographs, classified leader behaviour into two broad areas – *consideration* and *initiating structure*. *Consideration* is behaviour that involves human relationships and group maintenance;

initiating structure is behaviour that involves organizing and directing work.[41] These two factors are considered *orthogonal* (independent) variables in the Ohio State research; i.e., they can be present in a behaviour in varying amounts and relationships at different times. Many style models have been based on the Ohio State research, and extensive research has supported the concept of *task* and *relationships* as the two major behavioural areas.

Earlier, Murphy had identified two similar categories of leader behaviour, which he named 'social-situation leadership demands' and 'work-situation leadership demands'.[42] In the 1950s, Bales also identified two similar leader behaviours for small groups.[43] Studies at Michigan State University produced a continuum, ranging from *employee-centred* behaviour to *production-centred* behaviour.[44]

The widespread consensus on the division of leader behaviour into two categories – one that related to work (task), and one that related to people (relationships) – marked significant progress in administrative theory, although conflicting perceptions of both the role and the relationship of these two variables have persisted.

The two dimensions of leader behaviour appear in the work of Halpin,[45] Blake and Mouton,[46] Likert,[47] Cartwright and Zander,[48] Brown,[49] Fiedler,[50] Jennings,[51] Reddin,[52] Hersey and Blanchard,[53] and Hallal.[54] There are differences in opinion regarding the two factors, i.e., whether they are *separate*, *dependent*, or *independent* variables. The dominant current view is

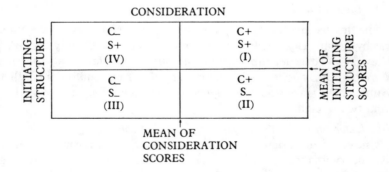

Figure 7 *A quadrant scheme for describing leaders' behaviour on the initiating structure and consideration dimensions. From Andrew W. Halpin,* Theory and Research in Administration *(New York: Macmillan Co., 1966), p. 99.*

that they are *orthogonal* (independent) rather than *bipolar* (dependent), or separate variables.

The futile search for the ideal style

Many early works had listed two contrasting styles; the implication was that one was good, while the other one was bad. These were variously described in bipolar concepts, such as *autocratic* versus *democratic*, *authoritarian* versus *participatory*, or *directive* versus *permissive*. Some studies indicated the superiority of the autocratic approach; others suggested the superiority of the democratic approach. The review of this body of research by Anderson, Sales, and others led to the conclusion that the 'either-or' approach was too simplistic. Neither of the two management styles is consistently superior.[55]

Multiple-style models with ideal styles

The Ohio State studies gave impetus to the development of multiple-style models based upon varying combinations of *initiating structure* and *consideration*.

Halpin, who participated in the Ohio State studies, developed a four-quadrant model that represented four combinations of *consideration* and *initiating structure* behaviours. His model suggests four basic styles, Quadrant 1 being the most effective or 'ideal' style. He says, 'We have seen that the most effective leaders are those who score high on *both* dimensions of leader behaviour.'[56]

Blake's grid,[57] which has been a useful management-training tool, is based on this concept, and it also suggests an 'ideal' style.

Likert also developed a four-style theory that describes four management systems in terms of a progression from 'Theory X' to 'Theory Y'. 'System 1' represents 'Theory Y' behaviours, which, in Likert's opinion, represent the most effective or 'ideal' management style.[58]

The ideal-style concept not defensible

There is enough research evidence now, however, to confirm that there is no one style that is universally effective in every situation. Fleishman and Peters concluded, from their research, that there was 'no particular combination of structure and consideration attitudes predictive of effectiveness ratings'.[59] Korman's analysis of twenty-five published studies of *initiating structure* and *consideration*, in relation to effectiveness, concluded that no one style is always better than another.[60] Various styles are effective in various situations; there is no ideal style.

Summary

The development of management thought has been an evolutionary process; hundreds of practitioners and scholars have contributed to it over the years. Research in organization and administration, primarily the domain of social and behavioural scientists, is a relatively new area of interest that has produced a substantial body of literature. Since World War II, administrative theory has grown to be an important area of study in educational administration. The work done in this interdisciplinary area is appearing increasingly in the educational literature. It is also being used in practical ways in educational organizations. Original contributions by scholars in educational administration have increased in recent years. There is a widespread belief that the modern educational administrator must have a theory-based preparation. The impact of this area of scholarly activity upon the improvement of educational administration is just beginning to be felt, and it should continue to grow in the future.

Notes

1. Taylor, Frederick W., *Principles of Scientific Management* (New York: Harper & Row, 1947).
2. Copley, Frank, *Frederick W. Taylor, Father of Scientific Management*, Vols. I and II (New York: Harper Brothers, 1923).
3. Gilbreth, Frank B., *Field System* (New York: The Myron C. Clark Publishing Co., 1908).
4. Clark, Wallace, *The Gantt Chart* (New York: The Ronald Press Co., 1922), p. 3.
5. Fayol, Henri, (J.A. Coubrough, translator), *Industrial and General Administration* (Geneva: International Management Institute, 1929).
6. Fayol, Henri, (Constance Storr, translator), *General and Industrial Management* (London: Sir Isaac Pitman and Sons, Ltd., 1949), pp. 19–20.
7. Urwick, Lyndall, *Elements of Administration* (London: Sir Isaac Pitman and Sons, Ltd., 1947), p. 118.
8. Haynes, W. Warren and Massie, Joseph L., *Management: Analysis, Concepts and Cases* (Englewood Cliffs, N.J.: Prentice-Hall, Inc., 1961), p. 45.
9. Drucker, Peter F., *The Practice of Management* (New York: Harper Brothers, 1954), *The Effective Executive* (New York: Harper & Row, 1967), and *Management – Tasks, Responsibilities and Practices* (New York: Harper & Row, 1974).
10. Mayo, Elton, *The Human Problems of an Industrial Civilization* (New York: Macmillan Co., 1933).
11. Roethlisberger F.J. and Dickson, William J., *Management and the Worker* (Cambridge, Mass.: Harvard University Press, 1947).
12. Barnard, Chester I., *The Functions of the Executive* (Cambridge, Mass.: Harvard University Press, 1938), p. 44.
13. McGregor, Douglas, *The Human Side of Enterprise* (New York: McGraw-Hill

Book Co., 1960), pp. 33–34. Cited in: Edwin B. Flippo, *Management: A Behavioral Approach* (Boston, Mass.: Allyn & Bacon, Inc., 1970), p. 94.

14. ibid.
15. Maslow, Abraham H., *Motivation and Personality* (New York: Harper & Row, 1954).
16. W.J. Reddin proposes a more pragmatic 'Theory Z' as an alternative to McGregor's 'Theory X' and 'Theory Y', *In* Reddin, W.J., *Managerial Effectiveness* (New York: McGraw-Hill Book Co., 1970), pp. 189–190.
17. Weber, Max (A.M. Henderson and Talcott Parsons, translators), *The Theory of Social and Economic Organizations* (New York: Oxford University Press, 1947).
18. ibid.
19. March, J.G. and Simons, Herbert A., *Organizations* (New York: John Wiley & Sons, Inc., 1958).
20. Parsons, Talcott, *Structure and Process in Modern Societies* (Glencoe, Ill.: The Free Press, 1964); and Etzioni, Amitai, *A Comparative Analysis of Complex Organizations* (New York: The Free Press, 1969).
21. Silverman, David, *The Theory of Organizations* (New York: Basic Books, Inc., 1971), p. 5
22. ibid.
23. ibid.
24. ibid.
25. Homans, George C., *The Human Group* (New York: Harcourt, Brace, and World, Inc., 1950), p. 1.
26. Reeves, Elton T., *Dynamics of Group Behavior* (New York: American Management Association, Inc., 1970), p. 11.
27. Lewin, Kurt, *Field Theory in Social Science* (New York: Harper & Row, 1951), p. 146.
28. Reeves, op. cit.
29. Bradford, L.P., (ed), *Group Development*, Selected Reading Series No. 1 (Washington, D.C.: National Education Association, National Training Laboratories, 1961); and Bradford, L.P., Gibb, J.R., and Benne, K.D. (eds), *T-Group and Laboratory Method* (New York: John Wiley & Sons, Inc., 1964).
30. Bennis, W.G., *The Marked Deck: A Non-Objective Playlet for Four Characters* (Washington, D.C.: National Education Associaton, National Training Laboratories, Subscription Service No. 2, 1963); Bennie, Schein, Berlew, and Steele, *Interpersonal Dynamics* (Homewood, Ill.: Dorsey Press, 1964); and Bennis, Benne, Chin, and Corey (eds), *The Planning of Change*, 3rd ed. (New York: Holt, Rinehart and Winston, Inc., 1976).
31. Miles, M.B., *Learning to Work in Groups* (New York: Teachers College Press, 1959), and 'Human relations training: Processes and outcomes', *Journal of Counselling Psychology* (7:301–306, 1960).
32. Odiorne, G.S., 'The trouble with sensitivity training', *ASTD Journal* (October: 9–29, 1963).
33. Argyris, Chris, 'T-Groups for organizational effectiveness', *Harvard Business Review* (March–April: 60–74, 1964).
34. Schmuck, Richard A., et al., *Handbook of Organization Development in Schools*

(Palo Alto. Calif.: National Press Books, 1972); and Schmuck and Miles, (eds), *Organization Development in Schools* (Palo Alto, Calif.: National Press Books, 1971).

35. Lewin, Kurt, *Field Theory in Social Science* (New York: Harper & Row, 1951), 'Frontiers in group dynamics: Concepts, method and reality in social science; social equilibria and social change', *Human Relations* (1:5–41, 1947), and *A Dynamic Theory of Personality*, (D.K. Adams and K.E. Zerner, translators) (New York: McGraw-Hill Book Co., 1935).

36. Argyris, Chris, *Intervention Theory and Method: A Behavioral Science View* (Reading, Mass.: Addison-Wesley Publishing Co., 1970), and *Theory in Practice: Increasing Professional Effectiveness* (San Francisco, Calif.: Josey-Bass, Inc., 1974).

37. Herzberg, Frederick, *Work and the Nature of Man* (New York: World Publishing Co., 1966).

38. Stogdill, Ralph B., 'Personal factors associated with leadership: A survey of the literature', *Journal of Psychology* (25:35–71, 1948).

39. Katz, Robert L., 'Skills of an effective administrator', *Harvard Business Review* (January–February: 33–42, 1955).

40. Lewin, K., Lippitt, R. and White, R.K., 'Patterns of aggressive behaviour in experimentally created social climates', *Journal of Social Psychology* (10:271–279, 1939).

41. Halpin, Andrew, *Theory and Research in Administration* (New York: Macmillan Co., 1966), pp. 97–98.

42. Murphy, A.J., 'A study of the leadership process', *American Sociological Review* (6:674–687, 1941).

43. Bales, R.F., 'The equilibrium problem in small groups', Parsons, T., Bales, R.F., and Shils, E.A. (eds), *Working Papers in Theory of Action* (New York: The Free Press of Glencoe, 1953).

44. Likert, Rensis, *New Patterns of Management* (New York: McGraw-Hill Books Co., 1961).

45. Halpin, op. cit., pp. 98–99.

46. Blake, Robert R. and Mouton, Jane S., *The Managerial Grid* (Houston, Tex.: The Gulf Publishing Co., 1964).

47. Likert, Rensis, *The Human Organization* (New York: McGraw-Hill Book Co., 1967).

48. Cartwright, D. and Zander, A., *Group Dynamics Research and Theory* (Evanston, Ill.: Raw, Peterson, and Company, 1960).

49. Brown, J.A.C., *The Social Psychology of Industry* (Baltimore, Md.: Penguin Books, Inc., 1954).

50. Fiedler, Fred E., *A Theory of Leadership Effectiveness* (New York: McGraw-Hill Book Co., 1967).

51. Jennings, Eugene E., *The Executive* (New York: Harper & Row, 1962).

52. Reddin, William J., The tri-dimensional grid. *Training Directors Journal* (July: 9–18, 1964).

53. Hersey, Paul and Blanchard, Kenneth H., *Management of Organizational Behavior* (Englewood Cliffs, N.J.: Prentice-Hall, Inc., 1969).

54. Hallal, William E., Toward a general theory of leadership. *Human Relations* (27: 401–416, 1974).
55. Reddin, William J., *Managerial Effectiveness* (New York: McGraw-Hill Book Co., 1970), pp. 35–39.
56. Halpin, op. cit., p. 98
57. Blake, op. cit.
58. Likert, op. cit.
59. Fleishman, E.A. and Peters, D.R., 'Interpersonal values, leadership attitudes, and managerial success', *Personal Psychology* (15:127–143, 1962).
60. Korman, A.K., 'Consideration, initiating structure and organizational criteria – A review', *Personal Psychology* (19:349–361, 1966).

CHAPTER 3.2

THEORY ABOUT ORGANIZATION: A NEW PERS-PECTIVE AND ITS IMPLICATIONS FOR SCHOOLS*
THOMAS B. GREENFIELD

In common parlance we speak of organizations as if they were real. Neither scholar nor layman finds difficulty with talk in which organizations 'serve functions', 'adapt to their environment', 'clarify their goals', or 'act to implement policy'. What it is that serves, adapts, clarifies, or acts seldom comes into question. Underlying widely accepted notions about organizations, therefore, stands the apparent assumption that organizations are not only real but also distinct from the actions, feelings, and purposes of people. This mode of thought provides the platform for a long-standing debate about organizations and people. Is it organizations which oppress and harass people or is it fallible people who fail to carry out the well-intentioned aims of organizations? The debate continues on issues such as whether it is better to abolish organizations, to reshape them along more humane lines, or to train people to recognize the goals of organizations more clearly and to serve them more faithfully.

In contrast, this chapter rejects the dualism which conveniently separates people and organizations; instead it argues that a mistaken belief in the reality of organizations has diverted our attention from human action and intention as the stuff from which organizations are made. As a result, theory and research have frequently set out on a false path in trying to understand organizations and have given us a misplaced confidence in our ability to deal with their problems. If we see organizations and individuals as inextricably intertwined, it may not be so easy to alter organizations, or to lead them, or

* Theory about Organizations – A New Perspective and its Implications for Schools, from *Administering Education – International Challenge*, Meredydd Hughes (ed), Athlone Press, 1975.

to administer them without touching something unexpectedly human. More importantly, the view that people and organizations are inseparable requires us to reassess the commonly accepted claim that there exists a body of theory and principle which provides the touchstone for effective administrative action in organizations. The belief in the reality and independence of organizations permits us to separate the study of organizations from the study of people and their particular values, habits, and beliefs. The common view in organization studies holds that people occupy organizations in somewhat the same way as they inhabit houses. The tenants may change but, apart from wear and tear, the basic structure remains and in some way shapes the behaviour of the people within. Studies have therefore focused largely on the variety of organizational structures and their effects upon people. These structures are usually seen as invariate over time and place, as universal forms into which individuals may move from time to time, bringing with them idiosyncrasies which colour their performance of the roles prescribed by the organization (Getzels, 1958, p. 156).

Organizational science and the profession of administration

The science of organization has found its way into studies of schools and influenced the training of those who are to administer schools. In this science, schools are a variety of the species organization which can be distinguished chiefly by the nature of their goals and their bureaucratic structure (Bidwell, 1965, pp. 973–974). The science of organization is, therefore, assumed to provide useful knowledge about schools even as it does about other kinds of organizations. Accepting this position, Griffiths (1964, p. 3) rejects 'the opinion that educational administration is a unique activity, differing greatly from business, military, hospital and other varieties of administration' and endorses (p. 118) a 'general theory which enables the researcher to describe, explain, and predict a wide range of human behaviour within organizations'.

In a profession of administration based upon organizational science, the task of the administrator is to bring people and organizations together in a fruitful and satisfying union. In so doing, the work of the administrator carries the justification of the larger social order (Getzels, 1958, p. 156), since he works to link day-to-day activity in organizations to that social order. In schools, the administrator may be director or superintendent, principal or headmaster, department head or supervisor. Whatever their titles, their tasks are always the same. They bring people and resources together so that the goals of the organization and presumably of an encompassing social order may be met (Gregg 1957, pp. 269–270). No matter what circumstances he finds himself in, the administrator mediates between the organization and the people within it. The task is difficult; he needs help with it. As the argument runs, such help is fortunately to be found in the emerging science of organizations. Since organizations do have a human component, knowledge about organizations is usually described as a social science. But social or not, this science like all others is seen as universal, timeless, and imperfect only in its incompleteness.

The claims for a science of organization and for a profession of administration based upon that science have in recent times made a marked impact upon education. For over two decades now, scholars have attempted to improve education by applying organization theory to the conduct of affairs in schools and by training educational administrators in that science (Culbertson and Shibles, 1973). Celebrating its emancipation from the press of immediate practical affairs (Griffiths, 1964), the field turned instead to discovery of the basic relationships and principles which underlie day-to-day concerns. The professor supplanted the practitioner as the source of valid knowledge about administration. If practitioners did not know or accept that they were no longer masters of the basic knowledge which underlay their craft, it did not matter. Even the scholar-practitioner, Chester Barnard, in introducing Simon's classic writings claimed that it was the scholar's knowledge of the 'abstract principles of structure' rather than the practitioner's knowledge of 'concrete behaviour' (Simon, 1957, pp. xlii–xliv). Things are not what they seem, in educational administration as in other realms of reality. We need the scientist and his theory to interpret them to us. His knowledge, though it may be incomplete and is certainly subject to improvement, has the virtue of universal applicability. Acting on this conviction, scholars in educational administration have sought to understand how organizations really work and to use this knowledge towards the improvement of educational practice.

It will surely come as no surprise to anyone who examines the references cited to this point that most of them are American in origin, since it was in the United States that the movement to conceive educational administration as a social science arose in the late 1940s. A decade later the movement had taken hold in Canada and some time later in Australia and Britain. As the concept of educational administration as a profession and social science gains ever wider recognition and acceptance, it becomes appropriate to examine the theory and assumptions which underlie the field. In particular we need to ask whether the theory and assumptions still appear to hold in the settings where they were developed before they were recommended and applied to totally new settings. Such an examination is not only appropriate but essential in the face of an alternative view which sees organizations not as structures subject to universal laws but as cultural artefacts dependent upon the scientific meaning and intention of people within them. This alternative view, which stems from nineteenth-century German idealism (Deutscher, 1973, p. 326), bears the awkward name phenomenology (Phillipson, 1972), though it might with equal justification be called the method of understanding, as it is in the work of Max Weber (Eldridge, 1971, p. 28). What we call the view is not important. What matters is that there exists a body of theory and assumption which runs squarely at odds with that which has provided the ideological underpinnings of educational administration as it has developed over the past two decades. The ideological conflict between these views rests on two fundamentally different ways of looking at the world. One is the established view both in the study of organizations generally and in the study of educational administration. In this chapter I will outline the alternative view and recommend its application both in organization and administrative theory.

Two views of social reality

The conflicting views on organizations of which I have been speaking represent vastly different ways of looking at social reality and rest on sharply contrasting processes for interpreting it. These contrasts are summarized in Table 3 in which I have compared the two views and suggested how they differ with respect to a number of critical issues. Each of these issues has implications for the theory of organizations and for research undertaken in line with such theory. Necessarily then, these contrasts also have implications for a number of practical questions in the conduct of affairs in organizations. Some of these will be explored in the concluding section of this chapter. Although there are no generally accepted names for identifying the two views contrasted in Table 3, it may suffice to note that the crux of the issue is whether social reality is based upon naturally existing systems or upon human invention of social forms. Social reality is usually construed as a natural and necessary order which, as it unfolds, permits human society to exist and people within it to meet their basic needs. Alternatively, social

Table 3　Alternative bases for interpreting social reality

What is social reality?

Dimensions of comparison	*A natural system*	*Human invention*
Philosophical basis	Realism: the world exists and is knowable as it really is. Organizations are real entities with a life of their own.	Idealism: the world exists but different people construe it in very different ways. Organizations are invented social reality.
The role of social science	Discovering the universal laws of society and human conduct within it.	Discovering how different people interpret the world in which they live.
Basic units of social reality	The collectivity: society or organizations.	Individuals acting singly or together.
Method of understanding	Identifying conditions or relationships which permit the collectivity to exist. Conceiving what these conditions and relationships are.	Interpretations of the subjective meanings which individuals place upon their action. Discovering the subjective rules for such action.
Theory	A rational edifice built by scientists to explain human behaviour.	Sets of meanings which people use to make sense of their world and behaviour within it.
Research	Experimental or quasi-experimental validation of theory.	The search for meaningful relationships and the discovery of their consequences for action.
Methodology	Abstraction of reality, especially through mathematical models and quantitative analysis.	The representation of reality for purposes of comparison. Analysis of language and meaning.
Society	Ordered. Governed by a uniform set of values and made possible only by those values.	Conflicted. Governed by the values of people with access to power.
Organizations	Goal-oriented. Independent of people. Instruments of order in society serving both society and the individual.	Dependent upon people and their goals. Instruments of power which some people control and can use to attain ends which seem good to them.
Organizational pathologies	Organizations get out of kilter with social values and individual needs.	Given diverse human ends, there is always conflict among people acting to pursue them.
Prescription for curing organizational ills	Change the structure of the organization to meet social values and individual needs.	Find out what values are embodied in organizational action and whose they are. Change the people or change their values if you can.

reality may be construed as images in the mind of man having no necessary or inevitable forms except as man creates them and endows them with reality and authority. In the one perspective, organizations are natural objects – systems of being which man discovers; in the other, organizations are cultural artefacts which man shapes within limits given only by his perception and the boundaries of his life as a human animal.

The systems notion posits an organizational force or framework which encompasses and gives order to people and events within it. The system – unseen behind everyday affairs – is real; it *is* the organization. The force of 'natural' in the descriptor is to evoke the view common in systems theory that organizational forms are shaped by powerful forces which in large measure act independently of man. The organizations so formed will be right and good, if the natural forces are allowed free play. Mayntz (1964, pp. 105, 115) has noted that such views in which an unseen organizational hand works for the greater social good are likely to be most congenial to scholars who share a faith in the ideals of the Western liberal democracies. In identifying organizations as social inventions, the alternative view identifies organization with man's image of himself and with the particular and distinctive ways in which people see the world around them and their place in it. This view is the perspective of phenomenology. In it organizations are the perceived social reality within which people make decisions and take actions which seem right and proper to them (Greenfield, 1973, p. 557). The heart of this view is not a single abstraction called organization, but rather the varied perceptions by individuals of what they can, should, or must do in dealing with others within the circumstances in which they find themselves.

Philosophical basis

The systems view assumes that the world is knowable as it is. Although the acquisition of such knowledge requires the intervention and help of scientists, theorists, and scholars, there exists an ultimate reality which may be discovered by application of the scientific method and similar forms of rational analysis. In systems theory, the prevailing image of the organization is that of an organism. Organizations exist; they are observable entities which have a life of their own. Organizations are like people, although sometimes the image is more that of the recalcitrant child rather than the mature adult. In any case, the theory endows organizations with many human properties. They have goals towards which they direct their activities; they respond and adapt to their environments. Nor can organizations escape the fate of organisms ill-adapted to their environments. Indeed, the fate of organizations depends upon their ability to adapt to an increasingly complex and turbulent environment. Following the Darwinian logic inherent in their image of the organizations, systems theorists (Bennis, 1968) see small, quick-witted, democratic organizations replacing the ponderous, bureaucratic forms now expiring around us. The fact that bureaucratic organizations appear as large, robust, and formidable as ever does not appear to shake belief in organizations as living entities subject to stringent laws permitting only the fittest to survive. Indeed, our belief in the living organization is likely to be so strong that we fail to notice that the systems theorists have shifted from telling us about the way organizations are to telling us how they ought to be. 'If only organizations were adapted to their environments,' the argument runs, 'imagine how quickly these bureaucratic forms would disappear.' In thinking about the dazzling prospect of a world in which organizations were creatures closely adapted to a benign, well-intentioned environment, we forget that the role of theory is to tell us the way things are rather than how they ought to be or how we should like them to be. Our image of the organization as an entity, as a living entity, rests upon an analogy. But we fail to draw the conclusion (Willer, 1967, p. 33) that the analogy is useless when discrepancies appear between the image and the phenomena observed.

The phenomenological view of reality contrasts sharply with that of systems theory. This view has its origin in the distinction Kant drew between the noumenal world (the world as it is) and the phenomenal world (the world as we see it). For Kant, a world of reality does indeed exist, but man can never perceive it directly; reality is always glossed over with human interpretations which themselves become the realities to which man responds. And man is always learning, always interpreting, always inventing the 'reality' which he sees about him. In popular form, the Kantian philosophy has been expressed as follows: 'Man does not create his world, but he does make it.' It therefore comes as no surprise to the phenomenologist that people are killed by 'empty' guns. But for the phenomenologist, beliefs are always of greater consequence than facts in shaping behaviour. The bullet may indeed be in the gun, but it is the individual's belief about an empty chamber which causes him idly to pull the trigger. Deutscher (1973) summarizes the phenomenological view as follows:

> The phenomenological orientation always sees reality as constructed by men

in the process of thinking about it. It is the social version of Descartes' *Cogito, ergo sum*. For the phenomenologist it becomes *Cogitamus, ergo est* – we think, therefore it is! (1973, p. 328)

The role of social science

The implications of the phenomenological view are of critical importance in shaping our views both of the social sciences and of a study of organizations founded on them, as may be seen in the contrasting positions taken by Weber and Durkheim (Bendix and Roth, 1971, pp. 286–297). For Weber, working within his 'method of understanding', 'there is no such thing as a collective personality which "acts" ', only individuals acting on their interpretations of reality. In contrast, Durkheim, convinced of an ultimate, knowable social reality, sought to eliminate the perceptions of individuals and to find 'the explanation of social life in the nature of society itself' (Bendix and Roth, 1971, p. 291). Thus Durkheim spent his life building a sociology around notions of 'elemental' forms which provide the invariable units out of which social life is built. Weber, on the other hand, explored the ideas, doctrines, and beliefs with which men endowed their organizations and which provided the motivation for action within them. Durkheim's path leads to generality, abstraction, and universality in the study of organizations; Weber's leads to the particularistic, the concrete, and the experience-based study of organizations. Durkheim's path leads to an asceptic study of organizations, Weber's to one which smells of reality.

The phenomenological view leads to the concept of organizations as 'invented social reality' (Greenfield, 1973, p. 556) and to the paradox that, having invented such reality, man is perfectly capable of responding to it as though it were not of his own invention (Silverman, 1970, p. 133). More basically, however, the phenomenological perspective questions the possibility of objectivity in what Weber calls 'the cultural sciences'. While it is possible for such sciences to pursue inquiry within a logically rigorous methodology and for them to take into account certain basic social facts such as where people live and what they do, it is not possible for cultural scientists to give us 'a direct awareness of the structure of human actions in all their reality' (Eldridge, 1971, p. 16). Thus the notion of discovering the ultimate laws which govern social reality becomes an ever-receding fantasy which retreats as we attempt to approach it. Such bogus 'laws' as the law of supply and demand were, both for Weber and Durkheim, 'maxims for action', advice to people on how to protect their interests if they wished to be 'fair and logical' (Eldridge, 1971, p. 18). In Weber's view, then, it is impossible for the cultural sciences to penetrate behind social perception to reach objective social reality. Paradoxically, this limitation on the cultural sciences is also their strength, since it permits them to do what is never possible in the physical sciences: the cultural scientist may enter into and take the viewpoint of the actor whose behaviour is to be explained.

> We can accomplish something which is never attainable in the natural sciences, namely the subjective understanding of the action of component individuals. . . . We do not 'understand' the behaviour of cells, but can only observe the relevant functional relationships and generalize on the basis of these observations. (Weber, 1947, pp. 103–104)

While the cultural scientist may not discover ultimate social reality, he can interpret what people see as social reality and, indeed, he must do so according to a consistent, logical, and rigorous methodology (Eldridge, 1971, pp. 9–10). It is such a discipline for interpreting human experience which provides the science in the cultural scientist's work, not his ability to discover ultimate truths about social structure. Thus the purpose of social science is to understand social reality as different people see it and to demonstrate how their views shape the action which they take within that reality. Since the social sciences cannot penetrate to what lies behind social reality, they must work directly with man's definitions of reality and with the rules he devises for coping with it. While the social sciences do not reveal ultimate truth, they do help us to make sense of our world. What the social sciences offer is explanation, clarification, and demystification of the social forms which man has created around himself. In the view of some (Dawe, 1970, p. 211), the social sciences may lead us to enlightenment and to liberation from the forces which oppress man. In the phenomenological view, these forces stem from man himself, not from abstractions which lie behind social reality and control man's behaviour within that reality.

Theory about what?

The two views give rise to opposing theories about the world and the way it works, since each sees reality in different kinds of things. Each approaches theory-building from a point of view which is normative rather than descriptive. In the natural systems view, the basic reality is the collectivity; reality is in society and its organizations. Assuming the existence of an ultimate social reality, the role of theory is to say how it hangs together or how it might be changed so that it would hang together even more effectively (Merton, 1957; Etzioni, 1960). Thus functional analysis – the theory associated with the systems view – becomes a justification of the way social reality is organized rather than an explanation of it. In this view, the theory becomes more important than the research because it tells us what we can never perceive directly with our senses: it tells us the ultimate reality behind the appearance of things and it establishes a view which is essentially beyond confirmation or disproof by mere research.

The phenomenological view begins with the individual and seeks to understand his interpretations of the world around him. The theory which emerges must be grounded (Glaser and Strauss, 1967) in data from particular organizations. That these data will be glossed with the meanings and purposes of those people and places is the whole point of this philosophical view. Thus the aim of scientific investigation is to understand how that glossing of reality goes on at one time and place and to compare it with what goes on in different times and places. Similarly organizations are to be understood in terms of people's beliefs about their behaviour within them. If we are to understand organizations, we must understand what people within them think of as right and proper to do. Within this framework we would certainly not expect people everywhere to have the same views. In fact, it is the existence of differences in belief structures which provides us with the key to interpreting them. People are not likely to think of their own views as strange. Indeed it is only in contrast to other views that we come to understand our own. Theory thus becomes the sets of meanings which yield insight and understanding of people's behaviour. These theories are likely to be as diverse as the sets of human meanings and understandings which they are to explain. In the phenomenological perspective, the hope for a universal theory of organizations collapses into multifaceted images of organizations as varied as the cultures which support them.

The view of theory as arising from our understanding is expressed by Walsh (1972):

> The point about the social world is that is has been preselected and preinterpreted by its members in terms of a series of commonsense assumptions which constitute a taken-for-granted scheme for reference. . . . In this manner factual reality is conferred upon the social world by the routine interpretive practices of its members. The implication of this is that every man is a practical theorist when it comes to investigating the social world, and not just the sociologist. (p. 26)

Thus, the naturalist tries to devise general theories of social behaviour and to validate them through ever more complex research methodologies which push him further from the experience and understanding of the everyday world. The phenomenologist works directly with such experience and understanding to build his theory upon them. As Kuhn (1970) points out, our theories are not just possible explanations of reality; they are sets of instructions for looking at reality. Thus choice among theories and among approaches to theory-building involves normative and – especially in the social sciences – moral questions. Choice among them is in part a matter of preference, but choice may also be made on the basis of which theories direct us to the most useful problems and which provide the most helpful insights into them.

Research and methodology

In the systems view, research is directed at confirming theory. Theory, in this view, is something which scientists build, largely from the armchair, by thinking up what must be the ultimate explanation for the phenomena observed. Contrary to accepted opinion, Kuhn (1970, p. 16) has argued that such theory is never open to disproof and serves instead as a 'consensual agreement among scientists about what procedures shall constitute scientific activity and hence which explanations will count as scientific explanations' (Walsh, 1972, p. 25).

From the phenomenological perspective, research, theory, and methodology must be closely associated. Theory must arise out of the process of inquiry itself and be intimately connected with the data under investigation. In this view, the aim of theory should be explanation and clarification. Thus research and theory which fulfils this aim must depend not only upon what is being explained but also upon to whom it is explained, and with what. Louch (1966) argues this view as follows:

> Explanation, in Wittgenstein's phrase, is a family of cases joined together only by a common aim, to make something plain or clear. This suggests that a coherent account of explanation could not be given without attending to the audience to whom an explanation is offered or the source of puzzlement that requires an explanation to be given. There are many audiences, many puzzles. (p. 233)

Research in the naturalist mode is prone to use experimental methods to establish relationships among variables. The research often substitutes mathematical models for the substantive theoretical model and is satisfied if statistically significant relationships are found among the variables of the mathematical model. The aim is to relate variables x and y, usually with a host of other variables 'held constant'. Little effort is spent on determining whether x and y exist in any form which is meaningful to or has consequences for actors within a social situation. Nor is there much effort to ask whether holding one or more variables constant yields an interpretable result among those remaining. In physical systems, we can understand what it means to hold volume constant, for example, while we raise the temperature of a gas and observe the effect on pressure. But what does it mean when we come to a social system and speak, as some researchers do, of holding social class constant while we observe the effect of school resources upon achievement? Whereas the physicist manipulates materials and apparatus in specific, understandable ways, the social researcher frequently makes no intervention at all in the social system which he is attempting to explain. Instead, he does the manipulation of variables in his mind, or in the workings of his computer. Can we rely on the suggestion that, if we manipulate variables in a social system, we will get the same results the researcher gets from his intellectual manipulation of them? The doubt is growing that we will not, as is apparent, for example, from critiques of school effects research (Spady, 1973, pp. 139–140) demonstrating that schools may account for a great deal or virtually nothing at all of pupil achievement, depending on which of several alternative but statistically acceptable procedures the researcher chooses for his analysis.

Phenomenologically based research, on the other hand, aims at dealing with the direct experience of people in specific situations. Therefore the case study and comparative and historical methods become the preferred means of analysis. These methods are perhaps found in their most developed form in the work Weber did in building ideal types for organizational analysis. These types should be seen as 'characterizations or impressions of ways of thought and styles of living' which permit comparison and understanding of them (Louch, 1966, p. 172). What Weber did in building these ideal types was to worm his way into the heads of bureaucrats, clerics, and commercial men in order to 'discern logical connections among propositions expressing [their] beliefs about the world' (Louch, 1966, p. 173). The moral consequences of these beliefs may also be made plain and checked against 'reality'. The close connection among theory, research, and ethics thus becomes obvious.

Thus an organizational theory based upon understanding rejects the emphasis which much of contemporary social science places upon quantification, more complex mathematical models, and bigger number crunchers in the shape of better and faster computers. As Burns (1967, p. 127) has pointed out, better manipulation of numbers cannot substitute for the emptiness of the concepts to which they apply. This fixation on numbers without concern for the concepts they are thought to represent leads to a sickness of social science which Sorokin has called 'quantophrenia' and which Rothkopf (1973, p. 6) likens to the *Leerlauf* reactions described by Lorenz. In these reactions, animals go through elaborate stereotyped performances for hunting or mating when no other living creature is there to see or respond to the performances.

If we move towards improved understanding in our research we might change our image of what constitutes *the* essential research tool and supplant the computer with Weber's notion of the ideal type. An ideal type provides us with an image of a social situation at a particular time and place. We may then surround this image with others made of different organizations or of the same organization at other times. By looking at these images comparatively, by seeing them almost as the frames of a motion picture, we begin to understand our world better and to comprehend its differences and the processes of change occurring within it. This direction in theory and research leads to an investigation of language and the categories it contains for understanding the world (Bernstein, 1971a; 1971b). It leads also to an investigation of the processes (Scheff, 1973; Garfinkel, 1964) by which we negotiate with each other and so come to define what we will pay attention to in our environment and our organizations.

Implications

Where do the ideas based on phenomenology leave the notion of 'organization'? And what of the science that studies organizations? And where does a profession of educational administration which bases its practice on this science now find itself? In conclusion, let me briefly develop some answers to these questions and suggest some directions for future study.

1 Organizations are definitions of social reality. Some people may make these definitions by virtue of their access to power while others must pay attention to them. Organizations are mechanisms for transforming our desires into social realities. But the transforming mechanism lies within individuals. It is found in individuals striving to change their demands or

beliefs into definitions of reality that others must regard as valid and accept as limitations on their actions. This notion of organizations as dependent upon the meanings and purposes which individuals bring to them does not require that all individuals share the same meanings and purposes. On the contrary, the views I am outlining here should make us seek to discover the varying meanings and objectives that individuals bring to the organizations of which they are a part. We should look more carefully too for differences in objectives between different kinds of people in organizations and begin to relate these to differences in power or access to resources. Although the concept of organization permits us to speak of the dominating demands and beliefs of some individuals, and allows us to explore how those with dominating views use the advantage of their position, we need not think of these dominating views as 'necessary', 'efficient', 'satisfying', or even 'functional', but merely as an invented social reality, which holds for a time and is then vulnerable to redefinition through changing demands and beliefs among people. Where then may we go from here? Let me suggest some lines of development.

2   We should begin to regard with healthy scepticism the claim that a general science of organization and administration is at hand. Such theories carry with them not only culturally dependent notions of what is important in an organization but also prescriptive ideas of how study and inquiry into organizational problems should go forward. The movement toward international associations for the study of educational administration should be welcomed, but these associations should open windows on our understanding of organizations rather than propagate received notions of organization theory. If the movement can provide a comparative and critical perspective on schools and on our notions of how they should be run, the association will serve a valuable role. Since the dominant theories of organization and administration have their source in the United States, it is these ideas which should receive searching analysis before they are blindly applied in other cultural settings. In Britain, this critical examination of theory and its policy implications has already begun (Baron and Taylor, 1969; Halsey, 1972), though one is hard pressed to find similar critical examinations in other national or cultural settings.

3   Willy nilly, the world does seem to be shrinking towards the global village. Yet there are still strong forces which maintain vivid cultural distinctions within it. Despite these forces, the interests of the mass media, which the academic community seems all too ready to ape (Perrow, 1972,

p. 198), direct attention more frequently to the symptoms of social problems rather than to their sources. While the mass media are usually ready with prefabricated solutions to these problems, students of organizations should doubt the utility of solutions which ignore their sources in the truly critical and powerful organizations of our societies. If we are unwilling to understand our own organizations, or if we regard acquiring such understanding as a trivial task, we should be aware that there are often others willing and waiting to apply their own preconceptions and answers to the tasks of defining the organization, identifying its problems, and prescribing solutions to them. Our own experience of our own organizations is a valuable resource. It is with this experience that the organization theorist must begin to understand the nature of organizations. Since an understanding of organizations is closely linked to control of them and to the possibility of change within them, the phenomenological perspective points to issues of crucial importance both to the theorist and the man of practical affairs.

4   The possibility of training administrators through the study of organization theory has been seriously overestimated. Such theory does not appear to offer ready-made keys to the problems of how to run an organization. Through credentials, such training does appear to offer sound prospects for advancement within administrative systems. While such training may increase social mobility, each society must decide whether it wishes to pursue this goal, and, if it does, whether this method is the most appropriate for doing so. If training of administrators is to serve its avowed purposes, then it seems clear that the nature of the training must move in virtually the opposite direction from that advocated in recent years. That is to say, training should move away from attempts to teach a broad social science of organizations-in-general towards a familiarity with specific organizations and their problems. That the training should continue to have critical and reflective dimensions should not conflict with this redirection of training programmes. It appears essential also for training programmes to develop a much stronger clinical base than is now common in most of them. In such training, both the theoretician and the practitioner must be intimately involved.

5   Research into organizational problems should consider and begin to use the phenomenological perspective. This redirection of research should awaken interest in the decision-making tradition of organization theory and in the institutional school of organizational analysis (Perrow, 1972, pp. 177–204) with its emphasis on the exposé and ideological analysis of

specific organizations (Bendix, 1956). In methodology, research should turn to those methods which attempt to represent perceived reality more faithfully and fully than do the present highly quantified and abstruse techniques. And researchers should avoid prescribing solutions to pressing social problems on the basis of prescriptive theory and research. For example, those who concluded on the basis of the Coleman study that the achievement of black students in American schools might be raised by integrating black and white students were dazzled by the naturalist assumption that a statistical relationship represents social reality. They therefore were led to the error of believing that social relationships may be manipulated in the same way in which variables from the research design can be manipulated. In doing so, they failed to reckon with the reaction of black students to greater integration as a 'solution' to their problems (Carlson, 1972). Indeed researchers and social scientists might consider the cultural imperialism which is frequently inherent in their recommendations for solving social problems and strive first to understand (Bernstein, 1971b; Sarason, 1971; Holbrook, 1964) the social and organizational world for which they hope to prescribe solutions.

What is needed for better research on schools is better images of what schools are and what goes on in them. 'Better' in this case means creating images of schools which reflect their character and quality and which will tell us something of what the experience of schooling is like. Since schools are made up of different people in different times and places, it is to be expected that images which reflect the experience of schooling must be many and varied. These images would be sets of 'one-sided viewpoints', as Weber called them, each throwing 'shafts of light' (Eldridge, 1971, p. 12) upon social reality in schools.

It seems appropriate, however, for students of schools as organizations to consider the meaning of their studies and to redirect them towards investigations which increase our understanding of organizations as they are before attempts are made to change them. Paradoxically, the efforts which promise to yield the most penetrating insights into organizations and the most practical strategies for improving them are those efforts (March, 1972) which deal with the way people construe organizational reality and with the moral and ethical issues involved in these construings.

If, as the phenomenologist holds, our ideas for understanding the world determine our action within it, then our ideas about the world – what really exists in it, how we should behave in it – are of the utmost importance. And if our ideas about the world are shaped by our experience, then the interpretation of our experience is also of paramount importance. It is this process, the placing of meaning upon experience, which shapes what we call our organizations and it is this process which should be the focus of the organization theorist's work. And unless we wish to yield to universal forces for determining our experience, we must look to theories of organizations based upon diverse meanings and interpretations of our experience.

References

Baron, G. and Taylor, W, W. (eds), 1969, *Educational Administration and the Social Sciences*, Athlone.

Bendix, R., 1956, *Work and Authority in Industry: Ideologies in the Course of Industrialization*, Wiley.

Bendix, R. and Roth, G., 1971, *Scholarship and Partisanship: Essays on Max Weber*, University of California Press.

Bennis, W.G., 1968, 'Beyond Bureaucracy', in Bennis, W.G. and Slater, P., (eds) *The Temporary Society*, Harper & Row, pp. 53–76.

Bernstein, B., 1971a, *Class, Codes and Control: Theoretical Studies towards a Sociology of Language*, Routledge & Kegan Paul.

Bernstein, B., 1971b, 'Education Cannot Compensate for Society' in Cosin et al. (eds) (1971, *School and Society: A Sociological Reader*, Routledge & Kegan Paul, pp. 61–6).

Bidwell, C.E. 1965, 'The School as a Formal Organization', in March, J.G. (ed) *Handbook of Organizations*, Rand McNally, pp. 972–1022.

Burns, T., 1967, 'The Comparative Study of Organizations', in Vroom, V. (ed) *Methods of Organizational Research*, University of Pittsburgh Press, pp. 118–170.

Carlson, K., 1972, 'Equalizing Educational Opportunity', *Review of Educational Research*, (42) 4, 453–475.

Culbertson, J. and Shibles, M. 1973, 'The Social Sciences and the Issues of Relevance', in Culbertson, J., Farquhar, R., Forgarty, G. and Shibles, M. (eds) *Social Science Content for Preparing Educational Leaders*, Charles E. Merrill.

Dawe, A., 1970, 'The Two Sociologies', *British Journal of Sociology*, 21 (2), pp. 207–218.

Deutscher, I. (ed), 1973, *What We Say/What We Do: Sentiments and Acts*, Scott Foresman.

Eldridge, J.E.T. (ed), 1971, *Max Weber: The Interpretation of Social Reality*, Michael Joseph.

Etzioni, A. 1960, 'Two Approaches to Organizational Analysis: A Critique and a Suggestion', *Administrative Science Quarterly*, 5 (2), pp. 257–278.

Garfinkel, H. 1967, *Studies in Ethnomethodology*, Prentice-Hall.

Getzels, J.W., 1958, 'Administration as a Social Process', in Halpin (ed) (1958, *Administrative Theory in Education*, Macmillan, pp. 150–165).

Glaser, B.G. and Strauss, A.L., 1967, *The Discovery of Grounded Theory*, Aldine.

Greenfield, T. B, 1973, 'Organizations as Social Inventions: Re-thinking Assumptions About Change', *Journal of Applied Behavioural Science*, 9, (5), pp. 551–574.

Gregg, R.T., 1957, 'The Administrative Process', in Campbell and Gregg (eds) (1958, *Administrative Behavior in Education*, Harper & Row, pp. 269–317).

Griffiths, D.E. (ed), 1964, *Behavioural Science and Educational Administration*, The Sixty-third Yearbook of the National Society for the Study of Education, University of Chicago Press.

Halsey, A.H. (ed), 1972, *Educational Priority: E.P.A. Problems and Policies*, Vol. 1, HMSO.

Holbrook, D., 1964, *English for the Rejected*, Cambridge University Press.

Kuhn, T., 1970, *The Structure of Scientific Revolution*, University of Chicago Press.

Louch, A.R. 1966, *Explanation and Human Action*, University of California Press.

March, J.G., 1972, 'Model Bias in Social Action', *Review of Educational Research*, 42, (4), pp. 413–429.

Mayntz, Renate, 1964, 'The Study of Organizations', *Current Sociology*, 13, (3), pp. 95–155.

Merton, R.K., 1957, *Social Theory and Social Structure*, Free Press.

Perrow, C. 1972, *Complex Organizations: A Critical Essay*, Scott Foresman.

Phillipson, M, 1972, 'Phenomenological Philosophy and Sociology', in Filmer et al. (1972, *Direction in Sociological Theory*, Collier Macmillan, pp. 119–163).

Rothkopf, E.Z., 1973, 'What Are We Trying to Understand and Improve? Educational Research as *Leerlaufreaktion*', invited address to the meeting of the American Educational Research Association, New Orleans.

Sarason, S.B., 1971, *The Culture of the School and the Problem of Change*, Allyn and Bacon.

Scheff, T.J., 1973, 'Negotiating Reality: Notes on Power in the Assessment of Responsibility', in Deutscher (ed) (1973, *What We Say/What We Do: Sentiments and Acts*, Scott Foresman, pp. 338–358).

Silverman, D., 1970, *The Theory of Organisations*, Heinemann.

Simon, H.A., 1957, *Administrative Behaviour: A Study of Decision-Making Process in Administrative Organization*, 2nd edition, Free Press.

Spady, W.G., 1973, 'The Impact of School Resources on Students', in Kerlinger, F.N. (ed) *Review of Research in Education*, No. 1, Peacock, pp. 135–177.

Walsh, D. 'Sociology and the Social World', in Filmer et al. (1972, pp. 15–35).

Weber, M. 1947, *The Theory of Social and Economic Organizations*, (Parsons, T., ed), William Hodge.

Willer, D., 1967, *Scientific Sociology: Theory and Method*, Prentice-Hall.

CHAPTER 3.3

ON THE WORKINGS OF GROUPS*
Charles B. Handy

Introduction

If a camel is a horse put together by a committee, why then do people spend so much of their lives in groups? On average, managers spend 50 percent of their working day in one sort of group or another. Senior managers can spend 80 percent.

There are more myths, more stereotypes, about groups and committees than about most subjects in organizations. There are the individualists, to whom groups and committees are an encumbrance and a nuisance. There are the team men, who want participation and involvement by all concerned. Does it matter? Are groups a fashion or a necessity?

What is a 'group' anyway? They vary from the formal – a work group, a project team, a committee, a board – to the informal – the *ad hoc* meeting or discussion, the luncheon group, the clique, the cabal. They are permanent or temporary. They are liked by their members or regarded as a waste of time. They can be a most effective device for blocking and obstructing new ideas, or the best way of putting them into practice.

What is the truth about groups? Is there any better understanding that we can gain about this universal phenomenon? Is there a diagnostic framework that we can apply to the working of groups which will allow us to understand more fully this part of organizational life?

In this chapter we shall look first at the *purposes of groups* – what they are used for, and by whom, what they are good at and when. We shall then consider *the determinants of group effectiveness* and conclude with some *conclusions and implications*.

* *Understanding Organizations*, Penguin Books Ltd., 1976, chapter 6, pp. 145–175.

The purposes of groups

We shall first need to define the types of group rather more precisely. A group, first of all, is any collection of people who perceive themselves to be a group. If this seems to be dodging the issue, reflect a minute. A dozen individuals in a pub by random chance are not a group, although they may be interacting (talking), have a common objective (drink and socialization), and be aware of each other. (These are some other definitions of groups.) But put those same people in an emergency situation, let them be trapped by fire in the saloon bar, then that random collection of people will become a group, will start to have some collective identity, because they will start to perceive themselves as a group, with another sort of objective and with needs for other sorts of interaction. All of us, at some time, must have experienced the formation of a group from random individuals, when danger seems to threaten, when the bus is marooned by snow, when the yacht loses its rudder, even in power cuts when one is trapped in the lift. Then we suddenly perceive ourselves to be members of a group. Common objectives, defined membership criteria, predetermined hierarchies, these are not enough without this self-perception by the members. So you will find that when the numbers get too large the members, perceiving themselves to be no longer a group but a crowd or an association, will start reforming into smaller collections. So it is that a name, even a jocular name, for the group becomes an important part of acquiring a perceived identity. Put random collections of peoples into groups – for instance on a management training programme – and they will, if they wish to be a group and it is important for them to be a group, start to find a name, or a private territorial sign, or a ritual, which will give them an independent identity. If they do not do this, it often means that membership of such a group is not important to them, that they are happy to remain a random collection of individuals.

The organizational purposes

Organizations use groups, or teams and committees, for the following major purposes:

1 For the distribution of work. To bring together a set of skills, talents, responsibilities, and allocate to them their particular duties.
2 For the management and control of work. To allow work to be organized and controlled by appropriate individuals with responsibility for a certain range of work.

3 For problem-solving and decision-taking. To bring together a set of skills, talents, and responsibilities so that the solution to any problem will have all available capacities applied to it.

4 For information-processing. To pass on decisions or information to those who need to know.

5 For information and idea collection. To gather ideas, information, or suggestions.

6 For testing and ratifying decisions. To test the validity of a decision taken outside the group, or to ratify such a decision.

7 For coordination and liaison. To coordinate problems and tasks between functions or divisions.

8 For increased commitment and involvement. To allow and encourage individuals to get involved in the plans and activities of the organization.

9 For negotiation or conflict resolution. To resolve a dispute or argument between levels, divisions, or functions.

10 For inquest or inquiry into the past.

Some of these functions may well be combined. Some will overlap. It should become clear from the discussion in this chapter that groups will behave differently and will need to be organized differently, managed differently, for each of these functions. Some of the major difficulties with groups arise because the same group is expected simultaneously to perform two different functions. A management meeting, for instance, which starts as a negotiation between functions will not proceed very satisfactorily to a discussion of the long-term plan of the organization. This does not mean that the same collection of individuals cannot perform two or more different functions. But they need to see themselves as a different group in order to do so. Thus the functions need to be separated by time, or place, or title. There is more sense than might appear in the comedian's stereotype of the small town functionaries who flit from committee to committee where all the participants are the same, and only the name of the committee changes.

The individual's purposes

Individuals use groups for one or more of the following purposes:

1 A means of satisfying their social or affiliation needs; to belong to something or to share in something.

2 A means of establishing a self-concept. Most people find it easier to

define themselves in terms of their relationship to others, as members of a role set with a role in that set.

3 A means of gaining help and support to carry out their particular objectives, which may or may not be the same as the organization's objectives.

4 A means of sharing and helping in a common activity or purpose which may be making a product, or carrying out a job, or having fun, or giving help, or creating something.

Again these purposes often overlap. They may also conflict. As many studies have shown, the social functions of work groups can get in the way of the productive functions. Rate-setting is the use of a group to set standards, achieve objectives, which may be contrary to the organization's objectives. The individual who is satisfying his affiliation needs through membership of that group must pay the price of conformity or be expelled.

The famous Hawthorne Studies in the Western Electric Company of Chicago demonstrated above all that membership of a group is important to most individuals and that the norms and objectives of the group will have a very large say in the norms and objectives of the individual who belongs to it.

The optimum, of course, is to see that the objectives and purposes of the individual, the group, and the organization all coincide.

Group effectiveness

In general, can we say anything about groups and the things they are good at? There are some things:

1 They are necessary in order to provide a psychological home for the individual. They are essential to organization effectiveness in that they provide the cells within the honeycomb. If they weren't required for the organization of work they would be formed by the individuals. Individuals will usually look to the work group, as a place of first resort, to satisfy their needs. Only if this fails will they turn elsewhere.

2 Groups produce less ideas, in total, than the individuals of those groups working separately. So much for the stereotype of brainstorming! But groups, though producing less ideas in total, produce better ideas in the sense that they are better evaluated, more thought through. A group will often produce a better solution to a quiz than the best individual in the group, since it can add the missing bits to the best performer. As we

shall see, size and the organization of the group are factors that can stop this happening.

3 Groups, rather surprisingly, take riskier decisions than the individuals comprising them would have done if they had been acting independently. Nobody is quite sure of the reason for this but it is either that: groups give a sense of shared responsibility; or risk-taking, within limits, being 'a good thing', we tend to behave more adventurously in groups than in private, where we do not have to live up to any public standard.

The determinants of group effectiveness

As with most features of organizations, the answer to the question 'what makes an effective group?' is 'it depends'. In the first place, it depends on the answer to the question 'effective for whom?' We have to remember that productivity and member satisfaction are two possible outcomes of group activity which may or may not be in double harness.

A point, however, worth stressing: although satisfaction does not necessarily lead to productivity, productivity can often lead to satisfaction. The pride and sense of achievement that comes from being a member of an effective group can lead to satisfaction if the individual values the group and the work that it is doing. This has been called a sense of competence, and 'competence motivation'.

We shall divide the determinants of group effectiveness as follows:

the givens	the group, the task, the environment
the intervening factors	leadership style, processes and procedures, motivation
the outcomes	productivity, member satisfaction

The implication behind this division is that there are some aspects of the situation which will affect the outcome but which are 'given'. They can be altered in the long or medium terms but in the short term they are constraints within which the group has to operate. The intervening factors are determinants of effectiveness which can be changed in the immediate present. The division is not absolute. Aspects of the group or of the task can often be altered in the short term, can become intervening factors. No one should assume that 'the givens' are given for all time. The successful man is the man who constantly appraises and challenges his constraints. The management of the 'givens' is one example of influence through ecology –

and a very important example of it. As a starting point for analysis let us accept the ecology as fixed for the medium term.

The group

Under this heading we shall briefly examine *size, member characteristics, individual objectives,* and *stage of development.*

Size

There are two, fairly obvious, conflicting tendencies in group size: (a) the larger the group, the greater the diversity of talent, skills, and knowledge and (b) the larger the group, the less chance of an individual participating.

In fact, under (b), participation does not diminish uniformly. Some people talk more easily than others in groups, individuals have different thresholds of participation. One man finds no difficulty in speaking in a group of twenty strangers, another will find a group of ten too large unless he knows them well, or has some official role in the group. Studies have shown that those who participate most in a group are perceived as having the most influence. This means that as a group gets larger the influence pattern will get distorted in favour of those with low thresholds of participation. This distribution of influence may not be in accordance with the distribution of knowledge or experience. The 'neglected resource' is a common feature of groups; the retiring expert whose views are never heard or never noticed because his participation level is so low.

The size of the group is therefore a trade-off. For best participation, for highest all-round involvement, a size of between five and seven seems to be optimum. However, in order to achieve the requisite representation, the required size may be considerably larger. If that is so then the leader or chairman must be particularly aware of the participation-influence problem.

In work groups, size tends to be related to cohesiveness, which in turn is positively related to member satisfaction. Large work groups tend to have more absenteeism and lower morale. Large in this context, however, seems to be twenty or over.

Member characteristics

First and most obviously, the members must have the requisite skills and abilities to do the job. So must the leader. But other things are known about the mix of characteristics and personalities.

People who are similar in their attitudes, values, and beliefs tend to form stable enduring groups. Homogeneity tends in general to promote satisfaction. Heterogeneous groups tend to exhibit more conflict, but most studies do show them to be more productive than the homogeneous groups. However, as one might expect, these groups were heterogeneous only in certain specific characteristics. One study pinpointed radicalism, adventuresomeness, and character integration as the variables which should vary amongst group members. Variety in sensitivity, suspiciousness, and aggressiveness impeded productivity. Variety but compatibility was the conclusion of another study, i.e., too many potential leaders was bad, groups with a mixture of assertive and dependent people were effective, for they had variety, but variety which could be organized.

Study of the teams playing a year-long business game at Carnegie Institute of Technology has shown that those groups where there was the greatest differentiation of influence among team members were highest in morale and also performed best. That is, teams whose players saw themselves as all about equally influential were less satisfied and made less profits than teams whose players agreed that some particular individuals were a good deal more influential than others.

There have been many studies concerned with compatibility in groups. It was found that compatibility became more crucial as the task became more complex. With simple routine tasks characteristics of the individuals could be as heterogeneous as you liked. Not so with complex tasks where interaction between group members is required. Compatibility can be achieved in various ways. An assertive leader with dependent followers makes for a compatible group. When the individuals all rate highly on warmth and affection it will contribute to compatibility. One common thread stands out. The need for consensus on a focal person, or leader. Two potential leaders do not make for compatibility in a group.

Individual objectives and roles

It is only common sense to assert that if all members of a group have the same objectives the group will tend to be that much more effective. Nevertheless most people bring hidden agendas to groups. These hidden agendas are a set of personal objectives, which often may have nothing to do with the declared objectives of the group. Hidden agendas can include:

Protecting the interests of one's subgroup
Impressing one's boss
Scoring off an opponent

Making a particular alliance
Covering up past errors

In most group situations it is not possible to satisfy all the individual and group objectives simultaneously. There has to be a trade-off. Unless, therefore, the individuals in a group make specific efforts to agree on common objectives and to prove a level of trust, they will tend to promote their own interests at the expense of the group. Naturally they will not normally do this to the extent of destroying the group or ensuring their own eviction from it – they will only promote their self-interest up to a point, a point where the group's performance 'passes', e.g., is not over budget.

Times of emergency, of crisis and mutual peril, tend to make us all sink our differences. Then it is that the 'common enemy' is dominant, groups become much more cohesive and productive. It is a pity that we have to rely on outside events to produce this change in the individual calculus. It might not have to be so if more attention were paid to the collective purpose and more time devoted to improving the trust relationship. Arising out of his objectives, each individual will assess his role in the group. He will decide to assume some combination of the roles of:

Strong fighter
Friend and helper
Logical thinker

In making this implicit or explicit decision about his behaviour in the group he is going to have to answer for himself three questions:

1 Who am I in this group? What is my occupational role here? What are the role expectations of me? Am I here to listen or to lead? Am I representative or present in my own right? Who is judging me on my role performance?
2 What is the influence pattern? Who has the power? What kind of power is it? Do I want to change the influence pattern? If so, how do I do it?
3 What are my needs and objectives? Are they in line with the group? Should they be? What do I do about them if they are not? If one of these needs is to be liked and accepted, how important is that for me?

Box 1   Behaviour analysis in a group

date: 24 March 1971   observer: SBT
group: C   task: 14

name	Jean	Mike	John	Mark	Peter	Jim		total
supporting	ЖЖ III	ЖЖ ЖЖ ЖЖ II	II	IIII	IIII	ЖЖ		
disagreeing		ЖЖ III	II	I	I	IIII		
building		IIII III	III	IIII	IIII	ЖЖ I		
criticizing		II			II	I		
bringing in	IIII	ЖЖ III				ЖЖ		
shutting out	II	IIII	II	III	II	II		
innovating		III				II		
solidifying	III	II	I	III		ЖЖ I		
admitting difficulty		II	I			I		
defending/ attacking		II						
giving information	ЖЖ ЖЖ II	ЖЖ ЖЖ ЖЖ ЖЖ ЖЖ ЖЖ I	ЖЖ ЖЖ ЖЖ II	ЖЖ ЖЖ III	ЖЖ ЖЖ ЖЖ III	ЖЖ ЖЖ ЖЖ ЖЖ ЖЖ ЖЖ I		
seeking information	ЖЖ II	ЖЖ ЖЖ ЖЖ ЖЖ ЖЖ ЖЖ I	I	ЖЖ ЖЖ I	II	ЖЖ II		
other								

From Rackham, Honey, and Colbert, *Developing Interactive Skills*, 1971.

In addition to the three roles outlined earlier, the individual in the group has another choice – to play no role, to withdraw. This withdrawal phenomenon often occurs as a result of *strain* (the role conflict or ambiguity in the group situation is too great) or *apathy* (the salience of the task is so low that the individual is not prepared to pay the cost of contributing to the group).

You cannot assume, without investigation, that the symptom of withdrawal is always caused by apathy although that is the frequent assumption by group leaders. The result of all these role considerations will show up as individual behaviour characteristics. One way of classifying these is shown in Box 1.

Stage of development

Groups mature and develop. Like individuals they have a fairly clearly defined growth cycle. This has been categorized as having four successive stages:

1 *Forming*. The group is not yet a group but a set of individuals. This stage is characterized by talk about the purpose of the group. The definition and the title of the group, its composition, leadership pattern, and life-span. At this stage, too, each individual tends to want to establish his personal identity within the group, make some individual impression.

2 *Storming*. Most groups go through a conflict stage when the preliminary, and often false, consensus on purposes, on leadership and other roles, on norms of work and behaviour, is challenged and reestablished. At this stage a lot of personal agendas are revealed and a certain amount of interpersonal hostility is generated. If successfully handled this period of storming leads to a new and more realistic setting of objectives, procedures, and norms. This stage is particularly important for testing the norms of trust in the group.

3 *Norming*. The group needs to establish norms and practices. When and how it should work, how it should take decisions, what type of behaviour, what level of work, what degree of openness, trust, and confidence is appropriate. At this stage there will be a lot of tentative experimentation by individuals to test the temperature of the group and to measure the appropriate level of commitment.

4 *Performing*. Only when the three previous stages have been successfully complete will the group be at full maturity and be able to be fully and

sensibly productive. Some kind of performance will be achieved at all stages of development but it is likely to be impeded by the other processes of growth and by individual agendas. In many periodic committees the leadership issue, or the objective and purpose of the group, are recurring topics that crop up in every meeting in some form or other, seriously hindering the true work of the group.

When the task is very important, when the individuals are highly committed to the group, or when individual and group objectives are identical, then these stages may become almost perfunctory. Certainly the group will 'grow up', will mature very rapidly and reach its optimum performance level. More often the issues are not dealt with specifically and the group's maturing process is driven underground, particularly the 'storming' stage. When this occurs you have the backstage covert politicking, the hidden agendas, the abuse of negative power. In other words, the storming, not culturally acceptable in the open, goes on all the same but often in a much more disruptive manner, concealed under the heading of *performance*. If group members were to rate themselves, as a group, on these scales they would have an overall indication of their level of maturity as a group.

Box 2   For 'self' or for 'group'

Fouriezos, Hutt, and Guetzhow studied the effects of low 'group task motivation' upon group productivity in the seventy-two conference groups in the Conference Research Project of the University of Michigan. The groups were rated on the extent to which the members expessed self-oriented needs, i.e., motives resulting in behaviour 'not necessarily directed towards a group's goals, or . . . a solution of group's problems' but 'primarily toward the satisfaction of the need itself, regardless of the effect on attainment of the group goal'. The experimenters found that the amount of such self-oriented behaviour correlated negatively with measures of member satisfaction. In other words, groups in which there was a high frequency of self-oriented behaviour were relatively dissatisfied with the meeting as a whole, with the decisions arrived at, with the procedures used to reach decisions, and with the chairmanship. These 'self-oriented' groups were also high in the amount of conflict they exhibited.

Finally, measures of productivity showed significant inverse relations with amount of self-oriented behaviour. For example, groups rated high on such behaviour tended to complete fewer items on the agenda, although their meetings lasted longer.

Abridged from Fouriezos, Hutt, and Guetzhow, 'Measurement of self-oriented needs in discussion groups', *J. Abnormal Soc. Psych.*

Low ratings would indicate that one or more of the stages of development had not been fully worked through.

Whether a particular group needs to be fully mature to do its job will, of course, depend on the importance of that job. In many instances the cost of developing a group to maturity, in sheer time, the displacement of other priorities, the displacement of other groups in importance to the individuals, will not be worth the increased gain in effectiveness. But in many instances – the start-up of a new operation for the top management team, or a new group resulting from a reorganization – it is worth spending time specifically to build a group. Many organizations now recognize the benefits in doing this. There are known techniques built around the theories of group dynamics which can help. Essentially these techniques help the group to analyse and improve its 'process', as opposed to its work on particular tasks, and to hasten its maturity by focusing specifically on each of the stages of development. Process consultation, T-groups, Coverdale training are some of these techniques.

The task

The 'givens' that must be looked at under the heading of the *task* are *nature of the task, criteria for effectiveness, salience of the task,* and *clarity of the task*. The implications of these are straightforward, but they must not be ignored.

The nature of the task

The types of task for which groups or committees are used have been listed above. Obviously, the type of task will affect the kind of group you can have. Information dissemination permits a larger group size than problem-solving. Task allocation allows a structured approach, idea formulation needs a more supportive style. The point was made earlier that to confuse two tasks in the one group is inadvisable. In particular this is so when the change in tasks involves a change in role for individuals. For instance, in work allocation or in an inquest situation the individual will be wearing his departmental, ambassadorial hat. For problem-solving or creativity he is expected to don his overall company apparel and to forget departmental politics. The switch in roles is not easy. The departmental hat will stay on. The creativity discussion will bog down in departmental quibbles. The individual will be castigated as narrow-minded and short-sighted. The group will be ineffective. Essentially it was a different group.

The people were the same but the roles were different. A different group needs a different identity – fixed by title, place, or time. Agendas or meetings could usefully be split by type of task, rather than all items lumped together in the order they were received by the secretary.

The criteria for effectiveness

In addition to the type of task, one has to consider the *urgency* with which results are required. Pressures of time or competition legitimize more structured forms of working, allow less freedom to develop a group or to deal with individual needs. As a result, the work will often be less accurate, or worse in terms of possible quality. One needs therefore to reflect upon the required *standards*. How, in short, is the effectiveness of the result to be measured? In quantity? In quality? In speed? In cost? In profit? The criteria for assessing performance is going to be a big determining factor on the way the group can operate as well as on what is meant by effectiveness at the end of the day.

Salience of the task

This aspect has already intruded into the discussion of individual objectives. The more important the task to the individual the more committed he is going to be to the group, the less concerned about his own objectives.

The more important the task to the organization the more attention they are likely to pay to the group's performance. If this attention takes the form of setting high expectations on effectiveness it will tend to increase the salience of the task for the individuals. If, however, the increased attention is accompanied by increased monitoring or controls then the implication is of lack of trust and confidence in the group. The group will then experience the pressure of control rather than the pressure of expectation. Pressure by control is demotivating. It is also expensive.

In general, the more salient the task is, the more you can demand of the group. But salience that leads to increased control will only cause strain within the group and within individuals.

Clarity of the task

The less ambiguous the task the more structured the leadership can be. A precise detailed and compartmentalized task implies no requirements in the way of homogeneity or compatibility. A precise task will assist the group through the forming and norming stages of development.

But not all tasks can or should be described so precisely. Ambiguous, open-ended assignments or objectives increase complexity, bring increased demands for compatibility, for time, for supportive leadership. Ambiguity increases stress, and therefore has implications for the kind of individuals required in the group and particularly in the leadership roles.

The environment

All groups work within an environment, usually the environment of the total organization. The environment imposes certain conditions or constraints on the way they operate. The principal 'givens' in this area are *the norms and expectations, the leader position, intergroup relations,* and *the physical location.*

Norms and expectations

The degree of salience that the task has for the organization, and the implications of that for the work group, has already been discussed.

In addition, however, every organization has some norms about ways of working, style of meeting, methods of reporting and coordinating. It is not always possible for a group or a committee to avoid conforming to these norms whether or not they are the most appropriate in their circumstances.

Leader position

Not only is it true that the more powerful the leader in the organization as a whole, the greater freedom he has to be flexible in his style, but he also has a positive effect on the morale of his work group. People like working under a respected chief. Just as civil servants appreciate a Minister who is effective in Cabinet, so in all organizations the leader who is effective in his ambassadorial role will do most to help, not only the ultimate effectiveness of the group, but also its internal *esprit de corps*. A leader who cannot give effect to, cannot sell, the product of the group or the committee is often sufficient grounds for the group members to turn the group into a social or casual group, rejecting the task goals as unrealistic.

Research studies support these commonsense conclusions. Studies have shown that in high-producing groups the leader is seen by his subordinates as possessing more influence with his superiors than the leader of the low-producing groups.

Intergroup relations

The standing of the group or the committee as a whole will affect its productivity and its morale. The degree to which the group is accepted as important, as helpful, as cooperative to the overall goals of the organization;

the influence wielded by the group with key figures in the organization; the degree to which it is perceived to influence events in the organization or outside; these factors are all important. No one wants to spend whole mornings in committees whose conclusions will never be noticed, or will be overruled.

The ambassadorial role of the leader has a big bearing on this. But so does the status of the individual members. The marginal group, the low-status group, the unnoticed group, is under a big temptation to activate their latent *negative power*.

Membership of a group which appears to make no difference to anyone will cause dissonance for most individuals. There are two possible ways for someone to resolve that dissonance, and bring his wishes into accord with reality:

1 He can reduce the importance of the group to himself. He can cease attending, or cease contributing.

2 He can activate the negative power of the group, its blocking or nuisance value, so that more people notice it. Its salience in the organization is then increased, if not its popularity.

This irritation factor in committees will always tend to arise if the committee is low in *centrality* in the organization, is not perceived to be useful or necessary or high in status by other groups.

The physical location

This is the simplest of the 'givens' but one very often ignored. There are specific aspects of the physical location of the group and the members of the group that must be considered:

1 Physical proximity increases interaction. One study showed that a flight of stairs interposed between the offices of members of one group reduced interaction of all types by 30 percent.

2 Interaction normally increases cooperative feelings. In the exceptional instances, where interaction leads to increasing dislike, divorce ensues and interaction ceases. Studies in a housing project showed that people whose doorways faced each other were more likely to become friends than others.

3 Physical barriers can prevent groups from forming. Assembly lines inhibit the formation of social groups at work. This is a drawback to

workers and one reason for their forming other groups, e.g., strike committees, purely social groups, etc. Concentration camps and prisons use the technique of isolation very effectively to prevent the formation of groups and to deprive the individual of a psychological home.

4 The location of a meeting gives out signals. The managing director's office reinforces his role. If it is off-site, in a hotel in the country, the signal is that people can forget their ambassadorial role for the time being, and be themselves, be individuals.

5 Shared facilities, even shared discomfort, does much to help group identity. Luncheon and coffee facilities, meeting places and conference rooms can be used deliberately for this purpose. The 'Nissen Hut' experience, groups crowded uncomfortably together, will often produce high cohesion. An isolated location, where all facilities have to be shared, will tend to create involvement in the group.

The intervening factors

These are the aspects of group work that can be changed or adapted in the short term, taking account of the 'givens', to improve group productivity or member satisfaction. They fall under the headings of:

Leadership style
Process and procedure
Motivation

Leadership style

There is no such thing as the 'right' style of leadership, but leadership will be most effective when the requirements of the *leader*, the *subordinate*, and the *task* fit together to give the 'best fit'. This has been underlined by all the foregoing discussion.

Process and procedures

For any group to be effective there is a set of processes or functions that have to be done by some person or persons in the group at some time or other. It is the ultimate responsibility of the leader to see that they are done – his choice of style will determine whether he does them, or whether the processes are shared out amongst other individuals. In certain types of group it would be quite appropriate for all the members at some point to perform each of these functions.

The processes or functions are usually grouped under two broad headings – *task functions* and *maintenance functions* – and comprise the following:

task	*maintenance*
initiating	encouraging
information-seeking	compromising
diagnosing	peace-keeping
opinion-seeking	clarifying, summarizing
evaluating	standard-setting
decision-managing	

Task functions

Particularly in any problem-solving situation all the listed processes ought to happen. Furthermore, they ought to happen in the order in which they are listed. Too often group discussions leap from initiating through rudimentary opinion-seeking to evaluation. The chairman states the problem, a solution is proposed, it is evaluated and a decision taken. The separation of information from opinion, of diagnosis from evaluation, greatly improves the quality of the solution. Evaluation is, at its heart, a comparative process. It compares one solution against other available solutions. To be well done it is therefore important that all solutions are known before any are evaluated. The stages of opinion-seeking, or idea generation, and evaluation should be separated. A mechanism for recording these ideas is also important – a blackboard, or large sheet of paper, some public recording device so that all members have available to them all possibilities before evaluation starts.

It has been shown in experimental studies that groups who attack a problem systematically perform better than groups who 'muddle through' or 'evolve'. The decision-making procedure is also of great importance. Will it be:

Decision by authority
Decision by majority
Decision by consensus
Decision by minority
Decision by no response?

Box 3   The ineffective management committee

The organization was having trouble getting its top management committee to act as a *management* group. It was composed of the senior divisional and functional managers. The M.D. complained that they could only think in departmental terms and in the short term. He could not get them to take a long-term, company-wide view. He attributed this to their personal incapacities. Investigation revealed that:

1 The committee meetings usually started with some form of 'inquest' which forced the managers into departmental roles. They found it hard to exchange these roles for company ones for the next item, which was usually of a different 'type'.
2 Decision was by authority rule. Discussion therefore was peripheral and mainly concerned to pinpoint departmental pit-falls.
3 The agenda was lengthy, the time available was short. Interjections therefore had to be short and factual. Philosophical discussions were not encouraged.
4 The offices of the departmental managers were all in the centres of their departments. This enhanced their ambassadorial or departmental role.
5 The meetings were run on a 'wheel' basis – thus accentuating the power of the chairman and providing the basis for authority rule.
6 Two of the members of the group were not trusted or respected by their colleagues. Everyone, including the two, was aware of this but the formality of the proceedings prevented its coming into the open.

Changes were made:

1 The committee was reorganized and renamed to exclude the two 'unrespected' members.
2 The offices of the others were then all situated on the fifth floor away from their departments. This not only changed their view of the role but also cut down their day-to-day interaction ('interference' said subordinates) with their departments.
3 The agendas were shortened, and the items divided by type.
4 The meeting times were lengthened.
5 The smaller number permitted the interaction pattern to change from the wheel to all-channel. The decision mechanism changed to consensus.

All agreed that the committee worked much more effectively and more like a management group. Levels of mutual trust went up. The M.D.'s appraisals of his managers were revised – upwards.

The last two are usually only negative. That is, an idea is suggested: either no one responds and it is dropped, or a minority bloc exercises its veto. Most group decisions are negative decisions and as such often pass unnoticed as decisions. If ideas are evaluated separately it can easily happen that each idea receives a veto or negative decision, the meeting then becoming totally unfruitful and very dispiriting to all present.

The kind of task procedure to adopt and in particular the decision-making process are two of the things that the group has to make up its mind on in the 'norming' stage of its development. The leader, by virtue of his position power, has great influence over choice of procedure (ecology), although he does not have to perform all of the functions himself.

Maintenance functions

Effective groups, be they problem-solving or producing, need maintenance. There are neglected resources in groups, they need encouraging; there are often opposing factions, they must be helped to compromise, to resolve or manage their conflict; individuals too often do not listen in groups, each man intent on preparing his own contribution; someone must clarify and summarize so that there is a common awareness of all that has happened. Lastly, the performance of the group will be vastly influenced by the kind of standards that it is aiming at. Someone has to set those standards and have them adopted by the group. Groups without standards will satisfice at the lowest level. Standards without groups, not accepted by the group as realistic for them, are meaningless.

Again, the leader does not have to perform all these functions himself, but they need doing. Groups in which these tasks and maintenance functions were observed to happen have been entitled cooperative groups. They were found, in one study by Deutsch, in comparison with 'competitive' groups to:

1 Be more productive in quantity.
2 Produce higher quality.
3 Have a stronger push to complete the task.
4 Have a greater division of labour and better coordination.
5 Experience fewer difficulties in communication.
6 Show more friendliness in the discussions.
7 Experience greater satisfaction with the group and its products.

Interaction pattern

The other factor that the group itself can control, and the leader can influence, is the interaction pattern, the pattern of communication between members. Is it, for instance, *a wheel, circle,* or *all-channel?* (See Figure 8.)

Well-known sets of experiments have been done by numbers of social scientists to demonstrate the relative merits of these communication patterns in small groups. The main conclusions are not unexpected:

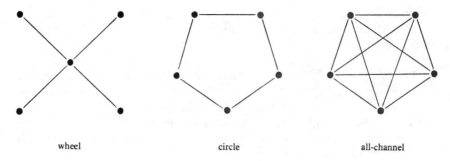

wheel   circle   all-channel

Figure 8

1 The wheel is always the quickest to reach a solution or conclusion, the circle is the slowest.

2 In complex open-ended problems the all-channel is the most likely to reach the best solution, the ability of the man at the centre of the wheel determining the outcome of that pattern. The wheel is usually inflexible if the task changes.

3 The level of satisfaction for individuals is lowest in the circle, fairly high in the all-channel, mixed in the wheel with the central figure usually expressing great satisfaction and the outlying figures feeling isolated.

One might suppose, although the research did not test this, that the feelings of satisfaction in the all-channel group would depend on the importance of the task. No one wants involvement in a trivial 'Mickey Mouse' assignment. Similarly, not all individuals react positively to being the central figure in the wheel – even in experimental situations people have been known to collapse and withdraw under the overload of communication.

Under pressure of time or competition the all-channel system either restructured itself into a wheel – or disintegrated. In general, then, wheels are good for speedy results where quality is not vital, but morale may be low for all but the leader. Circles are always bad, no coordination. All-channel systems are participative and involving and good for quality, but they take time and do not stand up under pressure. These conclusions can be seen at work in numberless committees where often, *pace* Parkinson, the wrong system is used for the wrong task – all-channel for the trivia of the parking lot, wheels for the big merger decision.

Motivation

As regards motivation in group settings, certain aspects need to be stressed:

1 Motivation is more than satisfaction. Satisfaction is one of the possible outcomes of groups. Lack of satisfaction will lead to absenteeism and turnover of members. But a satisfied group is not necessarily a productive group, although it helps. Satisfaction is a necessary but not sufficient condition of productivity. An individual will be satisfied in a group, will value membership of that group if:

(a) He likes the other members and is liked by them (friendship); or
(b) He approves of the purpose and work of the group (task); or
(c) He wishes to be associated with the standing of the group in the organization (status).

One or all of these will lead to satisfaction, depending on the psychological contract of the individual with that group and the particular needs subsumed in that contract. You can therefore have a satisfied and productive group in which condition (a) does not apply, in which the members do not particularly like each other.

2 Knowledge of expected results, or standard setting, is crucial if the motivation calculus of individuals is to operate. Hence the importance of realistic standards, of standards accepted by the group, of standards sufficiently high to give them a feeling of achievement when attained. Hence also the importance of knowing the results, of feedback. Both of these items are essential to the motivation of groups. Both are too frequently neglected.

3 Motivation by involvement will only work if the group and the task are important enough to the individual to justify his acceptance of additional responsibility. Otherwise it will be involvement by order – rules and procedures based on coercive or resource power and requiring control and maintenance mechanisms to make it work. One cannot assume that, because someone is nominated to a committee, he will do any more than attend its meetings.

Perhaps, however, the most important aspect of motivation in groups is the establishment of a 'common enemy', discussed earlier. Hopefully, the task assigned to the group will be sufficiently salient and clear to all members that it will automatically become a common enemy. But this cannot be assumed. The leader, particularly, may see the task as much more important than the other members. If the individuals put their own agendas in front of the task the productivity and morale will decline and the whole group will be much more difficult to manage. The leader therefore needs to do all he can either to:

Redefine the task so that it becomes a common enemy; or
Raise the individual's expectations of the task so that it dwarfs their individual needs.

A solution sometimes adopted, lacking a task of sufficient interest, is to make the building of a group the key task. This is:

Difficult, without an external task;
Counter to organizational interests since a group will be created whose primary goal will be its own satisfaction and survival.

Summary and conclusions

The complete model for the analysis of groups now looks like this:

Table 4

	The group	*The task*	*The environment*
	size	nature	norms and expectations
the givens	member characteristics	criteria for effectiveness	leader position
	individual objectives	salience of task	inter-group relations
	stage of development	clarity of task	
which all effect the intervening actors		choice of leadership style	
		processes and procedures	
		motivation	
which determine the outcomes		productivity	
		member satisfaction	

Are there any general conclusions that we can reach; or additional points to make?

The 'group' ideology

Groups fit well with a democratic culture, with representative systems of government. Participation and involvement go well with assumptions of man as an independent individual. Committees similarly are democratic and representative, but they are extraordinarily difficult things to operate effectively. The model presented in this chapter should help to give an understanding of many of the reasons. In addition, we must remember that:

1 Groups can be used by individuals, and by organizations, to diffuse, and even to lose, responsibility.

2 Committees are often better ways of 'recognizing' problems than 'solving' problems. A 'committee to investigate X' is a recognition of 'X' but that does not necessarily mean that it is the best way to solve 'X'. Committees are often, like Royal Commissions, a way of simultaneously accepting the importance of a problem but deferring its solution.

3 Group pressures have a powerful influence on individual conformity. They can be explicit or implicit in that merely being 'out of tune' with the group can itself be a pressure towards conforming. Even strong individuals can be reduced to impotence by a group. But weak individuals can be bolstered – it all depends on the norms of the group and its collective motivation and standards.

The problem is this: if groups or committees are convened or constructed for an appropriate task, or with impossible constraints; if they are badly led or have ineffective procedures; if they have the wrong people, too many people, too little power or meet too infrequently; if, in short, any one part of the model is badly out of line, frustration will set in and dissonance will be created. The result will either be an activation of *negative power* or a badly attended noneffective group, wasting people, time, and space. The chances of this happening are, in fact, very high. If 50 percent of managerial time is spent in groups, the cost of wasted time begins to look colossal, let alone the damage done by the use of negative power.

CHAPTER 3.4

FIFTEEN THOUSAND HOURS*
Michael Rutter, Barbara Maughan, Peter Mortimore, and Janet Ouston

Introduction

This is part of a longitudinal study of 5485 pupils in the Inner London Education Authority (ILEA) who are being followed from their primary schools through five years of secondary schooling. In 1970, before secondary transfer, these children were given group intelligence and reading attainment tests and were assessed on their behaviour and family background. About two-thirds of these pupils went on to twenty nonselective schools in the ILEA and these were retested in 1974 in their third year of secondary school. The schools were matched by a 'standardization formula' which adjusted for differences in intake. *'The differences between schools in their intakes did not explain the differences between them at fourteen because the schools with the most advantaged intakes were not necessarily those with the best outcomes' and, moreover, 'schools with very similar intakes had very different findings at fourteen'. How were these* school *differences to be explained? Twelve schools (containing 1487 of the original sample), varying in size, status, nature of buildings and facilities, were selected for detailed study in an attempt to answer this question. The main findings and some discussion of their implications are discussed in the edited and much reduced extract which follows.*

Summary of conclusions

First, secondary schools in inner London differed markedly in the

* *Fifteen Thousand Hours — Secondary Schools and Their Effects on Children*, Open Books Publishing Limited, 1979, pp. 177–205.

behaviour and attainments shown by their pupils. This was evident in the children's behaviour whilst at school, the regularity of their attendance, the proportions staying on at school beyond the legally enforced period, their success in public examinations, and their delinquency rates.

Second, although schools differed in the proportion of behaviourally difficult or low-achieving children they admitted, these differences did *not* wholly account for the variations between schools in their pupils' later behaviour and attainment. Even when comparisons between schools were restricted to children who were quite similar in family background and personal characteristics prior to secondary transfer, marked school variations remained. This meant that children were more likely to show good behaviour and good scholastic attainments if they attended some schools than if they attended others. The implication is that experiences during the secondary school years may influence children's progress.

Third, the variations between schools in different forms of 'outcome' for their pupils were reasonably stable over periods of at least four or five years.

Fourth, in general, schools performed fairly similarly on all the various measures of outcome. That is, schools which did better than average in terms of the children's behaviour in school tended also to do better than average in terms of examination success and delinquency. There were some exceptions to this pattern, but it appeared that in most schools the different forms of success were closely connected.

Fifth, these differences in outcome between schools were *not* due to such physical factors as the size of the school, the age of the buildings, or the space available; nor were they due to broad differences in administrative status or organization. It was entirely possible for schools to obtain good outcomes in spite of initially rather unpromising and unprepossessing school premises, and within the context of somewhat differing administrative arrangements.

Sixth, the differences between schools in outcome *were* systematically related to their characteristics as social institutions. Factors as varied as the degree of academic emphasis, teacher actions in lessons, the availability of incentives and rewards, good conditions for pupils, and the extent to which children were able to take responsibility were all significantly associated with outcome differences between schools. All of these factors were open to modification by the staff, rather than fixed by external constraints.

Seventh, outcomes were also influenced by factors *outside* teachers' immediate control. The academic balance in the intake to the schools was particularly important in this connection. Examination success tended to be better in schools with a substantial nucleus of children of at least average intellectual ability, and delinquency rates were higher in those with a heavy preponderance of the least able. Interestingly, however, while the balance of intake was significantly associated with pupil outcome, it did *not* appear to have any comparable influence on school functioning, as reflected in our school process measures.

Eighth, this effect of balance in the intake was most marked with respect to delinquency, and least important in the case of the children's observed behaviour in the classroom and elsewhere about the school.

Ninth, the association between the *combined* measure of overall school process and each of the measures of outcome was much stronger than any of the associations with the individual process variables. This suggests that the *cumulative* effect of these various social factors was considerably greater than the effect of any of the individual factors on their own. The implication is that the individual actions or measures may combine to create a particular *ethos*, or set of values, attitudes, and behaviours which will become characteristic of the school as a whole.

Tenth, the total pattern of findings indicates the strong probability that the associations between school process and outcome reflect in part a *causal* process. In other words, to an appreciable extent children's behaviour and attitudes are shaped and influenced by their experiences at school and, in particular, by the qualities of the school as a social institution.

School process: a causal influence?

We have suggested that there is a causal relationship between school process and children's progress. Firm conclusions about causation can only come from controlled experimental studies. In a nonexperimental study, the *pattern* of statistical associations can nevertheless provide quite good guidance as to whether a relationship is likely to reflect a causal effect.

In the present study, the existence of longitudinal data was particularly helpful in showing that the pupil outcomes were associated with experiences which occurred during the years of secondary schooling. Not only did the schools differ in outcome after controlling for the children's measured characteristics at intake, but also these differences in outcome were systematically associated with measured features of the schools.

But perhaps the most crucial point concerns the pattern of correlations with school process. The question here is whether schools were as they were because of the children they admitted, or rather whether children behaved in the way they did because of school influences. Of course, interactions will take place in both directions, but the much greater correlation between school process and children's behaviour/attainments at the *end* of secondary schooling strongly implies a greater effect of schools on children than of children on schools. We may infer that it is very likely that school processes *do* influence pupil outcome.

Of course it is not suggested that the links work only in one direction. Schools constitute just one element in a complex set of ecological interactions, and are shaped and constrained by a variety of societal forces outside their immediate control. They are likely to be influenced by the types of neighbourhood they serve; running a school in a remote country village is not the same as running one in inner London. Factors such as the extent of parental support and community involvement are also liable to influence how a school functions as a social unit. The teaching task in an academically selective school serving a prosperous middle-class district will be very different from that in a school with a heavy preponderance of less-able pupils from socially disadvantaged homes.

Our study was not able to look at variations of this kind, but they are clearly important issues. Even within a similar geographical area, external influences, and perhaps most importantly the pupils themselves, will play a part in shaping school life. The initial teaching task is shaped by the attitudes, behaviour, interests, and capabilities of the children in the class. Teacher actions then influence children's behaviour, which in turn modifies teacher behaviour, which then further impinges on the children. In this way, spirals of either improving or deteriorating behaviour (and attainments) seem likely to be built up.

The pattern of connections is complex. It is nevertheless clear that, within this network, schools have a considerable degree of choice in how they are organized, and that teachers have a similar choice in their decisions on how to respond to the children they teach. Our results suggest that these decisions on how to respond are likely to affect the chances of the children improving in their behaviour and attainments.

It is not argued that schools are the *most* important influence on children's progress. Nevertheless, we do suggest that schools constitute one major area of influence, and one which is susceptible to change. However, for this conclusion to be of much use to practitioners, it is necessary to go on to consider some of the possible mechanisms which may be involved. Our statistical associations need to be restated in terms of the processes and meanings which they may reflect.

Schools as social organizations

Evidence for an institutional effect

The school process measures which correlated with the four types of pupil outcome included a wide variety of factors. Doubtless, as we will come to consider later, they operated by a variety of different mechanisms. It was striking, however, that their *combined* effect was much more powerful than that of any individual factor considered on its own. For this and other reasons, we have suggested that some kind of overall school 'ethos' might be involved.

Before considering how the individual process variables might operate in the context of such an institutional effect we need to ask why it is necessary to talk in terms of an ethos at all. Could it not be that school process variables act by directly shaping the behaviour of individual children? Obviously, this does occur (as we will indicate) but there are three main reasons for arguing that there is likely to be a broader institutional effect as well.

Firstly, most of the individual process variables had only a most indirect connection with the outcome with which they were statistically associated. We found a host of school factors which correlated significantly with attendance, but many of these did not involve any kind of teacher or school response to absconding or truanting as such. Moreover, some school process and balance of intake variables were significantly associated with child behaviours completely outside the school itself – as, for example, with delinquency. The implication is that the style and quality of life at school was having a relatively pervasive effect on children's behaviour – an effect which went beyond any kind of immediate shaping by direct rewards and punishments.

Secondly, we observed (although we have few quantitative measures to document this) that the *same* teacher actions sometimes led to quite *different* results in different schools. For example, if children were left alone in lessons to get on with their own work, in some schools they did just that. In others, any relaxation of direct control led to an increase in disruptive behaviour. It appeared that there was something about the way children were dealt with in general which influenced their behaviour even when there was no direct supervision by staff.

Third, many of the variables did not refer to actions which bore directly on individual children. Thus, some were concerned with conditions in the school generally (e.g., care of the buildings). Others were involved with the management of groups (for example, the *dis*advantage of frequent individual interactions in class-oriented teaching) or concerned teacher behaviours which were not focused on any individual (e.g., the effect of frequently ending lessons early or beginning them late). We need to recognize that the way of responding to an individual child will have an effect on the *rest* of the class. This may be relevant, for example, in the case of unofficial sanctions. Experimental studies provide ample demonstrations of the fact that punishment can be a most effective way of controlling behaviour (see Walters and Grusec, 1977). But in a school context the ways in which punishment is used and the frequency with which it is given will carry messages to *other* children, and create an atmosphere which can run counter to the intended effect on the offending individual.

Taken together, these three aspects of our findings suggest that the importance of the separate school process measures may lie in their contribution to the ethos or climate of the school as a whole.

Concept of ethos

By introducing the concept of an ethos, we mean that it is valuable to think of schools in terms of their characteristics as social organizations (see Getzels, 1969; also Shipman, 1975). Numerous studies have documented the well-nigh universal tendency for individuals in common circumstances to form social groups with their own rules, values, and standards of behaviour (see Newcomb et al., 1969; Sherif and Sherif, 1969). Group influences tend to be quite powerful, and there is a general tendency for people to 'go along' with the majority (see Kelvin, 1969). Indeed, people going against the norm are likely to experience considerable anxiety (Hoffman, 1957). In approaching our findings on school processes we have drawn parallels with a variety of other somewhat similar studies of different institutions such as hospitals, hostels, children's homes, and the like. All these studies have shown that any relatively self-contained organization tends to develop its own culture or pattern; this also applies to secondary schools. We need to consider now how the individual process measures might operate in such a context.

Strictly speaking, in discussing the meaning of our findings on the effects of school values and norms of behaviour, we are restricted to the norms which were characteristic of the particular twelve schools we studied and to the four specific outcomes we measured. However, these measures should be seen only as *indicators* of school success and not as the sole, or even the most important, aims of schooling. Our fifth measure, of patterns of employment, adds an essential additional dimension to outcome, but even so work is just one aspect of life. Schools may see their educational objectives as applying equally to the fostering of an enthusiasm and interest in learning, of confidence and the ability to take responsibility, of adaptability to cope with life changes, of the development of personal relationships, or of individuality. Schools have a choice in the norms they select. Our discussion of the ways in which norms may be established and accepted by pupils is concerned with social mechanisms in schools generally and *not* with the particular norms we assessed.

Norms and values can be established in a variety of different ways. So far as secondary schools are concerned, the chief mechanisms are likely to be: (i) teachers' expectations about the children's work and behaviour, (ii) the models provided by the teacher's own conduct in school, and by the behaviour of the other pupils, and (iii) the feedback that the children receive on what is acceptable performance at the school.

Expectations and standards

Our results suggest that children had better academic success in schools where homework was regularly set and marked, and where the teachers expressed expectations that a high proportion of the children would do well in national examinations. It appears that both general attitudes and specific actions to emphasize academic expectations can play a part here. Children are liable to work better if taught in an atmosphere of confidence that they can and will succeed in the tasks they are set. Of course, in turn, the children's good work will tend to reinforce and support the teacher's high expectations of them.

The same mechanisms apply as much to behaviour as to scholastic success. Thus, giving children responsibility for looking after school books and papers conveys the teacher's expectations that they will behave responsibly, and will take good care of the school property. The findings showed that schools which expected children to take care of their own resources had better behaviour, better attendance, and less delinquency. In a similar way, giving children posts or tasks of responsibility (such as the post of form captain or participation in school assemblies) was associated with better pupil behaviour. The message of confidence that the pupils can be trusted to act with maturity and responsibility is likely to encourage pupils to fulfil those expectations.

Models provided by teachers

Standards of behaviour in school are also set by the behaviour of the staff. Our observations of good care of the buildings, and the willingness of teachers to see pupils about problems at any time, provide some examples of *positive* models. These actions convey the message that the school is valued and thought to be worth keeping clean and in good decorative condition; and that staff appreciate the needs of children sufficiently to give their own time to help them when they experience difficulties. *Negative* models would be provided by teachers starting lessons late and ending them early, and by their use of unofficial physical sanctions. If teachers react with violence to provocation and disruptiveness this may well encourage pupils to do the same. Similarly, if the teachers' own behaviour suggests that they disregard timekeeping, they can scarcely expect good timekeeping and attendance from the pupils.

Of course, teachers are by no means the only available models of behaviour. Secondary school pupils are likely to be influenced by their peers and, when younger, by the behaviour of pupils higher up the school.

Feedback

The feedback that a child receives about what is and what is not acceptable at school will also constitute a powerful influence on his behaviour. Our findings showed that the most immediate and direct feedback in terms of praise or approval had the strongest association with pupil behaviour. Prizes for sport were associated with good attendance but not with any of the other outcomes, and prizes for work were quite unrelated to any of the outcome measures. The amount of punishment showed only weak, and generally nonsignificant, associations with outcome, and when the associations did reach significance, the trend was for higher levels of punishment to be associated with *worse* outcomes. Our results showed some association between prizes and good outcomes – it was just that the effects of classroom praise seemed to be much greater.

Formal punishments (such as canings or being told off by the head) also suffer from drawbacks associated with delay, although the delays are usually less than is the case with prizes. All of the schools in our study used punishments and reprimands fairly frequently, and it is obvious that any school must have effective means of indicating firm disapproval of misbehaviour. However, it does seem to be important that there should be the right balance between reward and punishment. Both have a place, but an excessive use of punishments is likely to be discouraging and to lead to low morale. Praise, rewards, and encouragements need to outweigh the negative sanctions. When giving praise it is important, however, that the currency should be *real*. Children usually know when they have done well or badly and rewards for poor quality work rapidly become devalued and ineffective.

In this connection it is relevant to note that rewards come not only from praise or prizes which are given by staff, but also are implicit in the successful accomplishment of a job well done. It seems important to organize things so that most children are able to succeed most of the time, but, of course, providing a gradient of difficulty so that there is steady progress.

Consistency of school values

Expectations, models, and feedback are all likely to affect the ways in which pupils' behaviour and attitudes develop within a school. The 'atmosphere' of any particular school will be greatly influenced by the degree to which it functions as a coherent whole, with agreed ways of doing things which are consistent throughout the school and which have the general support of all staff.

We had several findings which suggested that this applied in the schools we studied. Outcomes tended to be better when both the curriculum and approaches to discipline were agreed and supported by the staff acting together. Thus, attendance was better and delinquency less frequent in schools where courses were planned jointly. It was not just that this facilitated continuities in teaching (although it did) but also that group planning provided opportunities for teachers to encourage and support one another.

Much the same applied with standards of discipline. Exam successes were more frequent and delinquency less common in schools where discipline was based on general expectations set by the school (or house or department), rather than left to individual teachers to work out for themselves. For obvious reasons, school values and norms are likely to be more effective if it is clear to all that they have widespread support. Discipline will be easier to maintain if the pupils appreciate that it relates to generally accepted approaches and does not simply represent the whims of the individual teacher. The particular rules which are set and the specific disciplinary techniques which are used are probably much less important than the establishment of some principles and guidelines which are both clearly recognizable and accepted by the school as a whole.

The importance of some kind of school-wide set of values and norms of behaviour was also reflected in our findings that in the more successful schools teachers reported that their senior colleagues were aware of matters such as staff punctuality and that they checked that policies were being maintained, as in the setting of homework. This was not a matter of intrusive control or supervision but rather a reflection that staff cared about the way the school functioned. It appeared that an efficient system within which teachers worked harmoniously towards agreed goals was conducive to both good morale and effective teaching.

This was also implicit in our findings on the pattern of decision-making in the schools with better pupil outcomes. The importance of a sense of direction was suggested by the observation that in schools with good outcomes decisions tended to be made at a senior level rather than in the staffroom. On the other hand, in these same schools teachers stated that their views were represented and considered. It seemed necessary that teachers should feel that they had some part in the decision-making process but also that they had sufficient confidence in the staff group as a whole, that they were content for their opinions and suggestions to be expressed by someone else.

It follows from our arguments on the value of cohesive social groups that most of the issues which apply to pupils apply similarly to teachers. They, too, will be influenced by the models, expectations, and feedback from senior staff (and also of course from pupils) and they, too, need to take responsibility in, to feel rewarded by, and to identify with the school. The findings showed that, in themselves, physical conditions (in terms of equipment, storage space, etc.) and time available (such as guaranteed free periods) were not vital – a conclusion which closely parallels that for children. The one feature which was significant was adequate clerical help, which seemed to reflect the extent to which schools took teachers' needs seriously, and attempted to meet them.

In short, it appears helpful for there to be some kind of consensus on how school life should be organized. For there to be an accepted set of norms which applies consistently throughout the school, it is necessary not only to have ways of ensuring that there is joint staff action but also that staff feel part of a group whose values they share.

Pupil acceptance of school norms

As we have seen, pupils are likely to be influenced both by the norms and values they are exposed to at school and also by the degree to which these appear to be consistent throughout the school. The question is what are the features of schools which make it more likely that pupils will share the educational perspective? Our own evidence suggests that the crucial influences will include (i) general conditions for, and staff attitudes to, the pupils, (ii) shared activities between staff and pupils, (iii) pupil positions of responsibility within the school system, and (iv) success and achievement.

General conditions and staff attitudes to pupils

The findings showed that pupil outcomes (especially with respect to behaviour and academic attainment) tended to be better when the schools provided pleasant working conditions for their pupils. This was evident in the significant association between good pupil behaviour and good maintenance of decorations and care of the building generally. Keeping the school clean, tidy, and well painted, with attractive pictures and plants, together with furniture in a good state of repair, seemed to encourage the children to respect their surroundings and behave more appropriately. Similarly, academic attainments were better in schools which provided good pupil conditions in terms of features such as access to a telephone, availability of refreshments, and being allowed in the buildings during breaks.

Staff concern for pupil needs seemed equally important. Thus, children's behaviour was better in schools where teachers were readily available to be consulted by the children about problems, and where many children were in fact seen by teachers. The same issue was evident in the positive association between good pupil outcomes and reports by a high proportion of children that they would consult teachers about a personal problem.

Another aspect of the prevailing atmosphere in a school concerns the staff's response to the children's behaviour and their general evaluation of the pupils' capabilities. We have already noted that outcomes were better in schools where the teachers expected the children to achieve well and where there was substantial use of praise and approval in classroom teaching. These variables were considered earlier in relation to different mechanisms – those associated with expectations and feedback. However, they are also likely to be important in setting the emotional tone of the school and hence in influencing pupil morale. Our findings suggested that pupils behaved better and achieved more when teachers treated them in ways which emphasized their successes and good potential rather than those which focused on their failings and shortcomings.

Shared activities between staff and pupils

We obtained very few measures on the extent of shared activity between staff and pupils, but it was found that schools in which a high proportion of children had been on out-of-school outings had better academic outcomes.

Pupil positions of responsibility

The study findings showed that schools in which a high proportion of children held some kind of responsibility in the school system had better outcomes with respect to both pupil behaviour and examination success. This was evident in terms of the proportion of children who had been form captain or its equivalent and also in terms of the proportion who had taken some kind of active role in a school assembly or other meeting. As already mentioned, giving children these responsibilities is likely to have benefits because it conveys trust in pupils' abilities and because it sets standards of mature behaviour.

Success and achievement

Especially during the later years at school, it is probably also crucial that the pupils are experiencing some success which is both holding them at school and providing them with satisfaction. We have few data which are relevant to this point, but it may be noted that school outcomes on exam success, pupil behaviour and attendance were fairly closely connected. Schools with good academic achievement tended to be more successful in maintaining good attendance and behaviour. It is also pertinent that school attendance rates fell off most sharply in the last school year when national examinations became a major focus for many children. Attendance rates in particular were associated with school factors not incorporated in either our process or balance of intake measures. A consideration of the schools with particularly poor attendance suggests that the relative lack of exam success may be one additional important factor.

Passing exams and being prepared for work may be the most obvious indicators of success at school, but preparation for other aspects of adult life is likely to be equally important. Achievements in activities as varied as sports, music, and drama all play a part in this. But success should not be measured merely in terms of specific task skills or paper accomplishments – even across a wide range of activities. The taking of responsibility in the school is also a most important area for success and a valuable training for the taking of responsibilities later.

Contra-school peer groups

The factors we have discussed up to this point have all related to ways in which schools may be able to increase pupil involvement in school-defined aims. Many other writers, however, have seen schools as inevitably, and perhaps even primarily, centres of conflict. But it would be wrong to see the tensions and conflicts as similarly intense in all schools. They are not. Our observations showed marked variations between the twelve schools in the ways they functioned and, as we have discussed, the results pointed to a variety of means by which schools could increase harmony, good behaviour, and academic success.

On the other hand, it would be misleading to see matters as entirely in the hands of the teaching staff. We found that outcomes tended to be worse (and especially that delinquency tended to be more frequent) in schools with a particularly high proportion of intellectually less-able children. Outcomes tended to be less good if the bulk of the school populations consisted of children in the lowest ability band (as determined *prior* to secondary school transfer).

The twelve schools included some which functioned very well and yet had intakes which were relatively disadvantaged. Of course, teachers' responses to their classes *are* determined in part by the characteristics of the children they teach. It would be simplistic to see the process as a one-way interaction. On the other hand, the measures of intake balance were much more strongly correlated with pupil outcome than they were with school process. The inference to be drawn is that the main mechanism was likely to be of some other kind – probably related to some aspects of the peer group itself.

In our school population, as in others which have been studied, there was a strong tendency for first offences to be committed in groups. It may be that, in this way, delinquency 'spreads' as children come into contact with others who are already delinquent, and who constitute a peer group in which delinquent activities are an accepted form of behaviour. The same process could operate with respect to patterns of poor attendance and lack of commitment to school work.

On the other hand, there are reasons for supposing that this does not constitute the whole explanation. It is pertinent in this connection that a socially disadvantaged intake to schools was *not* significantly associated with a high rate of delinquency in spite of the fact that, at an *individual* level, occupational level of the family was a good predictor of delinquency. In other words, the mix which most strongly predisposed to delinquency was *not* a mix of boys with the highest individual predisposition to delinquency. This suggests the operation of some other mechanism.

Perhaps part of the explanation lies in the effects of scholastic failure on feelings of personal worth. For children who are unlikely to gain any examination passes there may be few advantages in being part of an institution in which one of the explicit objectives is academic success and in which the norm is scholastic commitment. If the intake to any school consists of a very high proportion of less-able children there will be an increased tendency for the formation of nonacademic social groups indifferent or opposed to academic success.[1]

Several implications for educational practice follow. First, it is evident that there are considerable disadvantages in an educational system which allows such an uneven distribution of children that some schools have intakes with a heavy preponderance of the intellectually less able.[2] (Efforts to equalize social mix seem less important.) Second, there are likely to be problems in a system which is geared to success in exams which are set at such a level that two-fifths of the child population are expected to fail.

We found that delinquency rates were lower in schools where the majority of children remained in the same form or set throughout their schooling. Possibly, by ensuring the relative stability of pupil groups, these schools had increased the likelihood that the pupils would become involved with the school and its aims, in a way which other schools which lacked this kind of secure point for identification within the school had failed to do. It also seems possible that schools can do something to counter the effects of any contra-school peer group influence by increasing the rewards and satisfaction open to the less-able children in the school, and by taking steps to ensure that their particular needs are met. Although some conflict is probably inevitable (and may be useful) in all schools, it does seem that there may be a variety of ways in which it can be prevented from becoming counter-productive.

We may conclude from the whole study that the results carry the strong implication that schools can do much to foster good behaviour and attainments and that, even in a disadvantaged area, schools can be a force for the good.

Notes

1. Also, of course, the same factors may lead schools to redefine their objectives in terms other than academic success.
2. It has been ILEA policy for a number of years now to obtain a more even distribution of children of different measured ability in the schools.

References

Getzels, J.W., 1969, A social psychology of education. In Lindzey, G. and Aronson, E. (eds) *The Handbook of Social Psychology* (second edition), Vol 5: *Applied Social Psychology*. London: Addison-Wesley, pp. 459–537.

Hoffman, M.L., 1957, Conformity as a dense mechanism and a formal resistance to genuine group influence, *Journal of Personality*, 25, 412–424.

Kelvin, P., 1969, *The Bases of Social Behaviour: An approach in terms of order and value*, London: Holt, Rinehart & Winston.

Newcomb, T.M., Turner, R.H., and Converse, P.E., 1969, *Social Psychology: The Study of Human Interaction*, London: Holt, Rinehart & Winston.

Sherif, M. and Sherif, C.W., 1969, *Social Psychology*, London: Harper & Row.

Shipman, M.D., 1975, *The Sociology of the School*, (2nd edition), London: Longmans.

Walters, G.C. and Grusec, J.E., 1977, *Punishment*, San Francisco: Freeman.

CHAPTER 3.5

POWER AND PARTICIPATORY DECISION-MAKING IN SELECTED ENGLISH SCHOOLS*
James A. Conway[1]

This study attempted to clarify the relationship of power of school heads and participation of English teachers in school decisions. A deliberate sample of eight schools was drawn from the schools in the northwest of England. The major criteria for selection were: size (medium to large); location (urban-suburban and reasonably accessible from Manchester); and representatives of the types of schools found in that geographic area. A descriptive analysis indicated that English teachers do perceive themselves participating in most decision areas. At a second level of analysis the relationship between status and intensity of participation was computed with $r = .544$ for the 103 members of staff ($p < .001$). An implication is that competence is a criterion for status position, leading to involvement and hence power in the social system. The final analysis dealt with implications of use of power from a description of participation patterns. The clusterings found lend credence to the belief that English heads are controlling those areas of power where tangible rewards and punishments are evident. They appear to be supporting participatory management in such other areas as those where teachers do not desire involvement or those which carry minimal expenditure of organizational resources.

Introduction

Ever since the now classic studies by Coch and French[2] on overcoming worker resistance to change there has been an increasing emphasis placed on the participation of workers in certain areas of management decision-

* *The Journal of Educational Administration*, Vol XVI, No. 1, May 1978, pp. 80–96.

making. Such participation has been primarily noted in the industrial and business domains throughout the world but only recently is it evident in schools.[3] In England, Sharma documented that while teachers reported some participation occurring as early as 1963 these same teachers indicated that considerably greater participation was desired.[4]

In 1967 the Plowden Report urged more consultation between heads and assistant teachers at the primary level[5] while the Donnison Report in 1970 urged similar practices at the secondary level.[6] Despite this official urging from government and the business-industrial movement towards participation as a desired mode of behaviour, Musgrove in 1971 still saw fit to characterize headmasters as 'petty despots'.[7] One of his strongest conclusions was:

> Teachers, then, would like more say in the way schools are run. This is true of both secondary and primary teachers; but the latter see the head as wielding more power and would be prepared to have more in their hands.[8]

This view of the English head as a powerful figure is underscored by Easthope in his view in 1975 of the English head as a 'sovereign head'.[9] Easthope's conclusion is that 'the power exercised by the head in an English school is formidable, and the head can be compared to the sovereign of a state whose powers are limited only by the willingness of his subjects to obey his commands but whose right to give commands is not disputed by his subjects.'[10]

In contrast to this view of 'sovereign power' is the view expressed by George Baron in a paper prepared for the *Newsletter* of the University Council of Educational Administration in 1974. Drawing upon the narrative of a few heads of schools as indicative of his perspective Baron states: 'The distinctive English acceptance of the headmaster as "captain of his ship" has been long under challenge and various forms of participatory leadership have developed.'[11] Still further indication of the significance of participatory decision-making in the emerging leadership of schools is found through the Open University's *Management in Education* Units.[12]

It is around this difference in thought that the present study was formulated. That is, what is a reasonably accurate characterization of the English headmaster – petty despot or participatory leader? Is it likely that the type of leader that Musgrove depicts would support participation of teachers in the fundamental decision areas of the schools? Studies in both America and Ireland have indicated that participation appears to be a norm or at the very least an evolving norm.[13] Is this also the case for England and perhaps the fundamental support for Baron's observation? If in fact such is the case, that is, that participation is a norm as identified by teachers and masters, then a subsequent question is whether or not such participation is being conducted as the Donnison Report urges, 'with due regard for seniority and the primacy of the headmaster'.[14]

More precisely, the purposes of this study were:

1 to establish the type and extent of participation in decision-making in a cross-section of English schools;
2 to consider status levels of teachers within the hierarchy of the school as an indicator of power and the relationship to the school decision-making; and
3 to analyse the differences between present and desired participation by teachers to ascertain if a pattern of involvement by area is evident with implications for understanding the apparent dilemma of sovereign heads and participatory leadership.

Conceptual background

Participation

As was indicated earlier, participation has had much emphasis since the 1948 studies of Coch and French. Likert gave the concept central focus in his *New Patterns of Management* (1961) while Tannenbaum, Sharma, Bridges, Alutto-Belasco, and Conway continued development and refinement of the concept.[15] One of the more important distinctions that has been made is the effects of 'objective' participation versus 'subjective' participation.

The notion of *objective* participation is that an outside observer can identify actions and events that the *observer contends* indicate the type and level of participatory decision-making that is operating in the organization. Thus, for example, Tannenbaum and Schmidt identify a hierarchy of participatory behaviours that they associate with leadership. They have constructed a continuum from 'task-oriented leader' to 'relationship-oriented' that essentially includes the following hierarchically arranged examples of participatory decision-making behaviour that an observer *might* believe he is seeing:[16]

1 Leader makes decision and announces it.
2 Leader 'sells' decision.
3 Leader presents the idea(s) for the decision then invites question to clarify.
4 Leader proposes tentative decision which is subject to group modification.
5 Leader indicates precipitating problem, gets alternatives from group, then selects and alters for a decision.
6 Leader defines the limits for the decision and requests a decision within these limits from the group.
7 Leader permits subordinates to function in a decision-making capacity within the limits mutually defined by superior and group.

This approach to identifying participation obliterates the individual effects of the participation. We lose the results such behaviour elicits among those acting in the system. Thus, at level six above, an individual might feel that (s)he was being used or manipulated by the leader. That is, the participation was *objectively real*, but *subjectively false*.

The framework employed in this study was *individual-subjective* where each subject or participant identified whether or not participation was occurring for that participant, followed by a grouping of perceptions to attain an estimate for the school. For some persons, if the head should merely pass them in the hall and ask their opinion, they might feel that they have had substantial input to the decision outcome, that is, that they have genuinely participated. This might be contrary to what the outside observer sees but, nevertheless, the participation is psychologically real in that the effects are felt by the individual.

For this first part of this study the question to be answered was:

Q1: Is participation in decision-making perceived as occurring in all schools in the sample; that is, is participation a norm for the cross-sectional sample of English schools?

Power, status, and participation

While power is a term that is not consistently defined, it is generally recognized as a concept closely related to *authority* and *influence*.[17] Both power and authority are forms of influence. Authority is the right a manager has to make decisions and expect compliance. Power is the force that backs up the authority. Much managerial power is in the form of control over 'things such as pay, promotions, employment, termination, and so on'.[18] Thus the potential for compliance is likely to increase as the availability of sanctions through resources increases.

Empirically, Smith and Sandler found that in certain schools power was a significant contributor to the status of individuals in the school hierarchy.[19] But it also seems logical that the relationship would work both ways, that is, that those possessing status by virtue of position in the organizational hierarchy would be key elements in a communication hierarchy and therefore in a position of power.[20] Furthermore, it would seem likely that the administrative head would confer more frequently with those individuals within the organization who have the power to influence others.[21] Thus, assuming, as it seems reasonable to do, that the greater an individual's social power the higher the status, we could predict that there would be a direct and positive relationship between the level or intensity of an individual's perceived participation in school decisions and the status level of that individual in the school.

On the other hand, Conway found that in selected schools in Ireland the relationship between status and participation, while positive and direct, was only a weak association ($r = .16$ for $n = 55$). He offered as a possible explanation that the positions in the school hierarchy in that country may best be viewed as indicators of 'ascribed status' which may not be congruent with the social power or 'achieved status'.[22] Furthermore, while Smith and Sandler indicated that *perceived* competence was a major determinant of status,[23] they were apparently referring to *achieved* status. So too was Homans when he indicated that once a person has achieved status that such may then contribute to his ability to exert influence over others.[24] Thus it would seem logical to conclude that perhaps status positions in Ireland were assigned on the basis of criteria other than competence. Since this may well be the situation in any school organization or any country, a research question was posed to direct this phase of the study:

Q2:   Is the status level of English teachers positively associated with their self-perceived frequency of participation in school decisions?

Participation patterns and headmaster power

The third purpose of this study was to ascertain insights about any discrepancies noted between teachers' desires for participation and their present perceived participation in the school decision areas, followed by some speculation concerning the implications for the power position of the English head. By looking at the discrepancy scores for each area of decision-making for each of the schools in the sample, it should be possible to determine which decision areas tend to be reserved to the decision-making of the head. Of particular interest is the extent to which the areas of 'staff appointment' and 'staff timetabling' are shared with the relevant school personnel.

Blau and Schoenherr contend that in more modern organizations the area of recruitment of employees is a 'crucial responsibility and a major mechanism of control'.[25] They argue that an organization can recruit most anyone then rule with an iron fist, or the organization can be staffed with specialists or experts which then diminishes the need for tight-fisted control. They go on to indicate, however, that the *allocation of personnel* which is in essence what timetabling is about, is the 'ultimate mechanism of organizational control . . . in the sense that reliance primarily on it is the polar opposite of Weberian bureaucratic control through a chain of command backed with coercive sanctions'.[26]

The third question, then, is a general direction of concern to guide the analysis:

Q3: What are the patterns of involvement in the English schools sampled and what do they contribute to an understanding of headmaster power or control?

Procedures

Instruments

The primary instrument employed was an adaptation by Conway[27] of a Decisional Condition Questionnaire developed by Alutto and Belasco in 1972.[28] The adapted version contained the following eleven areas within which teachers could identify their involvement in decision-making:

1 Appointment of new staff
2 Preparation of school or department budgets
3 Textbook selection for department or school
4 Resolution of pupil academic or personal problems
5 Construction of individual teaching timetables
6 Resolution of staff grievances

  7 Adoption of new teaching methods

  8 Decisions about new building facilities

  9 Resolutions of problems involving community groups (as parent or citizen groups)

10 Resolution of problems with administrative services (as clerks, typists, etc.)

11 Decisions concerning general teaching policy

For each of the eleven decision areas a question was stated in the following format: (in this example for decision area 1)

  a When a new faculty member is hired in your school or department, would you be involved in making such a decision?
    Never — Sometimes — Often — Always —
  b Do you want to be involved in making such decisions?
    Never — Sometimes — Often — Always —

This adapted version of the questionnaire allowed for several participation measures. By counting only the 'a' portions of responses an estimate of the present level of participation that that teacher perceives may be computed. Viewing the difference between the 'b' (desired) and 'a' (present) provides a measure of how satisfied the teacher is with his or her involvement in decision-making.[29]

With each questionnaire the respondent was asked to indicate his position in the school hierarchy as:

1 Deputy

2 Department head

3 Graded post (a position of responsibility as Director of Games, etc.)

4 Teacher or assistant master/mistress

5 Other (with a request to specify his title)

Samples and subjects

A sample of nine schools was selected to approximate a cross-section of schools in the northwest of England. The following criteria were employed in making the selection: (a) size, such that medium to very large schools were represented; (b) location, that the schools were within reasonable access from Manchester; and (c) representatives of school types, that is, that there were comprehensive, grammar, and secondary modern schools included. It is recognized that since the schools were not drawn in a random fashion that extreme care must be taken in interpretation of data and in drawing generalizations. On the other hand the schools that finally participated (see Table 5) seem to be reasonably representative of the types of schools that are in evidence in that segment of England. All of the schools had good returns of the questionnaires except schools numbered 2 and 6. The low returns only take on importance when considering the school by school patterns which are discussed later.

Within the schools the head was interviewed and permission was requested to administer the adapted Decision Condition Questionnaire to the teaching staff. If permission was granted, as it was in 8 of the 9 schools, then the head was asked to distribute the questionnaires to a random sample of the staff. The returns of the teaching staff when viewed against their

Table 5 Schools, staff size, and percentage of returns

School code* no.	Type of school	Staff size		Percent† of returns
		Full-time	Part-time	
1	Urban infant	10	5	70
7	Suburban infant	6	7	83
2	Urban comprehensive	68	29	17
3	Urban secondary modern	43	5	40
4	Suburban girls grammar	43	26	77
6	Suburban boys grammar	43	12	27
8	Suburban comprehensive	54	20	70
9	Urban split-site comprehensive	91	18	70
5	Suburban comprehensive	94	7	—‡

* Code numbers were assigned as a school was visited and, therefore, indicate a sequence of visitation.
† Computed on the basis of a random distribution of thirty questionnaires to full-time staff.
‡ School number 5 was omitted as the head would not give permission to administer the teacher participation questionnaire.

position in the school (see Table 6) would tend to indicate that the upper levels of the status hierarchy may well be more heavily represented.

Table 6   Distribution of respondents among status levels

Status level	Assigned score	Number indicating this status
Deputy head	4	8
Department head	3	39
Graded post	2	35
Teacher or assistant master/mistress	1	21
	Total number of respondents	103

Results

The findings of this study will be presented to parallel the purposes stated earlier. First to be reported will be the descriptive outcomes, followed by the test of the research question of status versus participation, and finally the visual examination of participatory patterns for insights as to power and control of heads of schools.

Extent and type of participation

The average intensity of participation for *each* of the eight schools ranged from 'sometimes involved' to 'often involved'. In only one decision area in one school was there a case where no teaching staff saw themselves involved in the decision. That school was infant school 1 and the area where no one perceived any inputs concerned new building facilities. In general, then, it seems reasonable to respond to the first question with a positive response, that is, that some form of participation in decision-making seems to be evident in all of the school types sampled. Participation is definitely the rule rather than the exception for this cross-section of English schools.

Each of the eleven decision areas is considered next with a brief description of the finding and a possible interpretation.

1 *Participation in staff appointments:* This item was tied for eighth lowest in terms of present participation. While both infant and secondary staffs

indicated that some participation was evident, they went on to indicate that this was the second highest area of deprivation. That is, they generally desired considerably more input in this decision area than they were presently experiencing. Burgess has indicated that staff have traditionally had no input in the appointment of a new head.[30] It appears that this is also the case with respect to the appointment of new staff.

2 *Participation in budget preparation:* The participation for both infant and secondary staffs seemed reasonably high in this area. There was still, on the average, a considerably higher desired involvement (ranking fourth) although not as large a deviation as in the first decision area.

3 *Participation in textbook selection:* Textbook selection showed the least deviation from the desired level of participation and was also the highest for present level of involvement. In general, teachers indicated that they participated with high frequency in selecting texts and this was the amount of participation that they wanted. This was somewhat surprising since, in some communities in America, the selection of textbooks by teachers has been challenged by community people resulting in conflicts between administration and teaching characterized as infringements on academic freedom.[31]

The data for the English schools could mean that teachers regularly come together for selecting texts and thus all parties have input and with that input, an increased opportunity for coordination and articulation from one level to another. However, it would seem that if that were the case there would be more teachers expressing some discontent or discrepancy as such process would require some teachers 'giving in' or submitting to group demands thus leading to a somewhat higher state of dissatisfaction. Therefore, the more likely interpretation of the data is that English teachers enjoy relatively high autonomy in textbook selection. That condition may lead to the censorship-academic freedom conflict mentioned above.

4 *Participation in resolving pupil problems:* Both infant and secondary staffs indicated high involvement in this area at present (third highest) and also indicated a desire to maintain that level of involvement. This appears to be a very healthy picture and a very professional one. It would seem to indicate an acceptance on the part of staff of their responsibility for 'pastoral care' or the guidance function.

5 *Participation in constructing teaching timetables:* Timetable construction was anticipated as one of the more sensitive areas. One headmaster

commented that he constructed the timetables and he was not about to lose that area of 'power'. This decision area fell about in the middle for present involvement. While there was a considerable discrepancy between the present level and the desired level of involvement (third greatest deviation), it was still not as high as the above comment might have led us to anticipate.

6 *Participation in resolving staff grievances:* This was one of the two decision areas where some degree of saturation was evident. Saturation occurs when persons are involved in decisions to an extent *greater* than desired.[32] In one of the infant schools teachers indicated that they would prefer less participation than they presently experience in the resolution of grievances. In all other schools, the members of staff indicated that they presently enjoy about as much input as they want. It may well be that the staff realize that the difficulties of helping adults resolve problems are not necessarily rewarding and, though willing to help, assistant masters do not desire high involvement in this sensitive administrative area.

7 *Participation in adopting new teaching methods:* Teaching method selection is the one other area where some saturation was noted. In the suburban infant school the teachers indicated that they would appreciate somewhat less participation than at present. This was an open-spaced primary where, perhaps, the novelty and experimental nature of the school was now assuming a greater proportion of staff time than they felt it should. For the other infant school and the secondary schools the level of participation was quite high (ranking number 2) and the desired involvement only slightly higher.

8 *Participation in decisions about building facilities:* While this is the number one concern area (greatest deviation), it may be that the concern was escalated by the number of teachers responding from schools badly in need of repair. This was also the only area where an entire staff indicated that they presently have no participation at all and desire a very high level of involvement. It appears that those responsible for planning and refurbishing school buildings might well consider involving teaching staffs so that their teaching needs can be identified and met through the building structures.

9 *Participation in eliminating community group problems:* The English teachers responding in this study indicate that they were neither highly involved in resolving community problems nor did they desire such

involvement. This seems to be an 'urban' attitude of noninvolvement with community and might be contrasted if data were collected from some rural or semirural schools. The results might also indicate a disregard for the recommendations made in the Plowden Report that there should be more participation by parents in their children's education.[33]

10 *Participation in resolving problems with administrative services:* It may be that this is a continuation of area 6 (resolving staff grievance) for neither infant nor secondary members of staff expressed a desire for high involvement. Nor did they perceive themselves as substantially involved now. If this is associated with area 6, it would follow that the staffs do not see involvement with adult problems as their domain. Again, perhaps by default, this seems to be viewed as the responsibility of the school administrators.

11 *Participation in general policy decisions:* In both infant and secondary schools the present perceived involvement was, surprisingly, right at mid-point; that is, it was neither high nor low for either the present or desired conditions. The teachers see themselves reasonably involved now, desire somewhat more but do not want total participation in all policy decisions.

Teacher status and participation

The second question that directed this study asked if the status level of English teachers was associated with their self-perceived frequency of participation in school decisions. The status level of each respondent was assigned a number from 1 to 4 in accordance with the level that they assigned to themselves. An assistant master or mistress (teacher) was assigned the number one; two was given to those individuals who indicated they had a graded post position (such as 'games master' or 'communication coordinator', and the like); all department heads or house masters were assigned a three; and four was set for the deputy head. Some consideration was given to a differential assignment of numbers based upon the 'status' of the school as Easthope indicated for his study of school hierarchies;[34] but the concern in the present study was not the status position of the individual in a community of scholars or the society but rather the hierarchical or social power position within the school.

The correlation of the 103 members of staff was $r = .544$ significant at .001 even for a two-tailed test of significance. Thus, with a high degree of assurance, we can assert that the higher persons are in the status hierarchy of the school the more they find themselves involved in the school-related decision-making.

Patterns of participation

The third purpose of the study was to examine or determine whether there were patterns of participation that were discernible and, further, if such could provide insights for understanding headmaster power. The results relative to pattern are reported here while the discussion and implications for headmaster power are reserved for the final section.

The main levels of desired and present participation were computed for the participating schools. When the differences between the present and desired levels were examined together with the present levels of participation, there appeared to emerge three distinct clusters. These clusters are shown below in Table 7.

Table 7   Decision areas, present and desired teacher participation, and participation differences

Decision areas	Present participation	Desired participation	Degree of difference of desired vs present
Textbook selection	high	high	small
Pupil problems	high	high	small
Teaching methods	high	high	small
General school policy	mid-high	mid-high	small
Staff grievances	low	low	small
Community problems	low	low	small
Admin. staff problems	low	low	small
Appointment of staff	low	high	large
Building plans	low	mid-high	large
Budget preparation	mid-high	high	medium
Teaching timetables	middle	mid-high	medium

The first cluster is made up of those decision areas where the teaching staff on the average see themselves highly involved and further, that that level of involvement is consistent with their desired intensity of participation. The decision areas in the cluster are those directly related to the process or act of teaching where classroom decisions and teacher inputs would be a *sine qua non*. In the second cluster are areas where the staff have not found themselves involved to any extent nor do they appear to wish for much higher involvement. An examination of these decision areas shows them to be all associated with adult problems, indirectly affecting the teaching-learning process and apparently areas that teachers would prefer to remain in the domain of the administration or to have staff participate only as necessary or as invited to do so. The third cluster contains the decision areas of 'staff appointment', 'building plans', 'budget preparation', and 'teaching timetable preparation'. Here are found fairly substantial differences between present and desired levels of involvement and, as the areas are examined, they appear to be those where personnel selection, allocation, and physical resources are involved. The cluster appears to be composed of areas useful for reward or punishment.

In an attempt to further refine patterns the individual school scores for level of participation as well as the discrepancy measures for each school were computed and are reported in Table 8. To read the table the first school will be examined. School No. 9, which is the largest secondary school, had an average participation level of 2.33 for Textbook Selection. Since the range for participation is from 0 to 3 it can be seen that the 2.33 is a very high participation score. The high participation of teachers in that decision area for School No. 9 is further clarified by viewing the 2.33 against the average for all of the secondary schools (fourth column from the right-hand side of the table). Since the average for all of the secondary schools is 2.46 it is now possible to interpret the score of School No. 9 as high but lower than the average participation level. Inspecting further it is evident that all of the scores in the first cluster for School No. 9 are reasonably high but still lower than average. The second cluster scores are quite low, indicating that there is not very much participation by staff in two of the three decision areas. It should also be noted that there are no asterisks for the first two clusters, indicating that the teachers, for all of these decision areas, were reasonably satisfied with their level of input.

The last cluster is the one where asterisks are found most frequently for all of the schools. For School No. 9 the teachers indicate fairly low level of

Table 8   Decision Areas, Intensity of Present Participation, and Participation Differences by Schools

| Decision Areas | Secondary | | | | | | | Primary | | |
| | Schools Arranged from Largest to Smallest | | | | | | | | | |
	9	2b	8	4	6b	3	AVG.	7	1	AVG.
Textbook selection	2.33a	2.00	2.33	2.70	2.75	2.67	2.46	1.60	2.42	2.01
Pupil problems	1.95	1.60	1.91	2.00	1.75	2.17	1.90	2.20	2.71	2.46
Teaching methods	1.86	2.00	2.24	2.17	2.38	1.92	2.01	2.40	2.29	2.35
General school policy	1.38	1.80	1.48	1.74	1.50	1.67	1.60	1.80	2.14	1.97
Staff grievances	1.90	1.60	1.10	1.35	1.13	1.17	1.38	1.40	1.58	1.49
Community problems	.71	.80*	1.00	.74	.75	.75	.79	1.00	1.29	1.15
Admin. staff problems	.67	.20	.57	.39	.75	.33*	.49	.40	.40	.40
Appointment of staff	.86**	1.40*	1.43*	1.35	1.75	.67**	1.24*	.80	.42**	.60*
Building plans	.95**	1.20	1.00	.78**	1.38	.83**	1.02*	1.00	.00**	.50**
Budget preparation	1.43*	1.20	1.71*	1.48	2.25	2.08	1.69	1.40	.42**	.91**
Teaching timetables	1.29*	1.60*	1.38*	1.82*	1.60	1.25**	1.49*	1.80	2.71	2.23

* A single asterisk indicates the staff in the school felt *highly* deprived in their participation in this decision area.

** A double asterisk indicates the staff in the school felt *very highly* deprived in their participation in this decision area.

a The participation score has a potential range of 0 to 3.

b These two schools had returns lower than 40% and consequently must be interpreted with caution.

involvement for 'appointment of staff' and building inputs and these are two areas where these same teachers feel very highly deprived, that is, they would prefer a much higher level of involvement. With respect to budget and timetables they see themselves somewhat more involved but would still prefer a higher level of involvement.

Now in looking across the schools it appears that the two major areas of teacher dissatisfaction with their decision-making participation are for teaching timetable preparation (five of the six secondary schools indicated high or very high deprivation) and for appointment of staff (four of the six schools showed deprivation scores). There were too few primary schools to discern a pattern but it is interesting to note that in the two included here the greatest deprivation, on the average, was found in the decision areas relating to budget and building facilities. The implication of these and the other results reported above will be discussed in the next section.

Discussion and implications

As the results were reported in three sections, so too will they be presented for discussion. The first of these sections deals mainly with the descriptive data and responds to the question of whether or not participation is a norm for the schools.

Participation in English schools

The results indicated that all schools had at least minimal participation in all of the decision areas. This tends to support Baron's observation of an evolving participative leadership in schools in England.[35] This does not necessarily rule out the contention of Musgrove that the heads are essentially 'petty despots', but the results do indicate a sharing of power and a wide distribution of involvement. But what of the quality of involvement?

Musgrove has said that if schools are to be considered 'potent' then '. . . more teachers must be able to take final decisions, or have a genuine voice in such decisions which relate to the circumstances in which they work'.[36] The data from this study indicate that teachers perceive themselves significantly involved in a variety of decision areas. Do the data indicate teachers being able to take final action? to make final decisions? No, but Musgrove's alternative would ask then if their input is, indeed, *genuine*. As indicated earlier the notion of 'real' or 'genuine' input must be viewed from the perspective of the individual experiencing the participation and, therefore, the data would seem to support an interpretation of *genuine* or real involvement.

It should be noted again that the sample of schools was deliberate rather than random and thus generalizations should be treated as hypothesis-generating rather than hypothesis-confirming. Nevertheless, even with a deliberately selected cross-sectional sample, to find participation in all schools where entry was permitted, in all types of schools and of all sizes, in both urban and suburban locations, is noteworthy. At the very least we can suggest that participation is possible with even the largest of schools, contrary to the expectation which some promote that largeness and dehumanization are necessary correlates.

At a conceptual level the findings lend credibility to the view that participatory management is to be expected rather than suspected in school organizations. Miller has indicated that proponents of Theory Y or nonauthoritarian administrators '. . . firmly believe that organizational decision making will evolve in this direction . . .'[37] Indeed if the system perspective is adopted wherein the organization is seen as akin to a living organism, then it becomes obvious that a certain level of participation is a *sine qua non* for organismic existence. Cannon's concept of homeostasis might be considered as a form of decentralized decision-making where certain bodily functions are not exercised by the cerebral cortex but by lower levels of the decider system.[38]

Teacher status and participation

The result reported of a correlation of .544 between the status of the staff in the school and their intensity or level of participation is what might be expected in a system where worker relationships are of a personal nature *and* where there is a high discretion in the superior's application or enforcement of system rules. Gibson indicates that this particular system relationship, which he labels 'permissive personalism', tends to encourage conforming behaviour which in turn promotes an image of trustworthiness and thus enhances the individual's level in the system.[39] It would also seem to follow that the higher the status position in the school hierarchy the more these persons are perceived as holding social power. That is, these persons are seen as competent to influence a change in the system and they are, consequently, persons to be consulted with in making decisions. If true, this would indicate that more than length of service was used for promotion in the system, at least for those included in the study. Furthermore, conversation with heads of schools tended to support competence as a criterion for promotion. Some heads indicated that they would frequently reserve graded post allocations so that they could use these posts when they wanted to retain a particularly competent teacher.

In contrast to this use of power for rewarding competence it is useful to recall that, in Ireland, length of service has been employed as almost a single criterion for promotion to posts of responsibility. In the schools of that country it was found in a similar study that the relationship between status and participation of teachers was only .16.[40] Such single-criterion systems, where heads are either denied the power to reward and retain members of staff or also choose not to exercise such powers, may find the results dysfunctional in the longer course of time. It is certainly more advantageous for the head to know whom to consult with and expect that the individual will be not only competent but also hold influence in the system. This may be an example where the exercise of the heads' power in a reasonable fashion contributes to a cohesive end, especially as the power is shared within the system.

Patterns and power

If any generalization can be made from the data generated in this study it may be that teachers in secondary schools see the head retaining most control in the area of allocation and selection of human resources (appointments of staff and preparation of teaching timetables); while in the primary schools the control seems more in the physical resource areas of budgets and buildings. It may well be that the 'small group' atmosphere of the primary school facilitates teacher-head interactions and creates feeling of intimacy, but this may also force the head to maintain some visible vestige of power through the control of physical resources. This speculation is well beyond the data, however, for the infant schools were neither consistent nor of sufficient number to do more than speculate.

But there were sufficient secondary schools to see that management focused on control of human resources. But why this area for control? Is it that these schools are being administered from a modern management position as indicated by Blau and Schoenherr rather than the Weberian posture of bureaucratic control?[41] If so, then a highly developed training scheme for heads might be expected when in fact formal management training seems to be a relatively recent phenomena in the English system. Is it perhaps an indication of a philosophy of 'Theory X' management that *people* need to be controlled and directed, manipulated as things?[42] If so this might support both Musgrove and Easthope in the view of the head as a sovereign, petty despot who uses participation for control.[43] Or are the data indicative of a stage of organizational evolution where the last remnants of power are being retained by heads? Or at the evolutionary stage where heads are trying to create a participative climate at the same time as they seek ways to 'exercise control without overriding the professional autonomy of teaching staff'?[44] While the data do not permit a single explanation, we can state that the school heads have clearly retained control over that form of sanction that does most to increase their power and so increase the likelihood of subordinate compliance.

Final note

In summary it seems evident that heads in English schools in the northwest have tended to retain control of both physical and human resources at the same time as there has been development towards participative management. Members of staff perceive themselves sharing in the power, participating in decisions in relation to the position of the staff member in the power-status hierarchy of the school. However, while this study indicates that participation is a reality in the schools, it is important to recall that the manifestations or format of participation are self-defined. The teachers made the decision as to whether or not they were or were not sharing in the decision areas. Thus, while they have indicated that they are presently reasonably satisfied with their intensity of involvement, as they continue to participate and taste the fruits of power, it is likely that their demands for more visible, formal, or frequent participation will intensify. If that assumption holds, that is, that a taste of power increases the desire for more, then it would seem prudent that heads be prepared to facilitate the increased desires of involvement or suffer the cynicism and suspicions of staff with all of the consequences for learning and learners.[45]

The relationship or implications of the findings in this study to the shifts in political power and social expectations will likely be explored by those interested and affected by such shifts, that is, the three major political parties at the local level, the National Association of Schoolmasters followed by the Joint Four and more militant factions of the National Union of Teachers. The findings constitute only a small portion of the data these groups must consider for their political analyses and decisions.

Notes and references

1. The analysis for this study was partially supported by a fellowship from the Research Foundation of the State University of New York. I would also like to acknowledge the helpful comments of Professors R. Oliver Gibson, Mike M. Milstein, and Robert E. Jennings. The paper was first presented at the Annual Meeting of the American Educational Research Association, New York, April 4–8, 1977.
2. Coch, Lester and French, John R.P., 'Overcoming Resistance to Change', *Human Relations*, 1, 1948, pp. 512–532.
3. Musgrove, Frank, *Patterns of Power and Authority in English Education*, London, Methuen and Co., 1971, p. 68.
4. Sharma, Vhitsnhi L., 'A Comparative Study of the Process of Making and Taking Decisions within Schools in the U.K. and U.S.A.', Unpublished doctoral thesis, University of London, 1963.
5. Plowden Report, A Report of the Central Advisory Council for Education, Vol 1, *Children and Their Primary Schools*, HMSO, 1967.

6. Donnison Report, Public Schools Commission: Second Report, Vol. 1, *Report on Independent Day Schools and Direct Grant Grammar Schools*, HMSO, 1970.
7. Musgrove, F., op. cit., p. 70.
8. ibid., p. 79.
9. Easthope, Gary, *Community, Hierarchy and Open Education*, London, Routledge & Kegan Paul, 1975, chapter 3.
10. ibid. p. 37.
11. Baron, George, 'Trends in Educational Administration in Britain', *University Council for Educational Administration Newsletter*, VX, 3, February, 1974, p. 18.
12. The Open University Educational Studies: A Third Level Course, E321, *Management in Education*. See particularly Unit 3 'Schools as Organizations' and Units 4–5 'The Management of Innovation in Schools.'
13. See Conway, James A., 'Test of Linearity Between Teachers' Participation in Decision Making and Their Perceptions of Their Schools as Organizations', *Administrative Science Quarterly*, 21 March, 1976. pp. 130–139; and *Organizational Structure and Teacher Participation in Decision Making in Selected Schools in Ireland*, Social Sciences Research Centre Monograph 8, Galway, Ireland, 1976.
14. In Musgrove, F., op. cit., p. 73.
15. See Likert, Rensis. *New Patterns of Management*, New York, McGraw Hill, 1961; Tannenbaum, Arnol, S. (ed) *Control in Organizations*, New York, McGraw Hill, 1968; Sharma, C.L. op. cit. Bridges, Edwin M. 'Subjective and Objective Aspects of Demands for Involvement', *Administrator's Notebook*, 17, 6, 1969; Alutto, Joseph A., and Belasco, James A., 'Typology for Participation in Organizational Decision Making', *Administrative Science Quarterly*, 17, 1972, pp. 117–125; and Conway, J.A. op. cit.
16. Adapted from Tannenbaum, Robert and Schmidt, Warren H., 'How to Choose a Leadership Pattern', *Harvard Business Review*, March – April, 1958.
17. Bierstedt, Robert, 'An Analysis of Social Power', *American Sociological Review*, December, 1970, p. 733.
18. Sanford, Aubey, C., Hunt, Gary T., and Bracey, Hyler J., *Communication Behaviour in Organizations*, Columbus, Ohio, Charles E. Merrill, 1976, p. 104.
19. Smith, Kenneth B. and Sandler, Howard M., 'Bases of Status in Four Elementary School Faculties', *American Educational Research Journal*, 11, 4, 1974, 317–331.
20. Tronc, K.E., 'A Conceptual Model for the Study of Communication of Authority in a Bureaucratic Education System', *Journal of Educational Administration*, 5, 1967.
21. Tannenbaum, A.S., 'Control in Organization: Individual Adjustment and Organizational Performance', *Administrative Science Quarterly*, 7, 1962.
22. Conway, J.A., *Organizational Structure*, op. cit.
23. Smith, K.B. and Sandler, H.M., op. cit.
24. Homans, George C., *Social Behaviour: Its Elementary Forms*, New York, Harcourt, Brace and World, 1961.
25. Blau, Peter M. and Schoenherr, Richard A., 'New Forms of Power', in Salaman, Graeme and Thompson, Kenneth (eds), *People and Organizations*, London, Longman for the Open University Press, 1973, p. 16.

26. ibid. p. 17.
27. Conway, J.A., *Test of Linearity*, op. cit.
28. Alutto, J.A., and Belasco, J.A. op. cit.
29. ibid. Alutto and Belasco computed the test-retest reliability for the original questionnaire as .86.
30. Burgess, Tyrell, *A Guide to English Schools*, 3rd edition, Middlesex, England, Penguin Books, 1972, p. 73.
31. Hepburn, Mary A., 'A Case Study of Creeping Censorship, Georgia Style', *Phi Delta Kappan*, LV, 9, May, 1974, pp. 611–613.
32. See Conway, J.A., *Test of Linearity* for a discussion of the concept of saturation.
33. Tyrell, B., op. cit., p. 49.
34. Easthope, G., op. cit.
35. Baron, G., op. cit.
36. Musgrove, F., op. cit., p. 13.
37. Miller, James M., 'Living Systems: The Organization', *Behavioural Science*, 17, 1, January, 1972, p. 106.
38. Cannon, Walter B., *The Wisdom of the Body*, New York, W.W. Norton, 1932 and 1963, p. 318.
39. Gibson, R. Oliver, 'A General Systems Formulation of Work Relationships: Implications for Collective Negotiations', *ISR Journal*, 1,3, Summer 1969, pp. 158–171.
40. Conway, J.A., *Organizational Structure*, op. cit.
41. Blau, P.M. and Schoenherr, R.A., op. cit.
42. McGregor, Douglas., *The Human Side of Enterprise*, New York, McGraw-Hill, 1960.
43. Musgrove, F., op. cit., and Easthope, G., op. cit.
44. Davies, Digby, *Schools as Organizations*, Unit 3, The Open University Press, 1976, p. 27.
45. Assuming, of course, that the social-political climate for power sharing and participative decision making is of a supportive nature. See too the discussion on teacher organizations and policy-making in Jennings, Robert, *Education and Politics: Policy-Making in Local Education Authorities*, London, B.T. Batsford, 1977, pp. 106–110.

CHAPTER 3.6

THE SCHOOL AS A HIERARCHY*
Tim Packwood

Criticism of the hierarchy has become *passé*. Authoritarian, anti-individual, anti-professional, inflexible, ineffective, and outdated are just some of the epithets that are levelled. Yet work on the Homes, Schools, and Social Services Project undertaken by the Educational Studies Unit of Brunel University[1] demonstrated both the hierarchy's ubiquity and its complexity as an organizational form in the schools. This chapter, then, attempts to present a fuller picture of the hierarchy in the school situation, describing its components and arguing that the epithets mentioned above are not necessarily deserved.

As is well known, the hierarchy is a time-honoured form of organization for getting work done. While partnerships serve for small-scale operations and collegiates for some highly specialized individual services, the hierarchy is the general structure in all developed cultures for achieving work objectives that are beyond the control of the single individual. Through a series of manager-subordinate relationships it explicitly locates accountability for work.[2] The manager in the hierarchy is accountable not only for his, or her, performance, but also for the work of subordinates. And managers can only carry this accountability if they are given corresponding authority to sanction the work of subordinates – to have a voice in their selection, to assess their work, and to be able to initiate their removal from role.

Articles of management and rules of government made under Section 17 of the 1944 Education Act clearly place managerial accountability for the work of a school on the headteacher. He, or she, is answerable for what goes

* Hierarchy, Anarchy and Accountability: Contrasting Perspectives, *Educational Administration*, Spring 1977, Vol. 5, No. 2, pp. 1–6.

on to the LEA and the governing body.[3] Proponents of the autonomous, self-regulating collegiate should note that this clear locus of accountability would be sacrificed. LEAs and/or governors would be potentially required to have a direct relationship with all qualified teaching staff. This would inevitably make management complicated and time-consuming and would hardly satisfy those who argue for clearer, more accessible and responsive systems of accountability in our public institutions.

In the larger schools there will be additional levels of management in the sense defined above, but it is impossible to generalize regarding their location.[4] The Burnham system identifies salary gradings which, although reflecting judgements on competence and work, are not the same as managerial positions. So much depends on the individual institution; upon its history, geography, size, staff, and the preferences of its policy-makers. In so far as it is possible to speculate it would appear that secondary schools approach two levels of management, a headteacher with a head of department on the academic side and with a head of house or year for pastoral work. But there are many exceptions. Some teachers feel that only the headteacher can occupy a managerial position while in other situations deputy heads and/or heads of buildings or component subschools may well occupy intervening levels of management.

The presence of the managerial relationship does not necessarily imply authoritarianism. First, the formalization of authority in a working relationship says nothing about the style through which the authority is exercised. The presence of authority is a prerequisite for authoritarianism but it must be remembered that manager and subordinate, headteacher and teacher, are mutually interdependent. The success of the former depends on the latter and vice versa. Any manager, therefore, who consistently ignores or tramples on the feelings of his, or her, subordinates is most unwise. Secondly, there are limits to the application of authority. No manager can so define a subordinate's role that there is no room for the exercise of discretion and judgement. And if this were to be attempted the manager would in effect be doing the subordinate's job and thus neglecting other aspects of his, or her, own work. It is a strength of the hierarchy that managers can adjust the room for discretion in their subordinate's work to match emerging capacities and capabilities. As a general rule, newcomers to the institution have their work prescribed, and are watched, fairly closely. They are then given more scope when they have proved themselves.[5] In the teacher's case this discretion, inherent in work, is strengthened by that accruing from their professional status. As professionals it is expected that teachers are competent to decide how to meet the educational needs of the children with whom they work. Clearly this freedom is limited. There are regulations to be followed, syllabi and timetables will be laid down, and various resource constraints must be observed, but the art of actually teaching or providing pastoral care is a matter for the individual teacher alone. In England this professional area is not well defined. There is no one body to set and monitor binding standards, rather these emerge from the work of teaching institutions, from Her Majesty's Inspectors and local authority advisers, from the exhortations of advisory committees, and, perhaps most important, from the norms of local institutional practice. As Hughes has argued,[6] the headteacher can have an important role as leading professional as well as chief executive.[7]

Clearer enunciation of professional standards would certainly help define the teacher's freedom. Indeed all the signs suggest that if teachers do not take this on others will do it for them. Freedom would also be strengthened if there were a clearer recognition that all members of an institution, managers and subordinates alike, have an interest in the way that policy is developing. Jaques suggests[8] that institutions require a formalized procedure through which the most senior manager can negotiate the policy to be adopted with all the staff involved or their representatives. As has been implied earlier, without staff acceptance policy implementation is not going to be of the best.[9] Clearly there would be an important role for the teacher unions in this process. So far the argument has attempted to show some of the potential strengths within the managerial relationship and to rebut some of the criticisms so often made. Yet the hierarchy is far more than a system of manager-subordinate relationships, including a wide and complex structure of lateral relationships. Understanding of these is vital to any consideration of how total school services impact on the child. Here we can identify:[10]

* Managerial assistant relationships, the assistant being accountable for helping a manager perform some aspect of his, or her, work without taking on full accountability for the work of other subordinates or the authority to sanction their work. Two classes have been identified:

  staff officer, concerned with particular specialized aspects of work, for example, programming or personnel;

supervisory staff, potentially concerned with the whole range of the manager's work.[11]

* Coordinating relationships, where someone is made accountable for integrating a particular aspect of the work of others, but without taking full accountability for their work and on the basis of negotiation rather than directive authority.
* Monitoring relationships, where someone is made accountable for reviewing particular activities carried out by others, again without taking accountability for their work and on the basis of negotiating, rather than directing, any changes.
* Collateral relationships between organizational equals, that depend upon mutual agreement or reference of problems to a manager.
* Service-giving relationships, where service-seekers have authority to expect work that has been sanctioned by policy from others, without directing their work.

This potential richness in the hierarchy is seldom recognized by critics, or indeed by those who draw up organization charts, but the variations in accountability and authority are very real for those involved and make a great deal of difference to life at work. It would seem advantageous to recognize the differences and to be clear as to what is required. Deputy heads and senior masters or mistresses frequently occupy staff officer or supervisory, rather than managerial, relationships to other members of staff, yet this distinction is rarely made explicit. Similarly, if a head of building or subschool is expected to monitor the quality of subject teaching his age-range of pupils receive or the discipline in the classrooms, why not say what this involves? It may mean that the headteacher and his senior staff will have to get down to thinking about what constitutes satisfactory teaching and discipline, but that is no bad thing.

Secondary schools do present a particular complexity, not found to the same extent in other public and private sector organizations, through their role diffusion. This occurs widely, particularly where the school hierarchy is divided into separate pastoral and academic structures. Heads of subject departments may be tutors, and heads of house will be members of subject departments. While this duality of work is economic and indeed serves to link the two functions together, it inevitably fragments accountabilities. It is generally the case that there is no one in a management position over both the subhierarchies below the level of headteacher. There is no one, then, other than the headteacher who is able to cast authoritative judgement over the teacher's work as a whole. Inevitably this concern must pull the headteacher's attention down into the internal organization, leaving less time for that considerable part of the work concerned with negotiations across the school boundary.[12]

It would seem probable that as, and if, teaching becomes more professionalized, and as demands for staff participation[13] grow, there will be an increase in the use of coordinating[14] rather than managerial relationships within hierarchies. The vertical stereotype will thus give way to a broader, looser configuration, thereby emphasizing the freedom from direction that some see as part of the road to professionalism.[15] The last thirty years have also brought an increased use of meetings in the schools, which emphasize equality and bring together the various parts of the hierarchy to respond rapidly to emerging needs.[16]

The suggestion, then, is that the hierarchy is not outdated in our schools. Rather, it provides for the work of many to be integrated and for accountability to be identified and maintained. It can accommodate professionals and professional freedom and it is capable of recognizing, nurturing, and responding to its members' needs in ways that are beyond other forms of organization. There are many possible forms of working relationship within the hierarchy and this potential needs to be recognized in structuring. The need for looking at structure is continuous. Schools are made up of people. Changes in personal capacities and interactions with a changing environment require recognition and channelling in working arrangements. To neglect this is to encourage obsolescence and/or free licence.

This being so, it is dysfunctional that organization is so neglected in our training institutions and in so many of our schools. So much of a person's life effort goes into work and so much of his, or her, being is drawn from it that organization should be more than an area of knowledge that is 'picked up' or seen as of secondary importance. Many educationalists are proposing that future training should be more in-service orientated[17] and since discussion of organization is probably most meaningful within the particular local context, need and opportunity could be usefully matched.

Notes and references

1. The Educational Studies Unit was set up with DES finance in 1974 under the

direction of Professor Maurice Kogan. Work is currently being undertaken in two outer-London boroughs. Researchers are working with staff from secondary schools, social service departments, the Education Welfare Service, the School Psychological Service, the Careers Service, the Child Guidance Service, and the Juvenile Bureau to identify and clarify the gamut of issues surrounding relationships between the schools, homes, and other welfare agencies. Work is also being undertaken with pupils and parents.

2. Definitions of the managerial relationship, and other forms that are mentioned later in the chapter, have emerged from work carried out by Jaques and other members of the Brunel Institute of Organization and Social Studies in a wide variety of private and public sector organizations. See Jaques, E., *A General Theory of Bureaucracy*, Heinemann, 1976.

3. The immediate locus of accountability above the school is ambiguous, although hopefully the situation will be clarified through the efforts of the Taylor Committee. See Glatter, R., 'Reforming School Managements: Some Structural Issues', *Educational Administration*, Vol 5, No. 1. Also, Packwood, T., 'Permuting the Relating Game of Governors and Governed', *Education*, 29 August, 1975.

4. Managerial levels, in the sense of manager-subordinate relationships, should reflect the work that has to be done. The presence of a managerial position thus reflects a qualitative shift in activities. Rowbottom and Billis suggest that discrete qualitative categories of work can be identified in institutions 'across the board', and that ideally the various levels of work should be matched by levels of management. See Rowbottom, R., and Billis, D., 'The Stratification of Work and Organisation Design', *Human Relations*, 1976, 29, 11.

5. The process of initial assessment may be formalized in a probationary period, although a similar experience of close managerial attention is likely whenever a new activity is taken on.

6. Hughes, M.G., 'The Professional as Administrator: The Case of the Secondary School Head' in *Management in Education I*, Houghton, V., McHugh, R., and Morgan, C., (eds), Ward Lock Educational in association with The Open University Press, 1975.

7. Position in a managerial hierarchy clearly rules out individual autonomy for the teachers but it does not prohibit what Hill calls group autonomy, an assertion by professionals that they can only be managed by one of their own. It is unlikely that posts of headteacher could be widely opened to any but qualified teachers. See Hill, M., *The State, Administration and the Individual*, Fontana, 1976.

8. Jacques, E., *A General Theory of Bureaucracy*, op. cit.

9. Following the wider implications of this proposal there would be a need for directors of education, and perhaps chief executives, to negotiate the future local authority policy framework for education with headteachers.

10. It is quite possible that other relationships remain to be identified. The particular conditions of educational institutions may indeed throw up particular forms that are not duplicated elsewhere, but this is a matter for further investigation.

11. Many deputy roles prove to be built around the supervisory relationship.

12. Richardson, E., *The School, the Teacher and the Task of Management*, Heinemann, 1973.
13. Participation, like management, serves too general a descriptive use. It embraces a spectrum of interactions ranging from sharing in decision-making with managers, through consultation, to being 'kept in the picture'.
14. So-called matrix structures make use of coordinated teams in the sense defined in this paper.
15. Taylor, W., 'The Head as Manager: Some Criticisms' in *The Role of the Head*, Peters, R.S. (ed), Routledge & Kegan Paul, 1976.
16. Despite their peculiar character, meetings maintain the differentiations of working relationships. Whatever the style adopted, meetings with a manager have different properties from those with a coordinator or between collaterals. Strictly, the former are consultative since the manager cannot abdicate his, or her, own accountability to a majority vote.
17. See, for example, 'Back to Base' by Aitken, R., Director of Education for Coventry, in *The Times Educational Supplement*, 8 October, 1976.

CHAPTER 3.7

RECONCILING PROFESSIONAL AND ADMINISTRATIVE CONCERNS*
Meredydd G. Hughes

The defining criterion of an organization may be taken to be the existence of explicit procedures 'to coordinate the activities of a group in the interests of achieving specified objectives' (Blau, 1968, p. 298). The primary emphasis of classical management theory is therefore on deliberately designed procedures rather than on the interplay of uncoordinated activities. In traditional management theory institutional roles and their relationships are largely prescribed in official job descriptions and organization charts. The basic concepts are division of labour, span of control, and hierarchical structure with a single chief executive at the apex of the pyramid. A rational approach to the achievement of well-defined organizational goals leads to a clear specification of responsibilities (Gulick and Urwick, 1937), and the applications to all situations of widely agreed 'general principles of management' (Fayol, 1949).

Similarly Max Weber (1947) in his influential theoretical analysis of legal-rational bureaucracy as an ideal type also emphasizes hierarchical differentiation and control. Administration by bureaucrats, according to Weber, is the most efficient form of organization. Their disciplined behaviour, governed by rules and controlled by hierarchical superiors, ensures a rational and consistent pursuit of organizational objectives. The rationality and reliability are enhanced by the emphasis placed on establishing a detached, impersonal relationship among staff and between staff and the public, so ensuring that impact of the individuality of any given position occupant is minimal.

* Commonwealth Council for Educational Administration, *Studies in Educational Administration*, No. 13, December 1978.

As noted by several writers, schools and colleges conform to a considerable extent to Max Weber's specifications of the characteristics of a bureaucracy. There is usually a well-defined division of labour. A hierarchy of authority may be identified. A system of rules and regulations is often laid down and employment is generally based on technical qualifications. The further criterion of bureaucracy set out by Max Weber is the impersonality of relations among staff and between staff and clients and it is often claimed by critics of large schools that this characteristic also applies to such institutions. Many have quoted Barker and Gump's celebrated conclusion (1964) that 'a school should be small enough that the students are not redundant'.

It is only fair to note that there are studies which suggest that the bureaucratic emphasis in education may not necessarily be unwelcome to staff. Drawing his conclusion from case studies, Congreve (1957) claimed that staff members prefer formal impersonal administration to a more informal approach, the formal administrator being more consistent and positive in his methods. Similarly Moeller and Charters (1966) found that teachers in bureaucratic systems were significantly higher in their sense of power to affect policy decisions than teachers in less bureaucratized systems. The conclusion they drew is that bureaucracy provides a teacher with an orderly, understandable, and predictable milieu in which to pursue his profession and thereby makes it easier for him to feel able to influence the direction the organization will take.

There is also some support for the contention that bureaucratization increases with the size of organization. Anderson (1968) showed that staffing, impersonality, and resistance to innovation are positively and significantly related to the size of school. Similarly Cohen (1970), reporting a research project in England and Wales, found some support for his hypothesis that the size of school is related to bureaucratized role conceptions on the part of the headteacher. He found that the heads of larger schools laid greater emphasis than heads of smaller schools on the application of rules and regulations to govern procedures.

On the other hand there are writers who have argued on a number of grounds that the bureaucratic model and the corresponding models of classical management theory of themselves provide only a first approximation to an understanding of school organization. There are alternative perspectives, and at different times it has been argued that classical theory pays insufficient regard to one or more of the following:

1 the individual in the organization;
2 group relationships in the organization;
3 the dysfunctional consequences of structural aspects of the organization;
4 technical and environmental factors;
5 the problems posed by the employment of professionals in the organization;

In this chapter I shall be mainly concerned with the last of these viewpoints, though we may also have occasion to refer to some of the other perspectives.

There is no doubt that Max Weber, more perhaps than other early writers on organization, recognized the importance of highly qualified and expert staff in the rational and efficient organization of a large-scale enterprise. Specialization and expertise among staff and employment based on technical qualification are among the hallmarks of his conceptualization of bureaucracy. It seems however that he did not fully anticipate the consequences of staffing his model bureaucracy with highly trained technical experts. For the paradox is this: it is through the independent exercise of his trained judgement, irrespective of his formal position, that the expert makes his contribution to an organization. It is through precisely the same activity that the expert comes into conflict with the administrative hierarchy. Furthermore, it is unsafe to assume under all circumstances that technical expertise necessarily, or even generally, increases with position in the formal hierarchy. This self-evident truth applies at all stages of the educational enterprise. One cannot assume that a school principal who may be a specialist in history or in classics knows more about the teaching of science than his senior physics master. At the other extreme a wise permanent secretary may recognize that he knows less about professional educational matters than a chief inspector who is his surbordinate in the hierarchy. Such situations are liable to present difficulties, unless tactfully handled.

Before going further it is desirable to recognize that the definition of the term 'professional' raises difficulties both theoretically and practically because of status implications. A working definition of a professional for present purposes is that he is a person who carries out a specialized activity based on systematic knowledge and who is committed to his calling. Much has been written about strains and areas of conflict between professionals and organizations (e.g., Scott, 1966; Harries-Jenkins, 1970). I will confine myself to two aspects:

1 the professional's tendency to resist bureaucratic control;
2 the professional's conditional organizational commitment.

1 The professional's tendency to resist bureaucratic control

To most administrators, observed the American sociologist Abrahamson (1967), professionals are a major source of frustration. He was then summing up his observations of scientists in research establishments and noted that professionals as individuals and because of the nature of their work 'seem unreasonably resistant toward administrative control' (p. 82). Writing similarly about scientists in industry, Kornhauser (1963) reported that organizational efforts to coordinate clash with a professional staff's striving for autonomy. Drucker (1952) had previously observed, writing of commercial undertakings, that the very concept of supervision goes against the grain for professional people. He continued as follows:

> Professional people work as senior and junior, rather than as boss and subordinate. Of course somebody has to be in charge of the project or activity and be responsible for it. But the professional thinks of it as a group project, with each member of the team having independent responsibility clearly vested in him. Thus the superior should be a coordinator or a teacher, rather than a supervisor.

In similar vein, Wardwell (1955) observes that the bureaucratic type of organization is not suitable for a profession, the appropriate mode being 'the group of equals pattern'.

Similar views have been expressed in relation to the school system. Watson (1969) differentiates between office and expertise in the secondary school, and notes that tensions may exist between hierarchical structure and the attitudes of professional teachers which may be minimized by appropriate administrative action. Bidwell (1965) observed that:

> an important facet of school system organization is the autonomy granted to or perhaps demanded by the teacher as a professional to make discretionary judgements about procedures to be used during the time a student group is in his charge.

Another American author, Katz (1964), in discussing patterns of autonomy, has suggested that certain specific spheres of autonomy for the school's members are necessary if the school is to accomplish its missions. He proceeded to consider autonomy structures which are related to specialization and those which concern the affiliation of members, including affiliations outside the organization.

2 The professional's conditional organizational commitment

The standards by which professionals judge their work are likely to be closely related to the intellectual discipline of their specialist field and less directly to the instrumental expediences of their employing organization. Loyalty to the organization is thus liable to take second place to the concept of solidarity with professional colleagues outside the boundaries of the organization itself. An example from outside the field of education is provided by a research report on social agencies by Blau and Scott (1963). They found that the professional social workers were nearly twice as likely as the administrators of the agency to consider that the agency's assistance to clients should be increased. The more professional workers also tended to be critical of the agency's assistance to clients and were to that extent less loyal to the organization.

A similar tendency for professionals psychologically to face outwards and away from the bureaucratic structure was explored in the education field in Gouldner's study of the staff of a small liberal arts college in the United States. Gouldner (1957) found that high commitment to professional skills was positively related to having an outside reference group orientation but that both were negatively related to loyalty to the employing organization. There is tension, he concluded, between an organization's bureaucratic need for expertise and its social system need for loyalty. Gouldner thus differentiated between two kinds of professional, firstly the *cosmopolitans* who are high in commitment to specialist skills and in orientation to outside reference groups but who are low in organizational loyalty, and secondly the *locals* who are opposite in each respect.

Further study of the data presented by Gouldner suggests that the cosmopolitan/local dichotomy is an oversimplification, but it is a typology which unfortunately has been taken over uncritically by many later writers. By today it is evident – and this perhaps needs to be clearly stated – that a simple division of personnel into cosmopolitans and locals cannot satisfactorily be achieved (Grimes and Berger, 1970). Many persons are both locals and cosmopolitans in the sense that they manage to combine loyalty to the organization and to their profession. The contrast is not an either/or distinction, as Toomey and Child (1971) have commented, the results suggesting 'a more fragmented organisation of attitudes'. Neither can it be assumed that all teachers have a strong professional orientation. Simpson (1969) noted that while teaching 'offers opportunities for professionalism among individual teachers if they are professionally inclined' the majority of elementary school teachers in his study in the United States display attitudes and behaviours which are not compatible with professionalism. Likewise Corwin (1965) distinguished between two concepts of the teacher, the teacher as a professional and the teacher as a bureaucratic employee. He found that scores on the two dimensions were not significantly correlated, which accords with the scepticism expressed above about the validity of the cosmopolitan/local typology. At the same time it may be conceded that there is at least *some* tendency for organizational members who are committed to their profession psychologically to face outwards rather than to stress their local organizational loyalty.

Here then is the dilemma: it is by using his trained judgement rather than by suppressing his views when they are unpopular to the organization that the educational professional can make a contribution to the further development of the educational system. In doing so, he is liable to come into conflict with the organizational hierarchy and at least to give the impression that he is only conditionally loyal to the system because of his wider horizons and affiliations. It must therefore be granted that there are inevitable managerial problems for an educational system, because, by the nature of the case, the majority of the personnel it employs have a claim to be regarded as professionals. It may be presumed that as the educational enterprise becomes more complex and the teachers themselves become better trained and more confident in their professional roles, the possibility of such conflict will tend to increase. Fortunately though, there is no present necessity to surrender to bleak pessimism of the view that administrative and professional relationships are *inevitably* incompatible with each other.

It must be admitted that empirical data in this area is scarce, and there is clearly scope for research to be undertaken from differing viewpoints. A significant aspect is the perception of the situation held by the participants themselves, the way in which, to use the language of the phenomenologists, they construct their own reality (Greenfield, 1975). In any particular situation there will also be political and personal factors which will affect the applicability of the administrative-professional construct which I have presented in this chapter, while a further complication is raised by the growth of the concept of professionalism among administrators themselves. In many countries this is a sensitive area but for that very reason it deserves further study and dispassionate analysis.

Having recognized the gaps in our knowledge, and the urgent need for further research related to various educational systems, which would benefit from a comparative perspective, I wish in the latter part of this chapter to suggest and discuss three concepts which, taken together, hold out some promise of lessening conflict and thereby assisting in mobilizing the expertise of the professional staff of the education service towards the achievement of the wider objectives of the system. These three concepts are:

1 *structural relativism* as a useful new perspective in organizational theory;
2 *participation in decision-making* as an essential element in enlisting the wholehearted cooperation of professional staff;
3 *professional-as-administrator roles* as integrative and coordinative devices.

Firstly then, let us consider the emergence of structural relativism as a credible and viable alternative to the claimed universalism of Fayol's general principles of managment and of Max Weber's ideal-type conceptualization of bureaucracy. The doctrine that there is *one* right model of organization was first effectively challenged by writers in the 1950s who postulated a *pair* of ideal types. Gouldner (1955) differentiated between punishment-centred bureaucracy and a representative bureaucracy, while a different level of ideas, MacGregor's well-known 'Theory X' and 'Theory Y', provide two contrasting monolithic constructs (MacGregor, 1960).

Similarly, Burns and Stalker (1961) provide detailed specifications of two contrasting management structures, a mechanistic form appropriate to stable conditions and an organic or organismic form to handle problems which cannot be broken down or distributed automatically within the hierarchical structure. More recently Eric Hoyle (1975) has referred to two fundamental models of organization, which he calls Model A and Model B. Model A is characterized by closed boundary relationships, mechanistic internal relationships, and high specificity of role prescription. It may be clearly recognized as the classical organizational model. Model B, on the other hand, is characterized by open boundary relationships, organismic internal relationships, and low specificity of role prescriptions, and incorporates elements of a human relations model, i.e., horizontal patterns of authority, low specialization, minimum of general rules, and an emphasis on personal relations.

A further significant development is the recognition that different types of structures may be appropriate within the same organization. Thus Litwak (1961) differentiated between subsystems handling work of a nonuniform nature, for which a human relations model is applicable, and subsystems which deal with uniform events of a routine nature, for which a Weberian model is appropriate. In advocating a 'contingency model', Lawrence and Lorsch (1967) developed further the implications of the view that structures are contingent upon the problems with which they have to deal. They identified and produced measures of distinct subenvironments of the organization, matching each subenvironment to an appropriate subunit structure.

Structural relativism provides a new flexibility not found in classical management theory. It leads, for instance, to recognition that different control and supervisory procedures may be applicable according to whether the decisions one is dealing with are mainly administrative or mainly professional. One response to the resulting separation of administrative and professional decisions is a differentiation of roles, resulting in a clear distinction being made between positions in the line of authority and advisory staff positions (Dalton, 1950). The staff-line distinction provides one means of injecting professional expertise into an organization at different levels without involving the expert in the authority structure or in routine procedures. A necessary precondition for a satisfactory outcome is that the occupants of the two types of position, for instance, school inspectors and administrators in a Ministry of Education, should achieve a substantial measure of agreement on their mutual role definition. This is a proviso which is not necessarily always fulfilled, as Dalton's study well demonstrates.

A more elaborate arrangement, which also separates professional and administrative decision-making is the creation of an organizational subsystem such as a research and development department in an industrial organization in which the professionals carry out their specialist activities partially segregated from and without direct control by the rest of the organization. Inevitably such arrangements create communication and transferral difficulties. Thus Litwak (1961), in his discussion of models of bureaucracy which permit conflict, gave special attention to the occupants of 'transferral occupations'. These are the persons who mediate between sections handling work of a nonuniform nature, for which a human relations model is applicable, and those sections which deal with uniform events of a routine nature, for which a classical model is more appropriate. Organizational intermediaries have to handle contradictory forms of social relations and have special problems because of their exposure to conflicting expectations. This is a matter to which I return in discussing the role of the professional-as-administrator.

Secondly, we consider staff participation in decision-making as a decisive factor in obtaining the cooperation of professional staff. The professional not only claims the right to make decisions in his specialist field, but also expects his views to be considered in a wide range of matters which affect his work and his status. His desire to participate in wider system decisions may be regarded as an extension of his expectation to exercise independent judgement in his professional activities (Noble and Pym, 1970). Though some teachers are highly motivated professionally, studies in several countries suggest that not all teachers have the professional orientation which results in demands for participation in decision-making. Eric Hoyle (1975) usefully distinguishes between a restricted and an extended professionality. The restricted professional concentrates his attention on his work in the classroom and his relationship with his pupils. The extended professional is also a good classroom practitioner but is in addition aware of the wider dimensions of his task. A greater emphasis on extended professionality is, in his view, a likely outcome of organizational development strategies for the in-service training of teachers, such as those advocated by Schmuck and Miles (1971) in the United States and Richardson (1975) in Britain.

Industrial experience of worker participation suggests that to be involved in a substantially greater amount of participation than expected produces a negative reaction because of the threatening nature of the situation to the subordinate. According to Likert (1958), 'the best results obtain when amount of participation used is somewhat greater than expected by the surbordinates but still within their capacity to respond to it effectively.' This reinforces the case for organizational development and suggests that participative processes should be introduced gradually with plenty of preparation at each stage. It must be conceded, however, that there are difficult problems in determining the parameters and limits of staff participation. In Britain there has been much recent discussion of whether what is required is more staff consultation or full staff involvement in decision-making. There is wide support for the view that whatever procedures are adopted must be open and authentic rather than manipulative tactical ploys to secure support for predetermined policies. Inauthentic participation will be seen for what it is and will be quickly discredited. Experience related to the setting up of academic boards in colleges of further education in England and Wales suggests that in practice it is often unrealistic to seek to draw a sharp distinction between consultation and joint decision-making by the principal and his senior staff (Parkes, 1973). The point which emerges most clearly, however, is that whatever kind of organizational involvement of a professional staff is proposed, whether formal or informal, it can only be effective if there is an adequate programme for professional development through in-service training.

Thirdly and finally, we consider the integrative-coordinative function of professional-as-administrator roles. It will be agreed that it is a very frequent occurrence for professional educators to be appointed to administrative positions in education. I wish to argue that this can be a very effective means of lessening conflict in professionally staffed organizations. As Barber (1963) observed, the professional-as-administrator is in a position to play a key role in achieving accommodation between the organization's emphasis on superordinate control and the professional's desire for colleague control. Etzioni (1964) has similarly written of the professionally orientated administrator as follows.

> Because of his training he is more likely to understand the special needs of a professional organisation and its staff than a lay administrator and because of his personal characteristics he is more likely to be skilled in handling the needs and requests of his professional colleagues as well as those of administrative staff.

It may also be argued that the administrator who is able because of his thorough knowledge of the viewpoint of the professionals to be selective and discreet in his application of organizational restraint is likely to be rewarded with appreciation and loyalty.

Elementary school headteachers, principals of secondary schools and of institutions of further and higher education, senior staff of school boards and ministries of education, university vice-chancellors and deans of faculty, all these may be designated as members of the category professionals-as-administrators. These are the boundary roles of organizational intermediaries, the transferral occupations to which Litwak referred. The professional-as-administrator is thus frequently exposed to role conflict with divergent expectations from above and below and consequently he has to accept a degree of role strain to which the pure professional is not exposed. The pressures on the professional-as-administrator are considerable, as Abrahamson (1967) has observed: 'professional norms stressing autonomous integrity for practitioners still make a claim upon him which he considers legitimate, but so does the organisation's need for control'. One way of resolving the tension is for the professional-as-administrator to cut himself off from his professional past and to insist on regarding himself as a pure administrator. For this to occur is regrettable, however. If the man who has been a professional completely changes his viewpoint and his values when he becomes an administrator, the justification for his appointment may have largely disappeared. In view of his background, one criterion by which his success as an administrator is likely to be judged is the extent to which, as a professional, he actively encourages and helps to train his professional colleagues to become involved in the decision-making of the organization. Support for such a view is provided by some research which I have myself reported on the role of the secondary school head in England and Wales (Hughes, 1975). This showed that in the school context the professional-as-administrator fulfils his mediating role to a large extent by providing the kind of supervision of professional staff and the kind of organizational leadership in responding to external change which is acceptable to professionals. Other aspects of his professionalism such as an insistence on doing a substantial amount of regular teaching may be inappropriate and even counter-productive. I will therefore end by quoting from the conclusions of that report:

> Much therefore depends on the interpretation given by the professional-as-administrator to his professional role. If his professionalism is restricted and modelled on traditional stereotypes, his best endeavours could well exacerbate the problems of a large and complex organisation, subject to pressures from within and without. If the emphasis is on his leadership and encouragement of colleagues in their joint efforts, his contribution could be invaluable in enabling the combined expertise of a professional staff to be mobilised for the achievement of agreed organisational objectives.

I have argued in this chapter that structural relativism provides the organization framework for the harmonious development of an educational system, for which it will be increasingly true in the coming years that it is staffed by professionals. An essential aim will then surely be to involve the professional staff in the broad decisions of the educational enterprise. In achieving this the educational administrators, who are also educational professional leaders, will have a crucial role to play. In stating such a view, we are reechoing the words of Chester Barnard (1938), who observed that, though cooperation rather than leadership is the creative process, 'leadership is the indispensable fulminator of its forces'.

References

Abrahamson, M., 1967, *The Professional in the Organization*, Chicago: Rand McNally.

Anderson, J.G., 1968, *Bureaucracy in Education*, Baltimore: John Hopkins Press.

Barber, B., 1963, 'Some problems in the sociology of the professions', *Daedalus*, 92, pp. 668–669.

Barker, R.G. and Gump, P.V., 1964, *Big School, Small School: High School Size and Student Behavior*, Stanford, Calif.: Stanford University Press.

Barnard, C.I., 1938,.*The Functions of the Executive*, Cambridge, Mass.: Harvard University Press.

Bidwell, C.E., 1965, 'The school as a formal organization', in *Handbook of Organizations*, March, J.C., (ed), Chicago: Rank McNally.

Blau, P.M., 1968, 'Theories of Organization', in *International Encyclopedia of the Social Sciences*, 11, pp. 297–305.

Blau, P.M. and Scott, W.R., 1963, *Formal Organisations*, London: Routledge & Kegan Paul.

Burns, T. and Stalker, G.M., 1961, *The Management of Innovation*, London: Tavistock.

Cohen, L., 1970, 'School size and head teachers' bureaucratic role conceptions', *Educational Review*, 23, pp. 50–58.

Congreve, W.J., 1957, 'Administrative behaviour and staff relations', *Administrator's Notebook*, 6(2), pp. 1–4.

Corwin, R.G., 1965, 'Militant professionalism, initiative and compliance in public education', *Sociology of Education*, 38, pp. 310–331.

Dalton, M., 1950, 'Conflicts between staff and line managerial officers', *American Sociological Review*, 15, pp. 342–351.

Drucker, P.F., 1952, 'Management and the professional employee', *Harvard Business Review*, 30, pp. 84–90.

Etzioni, A., 1964, *Modern Organizations*, Englewood Cliffs, New Jersey: Prentice Hall.

Fayol, H., 1949, *General and Industrial Management*, London: Pitman.

Gouldner, A.W., 1955, *Patterns of Industrial Bureaucracy*, London: Routledge & Kegan Paul.

Gouldner, A.W., 1957, 'Cosmopolitans and locals: Towards an analysis of latent social roles – 1', *Administrative Science Quarterly*, 2, pp. 281–306.

Greenfield, T.B., 1975, 'Theory about organisation: a new perspective and its implications for schools', chapter 5 in *Administering Education: International Challenge*, Hughes, M.G. (ed), London: Athlone Press.

Grimes, A.J. and Berger, P.K., 1970, 'Cosmopolitan-Local: evaluation of the construct', *Administrative Science Quarterly*, 15, pp. 407–416.

Gulick, L.H. and Urwick, L. (eds), 1937, *Papers on the Science of Administration*, New York: Columbia University.

Harries-Jenkins, G., 1970, 'Professionals in organisations', in *Professions and Professionalization*, Jackson, J.A., London: Cambridge University Press.

Hoyle, E., 1975, 'Leadership and decision-making in Education', chapter 3 in *Administering Education: International Challenge*, Hughes, M.G., (ed), London: Athlone Press.

Hughes, M.G., 1975, 'The professional-as-administrator: the case of the secondary school head', chapter 3 in *The Role of the Head*, Peters, R.S. (ed), London: Routledge & Kegan Paul.

Katz, F.E., 1964, 'The school as a complex social organization', *Harvard Educational Review*, 34, pp. 428–455.

Kornhauser, W., 1963, *Scientists in Industry: Conflict and Accommodation*, Berkeley: University of California Press.

Likert, R., 1958, 'Effective supervision: an adaptive and relative process', *Personnel Psychology*, 11, pp. 317–332.

Litwak, E., 1961, 'Models of bureaucracy which permit conflict', *American Journal of Sociology*, 67, pp. 177–184.

McGregor, D., 1960, *The Human Side of Enterprise*, New York: McGraw Hill.

Moeller, G.H. and Charters, W.W. Jr., 1966, 'Relation of bureaucratization to sense of power among teachers', *Administrative Science Quarterly*, 10, pp. 444–465.

Noble, T. and Pym, B., 1970, 'Collegial authority and the receding locus of power', *British Journal of Sociology*, 21, pp. 431–445.

Parkes, D.L., 1973, 'Circular 7/70 and the government of schools', *Educational Administration Bulletin*, 1 (2), pp. 2–11.

Richardson, E., 1975, *Authority and Organisation in the Secondary School*, London: Macmillan.

Schmuck, R.A. and Miles, M.B. (eds), 1971, *Organization Development in Schools*, Palo Alto, California: National Press Books.

Scott, W.R., 1966, 'Professionals in bureaucracies – areas of conflict', in *Professionalization*, Vollmer, H.M. and Mills, D.L. (eds), Englewood Cliffs, New Jersey: Prentice Hall.

Simpson, R.L., 1969, *The School Teacher: Social Values, Community Role and Professional Self-Image*, Final Report, Cooperative Research Project, No. 5-0451, Bureau of Research, Office of Education, U.S. Department of Health, Education and Welfare. Quoted in 'Schools as Work Organizations', Pellegrin, R.J.

Toomey, D. and Child, D., 1971, *Sociological Review*, 19, pp. 325–341.

Wardwell, W.I., 1955, 'Social integration, bureaucratization and the professions', *Social Forces*, 33, pp. 356–359.

Watson, L.E., 1969, 'Office and expertise in the secondary school', *Educational Research*, 11, pp. 104–112.

Weber, Max, 1947, *The Theory of Social and Economic Organization*, Tr. A.M. Henderson and T. Parsons, and ed. T. Parsons, Glencoe, Ill: The Free Press.

SECTION IV

LEADERSHIP IN SCHOOLS

CHAPTER 4.1

LEADERSHIP STYLES AND JOB-SATISFACTION IN PRIMARY SCHOOLS
Jennifer Nias

In the absence of appropriate empirical studies those with an interest in educational management have often had to draw analogies from the literature on industrial and commercial management (Morgan, 1976). A recent study, by interview, of 93 primary school teachers with betweeen two and ten years' experience on the 'shop floor' suggests that there may be a closer fit between the views of those who work in schools, hospitals, offices, and factories than sceptics have sometimes suggested. These teachers, all of whom had made a positive decision to teach younger children and who wanted to get on with the job of teaching, were often frustrated by what they perceived as inefficient management or alienated by dictatorial leadership. In this they do not differ significantly from workers in other types of institution (Handy, 1976).

The questions that these teachers were asked in interview were designed to chart their views on teaching as a career, and their own present and potential place within it, and not to establish their attitudes to, or opinions about, school management. Yet their career plans were affected by their present satisfaction with teaching and this in turn was strongly influenced by their perceptions of the ways in which their schools were led and administered. In short their job-satisfaction depended not just upon their contact with their pupils but also, to a marked extent, upon the managerial context which was provided for their teaching. They saw the provision of that context as the sole responsibility of headteachers and as a result made judgements about the latters' success as leaders. It seemed important therefore that I should attempt both to understand their views on school leadership and to see how these views related to their expressed levels of job-satisfaction or dissatisfaction.

Their comments support the claim of Yukl (1975) that there are three independent dimensions of leadership style. These can be combined in different ways into leadership types, each of which has different effects upon the job-satisfaction of subordinates.

Data collection and analysis

Work with postgraduates training to teach in primary schools, and contact with them in their probationary years, raised for me several questions. How well did this slightly atypical group of people settle into teaching? For how long did they remain or intend to remain in the job? Why had they given up? What plans did they have for the future? Did they think of themselves first as primary school teachers or as graduates? What did they like and dislike about teaching?

Hoping to find some answers to these and similar questions, and in the process to throw some light upon the nature of professional socialization in general, I followed up, over a period of two years, a group of 99 graduates who, after a specialized one-year PGCE course, had taken jobs in infant and junior schools. Two-thirds of these had attended the same university PGCE course, the rest had between them been at seven other PGCE courses at university, polytechnics, and colleges of education. None had taught for less than two years or more than ten. They spread out fairly evenly, in terms of experience, between these two points. I also followed up those from the largest course-group who had given up teaching.

I contacted the sample by letter or telephone; six did not wish to be included. A further four, now teaching outside England, replied by letter and I subsequently held long telephone conversations with two of them. I interviewed 83 others at length (anywhere between $1\frac{1}{2}$ to 5 hours), using a semistructured approach and taking shorthand notes, and visited 53 in their classrooms. (Four of those still teaching did not wish me to visit their schools; 26 of those from the largest course-group were at home, with their own families.) Twenty-two also kept field notebooks on one day a week for one term. When I visited a teacher in his/her school, I also interviewed the headteacher. In addition, I corresponded with, or interviewed by telephone, as many of the headteachers as I could contact (70%) of any school in which any of the sample had taught during the previous ten years. Since, however, I was interested in their views on the socialization of their teachers and not on their own leadership I have not used their responses in this analysis.

Sixty-three of the 93 teachers in my study were described by their headteachers in terms such as 'much-above average', or 'highly competent'. Nine were classed as 'superb', 'exceptional', 'a key member of my staff'. Thus only fifteen were not perceived as being highly successful teachers, and of this number six were using teaching as a necessary avenue into educational psychology, and were not committed to a career in teaching. Even allowing for the vagueness and subjectivity of the criteria used by heads in assessing the competence of their staff, and the research weaknesses of obtaining these assessments in a face-to-face encounter with a virtual stranger, a clear picture emerges of a group of highly motivated, well-qualified teachers who had earned the professional respect of their head-teachers. Their comments upon their schools and the ways in which these were managed cannot therefore be interpreted as the self-justification of incompetent practitioners, ready to put the blame for their own inadequacies upon institutional factors. Nor is there much correspondence between the heads who thought highly of their teachers, and the teachers who commented favourably upon the leadership of their heads.

Since my chief focus in this inquiry was upon the professional socialization of teachers in mid-career, the material on which this article is based was gathered incidentally, and initial analysis of it was not made in the light of existing management theory. Indeed, I turned to the relevant literature only after I had formulated my own hypotheses. From a methodological point of view this raises two points.

First, the findings presented are an example of 'grounded theory' (Glaser and Strauss, 1967), with both the research strengths and weaknesses of this approach. Second, by referring to the theoretical works of others only after I had made sense in my own terms of the data I had collected, I was in a position to judge whether or not my analysis confirmed that already made by established management theorists. In other words, the ways in which I have categorized leadership style and leadership type are independent of previous research findings, and in this respect they reinforce the work of others. Indeed, the correspondence that I found between my own analysis of leadership style and that of Halpin (1966) and Yukl (1975) is so strong that this article should be regarded as presenting confirmatory rather than original material.

The same is true of teachers' reflections upon their levels of job-satisfaction and dissatisfaction. A fuller analysis of apparent causes for each of these is made elsewhere (Nias, 1979). Here I have used a simpler categorization which confirms, but was not initially drawn from, the work of Herzberg (1966). Like him, I found a distinction between 'satisfiers' deriving from the job itself, and 'dissatisfiers' which related primarily to the context in which the job was done. The removal of the 'dissatisfier' does not provide a 'satisfier'. Thus teachers' views on the leadership of their heads tend, by definition, to be expressed in negative terms. When they are satisfied with the management of their schools they do not mention it, because good management is not, under normal circumstances, a 'satisfier' in its own right. Bad management is, by contrast, a 'dissatisfier'.

Leadership styles

Leadership style has been analysed by several writers into two or more independent dimensions, though it is not clear to what extent these studies can be reconciled conceptually with one another. Early classification of leaders tended to follow Lewin's (1944) theoretical typology (democratic, autocratic, and *laissez-faire*) and to focus upon the relative degree of influence each type exerts upon its group's decisions. Subsequent work by management theorists has perpetuated this typology and advanced autocratic or participative decision-making as alternative institutional panaceas (Hicks and Gullett, 1976). Classical studies with children along these lines by Lippitt and White (1943) and Anderson (1943) are still widely used in initial teacher education in Britain.

By contrast, Etzioni (1964) saw management in terms of two independent dimensions – instrumental and expressive. This division was independently developed by Halpin (1966) as 'initiating structure' and 'consideration'. The existence of these dimensions has received considerable support in American empirical studies (see Gibbs, 1969). Burnham (1968), Richardson (1973), and Smith (1979) are among those who have used them to analyse management functions in British secondary schools.

Unfortunately, the terms 'autocratic' and 'democratic' have also been used to describe elements from both typologies (McGregor, 1960; Likert, 1961; Blake and Mouton, 1964). Thus, an autocratic leader can be seen as one who cares little for the feelings of others, personally oversees administration, *and* excludes others from decision-making, while a democratic leader may be helpful to his subordinates, delegates freely, *and* allows 'appropriate leadership acts to develop within the group' (Bates, et al., 1974, p. 91). The resulting confusion about the precise meaning of these labels has been confounded by the value-connotations which attach to them. Nor is this confusion relieved by relabelling into 'structuring' and 'supportive', as Handy (1976) suggests.

Yukl (1975) has, to some extent, resolved for management theorists the problems raised by the use of these imprecise, culturally biased terms. Instead of two leadership dimensions, he suggests a threefold typology which avoids the use of 'autocratic' and 'democratic'. He accepts Halpin's dimensions, and adds a participatory one, under the label 'decision-centralization'. Thus the three independent dimensions along which leadership can be distributed, according to Yukl (1975, p. 162), are:

> *Initiating Structure:* the degree to which a leader defines and structures his own role and those of his subordinates towards goal attainment.
> *Consideration:* the degree to which a leader acts in a warm and supportive manner and shows concern and respect for his subordinates.
> *Decision-Centralization:* the degree of leader influence over group decisions.

In general my findings support the validity of this threefold typology, and I have therefore used in my analysis labels derived from Halpin and Yukl. (See Table 9.)

Two other points need to be made. First, I have subsumed administration under leadership, even though it is customary (e.g., Hughes, 1975) to treat them separately. Hoyle and Bell (1972, p. 26) argue that an administrator is concerned primarily with maintaining established structures, procedures, and goals 'whereas a leader is concerned with changing the structures and procedures for attaining a school's goals, or with changing the goals themselves'. While this distinction ought logically to hold for the primary schools whose teachers I interviewed it does not seem to. Many of these teachers found the administrative inefficiency of their schools a major source of job-dissatisfaction and implied that the establishment and maintenance of good administration was one of the major tasks of a leader. On the other hand, another major complaint was the absence of an agreed set of school goals. It may be that, in particular schools, inefficiency and excessive teacher autonomy in goal-setting went hand-in-hand. Under these circumstances a headteacher who by good administration implicitly moved the school's goals from a collection of individual aspirations in the direction of a coherent policy could correctly be described as a leader. Similarly, it would be artificial to separate good administration from consideration, for

Table 9 Leadership styles and types

	Passive type (Disfavoured)	Positive type (Favoured)	Bourbon type (Disfavoured)
Style A Initiating Structure	Sets a low professional standard	Sets a high professional standard	
	Low level of personal involvement in school	High level of personal involvement in school	
	Does not monitor standards of teachers		
	Inefficient administration		Inefficient administration
Style B Consideration	Not easy to contact or talk to	Readily available, especially for discussion	
		Interested in individual teacher development	
	Does not support individual teachers		Treats individual teachers as inferiors
Style C Decision-Centralization	Has no perceived aims	Gives a lead in establishing aims for school	
		Encourages participation in goal-setting and decision-making	Does not encourage or allow participation in goal-setting and decision-making

inefficiency was construed by many teachers as a failure on the head's part to understand their difficulties or to make the schools a pleasant place for them to work in. In commonsense terms, it would clearly distort the teachers' meanings if, in deference to a semantic distinction, I omitted administration from a consideration of leadership style.

Secondly, I have made no use of another category often used in the analysis of leadership style. Contingency theory, deriving from the work of Fiedler (1968), relates leadership style to other relevant variables, in particular to the task and/or the work group and to the position of the leader within that work group. Since I did not initially set out to study leadership style, I did not pay sufficient attention to situational variables to be able to make any accurate or insightful *post hoc* use of the work of contingency theorists. This may be a major weakness, especially in view of Fiedler's suggestion that there is a strong correlation between appropriate leadership and the circumstances of both group and task. It could be that the leadership types described below offer different benefits in varying group-task conditions, and should not therefore be described on subjective criteria as 'favoured' or 'disfavoured'. (See Table 9.)

Leadership types

Individual leaders are differently positioned, and in respect of different characteristics, along each of the three suggested dimensions of leadership style. The resulting spread can be grouped into three leadership types. (See Table 9.) However, these characteristics are not mutually exclusive, despite a strong tendency to cluster. The suggested typology should therefore be regarded as exploratory rather than definitive.

I have used my own labels to describe these types, not out of any desire to add to the existing conceptual confusion, but because I could not find any others already in use which adequately described the characteristics which I felt emerged from the data. One leadership type, the 'passive', gave teachers more freedom than they desired. They perceived themselves as totally free to set their own goals, under heads whose professional standards did not match their own, and who offered neither coherence to the school as a whole nor support and guidance to individuals. The second, the 'Bourbon', was characterized by social distance, authoritarian professional relationships, and administrative inefficiency. The third, which I have described as 'positive', set teachers a high professional standard, adopted a dynamic but consultative policy towards decision-making, and actively supported the professional development of individuals. In all three types, respect for a head's leadership style on any dimension was independent of expressed personal liking for him.

Initiating structure

The items included in this category are remarkably similar to those used by Halpin (1966, p. 89) in measuring the behaviour of aircraft commanders. Of the fifteen items that he used, ten appear, almost verbatim, in my interview responses.

There is also a strong resemblance between the characteristics measured by his subtest for Organizational Climate (Principal's Behaviour: VII Thrust) (Halpin, 1966, p. 154) and those that I have described elsewhere as 'commitment' (Nias, 1980). This is not the place to analyse this concept in detail, even though it is a central one in teachers' thinking about themselves, their colleagues, and the job of teaching. It is however relevant to note that 'committed' teachers set themselves high standards in all aspects of their work. Often, the term also implies enthusiasm and idealism. Sometimes it is used synonymously with 'involvement' especially when reference is made to the headteacher (for example, 'To be a good head, you have to be totally involved, totally committed'; 'All the staff and the head give to the job; they're all involved, all committed.')

Two aspects of 'commitment' seem to distinguish 'passive' heads from 'positive' ones. In the first place, the latter are perceived as setting a high professional standard. 'The standards of everything in this school come from the head.' 'She had such a high standard herself. . . . She was never late, always ready to talk after school, could give you really practical help. If she did anything, like an assembly, you always knew it would be well done. There was always something to live up to.' 'The head here is outstanding. His enthusiasm is infectious, he's always around and he sets us a wonderful example of involvement and hard work.' 'He sets such a high standard that you feel you want to be equally committed.' 'With such high standards, mostly due to the headteacher, you don't want to let the others down.'

Secondly, 'positive' leaders display a high level of 'personal involvement with the school'. This characteristic, though never actually defined by an interviewee, seems to mean that heads are seen to be working long hours, to be occupied in school time with school matters (as opposed to union activities, or private concerns such as being a JP or a councillor), to be present at extracurricular events. 'To be a good head you have to be totally involved. . . . She is, so we all are.' 'It's his school really, but it isn't because he manages to make us feel it's all of ours.' 'The real impetus comes from the head; he's completely involved.' 'Involvement' itself may be conceptually related to 'scope' (Etzioni, 1964) and 'inclusion' (Argyris, 1964), high levels of both of which are claimed to be related to job-satisfaction. Be that as it may, responsibility for creating within the school an atmosphere of 'involvement' is laid at the door of the head, as these three representative comments suggest.

By contrast, 'passive' heads appeared to their teachers to have low standards (for example, of punctuality, assembly-presentation, efficiency), and to be lacking in commitment to the school. It was not always easy to disentangle one factor from the other. 'In this school, you feel as if all your efforts were wasted because the head is so uninterested, and it rubs off on the staff. She really couldn't care less any more about teaching. We never see her in the classrooms; in fact we don't see much of her in the school. She often comes late, gets her hair done in school time, and when she is in, sits in her office learning her part for her amateur dramatics. She can't be doing requisitions all the time. . . . If I can't move, I think I'll leave and have a baby. It gets so disheartening when you work hard yourself and there's no back up.' 'I got on well with the caretaker and cleaners who cared more about the school than the head did. They seemed to be more worried than he was by the low standards in the school. . . . He was away by one minute past four every day, and since we never saw him when he was in school, there was no leadership. . . . I was glad to leave that school. Here it's quite different. The head gives a lead and at least some of the staff follow.' Perceived absenteeism was as disheartening as perceived indifference. 'We never saw the head when he was in school . . . but mostly he was out anyway. . . . He was a key member of NAHT, I think, certainly he was always running off to meetings.'

Nor were comments such as these an indication of unapproachability or lack of consideration. 'She copes so badly, yet is so good with the children, it's impossible really to dislike her, although it's infuriating never getting a straight answer to questions merely because she doesn't know what's going on.' 'The sad thing was that he lost all interest in the school.' 'She's very nice, but a 9-to-4 head and never available to discuss anything. You have no incentive to improve when no one cares what you do.'

Equally damaging to teacher morale were the 'passive' heads who allowed their staff to 'get away with murder. I could have taught them Arabic all day and no one would have minded.' Statements like this one may not, of course, be objectively true, but as with comments on headteacher 'commitment' what matters to the classroom teacher is not the head's perspective but his own. The teachers in my survey felt that headteachers should be seen to be involved with the life of the school. In the same way, they wanted their heads to monitor the work that was being done. Nearly 25% of those interviewed made some comment which indicated the need they felt to be kept up to standard by informed surveillance. Their comments ranged from the vividly general ('In a system where you aren't supervised, the bad eggs run riot') to the self-critically specific ('After three years I decided to leave. The head never appeared in the classroom, never kept a check on anything we did. I was getting too good at papering over things, and he didn't notice,' or 'By Christmas I needed to be told to put things right, and wasn't strong enough to do it on my own. I'd got into very bad habits and really would have appreciated it if the head had come in and told me so'). It seems that many teachers, even those described in glowing terms by their heads, do not appreciate the extent of the professional freedom offered them by 'passive' heads. On the other hand, there was no mention among factors contributing to job-satisfaction of the obverse of this. Like inefficient administration, the absence of monitoring is a 'dissatisfier', but its existence does not serve as a 'satisfier' (Herzberg, 1966).

One aspect of school life which was unequivocally seen to be the responsibility of the headteacher (and not, normally, of the deputy) and against which, therefore, his own professional standards were judged was the overall administration of the school. The aspect of teaching most often mentioned as being irritating or discouraging, in some cases even as being a major reason for leaving the profession, was 'the inefficiency – that's the worst thing'. Nearly half my sample cited 'disorganization' or 'inefficiency' as one of the most frustrating aspects of their job. Examples given included broken, but unreported television sets or equipment, messages not passed on, incoming information (e.g., on courses) not circulated, lessons interrupted by children with notes, books, coaches, or films not ordered as requested, inadequate advance warning given of timetable changes, or of visitors to the classroom, mislaid equipment, sudden shortages of stock, expenditure which resulted in overgenerous provision of resources in some subjects ('All those A.V. aids gathering dust in the cupboard') and too little in others ('I even have to bring my own dictionary for the children to use – but you should see the P.E. equipment').

These and similar examples contributed to teacher dissatisfaction because they were seen as preventing teachers from doing their jobs efficiently and effectively. 'I'm fed up with organizing everything at the last minute, I like to plan ahead, and prepare my mind in advance, but we're never told anything until the last minute, so it's almost impossible to be organized yourself.' 'I find the bad organization in the school is really frustrating. You waste so much time that ought to be spent on important things.' 'I got so fed up one day that I kept a record for a week of time spent in my classroom on doing things which were due to the head's inefficiency, like walking the kids down to hall to watch a TV programme on a broken set and back again, and reading out notices about choir practices and lost sweaters. It came to over half-an-hour a day. And I could have heard six children read in that time.' 'I've almost given up planning anything in advance, I used to plan and prepare properly, but because of the constant chopping and changing, I found I could seldom do anything I'd planned. So now I don't plan – I don't do the job so well, as a result, and I find that very discouraging.' Commenting on a local induction scheme for probationers, one teacher said, 'I think it's an abdication of responsibility on the part of the heads. There's no substitution for a well-organized school. If we had that, probationers wouldn't need special help in settling in.'

Remarks such as these were made by 42% of those interviewed and as often in schools whose heads were in other respects 'Bourbon', as in those with 'passive' leaders. They reflect the anger which teachers feel when they are, as they see it, prevented from teaching as well as they could by inefficient administration and inconsiderate management. To be sure, they do not cite a well-organized school as one of the things they like about teaching, but they comment with discouragement, bitterness, and disillusion upon the effects on their work of working in a disorganized one. In this sense, administration is an aspect of consideration as much as it is of initiating structure. In either case it cannot be excluded from a consideration of leadership style.

Consideration

In consideration too there was a marked correspondence between the headteacher characteristics singled out for mention by the teachers in this sample and the items listed by Halpin, both in his Leader Behaviour Description Questionnaire (1966, p. 89) and as a subtest for Organizational Climate (Principal's Behaviour: VIII Consideration) (1966, p. 154). Although some of the items in both these lists relate to decision-centralization there is enough similarity between the remainder and the comments of teachers in my sample, to justify the inclusion of consideration as a major dimension of leadership style.

It is, of course, a truism that good leaders are concerned with personal relationships with and among their staff. In this study the 'positive' leader is personally visible and accessible, and seems to his staff to be concerned with the professional development of individuals, whereas 'passive' leaders are perceived both as personally inaccessible, and as unable or unwilling to offer support. In addition, 'Bourbon' heads maintain distant, and at times even abrasive, relationships with individuals.

One-sixth of the teachers to whom I spoke mentioned the personal accessibility of the 'positive' head as one of his valued attributes. This characteristic is welcomed by experienced teachers with specific problems ('You can always take a problem to her and she's ready to help'), and in a more general way by those with less experience. 'The head was great. He was always around without being interfering,' and, 'The head came in every day, usually after school; she suggested, praised, gave advice, I really appreciated that', are two typical comments. By contrast, 'passive' heads are often seen as obsessed with office routines or as 'hiding in the stock-room'. As a result, they are 'never available to talk to'. This leads teachers to the disabling conclusions that 'we never know what he wants, he doesn't seem to have a policy' and that 'we don't feel responsible to anyone.' It can also result in the frustration of innovative effort. As one teacher said, 'When I was given a Scale 2 post for Maths I tried to devise a recordkeeping system for the whole school, but I could never pin the head down to a discussion of it, and in the end I gave up trying.' Another described a similar experience with an abortive attempt to introduce team-teaching and concluded, 'We never see him; as long as he can tell visitors to the school that we've got team-teaching, I don't think he's interested in whether or not we actually achieve anything.'

The frustration resulting from lack of communication with and from 'passive' heads contrasts markedly with the satisfaction shown by teachers whose 'positive' leaders were not only known to be available in their offices, but who also made themselves accessible by constantly moving about the school.

Discussion arises easily with an accessible head, and it is probably no coincidence that individuals see 'positive' heads as being concerned with their professional development, and as contributing to this development through discussion. 'The biggest factor in my development has been my talks with the head,' said one teacher, while another spoke of 'the key role played by the head in my development; he was always ready to talk.' In general, heads who encouraged discussion, formal or informal, among their staff were all singled out for praise (e.g., 'I learnt such a lot by talking to the head after school'; 'The head here gives us so much opportunity for discussion, and joins in herself'; 'The head was marvellous. . . . He was always ready to talk').

It was not, however, so much the absence of discussion which led another handful of teachers to complain that 'passive' heads were not interested in their problems as a perceived lack of support. 'I learnt to ask the staff, not the head. You don't get any help from him, and it only gives him the impression you can't manage,' was a typical comment. 'I like the children and their parents,' claimed one teacher, 'but it isn't an easy school to teach in and you get no backing from the head. I'd move if I could, especially if I could feel I was part of a team.'

Little or no comment was made about the accessibility of 'Bourbon' heads, or about their readiness to support and guide their teachers. What was, however, the subject of anguished description, especially in answer to the question, 'What do you dislike about teaching?', was the authoritarian manner in which some relationships were perceived as being handled. There were only four examples of this, but each of them had made a profound impression on the recipient. Three teachers' views could be summed up by the comment of one of them: 'He was a bully. . . . He caned the children and shouted at us all. . . . I left the school as soon as I could.' The third I quote in some detail. This account does not give the head's view of the incident, and to that extent is only partial, but my concern is to show what aspects of leadership style may be 'dissatisfiers', not to establish the accuracy of personal testimony. Behaviour on the part of leaders which is seen by their subordinates as arbitrary, high-handed, or unkind is clearly a 'dissatisfier'. 'One day the head called me in and accused me of defying him in ignoring his written orders (over the teaching of English). I hadn't defied him, just hadn't realized that they were orders, not guidelines, but he wouldn't believe me, and said he wouldn't give me a good reference when I asked for one, unless I learnt to fit his mould better. Next day the adviser turned up, and told me that if I were a shop-girl I'd do exactly what my boss told me, and my situation here was exactly the same. It was sheer stupidity, he said, for me to defy my headteacher in so calculated a fashion. . . . I was too stunned to say much. . . . Later on I was told that being a competent teacher wasn't enough, a teacher had to obey the head.'

Decision-centralization

Belasco and Alutto (1975) have argued both that participation in decision-making has recently emerged as a central concern for teachers and that the desire to participate is differentially distributed among various groups of teachers. Thus one must not assume that the decentralization of decision-making will always increase the job-satisfaction of teachers. They advance evidence to suggest that age, sex, marital status, SES, type of school are all critical variables. It is likely that other variables to do with the nature of the staff group and social climate of the school are also relevant, but lacking evidence to support this contingency-hypothesis, I can show only that some teachers in my sample preferred heads who assumed a major role in decision-making, while others were happier with a greater degree of decentralization. All, however, condemned heads who totally devolved responsibility for making those decisions which radically affected the whole school. As Halpin (1966) showed, educational administrators who felt consideration to be a prime leadership quality in their job did not realize that their subordinates in fact wanted them to engage in more initiation of structure.

In particular, almost the greatest single cause of dissatisfaction among the teachers whom I interviewed was their sense of working in schools which lacked a sense of purpose. Seven explicitly mentioned the lack of 'common goals' or 'common standards' as one of the things they most disliked about teaching, eight complained of a lack of 'continuity', 'consistency', or 'direction' in school policy, ten commented on the absence of a 'coherent philosophy', twenty-three more named dissatisfactions related to a lack of common policy, and five claimed that the frustration thus induced was a major reason for their leaving their job, or teaching. Typically, 'There must be priorities in a school, even if the priorities are wrong. You must be able to see coherent responses, agreed by the staff and the parents. A school must be a unit, not just a collection of good groups,' and, 'I decided to move there because I had to get somewhere where I could feel that the school was achieving something purposeful. . . . A teacher must not only be good, but part of a coherent whole.' Put positively, this urge for coherence emerges as, 'What I do is worth it, because the next teacher is going to make use of it. It's worth the extra effort because you have something to build for. You see the standards of the children in the fourth year, and you know that you're setting them off along that path.'

Most laid discontents about the absence of school goals at the door of 'passive' heads. 'You couldn't pin the head down; he always seemed to be changing his ideas. There was no sense or aim in the school, no philosophy. In the end I came to feel that I was nothing more than a child-minder.' 'The head spends so much time following popular fashions, he's always chopping and changing his policies, and there is no sense of achieving anything.' 'The general attitude in the school is, "you do what you think", and that's not very helpful if you've got problems.' 'There was no ultimate purpose in what we did . . . he didn't know what we were educating for. . . . As long as we didn't annoy the parents, or let the kids get noisy, the head didn't seem interested.'

Implicitly, therefore, the head is expected to take a lead in establishing aims for his school. When he did so, this behaviour received appreciative comment from his teachers. Typical comments about 'positive' heads were: 'The headteacher set the direction of the school. He was an old-fashioned patriarch in many ways, but the staff were an open group, and the fact that the place was full of certainties made it a good place to start in.' 'It's much better at this school. We're given a lead. We're under quite strong pressure from the head to conform in certain ways, but that's better I think than at [his previous school] where you were left entirely to do your own thing.'

There is, however, a strongly expressed complementary feeling that, while the head should give his staff a lead in formulating school aims and policies, he should not take this entirely upon himself. Teachers reacted strongly against 'Bourbon' heads who denied them a part in decision-making. 'It was impossible to disagree with our last headteacher. But I'm happier now. There's more open discussion, and people are more involved in the school.' 'We all have to follow directives from the head. . . . All she wants from the staff and the children is obedience. That's really why I'm giving up. I don't feel any more that I have anything to contribute.' 'I used to smoulder in silence in staff meetings. . . . He wasn't interested in anything we had to say.' 'In future, I want to have a say on policy.'

Moreover, they were quick to spot, and to resent, what one described as 'mock democracy, based on length of service'. 'Staff meetings are disguised dictatorship', was a sentiment expressed by eight teachers, and given in different ways by five others as a major source of job-dissatisfaction. 'The staff can talk, but the school is run the head's way,' sums up discontent with this aspect of 'Bourbon' leadership.

By contrast, 'positive' leaders offered their staffs a chance to contribute to goal-setting and decision-making. 'It's good here, because you can work out with the head and the staff what the goals are.' 'We have staff-meetings every week, and we really feel that we can have a say in what the school is about. . . . Mind you, it's hard work, but it's worth it. Everyone pulls together, whereas at [her previous school] we all went our separate ways.'

'There's no conflict in this situation, but plenty of discussion. That's due to the head. He started us all talking to each other, and although he makes the decisions, he listens to what we have to say.'

Conclusion

The teachers in this survey had clear expectations of their heads, and were dissatisfied when these standards were not met, whether by 'passive', or, less frequently, by 'Bourbon' styles of leadership. A 'positive' style, by contrast, provided the context in which a keen teacher could get on with his chosen work and therefore contributed considerably to his job-satisfaction. 'Positive' leadership was characterized by: explicit aims for the school as a whole which were subject, within limits, to negotiation, a high standard of personal 'commitment' and professional competence, support and encouragement for individuals, the capacity to create a sense of cohesion within the school as a whole. In Yukl's terms (1975), a 'positive' head was high on initiating structure and consideration and fairly low on decision-centralization. By contrast, a 'passive' head was low on initiating structure, fairly low on consideration, and very low on decision-centralization, while a 'Bourbon' head was high on decision-centralization and low on consideration.

It is interesting to note that, despite the common belief that teachers value their autonomy highly, 'passive' leaders cause more (though not necessarily greater) job-dissatisfaction than 'Bourbon' ones. There are several possible reasons for this. It may partly be because, in my sample, there are more of the former. Another explanation is the nature of education itself, which makes the identification and agreement of goals very difficult and thus emphasizes for teachers the importance of leaders who concentrate their efforts upon the delineation of goals and the initiation of structures to achieve them. It may also be that the traditional autonomy of classroom teachers affords them protection from excessive control, while leaving them vulnerable to an overall lack of direction.

The essentially collective nature of education in schools may also be responsible for the demand for stronger leadership. Education in primary schools takes place to a large extent in groups and is often supported by a 'progressive' philosophy which gives primacy to social aims. Groups, by definition, have goals and means of attaining them. To some teachers the school is the significant group and leaders who fail to initiate group goals or the structures for pursuing them stand charged of ineffectuality. The attention of others is focused upon their classes. These teachers usually find no difficulty in stating their personal aims for their own teaching groups but resent the administrative inefficiency which makes goal-attainment difficult. In either case they are implicitly expecting their heads to provide more structure, though of different kinds, than the latter see the need for. Moreover, the more committed they are, whether to school or class goals, the more likely they are to press for the means to pursue these ends.

It is also possible that initiating structure may appear a more important leadership dimension than consideration in situations where teachers are driven into isolationism by the perceived absence of collective goals. In schools where teachers derive satisfaction from interpersonal relations with their pupils rather than with their colleagues, they are unlikely to set much store by the quality of their social relations with their head. In these cases what they want of their leader, beyond a minimal level of courtesy and sensitivity, is efficiency and perceived power within the larger educational system to procure for them the means for personal goal-attainment. 'Bourbon' heads probably create dissatisfaction in this context because they fail to provide a clear task structure while at the same time falling below individuals' tolerance levels on the consideration dimension.

Whatever the causes, initiating structure is obviously a key dimension in educational leadership. Its absence is a strong 'dissatisfier', and those aspects of it which relate to the head's own professional standards and involvement with the school also appear to be 'satisfiers'.

This is not to say that consideration is not important. Gross cases among 'passive' or 'Bourbon' heads of perceived aloofness, superficiality, or abrasiveness in personal relationships are strong causes of job-dissatisfaction. By contrast 'positive' leaders contribute to job-satisfaction by showing a concern for the professional development of their teachers and being readily available for discussion. It therefore looks as if lack of consideration should be seen as a 'dissatisfier' though, under some circumstances, its presence may also be a 'satisfier'.

Decision-centralization is more clearly both a 'satisfier' and a 'dissatisfier'. Unfortunately, I do not have the evidence which might clarify the circumstances under which it becomes one rather than the other. Fiedler (1968) suggests a distinction between executive and consultative decision-making which intuitively seems relevant, but much more information would be needed about the nature of the group and the context of the school before one could fully accept his hypothesis. Be that as it may, most teachers do not seem to want fully decentralized decision-making, and resent 'passive' heads who do not take the decision-initiatives which are a 'satisfying' characteristic of 'positive' heads. At the same time many teachers welcome active involvement in policy-making and complain when deprived of it by 'Bourbon' heads.

In conclusion, evidence drawn from discussion with 93 graduate primary teachers suggests that educational commentators place a higher value on complete freedom of judgement and decision-making for teachers than the latter themselves do. If these teachers are representative of the profession, it is clear that many would be willing to sacrifice a good deal of their autonomy in goal-setting in return for a greater sense of cohesion and of teamwork. Most of those whom I interviewed genuinely wanted to teach well, but many felt that, because of 'passive' leadership, they were dissipating their efforts. Their tendency therefore was to change jobs, in search in part of effective, 'positive' leadership. If they failed in their attempts to find this, they left teaching, or contracted their horizons, concentrating solely on teaching their own classes. Here they frequently continued to earn the golden opinion of their headteachers, but were themselves conscious that they were contributing little or nothing to the school as a whole, or to the development of their colleagues. For many, this became an additional source of frustration and discontent. Thus maximum job-satisfaction went hand-in-hand with humane but positive leadership, leadership to which teachers felt they were encouraged to contribute but which gave them in return the chance to perform effectively the main role for which they believed they were employed.

References

Andersen, H., 1943, 'Domination and socially integrative behaviour', in Barker, R.G., et al., (eds), *Child Behaviour and Development*, New York: McGraw Hill.

Argyris, C., 1964, *Integrating the Individual and the Organization*, New York: Wiley.

Bates, T., Bell, R., and MacKenzie, M., 1974, Decision Making in the School, Unit 12, E 221 *Decision Making in British Education Systems*, Milton Keynes: Open University.

Belasco, J. and Alutto, J., 1975, Decisional Participation and Teacher Satisfaction, in Houghton, V, et al. (eds), *The Management of Organisations and Individuals*, London: Ward Lock Educational.

Blake, R. and Mouton, J., 1964, *The Managerial Grid*, Houston: Gulf Publishing Co.

Burnham, P., 1968, The Deputy Head, in Allen, B. (ed), *Headship in the 1970s*, Oxford: Blackwell.

Etzioni, A., 1964, *Modern Organizations*, Englewood Cliffs: Prentice Hall.

Fiedler, F., 1968, Personality and Situational Determinants of Leadership Effectiveness, in Cartwright, D. and Zander, A. (eds), 1968, 3rd edition, *Group Dynamics*, New York: Harper & Row.

Gibbs, C., 1969, 'Leadership', in Lindzey, G. and Aronson, E. (eds), *The Handbook of Social Psychology*, Vol 4, 2nd edition, Reading, Mass: Addison Wesley.

Glaser, B. and Strauss, A., 1967, *The Discovery of Grounded Theory*, London: Weidenfeld and Nicholson.

Gray, H., 1979, *Change and Management in Organizations*, Driffield: Nafferton Books.

Halpin, A., 1966, *Theory and Research in Administration*, New York: Macmillan.

Handy, C., 1976, *Understanding Organisations*, Harmondsworth: Penguin.

Herzberg, F., 1966, *Work and the Nature of Man*, Pittsburg: World Publishing Co.

Hicks, H. and Gullett, C., 1976, 3rd edition, *The Management of Organisations*, Tokyo: McGraw Hill Kogakusha.

Hoyle, E. and Bell, R., 1972, Problems of Curriculum Innovation I, Unit 13, *The Curriculum: Context, Design and Development*, Milton Keynes: Open University.

Hughes, M., 1975, The Professional as Administrator: The Case of the Secondary School Head, in Houghton, V., et al. (eds), *The Management of Organisations and Individuals*, London: Ward Lock Educational.

Lewin, K., 1944, The dynamics of group action, *Educational Leadership*, 1, 195–200.

Likert, R., 1961, *New Patterns of Management*, New York: McGraw Hill.

Lippitt, R. and White, R., 1943, 'The Social Climate of Children's Groups', in Barker R., et al. (eds), *Child Behaviour and Development*, New York: McGraw Hill.

McGregor, D., 1960, *The Human Side of Enterprise*, New York: McGraw Hill.

Morgan, C., 1976, Management in Education – Dissimilar or Congruent?, E 321 *Management in Education*, Unit 1, Milton Keynes: Open University.

Nias, J., 1979, Job Satisfaction and Dissatisfaction among Primary Teachers, (forthcoming).

Nias, J., 1980, Further Notes on the Concept of Commitment, (forthcoming).

Richardson, J.E., 1973, *The Teacher, the School and the Task of Management*, London: Heinemann Educational.

Smith, I., 1979, *Management, School Organisation and Teachers*, Stirling Educational Monographs, No 5, University of Stirling.

Yukl, G., 1975, 'Toward a Behavioural Theory of Leadership', in Houghton, V., et al., *The Management of Organisations and Individuals*, London: Ward Lock Educational.

CHAPTER 4.2

THE ROLE OF THE PRIMARY HEAD*
A.A. Coulson

The prewar elementary school and the primary school of the immediate postwar years had a fairly clear and restricted purpose – the most important tasks were the teaching of the three Rs and the socialization of children in the then generally accepted values of society. Curricula and teaching methods changed only slowly, and the school's interaction with parents and the neighbourhood it served was limited. The head was often the best qualified and experienced teacher on the staff and in some schools he was the only qualified teacher. Apart from teaching, he performed a fairly narrow range of administrative and welfare functions; the comparatively stable and unchanging régime of school life made it possible for him to carry out all the school's nonteaching tasks himself. But in the last two decades educational change has been increasingly rapid. Primary school curricula and teaching methods have been transformed, and the school is now more integrated with the community. Moreover, established values and authority have been brought into question in every part of society. In general, heads have responded to these changes by taking more and more responsibility upon themselves. This chapter looks at some of the factors which sustain the traditional, paternal form of headship in the primary school, examines some of the pressures which are making this conception of headship less practicable and more strenuous for many heads, and puts forward an alternative which, it is hoped, is more rational and more in keeping with the needs of the schools of today.

    The term 'primary' is used here to describe the 23,000 or so county and voluntary schools which are attended by all or part of the five-to-twelve

* *The Role of the Head*, R.S. Peters (ed), Routledge & Kegan Paul, London, 1976, pp. 92–108.

age-group. Almost all heads of schools for infants only (children aged five to seven) are women, but in other types of primary school over three-quarters of the heads are men.

County and voluntary primary schools are managed according to rules drawn up by local education authorities. There is a tripartite division of the responsibility for each school between the local authority, which determines the general character of the school and its place in the local educational system, the board of managers, which is officially responsible for the general control of the conduct and curriculum of the school, and the head, who is responsible for 'the internal organisation, management and discipline of the school' and the supervision of teaching and nonteaching staff. The rules of management are made by the local authority under powers delegated to them by the 1944 Education Act (Section 17 III); they therefore lay upon the head inescapable legal duties. Although there are considerable local variations, and many local educational authorities have recently amended both the powers and the composition of their governing bodies, the control exercised by these bodies has hitherto usually been a mere form (Kogan, 1972). Moreover, since the head is an employee of the local education authority, the true authority relationship is the one between him and his director of education and the director's staff. Thus, although heads enjoy considerable freedom of action, they are not really autonomous – they act under legal and financial requirements and the extent of their discretion varies according to the policies and traditions which prevail locally. Nevertheless, the gentle manner in which the authority of both local and central government is customarily exercised gives to heads great latitude to administer and organize the schools according to their own convictions.

This freedom permitted to the head, and the consequent close correspondence between his preoccupations and personality and the character of the school, is a distinctive feature of British education. The traditional approach to headship is expressed by one of the heads quoted by Donaldson (1970, pp. 76–77): 'I feel that the underlying philosophy is mine and that everything stems from this: the school organization and the atmosphere generated are determined and controlled by this.' It is part of the traditional concept of headship in Britain that the head is considered a teacher rather than an administrator (an emphasis symbolized by the use of the term head*teacher*). Because of this, most heads subordinate administrative means of shaping their schools to interpersonal strategies. In particular, the head expects to influence teachers by his own example and to persuade them to identify themselves with his aims and methods. Besides working 'through' the staff, the head is expected to exert a direct influence on pupils. Thus, in addition to their contacts with the whole school in assembly, most heads stress the importance of knowing every child individually, at least by name, and of teaching classes or groups of children regularly.

Another aspect of the traditional concept of headship is that of a filter, through which outside influences enter the school. It is expected that the head will protect the staff from criticism and interference by parents, and the children from the pernicious effects of the community's values (Westwood, 1966). Major changes of all kinds customarily enter the school by way of the head.

The traditional concept of headship, with its characteristic blend of personal control and moral authority, has been handed on to state schools from the public and independent grammar schools of the nineteenth century in which the heads were often clergy. Furthermore, it has reached the present-day primary school by way of the elementary school within whose characteristically authoritarian ethos, as Dearden (1968, p. 4) points out, 'The content of what was taught was made dependent for its acceptability on having come from the appropriate authority. . . .' This concept of headship has much in common with the Victorian *paterfamilias*. Yet, in the contemporary primary school the image of the head as a father figure is still held in high regard, especially by heads themselves.

Since the head is generally presumed to be the pivot and focus of the school, it is expected that he will possess a 'strong personality' in order to mould the institution in accordance with his own views. Cook and Mack (1972) conclude that firm decision-making is characteristic of most heads and that the word 'authoritarian' might not be inappropriate to describe the type of personality likely to lead to successful headship. Of course it is probably true that in many schools the head's considerable authority is exercised in a fairly benevolent way. Nevertheless, the question still arises as to how far it is appropriate in modern society for so much authority to be concentrated to such a large extent in the hands of one person. This leads us, then, to the broader question of how adequate is the traditional, paternal concept of headship to meet the growing and increasingly complex needs of the schools of today.

In secondary schools the traditional concept of headship is undergoing considerable changes, and in most of society paternalistic authority is considered outmoded. Why, then, does paternalism persist in the primary school?

It is a well-established principle that the supervision of pupils should have regard to their age and experience (Barrell, 1975). Supervision in the primary school is therefore both closer and more supportive than is the case with older children. Thus, primary school heads (and teachers) stand more manifestly *in loco parentis* to their pupils than do their secondary school counterparts.

Because primary school pupils are immature and dependent, and the care of small children is culturally defined as women's work (Lortie, 1969), primary school teaching is mainly a feminine occupation. The work emphasizes nurturant skills and stresses the importance of a total response to the 'whole' child as an individual; in this respect it is close to the maternal role in the family. It is the preponderance of women (about 75 percent), the work styles they adopt, and the attitude of most of them towards teaching as a career, which gives to primary teachers as an occupational group a number of characteristics which help to preserve the traditional, paternal authority of the head.

Since a large proportion of primary school teachers combine teaching with family life or leave it for family reasons, they are normally less committed to work careers than men of comparable attainments. The high turnover rate among teachers means that the average primary school staff usually contains a high proportion of teachers who have had little teaching experience or whose commitment to teaching as a career is limited. Where long-range career ambitions are lacking, a higher priority tends to be given to the achievement of pleasant social relations at work than to personal advancement or professional development (Simpson and Simpson, 1969). Personnel who lack career ambitions are also less likely to incur the possible costs of questioning the established order in the school and more likely to be acquiescent in the face of authority. The traditional authority pattern which prevails in most schools tends to be more acceptable to women than to men because women have conventionally played more submissive roles in society than men and, as a result, have been more tolerant of authority. Furthermore, cultural norms, supported by both men and women, uphold male superiortiy where men and women work together. This applies particularly in the primary school where most teachers are women and the majority of heads are men.

The basic unit of the primary school is the class. Within the classroom the teacher enjoys a fairly high degree of discretion over her work. Because each teacher habitually works with the same group of children in the same place for most of the school day, she becomes closely identified with the group and the place (*my* class, *my* room). Also, since her main focus lies within the setting in which she spends most of her working life, her basic concern is with the actual processes of teaching her own particular class. In short, the primary school teacher lives in what Jackson (1968, p. 47) has called, 'a world of sharp existential boundaries'. Because of her preoccupation with the fairly isolated world of the classroom, the primary school teacher tends to be relatively indifferent to organizational matters involving the school as a whole. Lortie (1969) suggests that decision-making in schools is 'zoned'. Whilst the teacher has her own zone of autonomy inside the classroom, it is tacitly agreed that she accepts the head's hegemony over matters of general school policy and administration.

The teacher's immersion in teaching tasks contributes further to the maintenance of paternal authority by diminishing the intensity of her relationships with colleagues. School issues, which could, perhaps, promote solidarity among teachers working jointly to solve common problems, rarely assume sufficient importance to foster the collegial ties which might act as a counterweight to the head's paternalism (Leggatt, 1970).

Whereas the authority of the established professions, such as the law and medicine, rests to a considerable degree upon their command of theoretical and esoteric knowledge, there is no agreed body of generalizable pedagogic knowledge underlying primary school teaching. In fact, among primary school teachers and heads there is a widespread conviction that personal qualities, good relationships, and fondness for children are greater assets than knowledge, expertise, or intellectual rigour. The primary school teacher's concentration upon personal factors and upon the day-to-day practicalities of teaching is accompanied by a distrust of theoretical and abstract modes of thinking and a reliance, instead, upon intuition and 'common sense' (Jackson, 1971). This attitude may arise partly from the widely held belief that, especially for women, child-rearing is largely natural and intuitive. The prominence given in primary school teaching to intuitive responses and to close, warm, interpersonal relationships, together with the feminization of the occupation, draws attention to the similarity in organization between the school and the family and to the parallel between the paternal concept of headship and the traditional role of the father in the family.

It is argued, then, that most primary school teachers have a perspective which is limited to the immediate in time and place, are preoccupied with classroom events, and view teaching as an intuitive activity which utilizes skills drawn mainly from experience. These features are ingredients of what Hoyle (1973) has called *restricted professionality*. Adoption of this occupational perspective affects the teacher's attitude to authority and is conducive to a concept of headship in which the legitimation of the head's status rests predominately upon the personal qualities of the incumbent, his 'common sense' and his – presumably successful – practical teaching experience. (And perhaps upon his age too, since most heads are older than most of their staff.) Restricted professional teachers may defer to the head and commit themselves to the ideals and pursuits he wishes to foster, not on rational grounds, but because of his positional authority and because his experience is similar to, but greater than, their own. The comparability of the head's training and professional socialization with that of most teachers facilitates this process by providing them, to a large extent, with a common professional outlook. This shared perspective leads to a general expectation that teachers will identify themselves with the head's aims, and will follow his spontaneous intuitive responses in matters of policy. The personal involvement of the head in every aspect of school operation further reduces the need for those aims and policies to be rationally formulated or made explicit.

Movement by primary school teachers towards *extended professionality* (Hoyle, 1973) may eventually counteract the force of tradition and lead to a more rational concept of headship. *Extended professionality* embraces a perspective which sees teaching as a rational activity in which the teacher derives her skills from a mediation between experience and theory; in addition to acknowledging the importance of teaching and relationships with pupils, it also places value upon professional collaboration and upon involvement by teachers in nonteaching professional activities. The basic assumption underlying this form of professional outlook is that the work of the individual teacher should be seen in context as an integral part of a much broader social process. Wide acceptance of this extended form of professionality would inevitably lead to teachers wishing to take a greater part in educational decision-making and, especially, in shaping the schools in which they work. The present truncated nature of teacher professionalism, however, is unlikely to play any major part in reducing the potency of the head's authority.

Having looked briefly at some of the factors which help to sustain the traditional, paternal form of headship in the primary school, we turn now to a consideration of some of the changes occurring in society and education which are affecting the schools and bringing this style of school leadership under pressure. In particular, we will look at four areas in which the head has traditionally enjoyed a high degree of autonomy: socialization and values; the curriculum and teaching methods; the internal authority structure of the school; and external relations between the school and its environment.

Socialization and values

Perhaps the most important aspect of primary schooling is socialization, the shaping of the individual in the face of an existing set of social norms and cultural values (Danziger, 1971). In his early years at school the young child learns social values and principles of conduct: he must learn to live in a crowd, to take turns, to cooperate, to control desires, and to accept the value of learning and conformity. The school is essentially an evaluative setting and pupils learn to live under the constraint of constant evaluation, both academic and moral. Values, norms, and rules governing behaviour flow from the head, and every expectation and exhortation of the head connotes value. The stress upon character-formation and value-transmission which is traditional in British education (Musgrave, 1972) assumes that the values to be passed on are generally agreed. Nowadays, however, traditional notions about, for example, appropriate standards of dress and hair length, acceptable patterns of social behaviour, and methods of discipline are subjects of public debate. It can no longer be assumed that the head's own values will coincide with those of many teachers nor that they will necessarily receive the support of parents. Moreover, since judgements about such matters are not fundamentally professional ones, the head cannot presume to be much more of an expert at making them than anyone else. In view, then, of the lack of a consensus upon norms and values, both in education and in society, it is manifestly undesirable that the values upheld by a school and embodied in its social system should be so closely dependent upon the convictions, or perhaps the prejudices, of a single individual.

Curriculum and methods

As pointed out earlier, heads have received a training and professional socialization very similar to that of most primary school teachers – as nonspecialist class teachers. Because of the lack of specialization in the primary school, the head is traditionally considered qualified, by virtue of his more extensive or more successful classroom experience, to supervise and control the work of teachers. His direct influence on the curriculum and teaching methods confers on him much greater power and responsibility than has his secondary school counterpart. Whereas the latter does not normally supervise the teaching of subject specialists, the primary school head usually compiles or approves all schemes of work and personally oversees teaching.

In the primary school the postwar years have seen the traditional authoritarian and teacher-centred teaching techniques of the elementary school give way increasingly to more flexible and child-centred methods. The removal of the eleven-plus examination, which had acted as an outside levelling constraint on the curriculum of most primary schools, together with an acceleration of the movement towards placing the emphasis on 'learning' rather than 'teaching', encouraged the introduction of new subjects and teaching methods. Other heads, advisers, publishers, and agencies such as the Nuffield Foundation and the Schools Council, constantly add to the variety of new material from which the head, in his role of 'innovator', can choose his own particular curriculum mixture. Numerous courses and books advocating the latest fashions now compete for the head's attention, and an ideology of change is now almost indispensable if a school is to be regarded as successful and its head considered 'progressive'. Unfortunately, there is a danger that the actual innovations chosen may be determined as much by the head's own interests, and by whatever is currently fashionable, as by careful analysis of the needs of the school and its pupils. The superficiality of many of the changes, the often haphazard way in which they are managed, and the frequent neglect of systematic evaluation of the effectiveness of either new or old methods, raise important questions about the innovations themselves, about the rationale underlying their introduction, and, perhaps most important, about the organizational health of many of the schools (Brown, 1971).

Since the quantity of curriculum information now produced makes it increasingly difficult for an individual to keep his knowledge up to date, even in a fairly restricted field, the retention by the head of his traditional position as the focus of all curriculum decisions has become less and less practicable. Other teachers are now often better equipped to take these decisions, particularly in their own special fields of interest. Increased public concern about the effectiveness of teaching (particulary the teaching of reading and number) has underlined the necessity for systematic and informed thought regarding decisions about the primary school curriculum. Given the range and complexity of the issues now involved it will become increasingly difficult for heads to cope with these decisions adequately.

Internal authority structure

Compared with secondary schools, most primary schools are relatively small. And, until recently, their hierarchy of staff was limited to the head, the deputy head or senior assistant, and teachers. In the secondary school the distribution of authority is based upon its departmental subunits, each of which has its own hierarchy. On the other hand, in the primary school each teacher, except usually the head, has a class. The classroom units are relatively independent of each other and every teacher has more or less the same degree of authority and autonomy. The primary school head, therefore, has no tradition of delegation and the 'flat', class-based structure of most of the schools encourages teacher independence rather than teacher interdependence. The flatness of the school's authority structure and the lack of specialized teaching makes differentiation between teachers difficult. Consequently, salary additions for primary school teachers tend to be 'merit' allowances rather than payments attached primarily to specific duties and responsibilities. Genuine authority and responsibility are concentrated and remain in the hands of the head.

The traditional concept of the head as a teacher rather than an administrator and the commonly held belief that he is personally responsible for everything in the school restricts delegation. The head who takes this view maintains a high degree of overall control, makes the final decisions on all major matters himself, and relies heavily on personal influence through face-to-face communication with his subordinates. The power of the head who adopts this type of leadership is effectively limited in that it is dependent upon his presence or at least upon his close personal involvement; It cannot be mediated by others.

Most heads are promoted straight from the classroom (Kelsall and Kelsall, 1969, p. 31):

As things stand, those who assume these duties are, in the main, practising teachers who are judged, possibly often on inadequate evidence, to have the experience and capacity to undertake a role in which classroom teaching hardly figures at all.

The head's role is essentially learned 'on the job' and most heads have little knowledge of techniques of decision-making, delegation, or communication. However, as the internal affairs of the school become more complex and its external links and commitments expand, the head will come under more and more pressure if he continues to deal with almost everything himself. A rational distribution of tasks and responsibilities among the staff would relieve much of this pressure. At present, where delegation does occur it is usually of a limited, *ad hoc* nature which restricts the occupants of other supervisory positions in the school to the status of heads' 'aides'. The performance of delegated tasks is frequently accompanied by interference from the head, and deputy heads and holders of posts of responsibility complain that little action is taken on their decisions until teachers have sought and obtained the head's endorsement (Coulson and Cox, 1975).

Paradoxically, some of the changes occurring in the primary school, such as the introduction of team-teaching and open-plan architecture, tend to increase the concentration of authority and accentuate the highly interactive, paternal style of leadership already prevalent among primary school heads. In general, the removal of barriers between teachers and classes reduces the isolation of the individual teacher and consequently his autonomy. As the physical separation of classes decreases, the individual teacher's zone of authority and decision-making diminishes; decisions formerly made in the classroom by each teacher may now be made collaboratively, by team leaders or year-group leaders, or by the head. Moreover, since the head is responsible for creating the other superordinate posts in the school and for determining the extent of their responsibility and authority, in legal and formal terms these offices are almost nonexistent. Because the occupants of these posts are directly responsible to the head, there is a strong tendency for them to function largely as extensions of his own role. The selective recruitment of teachers to these positions is, of course, one very important way the head has of shaping the school according to his own views.

External relations

As well as being the focal point of communications within the school, the head is traditionally the main channel of contact between the school and its environment. His command over both internal and external communications accentuates his importance since he is the only person who is able to exercise overall control. His boundary position between the school and its environment serves to identify him with the school in the eyes of the community. The head's traditional function of protecting the school from the interference of parents and other outsiders, creating a community 'sufficient unto itself', is being transformed into one which is also very much concerned with introducing outside influences into the school and with articulating the school and the community it serves. This development, and the head's increasing involvement in social and welfare problems, involves viewing him more as a manager of educational and welfare services than as a paternal figure who, to some extent, decides what the community's educational needs are as well as how they should be met.

In the existing situation the head, more than anyone else, is responsible for attempting to harmonize, or at least to reconcile, the child's two socialization settings – the home and the school. He also discharges the school's welfare functions more directly than other teachers, and it is through him that the community's social and medical services are brought to bear on both children and their parents. In fact, as links between the school and the neighbourhood grow, in some areas it begins to look as though the head is paternalistic not only to children and teachers but to the whole district. The head's role as a curriculum innovator, bringing in ideas from outside, has already been mentioned. In addition, contacts with other schools (particularly through their own heads), relations with governors or managers and with 'the office', negotiations with educational suppliers, and liaison with local colleges and universities regarding teaching practices and in-service courses all add to the burden of work for which the head has in the past accepted virtually sole responsibility.

In recent years public interest in and concern about educational matters has steadily intensified. Consequently, schools and their methods are now much more open to public scrutiny. Parental interest in education has grown considerably and a substantial number of parents are now well informed about educational topics. Many of them not only expect teaching methods to be explained and justified but are also keen to participate in the educational process themselves. Bodies such as the Advisory Centre for Education and the Confederation for the Advancement of State Education provide information and advice for parents and draw attention to the shortcomings of existing practices in the schools.

The part played by schools in the training of teachers has already expanded, and it is probable that a substantial measure of the responsibility not only for the preparation and induction of new entrants to teaching, but also for the proposed growth of in-service training, will be placed upon the schools themselves (*Education: A Framework for Expansion*, 1972).

In the present-day primary school what, then, is the rational justification for the head's monopolistic position in regard to external relations? Is it merely that he is the only member of staff who has time for such matters because he is not teaching a class? Or is he necessarily better qualified to deal with them because he has an expertise other teachers do not possess? Is it really feasible or desirable for the head, himself, to deal with the lion's share of these steadily proliferating tasks as well as all his other jobs?

The persistence of paternalism

Despite the growth and diversification of the demands made upon heads, research indicates that, in general, they retain personal control over issues involving policy decisions, the supervision of teachers, and the introduction of change (Barker Lunn, 1970; Brown, 1971; Coulson, 1974); they tend to lack confidence in the ability of many teachers to perform their jobs adequately without supervision (Caspari, 1965; Cook and Mack, 1972); and they perceive a need to involve themselves personally in *every* aspect of school life (Donaldson, 1970; Cook and Mack, 1972). It would appear, then, that the anxiety which many heads now experience about the expansion of their role has not, to any great extent, led to the distribution of the additional workload among assistant teachers. Although most heads now affect a benevolent image and have made some moves towards 'democratizing' their schools, the traditional, centralized authority pattern persists.

At the root of the primary head's paternalism lies the ego-identification which he normally has with the school. He tends to think of it as 'his' in a very special way and therefore to feel a deep sense of personal responsibility for everything and everyone in it. Certainly there are considerable statutory responsibilities placed upon heads, and many of them claim that this necessitates a paternalistic, even an authoritarian, form of leadership, involving close supervision of every aspect of school life by the head himself. Nevertheless, legal obligations are not in themselves sufficient to explain the *way* in which heads fulfil their responsibilities. Perhaps the explanation lies in the closeness of the relationship between the primary school head and the institution he leads. This closeness may in turn be related to the nature of the goals of primary education.

Since the role expectations for members of an organization can be clarified only within the framework of the purpose or mission of that organization, the diffuse goals of the primary school, in which socialization and value transmission are prominent, lead to equivocal role specifications for heads and teachers. The existing lack of clarity is aggravated by the profusion of changes with which schools are now continually faced. In addition to the ambiguity both of its goals and the role specifications of its teachers, the structural coherence of the primary school is low because of the semiautonomous nature of its classroom units. As a result, aims and practices may differ widely from teacher to teacher. Heads, then, perceive a need to overcome these divergent tendencies and give the school a unity. Hence, among their tasks they place priority upon the provision of a recognizable direction and philosophy for the school (Donaldson, 1970; Cook and Mack, 1972). This 'philosophy' is very closely identified with the head's own personality and is therefore normally conveyed by personal precept and example rather than explicitly stated; thus the head tends to regard himself as the unifying element in the school. His expectations, therefore, tend to replace more tangible goals. The importance given to his involvement in *every* school activity (Donaldson, 1970) illustrates the close identification which exists between the head as a person and the ideology he tries to promote. Heads typically speak of 'generating commitment' or of 'fostering loyalty'. From the way most of them perform their tasks it is clear that the loyalty and commitment referred to is to themselves as individuals, as well as to the ideals and values they promote in the school. Because the school is the head's image in the community, then in his view, and perhaps in the eyes of the community too, it is 'his' school. He may therefore tend to overidentify with it and to hold an idealized and perfectionist view of teaching (Gray, 1974). This may lead him to strive constantly to keep an eye on everything in order to assure himself that the school is moving towards his ideal.

The high esteem in which this headship style of dedicated obsessiveness is held reemphasizes how impracticable it is becoming to expect more than a handful of exceptional people to possess all the skills and attributes which school leadership now demands, and to perform all the head's traditional functions on their own without experiencing anxiety and strain. However great the head's dedication, can he alone function competently as leader in so many different fields – teacher-training, management and administration, moral and social values, social work and counselling, home–school relations, curriculum development, and so on? And all this without training or preparation except teaching experience? Surely a careful analysis of the traditional function of headship is needed in order to determine which school matters, if any, he *must* decide and which can be left to others. Also, careful consideration should be given to the personal knowledge and skills needed for headship and to how heads should be appointed, prepared, and evaluated.

The case against heads continuing to exercise paternal authority is not, however, based solely upon the impracticability of paternalism and its doubtful relevance to the changing situation in the schools. It also rests upon the obstacle which the head's dominance presents to the professionalization of teaching; for as things stand at present, the other side of the coin of the head's freedom is the teacher's subjection. However benevolent and supportive the head's paternalism may be, it curtails the authority and responsibility of other teachers and therefore adversely affects their professional status. As Hoyle (1969, pp. 69–70) remarks, 'the present status of the head permits him to control the activities of teachers in a manner more appropriate to workers performing routine skills than to relatively autonomous professionals'. The head's power of veto and his prerogative of having the last word on everything in the school denies to teachers the full exercise of professional judgement and inhibits the growth among them of professional attitudes.

The primary school is a specialized institution set up by society to perform that part of the socialization and education of children which it is beyond the capabilities of their parents to provide. In view of the complexity of the educational enterprise in modern society, it is no longer desirable or practicable for the heavy responsibility of controlling and directing a school to be placed upon a single individual – the head. Although tradition exerts a very considerable force, and there may be many problems involved in changing existing practices, it is suggested that there are strong arguments for authority in schools to move away from a paternalistic pattern towards a more collaborative one.

Suggestions for change

It must be emphasized, straight away, that the abolition of authority in the school and the removal of the office of head are not advocated. It is,

however, considered essential that authority in the school should be decentralized and rationalized (Hirst and Peters, 1970, pp. 113–124). This, in
turn, will involve considerable modification of the traditional concept of
headship. In particular, it implies the termination of the at present very
close identification which exists between the head and the school (*my*
school) and the abandonment of the belief that the school should be shaped
by the largely interpersonal transmission of the head's norms and expectations – his 'philosophy'. While the head should remain the school's chief
executive, his right to dominate policy-making should cease and his leadership should rest upon rational influence rather than institutionalized
supremacy. In short, the essential reform advocated is the effective separation of the head's legislative and executive functions.

Collegiality

Apart from the emotional adjustment needed to accept a revaluation of
the institution of headship and the problems which have to be overcome in
regard to authority, influence, and representation, what are the arguments
against the idea of the head as the chairman of a school management board
or committee? Each senior member of staff could be accountable to the
committee, could assume responsibility for a different aspect of school
operation, and could have equal, collegial authority. At present many
teachers, especially those who hold nominally supervisory positions,
experience uncertainty about their duties and responsibilities and find it
difficult to perform their tasks without constant reference to the head. In a
collegial system each member of the group would have a specified sphere of
responsibility and authority and, within the terms of reference agreed with
his colleagues, the freedom to exercise initiative in that area. General lines of
policy could be worked out by the staff committee under the chairmanship
of the head, and teachers would be responsible to the committee, not to the
head personally. Careful planning and efficient systems of communication
would, of course, be vital. A collaborative situation, in which knowledge
and ideas are pooled and decisions are shared, would be mutually helpful for
teachers and, though more demanding, would be more motivating and
professionally satisfying. By capitalizing on the special knowledge and
aptitudes of individuals the enterprise as a whole would also benefit.
Current educational developments such as collaborative forms of teaching
and open-plan architecture make staff cooperation and interdependence
increasingly necessary. A collective type of authority would be more com-

patible with these recent trends than paternalism.

It is desirable for the task of coordinating the internal system of the school with its environment to be carried out by a specific, identifiable person who represents the school. Although he should not monopolize this boundary function, the head should have this as his most important responsibility. He should also have discretion, within the limits of generally agreed policy, to deal with matters arising in the course of the day-to-day operation of the school. However, the pyramidal hierarchy of staff, with the head always at the apex, would be replaced by a federation of temporary structures serving specific purposes (Gray, 1973). The leader of each of these groups should, logically, be the best qualified and most expert person in the subject area the group is to tackle, regardless of his position in the school. These groups could formulate policies for specific aspects of the work of the school, devise and adapt strategies for implementing them, and evaluate and review the results.

At present the way the head is appointed, and the legal arrangements which place the bulk of the responsibility for the school in his hands, sustain the traditional, paternal concept of headship and stand in the way of a more rational allocation of authority and responsibility. In a collegial system adequate provision would be necessary for teachers to participate in the appointment of the head (Hargreaves, 1974). In some areas steps are already being taken in this direciton. Many local education authorities have recently amended their articles of school government (or rules of management) to give governing bodies greater discretion over school policy, and have altered the composition of these bodies to include representatives of parents, teachers, and nonteaching staff. These changes may entail less autonomy for heads and, naturally enough, are opposed by many of them. Although from the point of view of the community and of the teacher's freedom and professional development these changes may be desirable, there was actually always considerable room for manoeuvre within the traditional framework: neither the old-style nor the new-style rules of management prescribe the school's internal management structure or require the head to act in a particular way. Nevertheless, it is unrealistic to expect any collective way of running a school to function adequately under circumstances which enable the head to be authoritarian if it suits him.

A much deeper problem is the restricted professional outlook and limited career commitment of many primary school teachers. For many teachers of young children it is plain that the basic satisfactions of the job are intrinsic, gained from the actual process of teaching (Lortie, 1969). It is likely, then, that an extended form of professionality, involving extensive participation in school policy-making and nonteaching professional activities, may appear too rationalistic and theoretical to many of these teachers. It will be essential, therefore, to evolve structures which will accommodate and satisfy teachers of either 'restricted' or 'extended' professional outlook. This may best be done by adopting a differentiated approach to staffing.

Differentiation between groups of teachers is not new and has been growing as a result of changes in the structure of teachers' salaries. An eventual separation between a nucleus of long-serving, highly qualified career teachers, engaged in recurrent professional retraining, and a larger number of more rapidly changing, less well-qualified assistant teachers, now seems increasingly probable (Taylor, 1969; Renshaw, 1974). Although such a division would, no doubt, be resisted by teachers, it might neverthe-less be fairer and more rational than the existing situation in which differentiation between staff lacks clear criteria and depends very much on the head's patronage. Besides supervising and coordinating the work of assistant teachers and collectively formulating policy, the career teachers could absorb many of the head's traditional administrative and public relations functions.

Training

Special training is desirable for the occupants of all supervisory and managerial positions in schools. A main function of training should be to assist heads and teachers 'to structure and analyse their own and colleagues' experience so that they may use it more effectively' (Glatter, 1972). Because such training should aim at encouraging fresh and critical thinking about the functions and organization of the school, it is important that it should not be directed primarily at heads and aspiring heads, merely arming them with increased managerial competence with which to function more efficiently within the existing paternalistic framework. Rather, it should consider and question the basic assumptions which underlie traditional modes of school organization and leadership, and should aim at developing rational strategies of management appropriate to the needs of today's schools and, hopefully, adaptable to those of the future.

References

Barker Lunn, J.C., 1970, *Streaming in the Primary School*, NFER.

Barrell, G.R., 1975, *Teachers and the Law*, Methuen.

Brown, M.R., 1971, 'Some strategies used in primary schools for initiating and implementing change', M.Ed. thesis, Manchester University.

Caspari, I.E., 1965, *Roles and Responsibilities of Head Teacher and Teaching Staff in Primary Schools*, Tavistock Clinic, mimeographed.

Cook, A. and Mack, H., 1972, 'The headteacher's role', in *British Primary Schools Today*, Macmillan, Vol 2, pp. 283–353.

Coulson, A.A., 1974, 'The deputy head in the primary school: the role conceptions of heads and deputy heads', M.Ed. dissertation, Hull University.

Coulson, A.A. and Cox, M.V., 1975, 'What do deputies do?', *Education 3–13*, Vol 3, No. 2, pp. 100–103.

Danziger, K., 1971, *Socialization*, Penguin.

Dearden, R.F., 1968, *The Philosophy of Primary Education*, Routledge & Kegan Paul.

Donaldson, P.R., 1970, 'Role expectations of primary school headteachers', Diploma in Child Development dissertation, London University.

Education: A Framework for Expansion (1972), HMSO.

Glatter, R., 1972, *Management Development for the Education Profession*, Harrap.

Gray, H.L., 1973, 'The function of a head of a school', *Journal of Moral Education*, Vol 2, No. 2, pp. 99–108.

Gray, H.L., 1974, 'The head as manager', *Education 3–13*, Vol 2, No. 2, pp. 81–84.

Hargreaves, D.H., 1974, 'Do we need headteachers?', *Education 3–13*, Vol 2, No. 2, pp. 24–27.

The Headteacher, 1973, 'An "Education" Digest', *Education*, 13 April.

Hirst, P.H. and Peters, R.S., 1970, *The Logic of Education*, Routledge & Kegan Paul.

Hoyle, E., 1969, 'Professional stratification and anomie in the teaching profession', *Paedagogica Europaea*, Vol 5, pp. 60–71.

Hoyle, E., 1973, 'Strategies of curriculum change', in R. Watkins (ed), *In-Service Training: Structure and Content*, Ward Lock.

Jackson, P.W., 1968, *Life in Classrooms*, Holt, Rinehart & Winston.

Jackson, P.W., 1971, 'The way teachers think', in G.S. Lesser (ed), *Psychology and Educational Practice*, Scott, Foresman & Co., pp. 10–34.

Kelsall, R.K. and Kelsall, H.M., 1969, *The Schoolteacher in England and the United States*, Pergamon.

Kogan, M., 1972, 'The government of education', in *British Primary Schools Today*, Macmillan, Vol 2, pp. 71–106.

Leggatt, T., 1970, 'Teaching as a profession', in J.A. Jackson (ed), *Professions and Professionalization*, Sociological Studies 2, Cambridge University Press, pp. 155–177.

Lortie, D.C., 1969, 'The balance of control and autonomy in elementary school teaching', in A. Etzioni (ed), *The Semi-Professions and their Organization*, Free Press, pp. 1–53.

Musgrave, P.W., 1972, *The Sociology of Education*, Methuen.

Renshaw, P., 1974, 'Education and the primary school – a contradiction?', *Education for Teaching*, No. 93, spring.

Simpson, R.L. and Simpson, I.H., 1969, 'Women and bureaucracy in the semi-professions', in A. Etzioni (ed), *The Semi-Professions and their Organization,* Free Press, pp. 196–265.

Taylor, W., 1969, *Society and the Education of Teachers,* Faber & Faber.

Westwood, L.J., 1966, 'Re-assessing the role of the head', *Education for Teaching,* No. 71, November.

CHAPTER 4.3

SHARING IT OUT: THE ROLE OF THE HEAD IN PARTICIPATORY GOVERNMENT*
John Watts

Why share?

A British head has traditionally enjoyed extensive powers. As 'captain of the ship', to use the stock title, he has had authority literally to flog and metaphorically to hang. Such autocracy is at present out of tune with the *Zeitgeist* and even those in positions where they continue to wield it tend to wear turtle-neck sweaters over their old-school ties.

But the autocracy of the head, however benevolent, is diminishing for reasons other than being unfashionable. Autocratic rule is also losing effectiveness, and although a head may survive being made to feel unpopular, this is tolerable for him if it is offset by a sense of being efficient in discharging his responsibilities. The complexity of any school is greater than it was twenty-five years ago, let alone in Thomas Arnold's day. This is particularly true of a comprehensive school (primary or secondary), catering as it does for the needs of all sorts, conditions, and ages amongst the young of a pluralistic society. The school is less isolated than in the past from its surrounding society: it has to cooperate with bodies as diverse as the probation service and university admission tutors, the Schools Council and Race Relations Boards. Any head must delegate or disintegrate.

However, delegation may be executed in such a way that no real authority, only workload, is passed out by the head. The crucial question is that of where the decisions are made and to whom decision-makers are accountable. Probably most heads today would claim that their decisions are made

* *The Role of the Head*, R.S. Peters (ed), Routledge & Kegan Paul, London, 1976, pp. 127–136.

in consultation, either with their deputies, some form of cabinet of faculty or pastoral heads, or even with their whole staff. Yet none of this consultation constitutes participatory government in the sense in which I wish to speak of it, and which has been practised at Countesthorpe since it opened in 1970.

At that time of opening, the question was asked 'How may we maintain an innovatory approach once we have embarked upon it?' It was not enough to have instituted a school with a number of radically new features: change was envisaged as a continuous process. Hierarchical organizations are relatively impervious to change. How were we to remain open to change? More particularly, whence would come the initiative and the inventiveness for change? If it were to come only from the top, how could it be adequate? However experienced a head and his senior staff might be, however reliable their judgement, what likelihood was there of their imaginations being fertile? 'Young men have visions and old men dream dreams.' Younger teachers are more likely to have ideas and innovations than their elders. The ideas may need the riddling of experience, expertise, and judgement, but they must keep coming.

The tendency in schools is to tell juniors to stay quiet and listen, not to make awkward suggestions or ask embarrassing questions. My experience with graduate teacher training left me worried about the number of young men and women, ones with initiative and a sense of service, who changed their minds about becoming teachers after the experience of school practice had revealed to them the extent to which the hierarchy in staff would stifle their ambition. 'Keep quiet and conform' was the message. They traded the securities of teaching for work with more risk but a high demand for showing within a year or two what they could do with some opportunity for enterprise.

So the need to attract young teachers who want to get something done argues for their being given increased opportunity and responsibility. New developments in school place increased demands upon the teacher, and in particular he is required to forgo much of the autonomy he formerly enjoyed in the classroom in order to plan and execute work jointly with groups of colleagues. What may have been acceptable in the closed classroom must be modified to balance the working of a team. With the general growth in the size of schools there is danger that the teacher may come to feel depersonalized and alienated. It is reasonable for him to expect, in return for meeting new demands, a new degree of control in determining the conditions under which he works (particularly concerning the distribution of available resources), whom he works with, and in what sort of atmosphere. Control of, and responsibility for, these conditions may be expected to produce increased satisfaction and dignity.

There are of course other arguments for reducing the powers normally invested in the head. Although a newly appointed head may be the most effective agent for rapid change in a school, his impetus will be lost within five years. The school may then have to wait for one or two decades to make another lurch forward. Public demands for changes in the school may lead increasingly to ways being found to bypass the head and introduce change agents from outside. These may prove to be less gentle than the advisers and Schools Council project officers encountered up till now. The school needs equally well to be protected from the destructive wake that may be left by the progressive reforming head who has failed to win a consensus of support from the staff, students, and parents. An authoritarian progressive will usually come unstuck when outside agencies can exploit the division he has created among his staff. When this happens the reform aimed for by the head is thwarted, the power passes out of the school even to the point of its closing down, and children suffer.

We are thus faced with the question of which way the head's powers will be redeployed. Will they spread to external authority, or will they be shared within school? In depicting what happens when shared internally at Countesthorpe, I wish first to outline the powers in question, then to consider the reshaped role of the head, then to look at the problems I have encountered in the process, and finally, to venture a forecast of further development.

The head's powers

Within normal terms of appointment, a head has usually enjoyed powers that can be considered under six broad headings. There is some variation in the extent to which governing bodies have retained control in any of these areas, and there are worrying current tendencies, that I shall refer to later, which threaten to take powers back from governors to local councils, but whoever holds these six cards is running the school, and where governors have trusted the head whom they have appointed, these are the cards that he has been dealt.

First, the head has defined the objectives and the values for his school. He will operate within the limits of what the governors and parents expect, but this is seldom a problem if they have chosen the head they want. (In other words, the constraints will not need to be spelt out as the chosen head will be presumed to have internalized them.) The head seldom needs to make his objectives and values explicit. In fact, part of his power lies in leaving them implicit, or expressed only in ritual, so that they are not then exposed to rational cross-examination and consequent modification. They can nevertheless be clearly understood and thus effectively govern the school. Wherever the objectives and values *are* explicit, the head still wins as he is the mouthpiece of the school in all public statement.

Second, the head determines curriculum, what is taught.

Third, distinguished but related, is control of the internal organization, by which the head has power over access to the courses of learning within the general curriculum. He decides who has opportunity to learn what, who can study Latin and who has extra woodwork. He controls the timetable. He decides how the pupils are grouped, who teaches them, and, within the statutory requirements, how long they stay at school.

Fourth, the head distributes the available money. Therein lies one of his greatest sources of power. He decides how capitation allowances from the local authority are used: he can starve one department to build up another. He virtually controls the distribution of special allowances to the staff, thus having authority over teachers' incomes outside their basic salaries. In some authorities this distribution of additional payment is made by the governors, but the head's recommendations to them remain crucial. This particular power can become, almost invariably does become, the most resented of all, especially when his distribution of favours remains secret. Through it the head can control staff by promises, threats, and bargains. At the same time, he is laid open to promises, threats, and bargaining from the lobbying of his staff. It becomes very difficult for a head to be sure when a teacher is being completely honest and frank with him, not saying what he thinks the head wants to hear, and it becomes difficult for the teacher behaving in that way to retain self-respect; which is the main reason for the usual isolation of the head: staff find it easier not to speak to him too often.

Fifth, the head chooses his own staff. The extent to which the local authority qualifies this varies considerably but the head can usually make his pick. In contrast with employees in industry, he cannot dismiss staff. But my main point is that it is the head who decides for his teachers whom they have to work with. They like his choice or lump it. This was all very well when we only had to tolerate each other in the staffroom and could retreat to the idiosyncrasies of our classrooms, but increasingly now we have to plan and work in close conjunction with these colleagues and feel a growing right to share also in their selection.

Finally, less obvious, but significant, is the degree of power that a head exercises through control of the media of communication. Quite apart from being the spokesman through the external media, via statements to the press, letters to parents, and so on, the head can assert his authority internally by such means as (i) control of paper and print for circulating notices; (ii) convening and chairing staff meetings; (iii) conducting assemblies; (iv) access to public address equipment; (v) installation and distribution of telephones; and (vi) preparation of policy statements and reports. All of this amounts to a one-way system of regulative communication, with negligible means of feedback for assistant staff or students.

Shared power: an alternative

At Countesthorpe we have changed all that. The major policy decisions that have shaped the curriculum and discipline of the school have been made by the consensus of the staff. Increasingly, students have contributed to this consensus, and in some instances parents and governors have participated. I accepted the headship in 1972 because I found the policies and the means of determining them attractive, and was prepared to answer for them externally while being accountable internally to the college. I remain as long as those two zones of accountability are compatible.

Within the college we have varied executive roles, many of them held interchangeably by staff other than myself and deputies, but without the conventional chain of authority. Our chain of authority links decision-making groups whose composition is not fixed. The body that establishes any ruling consensus is a general meeting, the Moot, which is open to all, including nonteaching staff and students. The Moot establishes its own constitution, procedures, and chairmanship. It meets as necessary, about once in six weeks. Other decision-making groups are responsible directly or indirectly to the Moot and any individual may challenge their decisions through the Moot.

The subgroups may be standing or *ad hoc*. The principal standing committee consists of one quarter of the staff with student representation and it holds office for one quarter of the year. Thus every member of staff has a period on committee. Standing committee meets every Monday after school to receive reports and take intermediary decisions. It issues minutes the following day. Other committees include finance committee which is elected annually to make and apply the budget, and *ad hoc* appointment committees set up with each vacancy to select whoever is finally recommended to the authority for appointment to staff. All meetings are advertised and open.

Stated this way, structures appear to dominate. In operation, all depends on the attitudes of the participants, their readiness to use, and if necessary, to modify the structures in order to exercise and take responsibility for powers placed in their hands through them. All six areas of power that I have listed become shared by these means. The Moot may finally decide major policy and organization, but in the preparatory ferment, the ideas may spring from any source. Working parties which eventually formulate proposals for development are open to all. Anyone may put forward a scheme. It will be tested for its desirability and practicality under the constraints of resources, staffing, space, and money. A final proposal will be the work of many hands, a modification of many ideas. Once it is ratified, though, everyone is committed to making it work, because no one has had it imposed from above without opportunity to shape it.

What remains for the head?

Far from becoming a lift attendant in a bungalow, the head has much remaining to him. When Countesthorpe opened in 1970, Tim McMullen, its first head, intended to make himself redundant. There are still those who would like to see the head phased out while accepting him as an unfortunate necessity for the time being. I do not share this view and will consider it further in my concluding section. Anyway, what do I do at present?

What I do not do is to allow myself to become the administrator. Except in small schools, where the head may still be general factotum, heads who allow themselves to become administrators must have a liking for admin. Otherwise they could perfectly well delegate responsibility for accounts, returns, repairs, requisitions, and all that square-footage. Most local authorities will appoint someone for that function, responsible to the head. I find a reliable bursar is indispensable. For a start it enables me to remain a teacher (at present I teach a 25 percent timetable) and a teacher-trainer, in the sense of having an influence upon the practice of less-experienced staff. However, this is a role played quite as effectively by a senior teacher, and there is more to my headship than that.

As head, I carry a particular responsibility for continuity. Where the curriculum and organization unrolls steadily, I need to maintain the diary of events to ensure that the flow is not checked for want of forward planning. I and the deputies (always called 'the executive' for want of a better term by staff) between us attend all meetings. We warn various chairmen of dead-lines, such as dates for appointments to be made, and initiate working parties before decisions have to be rushed or overtaken by events.

At any meeting, the head's influence is quite unrelated to his voting power. Some critics have expressed disquiet over my having one vote along with any probationer or fifth-former. This is beside the point: what one has to consider is what happens before any vote is taken. In that period, the head's influence may take various forms excepting only that it cannot be authoritarian, though it may be authoritative. That is to say, nobody has to accept the wisdom of my view on my say-so: nobody has to do or think what I tell them to because of my position. On the other hand, I do have the authority to give information available to me by right of position, such as rulings from local authorities and legal obligations. And there still remains the possibility of an authoritative (not authoritarian) voice allowed to me by virtue of accorded authority, that is, whatever the others may want to take from me simply because I am me. That authority is a trust that has to be won, can fluctuate and could be lost altogether, but it is real.

If that trust holds, then, as head, I have a crucial function as two-way transmitter of pressures. Whether staff want it that way or not, I am the one to whom external authorities refer. Their approaches differ hardly at all from the normal. If the director of education, or any of his many officers or political superiors, wants to extract information or commitment from the school, or to communicate either to it, they get on to me. If a parent is unhappy about the school, he identifies it through me. If the press wants a comment, they ring me. If the chairman of governors wants to pass on a comment, or sound out some proposed move, he buttonholes me. The transmission of pressure is through my bloodstream and I feel no guilt over being paid danger money.

Perhaps the most important aspect of this osmotic role is the extent to which I modify actions and decisions in school by sensitizing all the par-ticipants to outside reaction. There is a regard for my situation, and what might render it an impossible one, going beyond personal consideration (warming though that is, when it emerges) to an appreciation of what is possible within the tolerance of public opinion and those in political power. Teachers can remain unusually innocent over political realities, lacking, as they do, any continuous face-to-face contact with the adult world. They can usually leave that sort of thing to the head and then denounce his worldliness. At Countesthorpe, though we are not without our utopians, everyone has been forced to face realities. Their own idealism has been observed in practice (with wildly conflicting reactions), whilst the demands of outside forces have led them to make working compromises in order to survive and prosper.

In so far as this has succeeded – and after every kind of local hostility, we have survived and prospered – it has afforded me a changed kind of satisfaction. Instead of experiencing the gratification of seeing my own educational will take on flesh, as I had done in previous headship, I now feel that I have made possible, and participated in, a form of school in which teachers and school students have been able to enjoy an increase in dignity which results from their sense of determining, to a large extent, the conditions under which they work and grow.

Barriers and strategies

Problems abound. You solve one set only to encounter, and even create, new ones. Some can be surmounted while others remain as permanent constraints. Some I can identify as arising from the role of the head in a participatory government. The problem that most often is raised for me by others is that of possible conflict between head and Moot. This is an obvious one only because conflict between head and staff is normal: even under a liberal headship they advise and consent, while he consults and decides. But the participatory system depends upon initial agreement of aims. That is why it is very doubtful whether an existing school could go over to a participatory approach – I wouldn't recommend it. Countesthorpe was made possible by the first head's clear announcement of intention which enabled him to recruit a staff who wanted to work in that way. With head and staff agreed on basics, any conflicts can be resolved by open discussion with reference to them, provided all parties learn to tolerate conflict, use it to identify issues, and make compromises in order to reach consensus. Conflict → compromise → consensus → commitment. Real difficulty arises if ever we neglect to get together regularly for talk. If this should ever lead to insoluble conflict between me and Moot, either I should have to go, or the participatory system would.

A head gets used to just so much talk before he has to make his mind up.

Here, the decisions take longer to emerge. This puts a strain upon my tolerance that has made for occasional impatience. In my case the novel situation was made possible by a transitional period between headships as a lecturer at the London Institute of Education. There I learnt to tolerate ambiguity and delayed decision in growing to appreciate the strength of consensus. I took up smoking, otherwise I think it did me good. Others it might drive to apoplexy: participatory democracy would not be for them.

Another strain upon my psyche arises from the need to balance the self-effacement of participation with the firmness and fight so often needed on the school's behalf in outside dealings. This alternation of humility with aggressiveness has often required rapid changes of role and I am sure that they have often been confused. Though more obvious in critical times, this probably abides to some degree. One just has to let the problem be known to those who wonder why they have undeservedly been snapped at, and hope they will be understanding.

Of course, some teachers need an authority figure in order to rebel against him. The more mature will have learnt to internalize their enemy, but I have not entirely escaped those who will push one into an authoritarian role apparently in order to object to it. We did have one who boasted that he had taught children to stick pins into headmaster dolls, but he left when the rest of the staff discovered his inflexibility. So we do our best to appoint people who seem to be ready to carry their joint responsibilities.

Turning from the psychological problems to a sociological one, public opinion has a long way to go to catch up with the idea of a head who is anything but autocratic. More than in any other field, people's attitudes to schools are conditioned by the intensive experience of them in the formative period of their earlier years. The head as a stock figure is inevitably anachronistic. Men who have had to learn that negotiation between employer and employee is inescapable have yet to accept that, even if he should want to be autocratic, the head can no longer wield absolute authority, and in the long run will only make himself look ridiculous if he tries to. County councillors who would never risk sacking any of their own employees because they had been on strike will still demand of a head that he should instruct his staff not to strike or else prove himself inadequate. Everyone from the RSPCA to the anti-abortionists assume that if only the head has a word with the pupils in assembly, they will stop it, whatever it is. The only strategy in face of these pious hopes seems to be one of persistence, declaration, and publishing articles like this one.

Of course, power is enjoyable: it enables one to get things done. Even discounting the unreasonable expectations of those who ask for magic from a head, much remains for heads who do not want to relinquish power. I have argued for a spreading of this power, for sharing it with teachers before it is taken into the hands of noneducationalists. Nevertheless, it is not a popular argument with heads, and I run severe risk of antagonizing colleagues who see it as undermining their position. I need to reassure them that I do not perceive them all as power-drunk ogres who need to be told their job and deflated into the bargain. Indeed, if they will examine the foregoing they will see that, in their own positions, I would be extremely cautious about relinquishing power into dubious hands. How is this paradox going to be resolved?

Implications for the future

I do not at present see any maintaining authority entering into contract with a body of teachers on a collegiate basis. Their need to have the accountability of one person ensures the continued existence of the head for some time to come. Given examples of satisfactory stewardship by a head within a participatory system, the most we can hope for is a partnership between LEA and the staff of a school in selection of any new head. A rotating head (other than one who pernes in his own gyre, so to speak) is therefore not on, except in nonmaintained schools such as the Rudolph Steiner foundations.

Parents and teachers should be much less worried over the shift of a head's powers towards his school than over the more sinister threat at the moment of its removal into the hands of noneducationalists. His power has at least been checked and balanced up till now by governors, officers, and councillors with a special concern for education. With the establishment of the new enlarged authorities of local government, there has been a detectable pull of power towards their centres. Politicians claiming to act for their electorate have questioned the powers residing with heads and governors, even with education committees, and, in the name of efficient management, have sought to bypass them. Heads could become accountable direct to councils, and education officers give place to chief executives, civil servants with who knows what notions on education.

Not only does this situation call for vigilance, but it should be borne in mind by those of us trying to spread participatory school government. Any suspicion of irresponsibility on the part of teachers will strengthen the hand of those advocating central authority. Any attempt by teachers to dispense with the head and go it alone would gain no union support at present, and would have no legal basis. The result would only be confrontations that would be destructive to school staffs and damaging to school students. The critical issues therefore are these. Will heads prepare their staffs, students, and parents to share more power with them, or will it be removed to the centre? My own guess is that unless heads and teachers work together on this, they will all lose power that will be gathered in to county hall where the old autocratic head will then sit in all his remoteness under the new guise of efficient corporate management.

CHAPTER 4.4

THE CHANGING ROLE OF THE DEPUTY HEADTEACHER IN ENGLISH SECONDARY SCHOOLS*
R. Todd and W.F. Dennison

Introduction

Lack of role definition for deputy headteachers has been traditional in English education. That is, the behavioural pattern built around the rights and duties associated with the job of deputy headteacher has not been clearly defined, and in part this has arisen from a similar lack of role definition for headteachers, who have tended to exercise the powers of a paternalistic autocrat. As a result headteachers have viewed their deputies as extensions of themselves, and in doing so have deprived them of an authentic role. The key to the deputy role was the extent to which the headteacher was prepared to delegate and, because of their autocratic nature, this was minimal. An inquiry by Burnham (1964) involving 277 deputies in eight different LEAs confirmed the nonexistence of clear role definitions, and many in their replies complained that they were frequently reduced to carrying out a few minor technical or clerical duties which did not encourage, or even allow, the use of initiative and expertise. All too often, in their view, they were forced into formulating a role for themselves, and many were frustrated by gaining a position of considerable status within the school, while at the same time being denied the opportunity of fulfilling a role commensurate with their expectations. In addition the 'man in the middle' position – between the headteacher and his staff – was frequently a major source of difficulty and dissatisfaction.

With this particular problem in mind the theory of 'dual-leadership' was developed. In this, Burnham ideally cast the headteacher as the task-

* *Education Review*, Vol. 30, No. 3, 1978, pp. 209–220.

instrumental leader, with the deputy as the social-emotional leader of the school, and by separating leadership roles in this way the deputy could acquire an independent role for himself as head of the informal system of the school. It was 'as of right', and did not require headteacher delegation. Moreover, as deputies were shown by the survey to rank care and concern for colleagues as a major priority, this logically leads to the conclusion that many welcomed the opportunity of becoming social-emotional leaders within their schools. However, two recent and not unconnected developments must raise doubts about the whole argument. Firstly the comprehensive reorganization of secondary schools has considerably increased the average size of schools, and with this it was decided that larger schools should be allowed to appoint additional staff at deputy headteacher level. For example, schools of Group 10 size and above have since 1971, at LEA discretion, been able to employ three staff with deputy headteacher status – the original deputy, now referred to as the first deputy headteacher, the existing senior master or mistress (depending upon the sex of the first deputy), and a newly appointed second deputy (Department of Education and Science, 1971). Clearly this innovation called for a reassessment of the role of the deputy headteacher, and job descriptions, if they existed at all, had to be rewritten. It was no longer possible for schools to advertise a post at this level, and for candidates to apply on the basis that there was a traditional understanding of what the employment contract implied. Judging by the wording of job advertisements in the *Times Educational Supplement* this point has been taken and often the further particulars include a job description within a specific area of responsibility – notably curriculum development and pastoral care.

The survey, interviews, and results

In order to investigate this changing situation a questionnaire was sent to the deputy headteachers of the 11 reorganized high schools of a nonmetropolitan county in the north of England. The authority has introduced a three-tier comprehensive system (first, middle, and high schools – thirteen to eighteen age-range) on an area by area basis beginning in 1969, and the advantage of using a small and compact sample was that, by the time of the survey, all involved had experience of a uniform organizational structure of senior staff based upon a headteacher and four deputies – first deputy, second deputy, senior master or mistress, and an additional post, because of the community interests of the school, a deputy head for further education and youth service. Of the 44 possible correspondents 37 replied (84%) under six main headings:

1 Background information – including sex, age, educational background, further full- or part-time study, career experience.
2 The role of the deputy headteacher – official title, job description, duties performed, and degree of role clarification.
3 Role conflict – with self, colleagues, and headteacher.
4 Views on previous research into the role of the deputy headteacher – in particular the 'man in the middle position' and the thesis of dual leadership.
5 The future of deputy headship – including comment on the pastoral-curriculum division of responsibility, the interchangeability of roles, and preparation for headship.
6 General – areas of satisfaction and dissatisfaction in the job of deputy headteacher.

Because of the geographical and numerical restrictions in the sample the intention was not to use the returns to draw conclusions on a statistical basis; instead, taking the points of interest and differences of opinion that emerged as a basis for in-depth interviews with 12 of the correspondents, it was found possible to isolate three components, in the development of the role of the deputy headteacher, for analysis. These were:

1 The use made and value of job descriptions, with particular reference to the separation of responsibilities for curriculum and pastoral matters, (a) for the job satisfaction of deputies, (b) as a tool in the management of the school, and (c) as a preparation for headship.
2 The extent of role conflict, in particular; (a) conflict with self – a comparison of his role, as perceived by a deputy, with the actuality of his tasks and status and (b) conflict with other teaching staff – a consideration of his colleague's perceptions of his role, in relation to his own, with special reference to the 'man in the middle' viewpoint.
3 An analysis of Burnham's dual-leadership argument in the context of comprehensive reorganization and multiple deputy headships.

The continuum of job definition

Acceptance of the concept of more than one deputy in itself necessitated schools in a reconsideration of the traditional role of the deputy. The 'extension of the headteacher' arrangement had to be adapted. Some schools conceived jobs of deputies with reference to specific areas of responsibility, and adopted this strategy rigidly and with conviction, while others quite deliberately avoided this stance. Between these two extremes several intermediary positions were apparent, to the extent that it is necessary to construct a continuum with five recognizable differentiations. They, and the numbers of deputies associated with each area, are:

1   $n = 4$. A clear and definitive division of roles into two and sometimes three areas of responsibility; usually designated curriculum, pastoral care, and administration (sometimes called administration and resources, or organization). The characteristics of this continuum position are strict role delineation and a precise job description, with one deputy having sole responsibility for a particular task, and an almost total absence of tasks which involved shared responsibility with another deputy. In addition, to emphasize the particular area of responsibility, each deputy not only dealt with the main and obvious tasks, but also performed associated subordinate duties in the area. A deputy, with a curriculum role for example, would naturally supervise curriculum development, but also his tasks would include sole responsibility for school, homework, daily relief, and examination timetables. In this situation there is little evidence of any liaison or interrelationships among deputies within the school. Each, apparently, regard themselves as having a specific job which is either thought to suit a particular personality, or has been selected by the incumbent as the post he wishes to fill.

2   $n = 8$. The second position on the continuum again describes a policy in which deputy headteacher roles are clearly separated. Role delineation is as strict as in (1) and job description as precise, but there are characteristic differences. Although the roles are still described as curriculum, pastoral, and administration, some of the subordinate tasks are not closely allied to their natural or logical situation. A pastoral deputy may have responsibility for the daily relief timetable to cover for absent staff, while a curriculum deputy might accept tasks involved with registers and admissions. There remains little evidence for shared responsibility in particular tasks, but often it is thought desirable that, after a few years tenure, job descriptions should be

exchanged among deputies. Clearly there is no emphasis in this stance on certain jobs suiting particular personalities, and the conclusion must be that in these circumstances deputies wish and are able to fulfil any role. In contrast to (1) there is much more stress on liaison, cooperation, and interpersonal relationships between deputies, as each in settling into a new job must rely heavily on the experience and expertise of the previous job-holder.

3 $n = 12$. At the midway point of the continuum the division of duties is still often on a curriculum-pastoral basis, although reference to a third, administrative role, is usually absent. The division however is far more elastic than in either (1) or (2), and there is no attempt to underline and emphasize it by designating every single task to a particular responsibility area. Often there is a balance of sole and shared responsibilities for a deputy in this situation, in the firm conviction that many tasks are better performed on a shared basis. In the same way it is acknowledged that, as many tasks fall into the area of genuine overlap, close liaison and cooperation are essential. Emphasis is therefore placed on the opportunities available for the deputies of one school to meet as a team, and concern themselves with each other's area of responsibility. Often it is argued that a deputy has overall responsibility for a specific task area, a responsibility for ensuring that tasks are effectively completed, but that this does not preclude the possibility of a pastoral deputy involving himself in an area of interest in curriculum development.

4 $n = 8$. Once the midway point is passed, deputy roles are no longer described in terms of responsibility for a specific area. The curriculum and pastoral designations are abandoned, and, although the emphasis can vary, all deputies work in both of these major fields. When the sole responsibility does exist it is invariably restricted to minor tasks. The main characteristic of this continuum position is freedom to deal with administrative matters as they occur, and a high degree of cooperation among deputies.

5 $n = 5$. The fifth position on the continuum represents the philosophy that it is neither practical nor desirable to divide deputy roles on a curriculum-pastoral basis, and indeed a policy of avoiding such designations is pursued. The belief is that such a division is artificial, and the production of a curriculum or pastoral job description perpetuates that artificiality. Shared responsibilities are adopted almost exclusively in all tasks, and the intention is to allow deputies to gain

experience in every field of school organization. Obviously if this approach is to be effective, good interpersonal relationships between deputies are essential.

Obviously when job-satisfaction, organizational effectiveness, and preparation for headship are considered, in relation to the division of responsibility within the school, responses varied, depending upon the point on the continuum from which a deputy considered his reply.

Levels of job-satisfaction

In the main, deputies enjoyed job-satisfaction whatever the continuum position of their school, although it must be remembered that as many of the schools and posts had only existed for a few years – and usually years of stimulating institutional development – there had been little opportunity for the disillusionments associated with sameness and stagnation to occur. Nevertheless there did appear to be a genuine feeling of satisfaction with the job that they were doing throughout the continuum, but there were differences. Those deputies with more general areas of responsibility (generally positions (4) and (5)) were particularly pleased with the roles they were able to develop, considering themselves to be fully involved in all aspects of school life. Many of them thought that the restriction of their role to a curriculum or pastoral area only would, if it occurred, be a cause of dissatisfaction to them. The opposite reaction was not apparent – deputies with specific responsibilities did not view a move to a more general range of duties as a possible source of dissatisfaction. In fact a minority ($n = 8$) thought that the limitation of role to curriculum, pastoral, or administration issues did not provide a sufficiently broad-based experience. They tended to advocate either the opportunity to work in a broader area of school activity or opportunities for exchanging job descriptions within the school. However, even for holders of specific posts, this represented a minority view, and the more general feeling was that the main satisfaction in this situation derived from developing expertise in a specific area, and that in doing so they were meeting the job specification to which they had been appointed on the assumption that it interested them and suited their personality. To this majority, interchangeability of responsibilities at intervals received little support. The conclusion must therefore be that while job-satisfaction for the deputies is general at all positions on the continuum there is more potential discontent among job-holders in schools at the specific responsibility end of the spectrum, but even here it is possible to find personnel who are happy with a role which requires involvement only with a limited range of school activities.

The division of responsibilities and organizational effectiveness

The views of respondents as to the most appropriate arrangement of responsibilities in terms of organizational effectiveness were, as might be expected, strongly influenced by the continuum position of their schools. In other words those at end (1) thought that a clear delineation of roles was best, while those at the other end (5) were sure about the merits of the designation-avoidance philosophy. As no single person had comparable experience at different continuum positions, and as senior personnel committed to their schools, this correlation between working arrangements and opinions on its effectiveness is in no way surprising. Therefore, in general terms, deputies with particular responsibilities welcome the clarity with which all members of the school staff could see where, on each issue, responsibility resided. The existence of a clear point of reference for all colleagues, the avoidance of duplication of effort or the possibility of omission, and the opportunity of acquiring detailed expertise in specific administrative matters, were all cited as benefits which accrue to the whole school. Many who argued along these lines also pointed out, from a midway position on the continuum, that in practice there had to be liaison and cooperation among deputies, because they acknowledge the inextricable links between curriculum and pastoral interests. Often they emphasized the value of senior management meetings in this context.

Those deputies with more general responsibilities tended to view the curriculum-pastoral division as administratively neat, but practically unrealistic. One view was that the division reinforced that between the academic and pastoral staff generally and therefore detracted from the effective running of the whole school. Others pointed out the advantage of having any deputy deal with a matter as it happened, rather than leave it – as occurs with specific responsibilities – until the appropriate person was available. In the extreme of rigid areas of responsibility the management system of the school can break down completely in the absence of a deputy. Of course, at the other end of the spectrum without any role specifications, the same task can be performed by more than one deputy, or worse still, tasks remain uncompleted or even unstarted. Obviously objective evidence to support the effectiveness of a particular continuum position could not be sought in this survey, and the only conclusion that can be drawn is that if difficulties are to arise they are most likely at the two polarized positions of either end of the continuum.

Preparation for headship

Almost two-thirds of the respondents regarded their present job as a preparation for eventual headship. Those who did not thought they were either too old (and therefore likely to be replaced in the not too distant future by a younger person with increased expectations) or saw their deputy role (adult education and youth service) as not leading to school headship. Essentially a situation is therefore approaching, in this authority at least, in which three deputies see themselves in a preparation role for a single headteacher job. Therefore it is interesting that two-thirds thought the curriculum-pastoral division as unsatisfactory preparation because it was too limiting, and for thoroughness a potential headteacher required insight into, and experience of, both major areas. Despite genuine attempts at cooperation many holders of specific posts found it was virtually impossible to make a real and meaningful contribution to an area other than their own. However, a number did point out that although their limited role was not an adequate preparation, the division of responsibilities did benefit the school, and this was the first priority, relegating concern for their own career prospects to second place; but not all accepted this possible incompatibility between serving as a deputy and preparing for headship.

A small number of respondents ($n = 6$) thought there were too many deputy headteachers in their school, leading to the suggestion that some looked for tasks, with the result that several of those discovered were menial and contributed nothing as an introduction to the duties of a headteacher. Partly to combat this tendency, and partly to take into account the phenomena of three staff preparing for one job, the idea of a principal deputy (a potential headteacher) differentiated from subordinate deputies (perhaps including staff who viewed the job at a slightly lower level and status than at present, and as a position until retirement) was put forward. However, this ignores two points. Firstly, not all deputies surveyed accepted that there was insufficient work for the increased number of posts, and secondly, the view that much is gained by school and staff in the experience of working in a management team is difficult to sustain with deputies of unequal status.

It was left to three respondents to raise the issue that deputy headship is only one part of the preparation for headship. A person is not appointed as a deputy without previous experience. It may well be that someone finds a specialist role a satisfactory introduction to deputy headship because he has developed a different specialism in previous jobs. A head of department might be appointed to a pastoral job, a head of house to a curriculum deputyship, and so on. Equally, a satisfied generalist may already have fulfilled both curriculum and pastoral roles, because the questionnaire answers showed clearly that there is no recognized career structure in the preparation of a deputy headteacher.

The development of a deputy headteacher role

Writing in 1964, Burnham found the position of the deputy headteacher to be largely anomalous with little consistency from school to school. Where a job definition existed, it was often fragmented, and clerical and routine duties predominated. Headteachers were basically denying their deputies a role, and four years later (Burnham, 1968, pp. 169–196) he still suggested that:

> Much of the ambiguity, frustration and conflict underlying the position would be resolved if there was a realisation that the duties which should properly fall to the deputy head are not as a result of 'delegation', but by the 'right' of differentiating forces within the organisation.

Evidence from the questionnaire would suggest that this nonrole situation is changing, mainly as a direct result of the evolution of large secondary schools with multiple deputies. What has emerged markedly is the existence of policy and management teams, comprising deputy headteachers, and occasionally other senior teachers, under the chairmanship of the headteacher. Many replies emphasized the part played by individual deputies in this team, and often a team which was thought to have real power in influencing the planning and policy-making decisions of the school. Individually, many deputies enjoyed delegated powers in their own responsibility areas without the need for reference to the headteacher.

In addition to the structural explanations of increased size and more senior posts, other reasons were put forward to account for the changing pattern in the role of a deputy. As well as being larger, comprehensive schools, with their greater range of pupil abilities than the schools they replaced, have more complex problems, and it was thought that the headteacher found it necessary to rely on the sum total of experience and expertise available amongst his deputies. Others suggested that, as head-teachers became more aware of management techniques, this led to the adoption of consultative processes on the grounds that a policy agreed after discussion was far more likely to be implemented than one imposed from above. Some even went so far as claiming that democratic leadership was so fully accepted in their school that this automatically led to a system of shared decision-making, and obviously a definite decisional role for senior staff.

Therefore, in the view of many deputies a definite role has emerged. This is reflected in a clear job description, and colleagues' and their own aware-ness of what is demanded by this description. However it does not follow that satisfactory relationships with others associated with the role – the role set outlined by Merton (1957, p. 106) – must follow. Many people have legitimate rights on, and expectations of, a deputy headteacher and his role, and the possibility of conflicting role expectations always exists. The deputy may, for example, find his ideal role concept in conflict with the actual role he must fulfil, while the expectations of a superior – the headteacher – can easily become incompatible with that of subordinates – other teaching colleagues. It was these two potential areas of conflict which received maximum attention in the survey.

Conflict with self

Deputies were asked to comment on their concept of the ideal role for a person in their position, and compare this with the actuality of duties, responsibilities, time allocations, and relationships which characterized their working day. About three-quarters of them reported a considerable discrepancy, and this showed itself in three ways. Firstly, although it was generally accepted that they had found a new role in the management decision processes of the school, the image of the previous 'nonrole' was not completely lost. Many resented the petty administrative duties on which they had to spend much time, assuming that they could be adequately dealt with by a competent secretary, and tasks more appropriate to a caretaker or a bursar, such as minor plumbing repairs and transport of pupils, were regularly reported. More important was the view that these less important parts of the job required disproportionate amounts of time, so that that remaining for major activities – debate on the philosophy of curriculum development within their schools, for example – was greatly restricted. This inability to use their time as effectively as they would wish was a substantial source of complaint. Quite simply, having been offered a role many thought that, because of the associated and often trivial duties which were theirs, many going back to the time of the 'nonrole' situation, they did not have the opportunity to fulfil this role in the way which they would choose.

One of the reasons why time is so important to the administrative duties of the deputies is that they have continued as classroom teachers. Loads ranged from a quarter to just over a half of a full timetable, and, while they all welcomed this teaching as a positive contribution to job-satisfaction, to some extent this heavy commitment must conflict with their deputy roles. In particular there was a clash in that they could not spend as long in the classroom as they wished, yet their classroom duties restricted the time they could award to administrative tasks. Many thought that enjoyment derived from teaching had dropped because of the responsibilities of being a deputy. The constant interference during actual teaching, the need – often because of pastoral responsibilities – to work with less-able children and the inability to concentrate totally on teaching duties while struggling with organizational problems were all quoted as examples of conflict within the dual role of deputy and teacher.

The final source of self-conflict only arose for a minority of those surveyed, but for them it was very important. They felt that they had not yet acquired the organizational and decision-making status of other deputies in their school, and had therefore failed to achieve a role which they thought should be theirs. This situation occurred exclusively in those schools in which there is a pecking order of principal deputy and assistant deputies (although, of course, those names are not used). Under these circumstances assistant deputies often complained that they were not consulted before decisions were taken, and could not participate in discussion because of lack of information. As a result they did not have the responsibility to which they thought their status entitled them, and they were reduced to trying to create another role for themselves either on their own initiative or at the instigation of the headteacher, but this often led to difficulties when the new duties overlapped those of other senior staff, such as head of house or head of department.

Conflict with the headteacher and other colleagues

To ascertain the degree of conflict deputies experienced with colleagues and headteachers, respondents were asked to compare their own conceptions of their role with the conceptions thought to be held by other staff. The vast majority were confident that, while there might be difference in emphasis, their own view of their role coincided with that of their head-teacher. In this context the most interesting point to emerge was that half of those surveyed did not acknowledge any duties in respect of staff welfare, and those that did thought in terms of shared responsibility with other deputies. This contrasted with Burnham's previous findings (1964, chapter 4) that, while headteachers did not rate concern for staff highly, their single deputies, often striving for a social-emotional role in the school, did. Yet on this occasion even the interviews only elicited that while staff welfare was important it rated well below task-instrumental responsibilities. Deputies returned again and again to making decisions, administering and organizing the school as the characteristics of their present role, with the implication that these were the areas on which their superior wished them to concentrate.

When considering conflict with colleagues less than half of those surveyed felt they had experienced any serious difficulty. Reasons suggested were that the dual role of teaching and administering won respect from teaching staff who appreciated the problems and difficulties that were involved. The publication of detailed job descriptions, so that colleagues know who to approach when a particular situation occurred, was often viewed as a source of harmonious relationships. However, many deputies pointed out that, with anything from 50 to 80 colleagues, role conflict with some at least was inevitable. Several deputies as instrumental-task leaders had played a prominent part in the introduction of the high school – a comprehensive reorganization which had met opposition from many senior staff who were resistant to change. Some deputies thought that their colleagues lacked understanding and awareness of what was involved in running a complex organization such as a high school. This gave rise to remarks about too many deputies and the viability of workloads – comments which were echoed by a few deputies themselves. Further education and youth service deputies in particular were concerned about colleagues' appreciation of their roles when criticisms were regularly made of their lack of school commitment without a realization of their out-of-school responsibilities.

A specific role-conflict concerned female deputies. A number, of both sexes, reported that they thought colleagues would like to see them devoting more time to staff and their problems. However, it was a point made particularly by women who, despite their determination to abandon their traditional senior mistress role – mainly concerned with girls' discipline and female staff welfare at a fairly trivial level – found their colleagues reluctant to allow them to do so. Members of staff anticipated that women deputies would give some social-emotional leadership whereas, like their male colleagues, they have tended to opt for task-instrumental roles. The evidence of this survey is that they have, in their own view, opted successfully, and as members of management teams they can be solely responsible for a specific area and can be involved in policy decisions affecting all aspects of school life.

Occupying the boundary position

As occupants of a boundary position between headteacher and staff, deputies are clearly placed in a 'man in the middle' position. Similar situations exist in nonschool environments and industrial foremen, at the boundary between workforce and management, have been studied by Wray (1945, pp. 298–301) and Roethlisberger (1945, pp. 283–298) in their efforts to be loyal to both parties by understanding their difficulties and problems, and in their communications between the two groups. In the questionnaire deputies were therefore asked whether they did regard themselves as occupying a 'man in the middle' position, and if so to specify the difficulties this created. Significantly, only a minority saw themselves in this position, and even those that did reported only limited difficulties. They commented on the problems of reconciling divergent views, and not transmitting confidences, and the conclusion was usually drawn that if the boundary position did prove difficult it would be a reflection of poor communications between the headteacher and his staff. Despite these comments, however, a majority of deputies as members of the school management team did not believe that they occupied the traditional middle position. In fact involvement in the decisional processes allowed many to consider themselves closer to the headteacher than to the staff, and when they argued or reasoned with staff over school policy or a particular line of action this was not done, in their view, as headteacher's communicator but as part of their role as a member of a team which devised the policy or approved the action. The extension of this development into the creation of an 'us' and 'them' situation is a clear possibility in the view of a small number of deputies.

An issue frequently emphasized was that if a deputy had autonomy in a specific area then the 'man in the middle' situation could not possibly occur.

In this arrangement a number of deputies found themselves acting in an interchangeable role with the headteacher. If a deputy is allowed to work independently without reference to the headteacher, it is quite natural to find a member of staff trying to use the headteacher as an intermediary when disagreement occurs over a decision by the deputy. Previous head and deputy roles are then reversed; in other words the headteacher can find himself in the boundary position. Many respondents commented upon this changing role of headship. As schools have increased in size heads have in many cases not become the remote figures predicted, but, partly because of the delegation of task-instrumental duties to deputies, and partly as a result of democratization of schools, heads have tended to become increasingly accessible to staff; to some extent even seeing this as their primary role. By frequenting staffrooms and accepting availability to staff as a part of their socio-emotional role, many headteachers would appear to be filling the middle ground vacated by their deputies.

Modifying the dual-leadership theory

The 'dual-leadership' theory of Burnham is based on the premise of Stodgill and Coons (1957) that the two most dominant characteristics of leadership behaviour are initiation (the leader is concerned with establishing organizational arrangements, directing the work, clarifying the objectives and so on – task-instrumental leadership) and consideration (the existence of good human relationships within the organization – social-emotional leadership). According to Pierce (1962, p. 160) an organization is therefore concerned with task goals, and, as a means to this end, with the recognition and satisfaction of the needs of members. Given that there are two leadership functions to fulfil, Burnham suggested that in the ideal, as the headteacher was already providing task-instrumental leadership, his deputy, lacking an authentic role, should be the social-emotional leader – a situation which apparently was already occurring in many schools with deputies expressing concern for staff welfare. In terms of the relevant characteristics of many schools when the theory was formulated (relatively small, a headteacher acting as a paternalistic autocrat, and a single deputy) the adoption by the deputy of a socio-emotional role seems a natural development. However, even in these now hypothesized situations the surveyed deputies almost without exception could not accept the argument. They tended to agree with McIntyre (1972) that the concept was too theoretical and too narrow an interpretation, and that no single type of leadership was appropriate for all situations and every personality. In particular they could not accept that an effective task-instrumental leader would not be concerned for good human relationships, or that a social-emotional leader could ignore the organizational tasks of the school. In their view a headteacher and deputy would have to exercise skills in each other's area, and if a two-style leadership pattern were accepted then it would be necessary to move towards one or the other dimension in a manner dependent only on the circumstances of the situation. In fact other studies (Hughes, 1970) do confirm that effective leaders score highly in either dimension.

A few years later, after the first movement towards comprehensive reorganization but before multiple deputy headships, Burnham (1968) modified his 'dual-leadership' theory. The task-instrumental role would, he argued, tend to be divided between the headteacher, who would continue to make the major policy decisions, and a 'procedural' leader – the deputy – who would oversee implementation of those decisions. Social-emotional leadership was likely to fragment among senior staff – heads of house, for example – with some of it remaining with deputies. This modified version found little support from the surveyed deputies. Clearly, in their case the existence of four of them was an additional factor, but the issue which emerged most clearly was that the majority of deputies saw themselves as task-instrumental leaders only. The membership of the management team and their part in the evolution and implementation of policy were regularly mentioned. The headteacher is of course chairman of this team, but the view of many was that its democratic atmosphere allowed them a substantial task-instrumental role. In addition, within their own area of responsibility, deputies were frequently making decisions without reference to the head-teacher, and therefore acting as much more than procedural leaders, although some job descriptions contained elements of putting policy into practice.

If the team of deputies see themselves, with the approval of the head-teacher, as task-instrumental leaders this clearly has implications for the role of the headteacher. In addition to a thinking and planning element in their role, the view of the deputies is that they are increasingly taking on the role of social-emotional leadership. This is confirmed by work in other parts of the country and the majority opinion of those surveyed is summarized by Davis (1970, pp. 121–134).

The delegation of responsibility should leave the head free to attend to staff problems, to be about the school sensing atmosphere, to be seen to be available. Far from being dehumanised or remote, if the chain of command is working efficiently, he should be relieved of the burden of administration in order to be seen and known as a person, not dismissed as a mere business manager.

It does not follow that deputies do not recognize the importance of relationships in the performance of their duties. The low priority they award to social-emotional aspects of their role – a time-consuming task, if it is to be fulfilled adequately – probably is as much an indication of the emphasis they believe they must place on other duties, than an attempt to ignore this element of organizational management; particularly when it is recalled that deputies almost without exception complained that lack of time was their greatest dissatisfaction with their work.

Conclusion

While the findings reported here might have broader implications, the geographical and numerical restrictions in the sample cannot justify such claims. However, they do show that with larger schools and several deputies the role of the deputy headteacher is changing. This clearly is worthy of further study. In particular, an extension to other types of school (in terms of the size and age-range) and other arrangements of deputies than investigated here, and a survey of headteachers and teaching staff could have much to offer. There are also the issues of economic efficiency in employing four well-paid staff to perform often minor caretaking and clerical tasks, and the training of men and women appointed to positions without any provision for pre- or in-service preparation, who must therefore learn their jobs during the first years in office.

References

Burnham, P.S., 1964, *The Role of the Deputy Head in Secondary Schools*, Unpublished M.Ed. thesis, University of Leicester.

Burnham, P.S., 1968, The Deputy Head. In Allen, B. (ed) *Headship in the 1970's*, Oxford, Blackwell.

Davis, M.J., 1970, Delegation and communication in the large school. In Hughes, M.G. (ed) *Secondary School Administration: A Management Approach*, Oxford, Pergamon.

Department of Education and Science, 1971, *Scales of Salaries for Teachers in Primary and Secondary Schools, England and Wales*, London, HMSO.

Hughes, M.G., (ed) 1970, *Secondary School Administration: A Management Approach*, Oxford, Pergamon.

McIntyre, W., 1972, *Size of school as a factor in the role of deputy head*, Unpublished M.Sc. dissertation, University of Bradford.

Merton, R.K., 1957, 'The role set problems in sociological theory', *British Journal of Sociology*, 8.

Pierce, R., 1962, The dual function of the task group, *Journal of Educational Psychology*, 36, IV.

Roethlisberger, F.J., 1945, 'The foreman: master and victim of double talk', *Harvard Business Review*, 23.

Stodgill, M. and Coons, E. (eds), 1958, *Leader Behaviour: Its Description and Measurement*, Ohio State University Bureau of Research, Monograph No. 88.

Wray, D.E., 1945, 'Marginal men of industry: the foremen', *American Journal of Sociology*, 54.

SECTION V

MANAGEMENT OF THE CURRICULUM

CHAPTER 5.1

FRAMEWORK FOR THE CURRICULUM: A STUDY OF SECONDARY SCHOOLING*
Penelope B. Weston

Constraints on the curriculum

In asking one hundred schools to describe the outline and context of the third-year curriculum, the research team were aware that this might be a frustrating as well as a time-consuming exercise. For example, a school might be so hampered by the character and siting of its buildings that the staff would feel unable to introduce strongly desired curriculum changes, but unhappy at describing, without further explanation, the existing third-year curriculum. Even if the problem were generally less acute than this, it seemed a good idea to give respondents the opportunity to mention and perhaps enlarge upon proposed changes in the curriculum, and those constraints which inhibited present intentions and future plans.

Significantly, perhaps, over half the respondents felt it worth listing the constraints which prevented the introduction of desired curriculum changes.

* *Framework for the Curriculum* is a report on part of a study, made by a research team headed by Professor P.H. Taylor and financed by the SSRC, of the thirteen-fourteen age group ('the third year') in schools. The research took place over five years and was designed 'to discover and describe . . . what is taught; to whom; with what emphases; in what circumstances and to study the data obtained in order to make judgements about the "official" and "hidden" curricula, their interactions and their joint effects on the education of pupils' (p.10). Stage one of this two-stage study consisted of gathering information from a sample of a 100 West Midland schools using three questionnaires asking respectively for general data on each school, details of the third-year timetable, and the grouping of pupils across the curriculum and teacher attitudes towards the curriculum. At the same time a Pupil Opinion Questionnaire was piloted for use at stage two. This stage consisted of detached case studies of two schools and 'alongside that "background studies" via questionnaires and some visits, in eighteen schools – all carefully chosen to be as representative as possible of the main sample' (p. 10). (NFER, 1977, pp. 79–84, 104–119, 144–151.)

A closer look at the types of constraint which were mentioned shows that they fall into several well-defined groups. There were references to shortages in material resources – buildings, money, and equipment; to staffing problems; to timetabling difficulties; and to curricular issues. Some of these were mentioned more frequently than others as Table 10 shows.

Table 10 Classification of constraints on the third-year timetable

	Type of problem	Number of mentions
1.	Shortage of material resources	35
2.	Staffing difficulties	34
3.	Curricular problems	14
4.	Timetabling constraints	9

One school, of course, might mention several of these types of constraint and the particular problem described would vary, as a few examples will illustrate. Thus within the first category, there were frequent references to inadequate or inflexible teaching space, particularly for practical subjects – 'only one woodwork room', 'lack of facilities for girls' activities', 'accommodation is very tight'. Grounds as well as buildings might be inadequate. In one school a move towards more integration in the curriculum and more team-teaching was felt to be impossible because:

> The school is on three separate sites, one site a mile from the other two. Even these two have a main road in between. A system of double lessons helps.

In other cases, it was the general financial problem (probably felt even more acutely now) which was mentioned, usually along with other factors, as a notable constraint on curricular development.

If problems about the material resources and facilities of the school were prominent among the concerns of many respondents, there was almost as much anxiety about the numbers and quality of the staff. In many cases, it was simply a question of teacher-pupil ratio. Twenty-five respondents in all felt that they badly needed more teachers, either to lower the overall teacher-pupil ratios or to solve a problem in one subject area. There might be particular reasons for the problem; frequently, it was a question of teachers for given subjects simply not being available – boys' craft was mentioned several times in this connection; one respondent commented: 'remedial teachers are unobtainable'. It is perhaps more disturbing to note that some respondents felt that improvements in the curriculum were hampered by the quality of the existing staff; there were references to 'uninterested' or 'uncommitted' teachers, and this raises delicate issues about the teacher's 'vocation' and the circumstances in which he works. More often concern was expressed about staff struggling to cope with curricular areas for which they were not qualified, a problem linked with the shortage of specialists mentioned above. One respondent referred rue-fully to a more general problem for his staff:

> There is a lack of experience in mixed ability techniques among the staff (who are not keen anyway).

Clearly, satisfaction with a staff group is a very subjective matter, and it should be said that a number of respondents commented frequently in other parts of the questionnaire on the community spirit and hard-working loyalty of their staff, often in difficult circumstances.

It is perhaps interesting to note that nowhere in the responses to this item were the qualities or characteristics of *pupils* described as a constraint, a fact that might come as a surprise to the pupils themselves.

Most of the other constraints mentioned by respondents concerned par-ticular curricular organizational problems. Sometimes the cry was simple: 'not enough time!' In one case the shortage of time was linked to an important third-year issue – the options system by which subject choices for the fourth and fifth year were made:

> There is a lack of time during the year where the maximum number of academic subjects are taught to make possible an informed choice of options for the fourth year.

Questions concerning the balance of the curriculum, and in particular the tension between a common core and an option-based curriculum in the third year, disturbed several respondents:

> The third year timetable is inevitably a compromise. Conflict between a common curriculum with stable primary groups and increased specialisation

with the flexibility required, is most acute in the third year.

Looking forward to an examination-directed curriculum meant to some respondents that external examinations were casting a shadow down to the third-year courses. One school would have liked to introduce some grouping of subjects, but felt that this might not be helpful to the pupils:

> There are separate subjects on the timetable at present because we don't want to disadvantage pupils choosing for external examination.

Sometimes the problem was felt most acutely in cumulative subjects like maths and languages:

> Four years is not enough time for certain subjects, for example language teaching, where French in the middle school has too often led to pupils rejecting it before they arrive here.

Perceived constraints, then, were varied and occasionally somewhat intangible. A headteacher who felt pressed by an 'inherited staff and timetable', or tied down by the 'strong academic tradition of the school' might find these nonfinancial constraints just as overwhelming as the more obvious shortages of staff and resources. The force of these constraints can be examined from another angle; in an ideal world how would the status quo be altered? Responses to this question gave some indications of the variety of curricular aims which respondents set before themselves.

The clearest example concerned pupil grouping; six respondents wanted more mixed-ability teaching, but six others pressed for more setting. Even where the general aim was the same – nine schools expressed a strong desire for more practical work in the curriculum – it might be related to different groups of pupils. Thus the head of one girls' school wished for more space for practical and creative subjects in the crowded timetable of the more academic students, while another stressed the need to provide the less academic with more crafts, business studies, or music.

Some of the wishes expressed here were directly related to the constraints described earlier – at least nine schools would have liked to create the more generous provision for practical work which shortages of staff and resources at present prevented. Similarly, four schools pleaded for better facilities for remedial teaching.

It is interesting that many of the desired changes were particular rather than sweeping, concerning perhaps one or two subjects which, it was hoped, could be provided for some or all pupils – music, craft, and a second language were mentioned a number of times. Perhaps it is by developing one area at a time in this way, as opportunity arises, that the curriculum is changed in many schools, unless a radical change in the organization or leadership of the school provokes a revision of the whole school's curriculum.

The case study schools in context

A common curriculum for the third year

The two case study schools, Victoria Comprehensive and West Mercia High, had arrived by different routes at some common curricular destinations for their third-year groups. In neither school was there a totally common course for *all* pupils, but in both there was a common core in terms of subjects taught and the time allotted to them. In both schools, third-year pupils spent a considerable amount of time in classes with others who were considered to be of broadly comparable ability, although this was more closely defined and applied to a larger part of the week at Victoria than at West Mercia. In both schools pupils were preparing during their third year to choose from a much wider range of subjects which would be offered in the fourth year, so that in some sense the third year could be seen as the end of a foundation course; although at West Mercia most of this had taken place at the middle schools. For both groups of third-year pupils it was only in the area of modern languages that there was clear differentiation, with some pupils taking a second language (and some having little or no foreign language study). But while the third-year curriculum structure at Victoria seemed fairly stable and accepted, at West Mercia significant changes were being proposed for the third year. Even here, however, there is an unexpected point of similarity; both staff groups were deeply involved in discussion of a 'diagnostic period' for all pupils on entry to the school, but it was only at West Mercia that this referred to the group of pupils with whom we were concerned.

On many of these issues we had also received information from the eighteen schools which had been selected to represent the original group of 100 schools.

How did the two case study schools compare with the rest in the outlines of their third-year organization and timetable structure?

Whatever the difference between individual schools, the central issues of the curriculum remain much the same. For the third year, perhaps the most important is the question of the common curriculum, and how that should be interpreted. This raises thorny problems of definition: what is meant here by 'curriculum', and in what sense can it be common?

Our observations in the case study schools suggested that apart from those senior teachers who had responsibilities for planning the work of the school as a whole, most of the teachers considered their commitments (which might be very heavy) to be more particular: to their own subject, to some aspect of pastoral care or administration, to the social and cultural life of the school. Most new secondary teachers, whether they are graduates or not, come to a school to teach the subject in which they have themselves specialized, and that is naturally their prime concern, especially in the first year of teaching. But more experienced teachers can also be so dedicated to their subject that they remain somewhat detached from the rest of the curriculum except when it impinges on their own concerns. Every head of department knows the territorial infighting that can follow from a suggestion that one subject should gain or lose a period in some timetable reshuffle, but how possible is it for those engaged in teaching to look at the curriculum in the round? It is our experience that many teachers who are not heads of department have not had occasion to think about the whole curriculum either for the school or for a single year-group, and find it difficult to stand back and see it as a whole. During interviews with English, science, and art teachers in the two case study schools we showed them an outline of the third-year curriculum; the following response was typical of many:

> Well, this is the first time I've seen this. I haven't really summed up the third year curriculum . . . I'm not sure that my subject deserves X periods within that framework . . .

There may, then, be advantages in starting out with a limited definition of the curriculum as a programme of subjects (or courses, topics, or modules) offered to a group or groups of students and scheduled to occupy certain specified amounts of time and space. In these terms, a common curriculum would be an identical programme for some specified population of students.

With this definition in mind, some comparisons can be made between the third year curriculum in the two case study schools and that offered in the larger group of eighteen schools. As a first step, Table 11 was drawn up to show how much time was spent on all subjects by third-year pupils in all twenty schools. For this purpose, subjects were grouped into broad areas; for example, geography, history, and religious education were grouped under the heading 'humanities'. (Full details are given in the notes under the table.) The time spent on each is given in terms of 'curriculum units'[1] each equal to one-ninth of the timetable cycle (which can for practical purposes be thought of here as one school week). A single entry for a school against one 'subject' shows that all third-year pupils in that school have been given the same overall time allocation, although it could be used in different ways; for example, while all these pupils at Holly School had 1.1 units (five periods) of English, the single entry of 1.4 units for science at Poplar School conceals the fact that the top band of four classes followed an integrated science course for six periods while the other pupils there had two periods each of the separate sciences. Where two sets of figures are given, this indicates the minimum and maximum amounts of time that could be spent by third-year pupils in that subject area. Very often this represents differences between the curriculum of a number of ability bands, as for example at Oak School, where, although a minority of pupils took no foreign language, others might take one, two, or even three, according to which band and class they were in.

One can see from the table that some subjects are more likely than others to be given a common time allocation for all pupils. First of all, there are the 'core subjects' – English and maths – which are studied by all pupils below the age of sixteen, irrespective of age or ability. At West Mercia School, all third-year pupils had five periods (1.1 curriculum units) of English and maths respectively.[2] In this arrangement the school was typical of many others in two ways. First because there was a common provision within the school; sixteen of the twenty schools had a common allocation of time in the third year for maths, and fourteen for English. (Victoria School was one of the exceptions, in that there were some variations in the time spent on both English and maths by pupils in different bands.) Secondly, there was wide agreement *between* schools about the proportion of time to be spent on these basic subjects: eleven other schools among the twenty provided 1.1 curriculum units of maths for all pupils. Except where the structure of the timetable made this inconvenient, pupils tended to receive a daily ration of maths. This may surprise no one in the schools; least of all the pupils, who had probably been accustomed to this pattern for all nine years of their school life, but in the current atmosphere of urgent concern about standards in these basic subjects it is worth underlining the stability and consensus to be found in schools about the place of these subjects in the curriculum.

More interestingly, fourteen of the schools had made a common time allocation *within* the school for the humanities area, although the variation *between* schools was greater – from 1.0 to 2.0 units. Again, West Mercia School illustrates the pattern found in many schools. Here the humanities area was divided into three subjects, with an equal share of the total time for all pupils: $H_2 G_2 RE_2$.[3] Other schools varied the total amount of time and the balance between subjects – for example $H_3 G_3 RE_1$ – but often had the same pattern for all third-year pupils. Victoria School again illustrated a different approach, with humanities tailored to fit the requirements of each band, so that while the A band had $G_2 H_2 RE_1$, Class C1 had $G_3 H_2 RE_2$. One school did not include RE in the third-year curriculum at all, and in another personal relationships was offered in its place. But history and geography appeared in every school, with either two or three periods allocated to each. The only integrated humanities course was at Pinewood School where the four C Band classes had six periods of social studies.

But in the time available how much detailed study could be made of each subject? What were the main aims for these humanities subjects at the third-year stage? The head of history at West Mercia School had made it clear that the main purpose in those particular circumstances was to get pupils enthused with the idea and 'feel' of history. All three subjects would go into the options pool for the fourth year, to be joined by a new hybrid in the humanities area, social studies. So in the third year, as at many other schools, some pupils might be studying one or two of the humanities subjects for the last time in their school career. It seems as if the inclusion of these familiar subjects in the third-year curriculum may have been serving at least two purposes; to complete a basic grounding, a 'foundation course', for those pupils who would 'give up' the subject at the age of fourteen; and to ensure that all pupils had a sufficiently clear idea of the identity of each subject to enable them to make choices for the fourth and fifth years.[4] In fact the contrast between the place of humanities subjects in the third-year curriculum on the one hand, and in the fourth- and fifth-year curriculum on the other, is interesting. At the two case study schools, in the fourth year, subjects which had been chosen as options became much more nearly

Table 11 Twenty schools: time allocated to subject areas in the third-year curriculum

School	English	Maths	Languages	Science	Humanities	Aesth/Pract.	PE	Pastoral, etc.
Elm	1.0	1.3	1.8	1.5	1.5	0.8	1.0	–
Yew	0.9	1.1	1.1–2.3	1.4	1.6	1.1–2.0	0.5–0.7	0.2 (Library)
Beech	1.0	1.3	1.5	2.3	1.5	1.0	0.8	–
Cedar[1]	1.3	1.3	2.3	2.3	1.5	– see note	0.3 see note	–
Willow	1.1	1.1	2.0	1.4	1.6	1.1	0.7	–
Oak	0.9–1.4	1.1	0–2.8	1.4	1.6	0.7–2.5	0.7–0.9	0.2 (Careers/Library)
Ash	1.1–1.6	1.1–1.4	0–2.3	0.9–1.4	1.1	1.1–3.2	0.9	–
West Mercia	1.1	1.1	0.9–2.0	1.6	1.4	1.1–2.0	0.9	–
Pinewood	1.1	1.1	0–2.0	1.4	1.6–1.8	0.5–1.8	0.9	–
Hazel[3]	1.4	1.1	0–0.9	1.4	1.4	1.8–2.3	0.9	0.2 (Careers)
Sycamore	0.9	0.9	1.4	1.4	1.4	2.3	0.9	–
Lime[2]	1.1	1.1	0–1.8	0.9	1.6	1.8–3.2	0.5–0.9	0.2 (Tutor period)
Redwood[4]	1.1–1.5	1.1	0–0.7	1.1	1.9	1.9	0.4–0.7	1.1 (Pastoral, Careers)
Poplar[5]	1.4	1.0–1.4	1.1	1.4	1.1–1.4	1.8	0.5–0.9	–
Victoria	1.0–1.3	1.0–1.5	0–1.8	1.5	1.3–2.1	1.5–2.3	0.8	–
Hawthorn[6]	1.4	1.1	0.7	see note	1.8	see note	0.9	0.2 (Careers)
Hornbeam	0.9–1.4	1.1	0–1.8	1.4	1.6–1.8	1.6–2.5	0.7	0–0.2 (Library)
Rowan[7]	1.0–1.8	1.1	0.2–0.9	0.9–1.4	2.0	1.8	0.7	–
Holly	1.1	1.1	0.7–1.1	0.5–1.4	1.6–2.0	1.8–2.8	0.9	–
Maple	1.1	0.9–1.1	0–1.6	0.9–1.4	1.4–1.8	1.4–2.8	1.1	–

Notes:

Entries are made in terms of notional 'curriculum units', nine of which make up one timetable week.

Humanities = Geography, History, and Religious Education.

Aesthetic/Practical = Music, Drama, Art, Craft, Woodwork, Metalwork, Technical Drawing, Domestic Science, Home Economics, Needlework, Pottery.

1. In this boarding school games take place outside timetabled hours; all boys take a six-week art course during the year; craft subjects are organized on an individual basis outside timetabled hours.
2. There is also a remedial form whose timetable includes 14 periods (3.2 units) of integrated studies.
3. In addition to those pupils taking French and/or German some will take an Asian language or English as a second language.
4. Every class has two periods of 'pastoral' and one period for careers advice; there is a remedial form with an integrated course 'Activity' of 4.5 units (12 one-hour periods).
5. This includes a remedial form who have, in addition, Lib. Drama.
6. All third-year classes are regrouped for 9 periods, i.e., three 'triple' periods, for art, science, and craft subjects.
7. This includes a remedial form who have, in addition, general studies.

equivalent in terms of time allocation to the 'core' subjects (English and maths at Victoria; English, maths, and science at West Mercia). Most main subjects took up about one curriculum unit (4 or 5 periods; 7 periods for science at West Mercia, 6 for English); any one pupil would have seven main subjects and a supporting programme of 'nonexamination' activities – P.E., careers, R.E., and so on. This change – for example from 2 to 5 periods a week for one subject – might seem like a transformation to some teachers in the humanities area; now there was ample time to begin a thorough study of the one subject. (At the same time English teachers whose subject was to lead to a double entry at public examination might feel hard pressed with 5 to 6 periods.) So by the fourth year, each of the subjects within this area was on a par, from the point of view of time allotted, with basic subjects like maths and English whereas in the third year all the humanities subjects together might only take up slightly more of the total time than English on its own.

In science, too, many schools seem to have found it possible and satisfactory to lay down a common outline for all pupils. Here Victoria School exemplified the most widely found pattern: for all pupils there was a double period for each of three subjects – physics, chemistry, and biology.

By contrast, the greatest variations in time allocations within and between schools came in languages, and the composite aesthetic/practical area. In the latter area, even with the inclusion of music (offered by all schools to some pupils), some pupils only received 0.5 units (2 out of 40 periods); on the other hand, there was a possible maximum of 3.2 units (14 out of 40 periods). Provision in this area varied in other ways; in type of work (art, music, separate or integrated craft subjects); whether this was to some extent determined by sex (for example, metalwork *or* needlework); the size of the group; and the range of specialist rooms and staff available. There were differences between the schools on all these points. In one or two schools the information supplied made it clear that pupils could choose freely between craft subjects, but in others the timetable itself showed that boys' and girls' crafts were organized separately. In some schools with a 'banded' curriculum, lower-band pupils were given more time in this area than top-band pupils. For example, at Pinewood School there was the following pattern: A Band classes, C_2; B Band, C_5; C Band, C_8. At Hornbeam School, where there were six third-year classes arranged in A, B, and C bands, a different approach was adopted for craft subjects. Time spent within this subject area depended partly on whether pupils were taking two languages (some A Band pupils), one language (some B Band pupils), or none (some B Band and all C Band pupils), but within the time available pupils were able to choose freely between the subjects offered. Information from the school giving the exact number for these teaching groups showed the results of this choice:

3B2/3C2 (20 boys, 35 girls)

Choice 1			Choice 2		
Art	6 boys	9 girls	Woodwork	9 boys	9 girls
or Metalwork	14 boys	9 girls	or Technical Drawing	11 boys	7 girls
or Needlework		17 girls	or Home Economics		19 girls

The approach to aesthetic and practical subjects at West Mercia School was rather different and was designed to fit the circumstances of thirteen-plus entry. Thus in their last term at middle school it was explained to pupils that they would be given the opportunity to sample a wide range of practical courses during the year, before making more definite choices for the fourth year. But in practice there were several restrictions on this 'sampling' procedure. In the first place, some craft subjects were restricted to one sex, an outcome made more likely, though not inevitable, by the division of pupils into separate boys' and girls' groups for all practical subjects. Secondly, those pupils who chose on entry to the high school to take a second language (or special music) only had half as much time for practical subjects as the others; this made it more difficult to ensure that they covered all areas. Thirdly, staffing and facilities varied for the various practical subjects: for example, there were three teachers and three rooms for art, and one teacher and one room for rural studies.

It was characteristic of many of the schools that foreign languages and practical subjects should complement each other. It might be a straightforward alternative, as at Yew School, a girls' direct grant school, where two classes took a second foreign language and the other two had home economics and needlework. More often, as at West Mercia, it was a question of stretching the time so that pupils covered both subject areas but for shorter periods of time. In fact, foreign language provision at the third-year level can be one of the most problematic areas for those planning the curriculum. Should all pupils take a foreign language at this stage? What proportion, if any, should study two languages? How is time to be provided for minority subjects?

Still thinking of the curriculum, for the moment, as a programme of subjects, it seems from the evidence reviewed here that there is a high degree of unanimity about the outlines of what should be studied by all third-year pupils in all types of school, although some subjects are more firmly established in the canon than others. In fact, the stability of a subject may be revealed by the degree of consensus between schools about how much time should be spent on it. Only in two of the broad subject areas employed in Table 11 were there wide variations, with some pupils (or schools) spending a large amount of time on foreign languages and very little on craft and the aesthetic side, while others might have no foreign language study at all.

But at the more particular level of school subjects in the third-year curriculum, the reasons why many subjects hold their place there may be more prosaic and easier to trace. For instance, the 'proper study of mankind' advocated in the Newsom Report could be carried out through a variety of programmes: in many junior and middle schools it would probably be more common to find this subject matter dealt with under labels like 'environmental studies' or 'integrated studies' than as separate subjects like history and geography, and in the first and/or second year of a number of secondary schools, humanities time might be taken up by a general course like 'Man, a Course of Study' (MACOS).[5] So why the more traditional history/geography/RE in the third year? One reason has already been suggested; that is, the need to establish the identity of individual subjects before the pupils make choices for the fourth year, and this was the reason explicitly given, in the questionnaire reply from one school, for not introducing the grouping or integrating of subjects in the third year. There is also the argument that this may be a terminal course in a subject, for those who do not choose it as an extra option in the fourth year. In some cases it may be necessary actually to begin public examination courses in the third year, so that the change from more general programmes (humanities, general science) to the individual subjects that may later be taken for public examination (geography, chemistry) may take place at the end of the second year. In either case it may be pressures from within the school system, particularly the public examination system, that are helping to shape the way in which the general aims are translated into the subject-orientated third-year curriculum.

Other pressures more remote from the immediate concerns of the school can play their part in maintaining the consensus about what subjects should be taught as well as keeping open the areas of debate. Thus tradition holds that there are boys' crafts and there are girls' crafts, and at a time when there is a shortage of staff and facilities for subjects like metalwork and woodwork there is not great incentive to go against tradition. Parents (and pupils) if asked what should be included in curriculum will tend to think in terms of subject labels with which they are already familiar, concentrating always on the 'basic subjects' of English and maths.

It might not be difficult, then, to secure a wide measure of agreement *between* schools about the broad subject areas that should be included in the third-year curriculum of all secondary schools, and in some cases the consensus might extend to individual 'subjects'. What about the 'common schools', the comprehensive schools, taking in all the children who presented themselves; was it possible to provide a common curriculum – still defined in terms of a common programme of subjects for pupils of all abilities – *within* the school? Returning for a moment to Table 11, if a school provided a common programme for all its third-year pupils this would show up as a line of single entries. On this criterion the only nonselective school to offer a common programme was Sycamore School, a large eleven–eighteen girls' comprehensive school. The arrangements made here were interesting in several ways. At the moment it is sufficient to point out that the third-year course was planned in broad subject areas of the sort used for this table, so that for example all pupils had 1.4 units in the language area, but this time might be spent in different ways by different groups. This concept – of sketching out the curriculum in terms of 'areas of experience' for all, with differentiation within them – had been the one adopted at the outset at West Mercia School, under the direction of Mr. Rutherford, the first headmaster. Although the plan was never fully realized, the outline remained in the form of common time allocations in five of the seven subject areas of Table 11. Another approach would be to provide a common programme defined in terms of subjects for all but a small minority of pupils, and this had been done in several well-established comprehensive schools like Hazel School, for example, where all but two of the twelve classes had an identical curriculum outline.

In many other schools there were variations in the course outline because the approach to curriculum planning was that employed at Victoria School. This approach could be summarized in the following terms: within the framework of a general education, consider the varying needs of pupils; establish groups of pupils whose needs are broadly similar, and then adapt the general outline to suit these groups. Obviously there could be a common programme for all bands (as was the case at Hazel School), but there was a tendency for those variations which we have seen to be fairly common in the third-year curriculum to be related to the band structure: only one band takes two foreign languages, one band spends more time than other bands on practical subjects. In this way the form of grouping may come to have an important influence on what is learned by different groups of pupils.

It seems, then, that in any school which caters for a wide range of ability there is unlikely at the third-year level to be a wholly common curriculum, as we have defined it; that is, all pupils taking the same subjects for the same amount of time. There is likely to be *some* differentiation either in the subjects studied or in the time spent on them. A wholly common programme can be drawn up, under certain conditions; for instance, it may be agreed that *all* pupils should study one foreign language, and none should take two. This would immediately eliminate one set of planning problems. Alternatively, the programme can be planned as a common framework, within which different courses can be accommodated – the approach adopted at Sycamore School. In any case, even with a common programme, there is still room for many answers to the question 'Are all the pupils following the same course?' As we saw at West Mercia School, within the seven periods that all third-year pupils spent on science, two courses were run: SCISP for the majority and a flexible general science programme for the H Band. In this respect, the common programme had been interpreted in relation to another set of planning decisions – about how pupils should be grouped – and two separate courses provided for prespecified groups of pupils. So, after all, it is inadequate, even at this general level, where the complex issues of classroom experience are not under discussion, to define the 'curriculum' simply in terms of content – subjects to be studied. 'What should be taught, studied and learned' (which Walker, 1973, described as the central problem of the curriculum) may be vitally affected by organizational decisions taken before the school year begins.

Devolution in curriculum planning: the use of time

This concept of devolution in curriculum planning can be applied to other areas besides pupil grouping. One of these is the organization of time within the school day. While we were in the case study schools we spent some time early in the year with single classes, joining them for a day at a time and going round the school with them to all their lessons. The most immediate experience, to us as adults, was one of fragmented time – up to eight different lessons, in different parts of the school, quite apart from assemblies, meals, and other breaks. Of course there were exceptions – two, or even three, periods spent in the workshops, laboratories, or the art room – and many pupils said they liked the variety, but the experience did draw one's attention to this aspect of timetabling. There seem to be two issues which are related. In the first place, who decides how each period is spent, and secondly, into what size of unit is the school day to be divided? One set of answers to these questions leads to the jigsaw model of the timetable, a painstaking compilation of many small pieces, which should leave no one in doubt about where he should be at any given time. Because of its complexity it must all be compiled centrally, under one person's direction, taking into consideration the special requirements of all departments.

Another set of answers can result in a modular or open-plan timetable, where fairly large units – possibly of groups of pupils or subjects, but probably also of time – are outlined on the timetable, the details to be filled in later by other groups of teachers. As usual, few real third-year timetables that we looked at conformed neatly to such models. At West Mercia, for example, time for practical subjects was arranged in this modular way; units of seventy minutes or more were blocked across five or ten classes, a group of up to twelve teachers was listed, and the disposition of pupils within this time was left to the teachers concerned. Subjects which were set by ability, like maths and modern languages, also had some leeway on the timetable, but for most of the third-year timetable the pattern of teachers and classes interlocked with the pattern for other year-groups, so that it resembled more nearly the jigsaw model. This was also the case at Victoria Comprehensive School where the struggle to find time for all the subjects had led to a move away from the 35-period week to a 40-period week. Indeed, if the length of the basic time unit is increased – as it had happened in practice at five comprehensive schools[6] – either the individual subjects have to be grouped or integrated in some way, or the timetable cycle itself has to be extended, as had been done at Hazel School where there were 40 lesson units, each of 70 minutes, in a ten-day cycle.

The Newsom Report spoke of the 'different rhythm of work which is appropriate for different subjects,'[7] while considering that by the age of fourteen most of the pupils were able to concentrate for longer than an hour and a half 'when the nature of the work makes this natural'. In the light of some third-year timetables, even an hour and a half may be considered a large unit. But the way in which units of time are regarded may be much more important than their absolute length. Spans of time which may appear long on the timetable can be broken down into much smaller units of different types of activity at the classroom level, as they might be in the primary class or at an adults' day conference. These decisions about how a span of time should be broken up – the activities to be pursued, the size and type of group appropriate to these activities, the sort of supervision that is required – can be taken at departmental level, as long as the centrally devised plan provides the framework; what is more, the plan can be changed fairly easily without disturbing that framework in any way.

In fact this sort of departmental planning may be common practice in certain departments; for instance, for P.E. and games a large group of pupils, possibly of mixed (academic) ability, may be allocated to a team of teachers. It is then up to the teachers concerned to divide the total group into subgroups according to the activities they want to teach during the allotted time. In this case, the influence of other factors – the season, the weather, the facilities available (is the sports hall needed for public examinations or special competitions?) – makes a flexible approach essential, and this is not considered remarkable. Moreover, in this area of the curriculum it is often accepted that pupils will spend varying amounts of time on the activities provided, and that what is laid down on the timetable should be seen as a minimum requirement. Thus, extra practices for school teams or individuals as well as voluntary lunch-hour clubs and Saturday matches are seen as hovering on the borderline between 'curricular' and 'extracurricular' activities. A similar outlook may prevail in the aesthetic/practical area, where time is almost always allotted in units of at least 60 or 70 minutes and quite often longer – perhaps a whole afternoon or morning. Of course this time may then be broken up into conventional, monotechnic units – one group, with one teacher, following through one activity for one (long) session in one place. But a group of teachers with a fairly large group of pupils and perhaps several work areas may be free to use these resources of space and time in a variety of ways.

What may be fairly common practice in the 'nonclassroom' subjects may seem less desirable or convenient for the rest of the curriculum. For a start, what length of unit is appropriate for each subject – or each class? It is often argued that some types of learning are best absorbed on a drip-feed principle, in small daily doses. Thus modern languages may demand regular short practice sessions and maths may flourish in a similar régime. In fact, it was the problem of reconciling the different sorts of time required by the language and practical areas that led the timetable planners at West Mercia to group third-year 'second language' and 'practical' pupils into two bands with different timetable rhythms. But arguments have also been made for a totally different approach to language teaching; for instance, the provision of intensive courses lasting a week or so where the language is used all day in a variety of situations. In the third year, science is commonly allocated a number of double periods, on the assumption that it is a 'practical' subject and units of this length are needed for experimental work. But if the work in hand is of a more theoretical nature, 80 minutes can be a long time to sit on a laboratory stool. For English and the humanities subjects, attitudes to time seem less clear-cut; a single period of 35/40 minutes may be too short for work involving the use of resource materials, but on the other hand if the two periods allotted, say, to history in the third year are allocated as a single unit of 80 minutes, teachers may feel that this makes the whole subject too vulnerable to the vageries of half-term, open days, or other occasional events. And what about the other sorts of activities that teachers of these subjects might wish to undertake? If the period length is short and is part of a highly structured school day, how feasible is it for teachers to take pupils out of the classroom, let alone out of the school? Any such diversion from 'desk work', however integral to the curricular programme, may need advanced planning of a high order, involving a number of teachers in other subject areas. It is not altogether surprising that it is in June and July, when during and after public examinations the normal routine has to give way to special orders posted on the staffroom noticeboard, that there is a sudden flurry of history and geography expeditions for the lower part of the school. While the limitations on such expeditions outside the school may be primarily related to financial and logistic considerations rather than to the timetable, more modest activities outside the classroom but on the school premises can be difficult to arrange within a timetable structure based on small units of time.

It is understandable that attitudes to the use of time may vary from subject to subject, and from school to school. But perhaps some of the everyday timetabling problems – periods too short, too long, unfairly distributed through the week, unrelated to the geographical realities of the school – are exacerbated by the underlying conception of how time has to be structured in the secondary school. Walton (1973)[8] suggests that the basic problem in this situation is that no allowance is made for 'slack', that is, time which is not tightly programmed. The concept of 'slack' was borrowed by Shaw (1972)[9] from industry, where it could be defined as surplus productive capacity which could be mobilized to meet sudden fluctuations. In education 'slack' could be seen as time that is not highly programmed. 'Slack does not mean idle or waiting time; it is simply not programmed in advance.' Shaw suggested that in educational settings other than the secondary school there is generally a more flexible outlook. In the early years of the primary school, slack might consist of expressive and semirecreational activity amounting to perhaps 20 percent of the time.

The secondary school, on the other hand, 'programmes all the time for all the pupils'. Why is this? Walton considers that it may be the result of several pressures: the dominance of the curriculum by public examinations, the increase in the number of secondary school subjects, and the tension between vocational demands and the attempt to give a general education. These could all be related to the problems presented by mass formal state education, and the apparent necessity for schools to deliver an agreed 'package' within a limited period of compulsory schooling: 'a lot of children have to be taught, as economically as possible, that knowledge which society considers to be desirable.'[10]

More pragmatic considerations might be put forward within the schools. Any organization providing a variety of activities for some hundreds of individuals within a limited space and time has to be well structured if productive work is to be carried on and anarchy avoided. But perhaps this need for sound planning has become caught up too closely with the detailed specification of the curriculum. If the tendency is more pronounced within secondary schools, it may be most obvious at the third-year level. Thus for the pupils in the first two years – eleven–thirteen – the timetable may look more 'open' because of planning decisions about the needs of children at this age; perhaps pupils should spend blocks of time with one or more teachers in a 'home base' to ease the transition from primary school, or the work time may be divided between large integrated subject areas. Again, even with the pressure of public examinations, it may be possible to sketch out much of the timetable for the fourth- and fifth-year pupils in terms of 'option blocks' occupying equal amounts of time, and for the sixth form a more flexible approach to time is often considered an appropriate way of encouraging a more mature response from students. But for the third year, the planners in a comprehensive school may have to take into account two pressures that tend to fragment the time. In the first place, there are pressures to include a large number of individual subjects, as we have already seen. Secondly, faced with this array of subjects, teachers and parents may well consider that it may be appropriate for pupils of thirteen–fourteen to follow slightly different paths according to their ability and interest. In the effort to meet these requirements the timetable planner may find himself back to struggling with the jigsaw, and any idea of building 'slack' into the whole picture seems irrelevant if not laughable.

Is there any way out of this problem? As long as certain conditions have to be met – specified numbers of pupils and staff to be occupied on the premises within specified hours – then in one sense those in charge of the school have to programme all the time for all the pupils. That is, everyone has to follow an agreed schedule. But if, as I suggested earlier, the 'master schedule', the timetable for the whole school, is laid down in outline terms initially, then the 'slack' can be built into the programme as the details are worked out at various levels – by department, by teams of teachers, by teacher and pupils within the classroom. In the crowded third-year timetable of many schools at present, slack of a sort may be introduced into the day despite rather than within the system, in a number of ways with which teachers and pupils are only too familiar: dawdling between classrooms; finishing a cup of coffee after the bell has gone; 'tidying up' or 'putting away' and innumerable other 'coping strategies'; but all this is recognized to be a misinterpretation or even a direct contravention of the official programme laid down in the timetable, and usually provokes recurrent waves of 'tightening up'. With a more flexible approach, where many teachers (and perhaps the pupils themselves) are involved in planning how time should be used, it may be easier to provide for the varying curricular needs of groups of individuals, and to replace the frenzy of the interlesson 'all change' with a more varied rhythm of work within the larger time blocks. In the third-year context, it may only be the remedial teachers at some schools who are given this degree of control over their timetable.

Once again, the key to a more flexible approach to the use of time of this (or any) year-group seems to lie in devolution – devolution in the detailed working out of the timetable. The analysis of third-year timetables in the twenty schools brought out the tendency of many larger schools to use longer time units for much of the week. If these longer 'periods' are still allocated from the centre to individual teacher/class units, then the problem remains the conventional one writ slightly larger: how the individual teacher structures time in his own subject with his 'own' class. But if groups of teachers are encouraged to plan these, or even longer units, together, then they may produce new solutions to the problems of providing for all the needs of all the pupils.

Notes

1. See Davies (1969), p. 68; the curriculum unit or 'notional class' is there set at one-ninth of the week, partly because he found this to be a common pattern in many schools where each pupil joined nine 'classes' per week. It provides a useful common unit for comparing timetables which use different units of measurement.
2. But some of the teachers at West Mercia were not satisfied about this and thought that the H Band – the slower learners – should spend more time on these basic subjects and less, for example, on science where there was also a common allocation of 7 periods for all the third-year pupils, in 1975–1976.
3. In this case we know that the common timetable outlined was complemented by a common syllabus in history, geography, and r.e. respectively, and (for eighty percent of the pupils) a common examination in the summer term.
4. At one school which was involved in an earlier part of the study, pupils followed an integrated humanities programme up to the end of the third year. When they came to make choices for the fourth year some of them were confused by subject names which they had not met before, in the school, and wanted to know what 'geography' and 'history' would be about.
5. *Man, A Course of Study* (MACOS), 1968, Curriculum Development Associates, Inc., Washington, DC/Centre for Applied Research in Education, University of East Anglia, Norwich.
6. There are of course obvious practical advantages in longer lesson units in large schools, as anyone who has stood in a busy corridor at changeover time will testify. Even with a clear passage it may take several minutes to get from one teaching area to another, or considerably longer if the school is on a split site.
7. Newsom Report, 1963, p. 126.
8. Walton, J., in *The Curriculum: Research, Innovation and Change*, edited by P.H. Taylor and J. Walton, Ward Lock Educational, 1973, pp. 125–135.
9. Shaw, K.E., in *The Secondary School Timetable*, edited by Walton, J., Ward Lock Educational, 1972, pp. 50–57.
10. Walton, J., in *The Curriculum: Research, Innovation and Change*, 1973, pp. 128–129.

CHAPTER 5.2

TIMETABLING*
H.M. Inspectorate

To amend Gertrude Stein, 'a timetable is a timetable is a timetable'; that is, it is a mechanical device for executing decisions about teachers, teaching groupings of pupils, and, to a lesser extent, the content of lessons. No particular timetable has to do with a common curriculum, though some timetabling techniques are more inimical than others to the effective operation of a chosen curricular pattern. It does not follow, however, that a timetable which is helpful to common curriculum working will be used in this way. The best which can be hoped for is that the timetable does not inhibit more than it must; and that, where it must, it is still as nonspecific as possible: for example, it moves from the extreme specificity of a single period of a given subject with one named teacher to a departmental or faculty arrangement which does not precommit to the same extent.

A timetable, above all, is not to be seen as a problem but as a vehicle for extending opportunities to teachers to incorporate what they will into their teaching method and content. Any paper on timetabling, therefore, must not be seen as offering a single solution, applicable anywhere.

Timetabling as an enabling device

Curricular change – in the sense of the substitution of one subject for another – has often resulted in timetable substitution, not change; and this substitution has not always been able to take into consideration the different needs of the new subject.

* Supplementary Paper 3 Timetabling, from *Curriculum 11–16*, Working Papers by H.M. Inspectorate, pp. 63–67.

Curricular development – the extension of existing subjects in some ways by integration, by new schemes, by fresh considerations of function – has not always been accompanied by timetabling change; and where such changes have taken place, they have often been to alleviate constraints other than those imposed by the curricular development.

This chapter examines constraints on timetabling, assesses new requirements from curricular change or development, and identifies certain features which will allow a timetable to become an enabling instrument to assist teachers rather than a straitjacket which inhibits them. In examining these constraints it will also show timetabling techniques which can readily be related to schools introducing a common curriculum.

Existing constraints arise from the accommodation available, the teaching staff, the time available, and factors external to the school. Each of these in itself contains a variety of different kinds and degrees of constraint. It has always been – and even with computer assistance, will always be – the task of the timetabler to analyse the constraints and place them in priority order for solution. No one timetabler has ever produced a perfect timetable (that is, one entirely satisfactory to its creator and all the consumers). The basic rule of educational decision is always in force – when you have decided to do x, it is no longer possible to do y and z; and it is almost an invariable rule that x and y and z are all desirable.

Constraints

An examination of each of these constraints and a set of questions about each follows.

Accommodation

Virtually every secondary school is short of some accommodation. The schools most adversely affected are often those where the provision of permanent accommodation overall is short. But the constraint of being short of, say, two laboratories or two workshops or one gymnasium can represent initially such a major constraint for the curriculum planner that much of the timetabler's room for manoeuvre is forfeited. On the other hand, certain features, endemic in secondary school organization, work against the best use of available space. In particular, the association of one teacher with one room will tend towards the underemployment of 'pupil stations'. To teach a group of up to a dozen in a room capable of taking up to

30 may well create a timetable difficulty somewhere, even if the timetabler overcomes it. Equally, internal redistribution of rooms for activities is frequently hampered by the forces of tradition. Recent thinking, too, in architectural planning is in some cases serving to restrict the use of rooms in some ways and hence to impose a certain teaching style. 'Boxes', continuous suites without separate entrances, or large open or semiopen spaces all have their limitations for the timetabler. Planning is affected, too, by any dual-use feature of the accommodation, particularly in spaces used for dining and teaching, and for day and evening activities (youth wings, sports centres, community activity rooms).

The timetabler must first examine the proposed curriculum to see whether it is practicable within the total accommodation. If we suppose that a draft curriculum for an eleven–sixteen school involves, at first sight, 1200 'meetings' in a school which can apparently produce only 1000 'meeting spaces' in a full week, it does not follow that this curriculum cannot be timetabled: what may have to change is the teaching arrangement for that curriculum. If, on the other hand, a draft curriculum throws up a requirement for 360 periods for average-size groups of 20 in craft, and the school has only five craft rooms, then a curricular rearrangement is imperative. A demand for, say, 180 periods of science in a 40-period week in three laboratories may however be met, given that not all this science will be taught in laboratories.

The decision as to which periods may be allocated in the laboratories must be the timetabler's: he must bear in mind factors about loadings elsewhere, not known to the head of science, who would therefore be in no position to make a decision; but the decision as to which teachers should be deployed with which groups in the laboratories is one which belongs to the head of science – and if the timetabler, by his method of construction, has not enabled the head of science to reach this decision, he has preempted the flexibility to which the subject is entitled in a good timetable and (possibly not as a scientist himself) has preempted decisions about what the science department will be doing. Thus, enablement must be the first precept for the timetabler.

Questions

Questions which the timetabler may ask, some of which will be subject to answers from others, include:

Is the school's administration housed for optimum functional discharge of responsibilities and, at the same time, most economically?

For example: Is the school office sited well? Is the head's room larger than needed? Would a change of use yield more teaching space? Has the foyer been allocated to a department (art, commerce, home economics)?

What use is made of central facilities?

For example: Is the library open outside lesson times? If so, is it more rather than less likely to be usable for class purposes? Is it designed to accommodate teaching groups? Is the assembly hall used except for assembly? Does the nature of the gymnasium mean double provision of space on the timetable for inclement weather? On a split (or scattered) site, has all unnecessary duplication of accommodation been avoided and is all necessary duplication present? Do dual-use arrangements for dining/teaching spaces allow one period for setting and another for clearing or has some study of the actual time involved been undertaken? What is the accommodation function of the resources centre?

What is the potential of the school's teaching spaces?

For example: Given 12 'boxes', are they all furnished identically, so that the nature of the work is controlled by the furniture? Is any space carpeted? Have any departments indicated that they wish to organize noisy and/or dirty and/or moving activities at some times so that their usual accommodation will be unsuitable? How much time is spent in registration and how far does this affect furnishing and disposition? Which sets of rooms between them provide enough outlet sockets, water supply, and semipermanent equipment to satisfy individual departments, even if these rooms are not contiguous?

What is the potential of the rest of the school's accommodation?

For example: Are corridors employed only for circulation and is there a chart of pupil movement through spaces? Is storage space allocated upon a basis of request or by tradition or rule-of-thumb? What is the actual loading of pegs in cloakrooms on (a) a wet day (b) a fine day? If locker desks are provided, what do they contain? How often are contents of cupboards reviewed and what process is there for disposing of lumber? How far is the provision of separate offices for middle management the result of previous timetabling policy? How far could temporal and physical coincidence of many ancillary functions be eliminated? When was the last assessment of the accommodation needs of the ancillary staff undertaken? Is the teaching staff housed in its common provision most economically, effectively, and comfortably?

What is the impact of the accommodation and its use on visitors and new pupils?

For example: Is there display? If there is, is time provided for pupils to study it? Is direction-finding made easy? What sorts of activities will the visitors first see? What sort should be available?

The teaching staff

The major constraints on the timetabler from teacher deployment are of two kinds – those arising from the existing staff (about whom he may believe that he knows too much) and those from the new staff (about whom information may be scanty). If, however, the principle of devolution – to heads of departments or faculties or their equivalent – is observed, again the timetabler will not be preempting decisions which are not properly his to make. More useful than endeavouring to deploy specific teachers with specific groups would be the detailed knowledge of the interests, talents, and capacities of all teachers which may not be revealed in their subject specialisms. If the school has a pastoral system which requires year teachers, for example, to teach their own groups, the timetabler will need to bear this in mind, but even here (since heads of departments will also be aware of this requirement) as little as possible that is specific should be set down. Not many schools now believe that new entrants to the profession must be confined to younger pupils only; and if the school does not subscribe to this view the timetabler has less of a problem. If it does, then he can become an agent of change by deploying a group of teachers for subsequent specific deployment by senior subject teachers, but this 'last move' deployment will at least have to be across the year-groups which the timetabler has specified. As with accommodation, the practicability of the curriculum draft needs to be investigated; and, equally, an early rejection of a draft on the grounds that the statistics do not match must be avoided. In a structure in which senior subject staff are enabled to take decisions, 140 periods of, say, 'languages' on a staff of three linguists may well be possible;

in a system of specific individual deployment in individual periods, such a draft is impossible to implement unless decisions about pupil performance are to be taken in advance of that performance.

Part-time teachers usually represent a major constraint, and often adversely affect timetable quality, especially from the pupil's point of view. Whether constraining the whole timetable on these grounds is wise or in the school's best interest is doubtful, and to set up the timetable with other constraints in mind, and then to see what effect this has on part-time teachers, is the better course of action.

Of considerable importance to the timetabler is the value of the contact ratio, that is, the proportion of the time available which teachers spend teaching. The range of nonteaching periods may be total (some with all 'free' and some with none): this matters less to the timetabler than the total nonavailability of teachers for teaching. When the school structure is itself devised as an enabler, the timetabler will be able so to dispose of the teaching power that the nonteaching time is found from faculty or departmental resources, as will be 'cover-periods'. It is easiest (and it is worth remarking that in timetable-making 'easiest' is often tantamount to 'most effective') for the timetabler to have to deploy a very few teachers with hardly any teaching, most teachers having an initially and nominally full load; relatively easy if there is a rather larger number with fairly substantial amounts of time; and most difficult when some principle of equity dictates equal rations of nonteaching time for all.

The timetabler will also have to pay special attention to the deployment and loading of new entrants, although the total number is less important than the proportion to be found in any one department. The implication of this for the creation, wherever convenient, of larger departments or groups is clear, and this of itself will help a school in coming to those fundamental questions implied in its wishing to implement a common curriculum.

However detailed the knowledge, no timetabler is likely to know everything about each teacher, and the timetabling should reflect this. For example, it is unlikely that among a group of, say, eight English specialists, they will all be equally gifted in teaching poetry, drama, prose, or 'skills'. A timetable which allocates each teacher separately and unalterably to one group for one year is making no allowance for these differences and may well be skewing the pupils' English diet. It follows that planned and purposeful fragmentation may not be evidence of bad timetabling. Where such fragmentation is haphazard, it is generally an indication of at least one constraint too many on the timetabler, but even in these cases, it is worth looking for the benefits which may accrue. Timetablers are peculiarly well placed to make virtues of necessities.

Since most teachers are most successful and confident when performing in what they regard as their own best field and circumstances, they are most likely to respond to a timetable which allows them as much freedom as possible and meets their criteria. Equally, dynamism, rethinking, and a redefinition of objectives may not flourish if the timetable encourages the static to remain so and stultifies invention. The timetabler who wishes to make the timetable an instrument of policy cannot wait for consensus or plunge simultaneously into a variety of shifts in emphasis which, taken together, may be destructive of the teacher's confidence. It is very important, therefore, that discussion, assessment, and analysis of the timetable and its successor involve all teaching staff continuously. If the period of thinking about the timetable is confined to the time it takes to produce it mechanically – and this is regrettably true about a number of timetables – then the timetabler and the teachers are the poorer. In particular, an assessment of timetable quality needs to be made on different levels and from different bases – the curriculum, the teaching force, the pupils, the accommodation, the agencies external to the school: all these must be separately assessed.

Questions

The following questions might be asked:

Does the timetable satisfy and encourage, (a) curriculum policy and future developments, (b) the teachers, (c) the pupils?
How long did its mechanics take?
How many alterations have been made?

How many of these arose from factors outside the timetabler's control (for example, fire, sudden death, or prolonged illness)? How many have been made to satisfy teacher predilections, such as room changes, set changes? Who has assessed the effect of such changes on the pupils?

To what sort of loading are new entrants to teaching subject in pupil-loading terms? What is the pupil-loading range over the staff as a whole? What is the mode?

Has the pattern of (a) pupil absence, (b) staff absence been charted against the timetable? Does any explanation for absence emerge from such a chart?

Who coordinates the timetable and other centrally required rotas?

For example. Who coordinates break/lunch supervision, bus duties, homework timetables, extracurricular activities? Do they appear to be logically compatible with each other?

The time available

The time available to the timetabler is likely to be viewed in more traditional terms than almost any other feature of the school's structure and organization. The heat and noise generated by a proposal to lengthen the school day by five minutes are frequently observed phenomena; and usually far exceed the heat and noise generated by far more fundamental changes, such as 'going mixed-ability' or dropping or including a new subject in the curriculum. Some years ago, the debate on time centred on the simple advantage/disadvantage arguments about 35 forty-minute periods or 40 thirty-five minute periods. In either case, 1400 minutes was the total available to the timetabler, over a maximum of 38 weeks in the year, which such items as first and last days of terms, school functions, and so on frequently effectively reduced to 36.

On this count, each single period in a 40-period week produces an annual contact of 21 hours – about half the standard working week for most adults. A 4-period option, introduced newly in the fourth year of a secondary school (e.g., commerce, economics, Spanish) thus aggregates to itself in the approximate 66 to 68 weeks available before the public examination a total of about 160 hours of study, or approximately 4 normal 'working adult' weeks.

The state of basic subjects is not markedly different. In a 40-period week, 5 is the most usual number allocated to mathematics and English, say 3 hours per week for five years. This amounts to some 520 hours of study or about 13 normal 'working adult' weeks. If religious education is allocated one period for five years, it accrues about two and a half normal 'working adult' weeks in those five years.

All these figures relate to available teacher/pupil contact time. They do not include any work done outside school hours – mainly by pupils. Equally, full attendance is assumed throughout. It is interesting to note that one two-week absence – the result of influenza, perhaps – from an option in years four and five represents a loss of time greater than 2.5 percent of the total available for the whole course; a lengthening of the school day by five minutes is tantamount (if the extra time is used for teaching) to increasing the teaching time by just under 2 percent: this is equivalent to extending each hour of teaching by just over a minute!

Other developments have, however, been introduced in some schools in recent years. These include the 4-period day, the 5-hour day, the continuous day, and the division of the day into equal modules. Advantages claimed by their proponents are many. In fact, many of these systems were introduced to offset an accommodation problem and the advantages have been identified subsequently. In only a very few schools has prior consideration been given to the whole question of time and its disposition, before a structure or a curriculum (and particularly the content of that curriculum) has been settled. It is this fact which has caused the general dissatisfaction with the marginal adjustments in time which have taken place. It is, too, this fact which has inhibited much curriculum development other than at the margins. A move towards a common curriculum requires questions to be asked about time allocations, frequency, periodicity, and objectives and these may require a new concept of the ways in which time may be used.

Questions

Most of the questions to be asked by the timetabler must be concerned with the justification of the use to which a school wishes to put the time at its disposal. They might include:

Have heads of departments/faculties been invited to produce a distillation of their proposed content – a sort of irreducible minimum – and then been asked to justify the time requested for its discharge? Have they considered this irreducible minimum as being the basic entitlement of all pupils?

Has a discussion taken place about allocation of nonteaching time? Has it included information about sizes of groups possible with certain contact ratios?

Does the school view the whole of its 'attendance day' (for example 9 am to 4 pm) as available?

Is the length of the mid-day break based upon the percentage dining at school?

If transport is a problem, have detailed studies, including costings, been made of quite different 'school-days'?

How far has consideration been given to the different kinds of time disposition needed by subject teachers to fulfil the first question?

Is the school day so constructed that pupils are inevitably late on a number of occasions?

Factors external to the school

A number of external factors have already appeared above, because it is difficult to separate clearly internal and external factors, and increasingly so as schools become less touchy about what used to be called 'outside interference'. In general terms, the outside factors may be divided into professional and nonprofessional. The latter are often easier to identify and tend to be more intractable – ranging from the nature of the chairman of governors' employment (and his consequent availability) to the problems of the bus contractor. Intractable as they may be, there seems little justification for letting any portion of a small tail wag the whole dog, yet it is true that schools will frequently say that nothing can be done, when in fact the problem has never been considered from first principles.

The professional factors often impinge upon far more sensitive areas. LEA advisory services, the careers service, the rules governing caretakers and cleaners are all clearly external and yet tightly control any school's manoeuvrability. Other services – probation, fire, and particularly now, social services – are sometimes seen as extraneously supportive or intrusive, seldom as integral. Schools, in session for comparatively so little of the year, do not appear to have yet understood that their role may have to be subordinated to those of services which are available and functional for 365 days a year.

The irregular incidence of matters related to external agencies is confusing and annoying to the timetabler. Once again, if the timetable is invested by the principle of flexibility, fewer problems will occur and there will be greater readiness for a school to make positive use of external agencies and a consequent greater productivity from the time employed, which will no longer be seen as lost. For the common curriculum school, every contribution can be viewed only as a gain, since that curriculum sets out to use positively all experiences available in schools.

Questions

Questions about external factors are few, but fundamental:

Does the school know as much about its regular external visitors as it does about its own staff?

Does timetable provision enable casual visitors/speakers to be absorbed readily into the organization without upsetting a variety of subjects or teachers?

How far does the school view external agencies as intrusive?

Who arranges times for governors'/parents'/staff meetings? And what is the consultation process in forming these decisions?

Is the offering to the school's resources which outside agencies with regular contacts can make restricted by the timetable?

Timetabling

The assessment of new requirements from curricular developments will always be a matter of guesswork and interpretation of the motives underlying the change. It is important that the timetabler does not assess innovation on the grounds of the extent to which the timetabling problem is increased or lessened by the change. The main requirement is in the initial thinking about the structure; if this is conceived so as to accommodate ideas and methods, rather than so many subject places, the timetabler might be able to absorb major shifts in a school's curricular emphases.

Integrated studies

A particular case where an innovation may be trammelled by ossification in the timetable occurs in 'integrated studies' (whatever it is called from school to school). One of the underlying reasons for such an introduction is often a desire to promote more interdisciplinarity, of which a loose definition might be 'gaining professional recognition on a wide front of the fact that separate subjects tend not to take cognizance of the contribution of other subjects'.

Often welcomed by the timetabler because integrated or interdisciplinary arrangements are time-saving, subjects may still be seen by him as separate and needing separate provision. The task is a different one in fact: it is to provide a framework which, while taking nothing from the separate subjects, allows such developments and overlap as both teachers and taught are capable of implementing and comprehending. Since this is likely to vary from week to week, the scheme must provide developmental chances.

Another curricular peril of integrated studies is the creation of groups of subjects to the exclusion of others which might have been integrated in the past. For example, it is common to find history, geography, and religious education put together under a humanities umbrella and so timetabled; and in many cases the former interdependence of religious education with music, art, and drama is specifically excluded within the timetable. It must be stressed that the common curriculum is almost certainly interdependent in concept, though this is not a necessary condition for its timetabling. However, this interdependence will spring from the 'minimum entitlement' idea, and has no connection with any, quite separate, organizational arrangements for timetabling certain subjects or subject staff together to produce integration. The common curriculum is concerned, in short, with integrated attitudes and a self-consistent conceptual framework: it is not concerned with subjects, whether integrated or not, except as labels of convenience and the timetabler must not make the mistake of confusing the substance and the shadow.

It is also worth noting that the timetable may be so constructed as to facilitate a teaching staff's early explorations into interdisciplinarity, without compelling this to happen *every* week for an *entire* year. Experiment is then allowed without the need to adopt a predetermined stance to show success or failure; an enabling timetable provides elements of privacy.

Other factors

Certain features in any timetable represent more than the allocation of teacher/class/space. Implicit will be an indication of the expected style and knowledge about content domination, relationships of teacher and class, and objectives. Factors not commonly built into timetables are those which do not appear to matter – for example, relationships between pupils in a group – or which have not taken place (although it is known that they will take place) by the date of the timetable's construction – for example, the development of pupils in a subject, their increased age (and maturity?), the nature of the summer term, particularly after public examinations. Other features often take no account of external factors – such as the incidence of half-term breaks, the regular late arrival of some public transport, the regular visit of careers advisory officers – which may diminish time for certain pupils or certain activities quite markedly.

The temporal order of a timetable's construction may also be apparent. When the requirements of the sixth form – however extravagant and unrealistic – are met first, the adverse effect is often visible in the lower school. The claims of option systems, particularly when these are, as is so common, overelaborate, result in the absence of any internal balance for some pupils elsewhere; for example, when a second-year class enjoys one day of eight consecutive sitting periods and spends the next day in frenetic movement through eight activity periods. It is unlikely that the timetabler is unaware of the importance of a balance of activities for each pupil during each day; and that this balance seems more important for younger rather than older students. When this balance is lacking, it must be assumed that other constraints have taken priority. Is concentration on the supposed needs of the older pupils, in curriculum or choice of teacher for a group, or preferential timetabling, not a self-defeating activity which may be a major cause of the annual missing army (those who, at sixteen-plus, turn their backs, ungratefully but with relief, on education in any form in any institution)?

CHAPTER 5.3

WILLIAM TYNDALE JUNIOR AND INFANTS SCHOOLS PUBLIC INQUIRY: A REPORT TO THE ILEA*
Robin Auld, QC

The junior school –
Mr. Haddow's class options scheme

About the end of February 1974, just after the half-term, when the secondary transfer reports had been completed, Mr. Haddow decided to make some radical changes in the teaching of his own fourth-year class. He decided to introduce a system of class options which gave his pupils – all aged about ten to eleven – a very wide choice as to how they would spend their day at school. As events turned out, this innovation had serious repercussions throughout the school; and, in my view, was the initial cause of the considerable parental discontent which began to grow towards the end of this term and the beginning of the summer term.

Mr. Haddow took this course after discussing it with Mr. Ellis and obtaining his agreement. However, Mr. Haddow did not, prior to its introduction, discuss it or even inform the staff as a whole of his intentions at one of their regular staff meetings. Mrs. Chowles, for example, only learned of Mr. Haddow's class options scheme when it started. It is surprising that Mr. Haddow made, and that Mr. Ellis allowed him to make, so radical a change in teaching arrangements without first consulting the staff as a whole. I say that for two principal reasons:

(i) with their respective teaching experience, both Mr. Ellis and Mr. Haddow must have known that so fundamental an innovation in the teaching of one class was bound to affect directly and indirectly the

* Inner London Education Authority, July 1976, pp. 60–67, 77–78, 148–154, 187–188.

teaching of other classes in the school; and

(ii) both Mr. Ellis and Mr. Haddow have always maintained a firm belief in the principle that the teaching policy of a school should be one to which its staff as a whole should work so as to ensure a consistency of approach in the teaching of the children. Having regard to the nature of the regular staff discussions that had taken place, both men must have known that this was an innovation on which there was likely to be hotly opposing views.

It is not clear how much Mr. Haddow did to inform the parents of his class children of his proposals or to explain to them exactly what they amounted to. He gave some indication to the parents by sending them a letter informing them that he felt it was time to increase the range of activities that he could offer to the children, inviting their help in running these activities, and suggesting that they should call into the classroom at any time to discuss the sort of help that they might be able to give. It appears that this invitation produced little response from the parents though, no doubt, Mr. Haddow had plenty of opportunity to inform some of the parents what he was doing as and when he saw them in and about the school.

Let Mr. Haddow describe in his own words what his purpose was in introducing his class options scheme and what it amounted to:

Terry Ellis and I had many educational discussions and after the half-term we decided that the school would need to develop in a different way if it were to meet the demands of all the children. It was agreed that I could develop a wider approach to the curriculum within my fourth-year class. With the children I decided on a range of 20 activities to be set up for them. They had the choice to move freely to the one they wished to do. I expanded these activities from the classroom into the hall outside. . . . Where necessary I would intervene and give direction to the children's learning.

. . . Each day we would meet in the classroom, I would say what I was able to provide for that day, talk with them about what they wanted to do, give them a general discussion on how this would affect the rest of the school (e.g., keeping the noise level low). I had a timetable on the wall of fixtures which I provided every day, e.g., TV programmes, games, visits. *It was a partial opting-in system for the children.* (my italics)

Mr. Haddow said that there were about 20 activities from which the children could choose. The following list, which he provided in evidence, gives some idea of the variety:

English work,	Music,	Reading,
Mathematics,	Board games,	Dancing,
Topic work, .	Table tennis,	Science experiments,
Cookery,	Woodwork,	Football games,
Painting,	Drawing,	Modelling, and
Pottery,	Diaries,	Tie-dye.
Improvised drama,	Needlecraft,	

In addition to providing this range of options for the children, Mr. Haddow expanded his teaching area, as above indicated in the passage quoted from his evidence, so as to allow some of the activities to take place outside his second-floor classroom, in the corridor, and in the second-floor hall.

Mr. Haddow saw the new system as being of particular benefit to the socially deprived and emotionally disturbed children in that, according to him, they were able to develop far greater self-sufficiency in this freer atmosphere than under the more conventional classroom system that he had followed in the previous term. As to the brighter and more academic children, Mr. Haddow's evidence was that they continued to work in much the same way as before, being already inclined to choose the academic options, and that they did so. He did recognize, however, that there was a 'middle group' who did not benefit immediately from the new scheme, and who, because they lacked a wish to learn, tended to drift, choosing the easier options such as watching television films and playing table tennis. Mr. Haddow accepted this as a stage through which this group of children would have to go before they became inclined to opt for more worthwhile activities, a development which he said began to take place towards the end of the summer term, 1974.

Mr. Haddow's sanguine and rather casual approach to the changes that he had introduced for his own class was not shared by some of the parents of children in that class, who noticed within a very short time a deterioration in the attitudes and behaviour of their children. These parents found their children becoming rude and unmanageable, failing to understand why their new-found freedom at school was not available to them at home. Some children, far from being stimulated by the freedom of choice that had been given to them, soon became bored and listless; others, who had been keen readers and who had enjoyed going to school, lost interest in reading and expressed a dislike of the new system. However, there were also some parents who claimed to have seen a change for the better in their children since Mr. Haddow had abandoned the conventional classroom techniques of teaching.

The unsettling effects of Mr. Haddow's new system spread beyond the confines of his own class. In the first place, there was a great increase in activity and noise caused by children choosing and changing the options available to them whenever they felt like it in the course of the day. And, because some of the optional activities took place in the corridor and in the hall, in addition to the classroom, there was a constant thoroughfare about the second floor which was evident to children in other classes and which disturbed their lessons. The other children saw the new freedom which Mr. Haddow's class was being given, and they resented and reacted against the fact that they were not included in these changes. In some cases, these children absented themselves from their classes and tried to join in the freer régime offered by Mr. Haddow. This happened to such an extent that, in a number of cases, the only way to deal with the children was to permit them to leave their own classes and join that of Mr. Haddow. Significantly, Mr. Haddow, in his proof of evidence to the inquiry, said that, as the year progressed, he attracted children from other classes. . . .

It took some time for the full significance and impact of Mr. Haddow's new class options scheme to become apparent to the parents and to the managers of the school. In the early stages many parents may have been somewhat wary of the change, but at least prepared to give it a try. Those managers who had regular contact with the junior school at that time, notably Mrs. Burnett, the chairman, Mrs. Dewhurst and Mrs. Gittings, also do not appear to have been unsympathetic to the new venture. It was not until the end of the term and the beginning of the summer term, when a number of parents began to voice their discontent, that some of the managers began to take a closer look at what was happening and to express their own concern. . . .

The junior school –
the reading groups scheme

There was undoubtedly a reading problem in the junior school at the time when Mr. Ellis took over. Out of a total of 217 on the school roll there were about 80 children who were receiving remedial reading tuition from Mrs. Walker working on a part-time basis. Although Mrs. Walker's work over the previous years had been successful and much appreciated by the parents whose children had been under her care, the amount of time that she, as a part-time teacher, could devote to the numbers needing her help was necessarily very limited.

Mr. Ellis felt that, because of the size of the problem, it was something that would have to be tackled by the staff as a whole. He also felt – and this is a part of his general approach to teaching – that, so far as possible, children with difficulties of any sort should not be segregated from other children, but catered for in the ordinary teaching arrangements made for the whole school.

Accordingly, in late January or early February 1974, Mr. Ellis introduced to the staff discussions the idea of a reading group scheme under which, for the purpose of teaching reading and language skills, the whole school would be organized for certain set periods into groups according to reading and language ability instead of into class groups according to age. There was nothing very revolutionary in this idea; if properly organized, there was no reason why it should not have worked well. Its two principal advantages were:

(i) Each teacher would be able to concentrate upon children within a narrower range of ability and thus could use his or her teaching time more effectively than in the case of a mixed-ability class. This would result in more remedial help for children in need of such help and a greater extending of the brighter children.
(ii) Having regard to the integrated day method of teaching largely in use at the school, it would ensure that each child spent a regular and fixed amount of time learning reading and language skills.

One of the possible disadvantages of the scheme was that such groups, each of them spanning as they would a wider age-range than found in a class grouped by age, might not be entirely successful in the case of some of the older children with learning difficulties. They might resent being grouped with very much younger children of average or above-average reading abilities.

The junior school staff as a whole welcomed the idea, and over a period of time and several meetings, discussed how it should be put into effect. In addition, the scheme was canvassed with some of the managers who were in regular contact with the school and with the parents. Mrs. Dewhurst, the parent-manager for the junior school, produced, in February 1974, a newsletter for both schools which informed the parents of the proposed reorganization and of the intention of the junior school staff to call a parents' meeting after half-term at which the scheme would be explained. About the same time Mr. Ellis arranged to have prepared and circulated to all the parents some notes of suggestions for the organization of the scheme pointing out some of its advantages, and inviting the parents to express their views.

The organization of the reading groups scheme required careful planning. Mr. Ellis took the opportunity to discuss it with Miss Elisabeth Biek, the senior remedial teacher for Islington, on one of her visits to the school in early February 1974. She advised him that, before such a system was introduced, some form of assessment of each child's reading standards would have to be made. She advised him to use a well-known form of reading test called the 'Neale Analysis of Reading Ability', and offered to advise him on grouping and methods of teaching once the results of the test had been obtained. Mr. Ellis followed her advice, though not completely, for, although he tested the reading of every child in the school, he did so using another, equally well-known, test known as 'The Schonell Reading Test'. It is enough for present purposes that Mr. Ellis, having tested each child in the school, was able to compile a list showing, in accordance with the test used, the reading ages of all its children.

The next stage was to decide on the number and ability-ranges of the groups and on the teaching methods to be adopted. It was particularly important that a common teaching method should be used by the staff in order to ensure a consistency of teaching approach as between the reading groups and the ordinary class groups in which the teaching of reading and language skills would necessarily continue, if not as distinct subjects, as part of the general class teaching activities.

Mr. Ellis invited Miss Biek to return to the school to discuss with him and the staff how the scheme should be organized. She attended a meeting there with him and the staff at the end of February, just after half-term. Miss Biek's account of this meeting gives a useful illustration of the way in which matters of importance in practical organization of the school were dealt with in meetings of the staff at that time. Her evidence was that she found it very difficult to get down to 'brass tacks' in the discussion about the way in which the reading groups should be organized and as to the methods of teaching to be adopted for them. It appeared to her that the staff had given little thought before the meeting to the practicalities of the scheme and that they were disinclined to consider them at the meeting. Her recollection was that Mr. Haddow did most of the talking for the staff, and that he kept steering the discussion into what she regarded as too general a line. While she tried to advise the staff on the practical aspects of the scheme, he appeared to be more interested in discussing such things as the advantages of an 'unstructured' as opposed to a 'structured' system of teaching, and the 'rationale' behind various methods of teaching reading. At the end of the meeting, and at a subsequent chance meeting with Mr. Haddow, Miss Biek offered to return and give further help in relation to the scheme, but she was never invited to do so.

There is very little precise information on the scheme eventually agreed upon by the staff, certainly nothing in writing indicating the method of organization or timetable. Such evidence as was given on the subject indicated that the school was divided up into reading groups in an ascending scale of ability and with no restriction of age within any group. Each member of the staff, including Mr. Ellis and Mrs. Walker, was allocated a group. Mrs. Walker had one of the groups with the lowest reading age, the intention being that she would be able to continue her remedial reading tuition, but in a much more concentrated way with that single group, rather than trying to cope with about 80 children as she had done up till then. The plan was that there should be a group reading session throughout the school at a regular time each day.

Towards the end of March 1973, Mr. Ellis called a meeting of parents in order that he and his staff could explain the scheme and answer any questions that the parents might have. It was the first general meeting at which the parents had an opportunity to meet the new headteacher, and, by all accounts, it was well attended and quite a success. A number of parents queried one or two aspects of the proposals, but all the evidence indicates that the parents attending the meeting appeared to be content that the scheme should be tried and welcomed the explanation that Mr. Ellis gave of it.

Following the meeting, the junior school staff started the reading groups scheme about one week before the end of term. There was not, and could not have been, any indication in the short time left that term how the scheme was going to work. However, the staff, the managers, and parents alike finished the term with the feeling that some progress had been made in giving the school a new sense of direction and that there was a good chance that these reading groups would bring about a significant improvement in the reading in the school.

The failure of the reading groups scheme

The reading groups scheme, which had been started just a week before the end of the previous term, did not survive very long. It was suggested in evidence by Mr. Ellis and Mr. Haddow that it had lasted much longer, but the overwhelming weight of evidence is that the reading groups had petered out within a few weeks of the beginning of the summer term. There is support for this conclusion in Mr. Ellis's own account of it given in his report to the managers at their meeting on 3 June 1974, that is five weeks into the summer term – when he informed them that: 'The new organization was experiencing certain "teething" troubles but it was hoped that it would continue *in some form* in the future.' (my italics)

The reading groups scheme did not survive because:

(i) The scheme was not planned properly. If more than one member of the staff was absent, the entire reading groups for the day were cancelled. No arrangements were made for reallocation for the day to other reading groups of children from reading groups whose teacher was away. Moreover, the fact that Mr. Ellis had undertaken responsibility for one of the groups meant that he was not available as a 'spare' teacher to take a group whenever necessary. On such occasions the children were frequently allowed out into the playground to play for the reading group period. Apart from teacher absences due to illness, this problem was aggravated by strike action that was taken on a number of days in May and June by the staff in support of an increased London weighting allowance for teachers.

(ii) Some members of the staff did not always use the reading group sessions to teach reading or language skills, but allowed the children to follow other activities. Mrs. McWhirter, for instance, who was responsible for one of the two groups with the lowest reading ages in the school, spent some of the time with her reading group encouraging the children 'to work together socially' in such activities as playing musical instruments and cooking instead of getting down to the purpose for which the reading group was set up. Another teacher, Miss Richards, on at least one occasion, wrote up on the blackboard, 'I hate reading groups', and sent her reading group out into the adventure playground to play instead of using the period for language purposes.

(iii) Some members of the staff had little experience or knowledge of how to conduct reading groups, and, as Miss Biek's evidence to the inquiry suggests, had not been very methodical in preparing themselves for this new scheme of teaching language skills. . . .

The cooperative teaching system for the second- and third-year children

The cooperative teaching system was organized in the following way. Four teachers, Mr. Haddow as 'the coordinator', and Mr. Austin, Miss Green, and Miss Richards, assumed a collective responsibility for teaching all the second- and third-year pupils – about 80 children. The children were divided into three groups, each group made up of children of the two age-groups. These three groups were called 'base groups', and each had its own teacher, Mr. Austin, Miss Green, and Miss Richards respectively. Each 'base group' also had its own classroom, the three classrooms being grouped together on one side of the upper floor of the school and leading off the same broad corridor. The corridor and upper hall were also used for the various activities of the whole cooperative teaching group.

The schooldays were divided into four sessions of about one hour each. These sessions were 'closed' and 'open' sessions alternately – the first half of the morning being a 'closed' session and the second half an 'open' session, and similarly in the afternoon. The scheme was that each 'base group' would spend the 'closed' session in its own classroom with its own teacher concentrating mainly on the basic skills of reading, writing, and mathematics. In the 'open' sessions the individual 'base groups' disbanded, and the whole group of about 80 children were presented with a variety of activities which they could individually choose to follow. The choice of activities was wide and could consist, for instance, of various forms of art and handicrafts, drama, sports and games of various sorts, visits, and also a continuation of work that had been started in the 'closed' sessions. These activities took place not only in the three 'base groups' classrooms but also in the upper hall and corridor. The whole arrangement was extremely flexible, Mr. Haddow and his group of teachers, individually or together, guiding or assisting particular groups of children in their chosen activities, moving from group to group as necessary. In some cases the children were left to get on with what they were doing on their own. The children were also free to change their activities as and when they liked in the course of a single 'open' session.

As his title 'coordinator' suggests, Mr. Haddow's job was not to take individual responsibility for any one of the three 'base groups' or classes. He did, however, assist during the 'closed' sessions, for example, by taking certain children out of their 'base groups' for such work as extra reading or what he has described as 'general discussions to extend the more able children'. In addition, he would from time to time join in and assist the work of one or other of the 'base group' teachers during the 'closed' sessions. The other aspect of his work as 'coordinator' was to take overall responsibility for the organization of the range of activities that was offered to the children at each of their 'open' sessions. He and his colleagues would start each 'open' session by gathering all 80 children together in the upper hall and explaining to them the activities the teachers were offering to provide for that session. The children would make their respective choices and disperse in groups or individually to the various areas available to them for their chosen activities. Mr. Haddow also made use of these gatherings at the beginning of each open session to invite discussion about matters of particular interest to the school as a whole or to the cooperative teaching group in particular, and also to talk about the work that had been done by the children.

This particular scheme of cooperative teaching, both in the form which it took and in the way Mr. Haddow and his group ran it, was not a success. For convenience, I will set out in one place here its defects in conception and – anticipating some of the events of the autumn term – the defects in its operation by Mr. Haddow and his colleagues.

Defects in conception

First, it was not really a cooperative teaching system at all. It was more an uneasy combination of class teaching and of the 'free activity' method of teaching that Mr. Haddow had practised in his fourth-year class in the previous spring and summer terms. Mr. Haddow, as coordinator, appears to have given little thought to a basic principle of cooperative teaching, namely that all members of the teaching group should have a common approach to the teaching methods and discipline to be employed, whether working in the 'closed' or 'open' sessions. His own evidence to the inquiry was that in the 'closed' sessions each of the three teachers worked 'in his or her chosen way'. It is for this reason that I am reluctant, even for the sake of convenience, to call the scheme introduced in the autumn term of 1974 'a team-teaching' scheme. Mr. Haddow did not act as a team-leader, or indeed as a coordinator, in the sense of giving a lead to the group of teachers working with him as to the way in which their individual approaches to teaching and discipline in the 'closed' sessions should correspond with their collective approach in the 'open' sessions. As it happened, the three teachers' individual teaching methods and attitudes to discipline differed in some respects. As a result, some of the children tended to become confused by the different methods of teaching and attitudes adopted towards them according to whether they were being taught by their own 'base group' teacher in the 'closed' session or by one or more of the other teachers in the 'open' session.

Secondly, the system adopted of two 'closed' and two 'open' sessions each day entailed too frequent a change-over for the children and was time-wasting and disruptive for them.

Thirdly, there was no adequate planning of the practical working of the scheme. One of the features of cooperative teaching is that it requires a very great deal more planning and preparation if it is to be successful than in the case of conventional classroom teaching. To do the job well, so that the children can derive the maximum educational benefit from such a flexible system, demands a great deal of advance preparation on the part of the teachers responsible for it. If that initial work has not been put in, and the scheme is not properly organized from the beginning, there is a real risk that the children will sense the lack of direction and become aimless, bored, and troublesome within a very short time. The lack of planning here was particularly evident in relation to the provision of options for the children in the 'open' sessions. No scheme appears to have been worked out to provide even an approximate programme, say on a weekly basis, under which the teachers could make adequate advance preparation for and inform the children of the range of activities from which they could choose on any particular day. The result was that a great deal of time was wasted – usually about ten minutes to quarter of an hour – at the beginning of each 'open' session while the 80 children assembled together; while they were told the range of activities from which they could choose; while the children discussed and decided what they wanted to do; and while the teachers and the children then set about organizing themselves to pursue the various activities selected for that session.

Defects in implementation

The defects in the way that Mr. Haddow and his colleagues worked their cooperative teaching scheme sprang partly from the shortcomings of the scheme itself and partly from their failure to put enough thought and work into the daily organization of the scheme once it had started. . . . Their time would have been better spent attending to their teaching and to the particular demands imposed upon them and upon the school as a whole by the new cooperative teaching scheme that they had introduced. The following are the principal respects in which Mr. Haddow and his group of teachers failed to work the scheme properly.

First, there was a continuing failure on the part of Mr. Haddow to coordinate the group of teachers so that they planned together in good time a balanced range of optional activities for each day from which the children could choose what they wanted to do. The result was that very often a large proportion of the children did not, or were not encouraged, to take part in activities with much of a learning content in them. For example, many children were able to spend a good deal of their 'open' session periods playing table tennis, draughts, or games out in the playground.

Secondly, Mr. Haddow introduced no system of recording or monitoring the 'open' session activities of the children so as to ensure that:

(i) with such balance of options as was provided, each child was choosing on a reasonably regular basis an activity with some learning content, and not just using each 'open' session for play; and
(ii) an adequate record was kept of the development and progress of each child.

I accept that it would have been impracticable to keep detailed records of the daily 'open' session activities of about 80 children. However, some rudimentary form of recording the children's choices and work done could have been instituted. Mr. Ellis and Mr. Haddow maintained that it was sufficient to keep records in their heads. No doubt Mr. Haddow and his colleagues had a good idea of the individual progress and interests of most of their charges; still, with some 80 children to provide for, that knowledge was not sufficient to prevent a number of children consistently choosing, and being allowed, to avoid doing any work in the 'open' sessions.

Thirdly, and quite apart from the failure to plan collectively in advance a balanced range of options from which the children could choose, the teachers failed individually to make adequate preparation for the optional activities that they provided to the children each day. The only exception to this criticism of Mr. Haddow and his group is Mr. Austin. Mr. Austin impressed most people who saw him at work as being conscientious and thoughtful in the way in which he prepared and presented his work for the children. Unfortunately, his individual efforts were not matched by those of his colleagues and were hampered considerably by the overall defects of the scheme already described.

Fourthly, although the idea of the 'open' sessions was that they should be relaxed and flexible periods in which the children could be encouraged to develop their own interests and learn in their own way, they were allowed too much freedom. Those children who wanted to work or had settled at a particular activity or project often found it difficult to concentrate because of the noise and constant movement of other children about them, some constantly changing what they were doing, others following noisy activities or playing games nearby, and others simply misbehaving.

Some advantages

Although the cooperative teaching scheme introduced in the autumn term had many drawbacks, there were some advantages. One of its single successes was to provide a stimulus for, and give confidence to, many of the children in the group who were of below-average ability and/or who were disturbed children. For some of these children the new régime did begin to produce a change for the better both in their attitude to learning and in their general behaviour. It took time for this to become evident. However, if the scheme had been properly planned and implemented by the teachers concerned this would possibly have been just one of several marks of success.

Other considerations

It appears to be generally accepted by teachers that when there is a fundamental change in the organization of a school, such as from conventional classroom teaching to cooperative or team-teaching, there is bound to be a transitional period of disruption for the school. If that is so, it is of the highest importance, particularly to the children who are most directly affected by the change, that such a disruptive transitional period should be as short as possible and that the disruption should be kept to the minimum possible. Mr. Ellis, who had had some experience of cooperative teaching, knew that, and Mr. Haddow, who also had some experience of a modest form of cooperative teaching, was also aware of it. In addition, both men were only too painfully aware of the troubles that had been caused earlier on in the year with the introduction of Mr. Haddow's class options scheme and the abortive reading groups scheme. With that knowledge and with that experience it was, in my view, foolhardy of them to introduce such a radical reorganization at a time when the school was already in a state of severe disruption after only six months of Mr. Ellis's headteachership.

Moreover, given that they did introduce this radical change at such an unpropitious time, it is extremely surprising that they did not:

(i) ensure that the cooperative teaching scheme was meticulously planned so as to minimize the extent and duration of the necessary disruption that it would cause;

(ii) inform the managers of, and consult with them on, the precise arrangements that were proposed *before* the new teaching system was introduced;

(iii) inform and discuss with the parents of the children concerned the precise arrangements that were proposed *before* the new teaching system was introduced;

(iv) ensure that there were staff of sufficient experience to make a success of the new teaching system before introducing it; and

(v) ensure that the new teaching system once introduced was made to work properly by proper coordination of the work of the teachers concerned and by adequate preparation by them individually and collectively of the work that it entailed.

As to the planning of the cooperative teaching scheme, Mr. Ellis and Mr. Haddow and others of the staff had been discussing it and making plans for it since at least May 1974. If they were determined to go through with it, as they clearly were, such plans should have been prepared in sufficient detail to inform the managers and parents of them before the end of the summer term. Mr. Ellis was studiously noncommittal at the parent-teachers' meeting of 9 July 1974 about what was proposed. And, according to him, he did not discuss the proposal in any detail at any staff meeting after that meeting and prior to the end of term. Even though Mr. Austin and Mr. Felton were not appointed until the very end of term, there was no reason why Mr. Ellis and his staff could not then have prepared for the reorganization of the autumn term on a contingent basis and given full information to the managers and the parents on that basis. In the event, and notwithstanding the considerable loss of confidence in the school of which he was aware, Mr. Ellis made no attempt at the end of the summer term or during the early part of the holiday period to draw up plans with Mr. Haddow and the staff so that adequate information in advance could be given to the managers and the parents of what the new term was to bring. The alternative course of postponing the introduction of the scheme was apparently not considered.

It was only in the last week of the summer term that Mr. Ellis and Mr. Haddow and the staff concerned began to make active preparations for the reorganization of the teaching of the second- and third-year children of the school. Even those plans, inadequate as they were, were not communicated at that stage to the managers or the parents.

Of the members of the new cooperative teaching group, none had much experience of cooperative teaching. Mr. Haddow, the coordinator, had only had one year's experience of a very modest form of cooperative teaching at his previous school. Mr. Austin had had some experience of cooperative teaching work about five years previously when he was a newly qualified teacher. Miss Green had had a nominal, and not very happy, involvement in a so-called team-teaching scheme at the junior school in the year 1972–1973, and Miss Richards, who had just completed her probationary year of teaching, had no experience of cooperative teaching at all. Although there are undoubtedly advantages both to children and to the teachers of having a cooperative teaching group consisting of a mixture of teachers who have and who have not had experience of cooperative teaching, such a group should have at least one or two teachers of sufficient experience to cope with the additional organizational and teaching skills that it involves. In my view, Mr. Haddow lacked the experience and application that the post of coordinator of this group required, and his colleagues between them did not have sufficient experience to make up for the lack of effective leadership from him.

Mr. Ellis, on the other hand, did have considerable experience of running successfully a large cooperative teaching group at his previous school. In evidence to the inquiry he said that he had involved himself to a certain extent in the planning and organization of the cooperative teaching group at William Tyndale Junior School. He also said that, whenever he could, he joined in and gave a hand in the work of the group. Unfortunately, despite his previous experience he did not, in my view, take the care that he should have done to ensure the successful organization and running of the scheme, particularly having regard to the circumstances and the time at which it was introduced. . . .

The cooperative teaching scheme continued to suffer from many defects in planning and organization. On Mr. Haddow's evidence to the inquiry, it was not until May in the summer term that it was working well education-ally. In the spring term the problems of lack of consistency in teaching and disciplinary methods among the teachers in the cooperative teaching group continued to cause a certain amount of friction between them and confusion for the children. Also, it was still possible for many children regularly to avoid doing any work in the daily 'open' sessions. This possibility was increased when Mr. Haddow and his group introduced a number of perma-nent daily options available to the children at each 'open' session, in addition to those that varied from day to day. Among these permanent options were skating, boating, swimming, drama, library visits, games, art, and 'follow-up work' from the 'closed' sessions. However, I should also mention alongside this list that Mr. Haddow also introduced this term a remedial reading tuition option to the 'open' session for each day. Accord-ing to his evidence to the inquiry, about 12 children a day on average took advantage of this option.

There were two other principal defects that continued in the system of options for the open sessions. First, apart from Mr. Austin, the teachers usually did not prepare sufficiently in advance the varying options that they offered to the children each day. This frequently resulted in a waste of time during the 'open' sessions while the teachers and the children sorted out the necessary equipment, etc., and it sometimes led to confusion because the teachers had not previously arranged with each other what they were going to do. Secondly, there was still a great waste of time at the beginning of each 'open' session, when all 80 children were gathered together in the hall for a quarter of an hour or so to choose their activities.

Mr. Rice had considerable reservations about the organization and work-ing of the cooperative teaching scheme. He felt that it lacked a strong enough group of teachers and that it lacked clearly defined educational objectives. He expressed these views to Mr. Ellis in January 1975, urging upon him that such a scheme required considerable organization and care if it was to work properly in a junior school. It sounds from the evidence given by both men to the inquiry as if Mr. Rice was inviting Mr. Ellis to reconsider the whole idea of cooperative teaching, at least until he was more firmly established and had a more experienced staff who could work well together. Mr. Ellis, however, relying upon his own past experience at Charles Lamb School, was not inclined to take Mr. Rice's advice, and appears to have regarded him as being overcautious in the anxieties that he was expressing. At all events, the cooperative teaching scheme continued.

CHAPTER 5.4

PERSPECTIVES ON PASTORAL CARE*
R. Best, C. Jarvis, and P. Ribbins

In this chapter we wish to do three things: firstly, to draw together a number of themes which usually underlie discussions on pastoral care; secondly, to discuss a variety of suggestions as to how the practice of pastoral care within the secondary school might be improved; thirdly, to consider 'grey areas' which continue to exist in discussions about pastoral care and which will require further attention in future studies.

Underlying themes

Perhaps the most widely shared theme among those who often contribute to the discussion of pastoral care is that the status quo of pastoral care in many schools has been characterized by a well-intentioned but insufficiently considered approach to meeting the welfare needs of children; that, furthermore, many teachers, and especially those with pastoral-care responsibilities, are uneasily aware of the limitations of existing provisions within their own and other schools. Such teachers are also well aware of the fact that much of the available literature on pastoral care is not of immediate relevance to the actual situations they encounter. All too often it deals with general principles and organizational patterns rather than confronting the problems they, as teachers, are actually struggling to overcome. In short, many teachers are unhappy about their existing practices but have become increasingly doubtful if much real help is to be expected from the sort of

* This article is reprinted from Best, R. et al. (eds), 1980, *Perspectives on Pastoral Care*, Heinemann Educational. It is the concluding chapter of a collection of readings on pastoral care. In it the editors of the reader summarize some of the major issues that have been raised in the book and suggest areas for further consideration.

accounts which now represent the 'orthodox' view of pastoral care.

How has this gap between analysis and prescription on the one hand and practice on the other developed, and what are its characteristic features? To answer this question it is necessary to look back at the historic development of pastoral-care provision within the secondary school and to describe the emergence of a prevailing orthodoxy which has come to dominate the literature of pastoral care in recent times.

During the course of this century schools have become the focus of much welfare effort, partly at least as a response to powerful humanitarian imperatives. This effort, particularly in the case of the comprehensive school, has culminated in the setting up of elaborate systems of pastoral care. In no real sense anticipating such developments, a dominant conception of pastoral care has gradually emerged. It is this which we have depicted as 'the conventional wisdom'. For a time pastoral-care developments appealed to and were justified in the terms of that wisdom. However, it has gradually become apparent to some theorists and many practitioners that the conventional wisdom presents a partially or even seriously distorted view of the realities of pastoral care in the secondary school. We suggest that pastoral care is a much more complex and problematic activity than the simplistic, child-centred notions of the conventional wisdom would allow. Further, to the extent that the conventional wisdom offers a narrowly prescriptive conception of pastoral care, concerned only with its manifest functions, it will be of limited practical value to chalk-face practitioners struggling with the day-to-day reality of the situations and pressures they actually face. This is not to suggest that the limitations of the conventional wisdom are entirely practical or empirical. It can also be argued that its conceptual and behavioural assumptions are more doubtful than its devotees are commonly prepared to admit. The interesting question remains: why has such a view of pastoral care continued to be so influential in the face of increasingly destructive criticism of the conceptual foundations and growing doubts of the empirical validity of the sort of child-centred approach which it seems to assume? There are a number of possible answers to this question. Firstly it is arguable that such a concept of pastoral care is now essentially employed in the ways in which schools publicly describe and legitimate their activities rather than as a guide to what they actually do. Certainly it must be admitted that its optimistic, child-centred, consensual, and unproblematic depiction of school life presents a very attractive picture. Secondly it should also be recognized that schools have lacked realistic alternative perspectives worked out in any detail against which to evaluate their existing caring activities and to guide their practical future endeavours.

Though it was never either our wish or hope to offer a comprehensive alternative orthodoxy of pastoral care in opposition to that of the 'conventional wisdom', we did hope to suggest ways in which practitioners might evaluate their own activities more realistically and perhaps even to make a number of suggestions as to how things might be improved. Much of what is discussed here can be viewed as a debate between those who believe that schools have merely failed to develop, or have insufficiently considered the implications of, certain of their pastoral-care practices, and those who hold that in some respects schools have been badly misguided and have seriously misconceived the relationship between care and education on an altogether more fundamental level. Basically, what is at issue is whether the shortcomings of existing pastoral-care practices spring from a failure to put into effect existing policies, or whether those policies themselves are located in fundamental misconceptions of the nature of pastoral care itself.

Pastoral care as inadequately developed and insufficiently considered

Perhaps the great majority of those who have reservations about pastoral care and its organization in the secondary school take this kind of view. Although they may trace the 'problems' of institutionalized pastoral care to apparently very different factors (and may accordingly point to very different 'solutions') they do seem to share a belief that in its essentials schools have got things more or less right. Not that existing systems and practices do not have limitations, but these can be corrected by supplementing and strengthening what exists rather than by fundamentally rethinking or reshaping them. Such analysis reveals a number of weaknesses and suggests a variety of ways in which existing practice might be improved. It is worth noting three of the areas of weakness which are discussed. (An analysis of the solutions which are offered is left mainly to the next section.)

(i) Inadequate or inappropriate use of the 'expert'

This argument has various aspects, some of which are not easily reconcilable. Firstly it is held that some of the failings of existing pastoral-care systems are due to the fact that teachers encounter children who have problems which are beyond the training and capacity of the ordinary teacher to deal with. There are at least two unsatisfactory solutions to this kind of situation. Either the teacher tries to deal with such problems unaided (and often does so inadequately) or else he ignores the problem as being beyond his capacity and hopes that it will eventually be resolved of its own accord. Neither kind of response will do. In such a situation what is needed is somebody with appropriate skill, experience, and training to whom the teacher may turn (a school counsellor, home-school liaison officer, or the like). In short what is needed is an *expert*. This issue will be considered in greater detail in the next section. What does need emphasizing here is that, in such a conception, the expert is seen as strengthening and supplementing existing systems rather than in any fundamental sense replacing or even significantly reshaping them.

(ii) Inadequacies in the role of the tutor and the pastoral head of department
The contribution made by teachers as tutors or as heads of pastoral-care departments is often said to be crucial if pastoral-care systems are to operate effectively. However, for many such teachers statements of this kind represent little more than empty rhetoric or pious moralizing. They are given little guidance as to what is expected of them and face conflicting demands as to what they should be doing. Furthermore they are often allocated few resources to carry out their responsibilities and given little opportunity to develop the skills and knowledge which they require. However, in spite of all this it can be argued that the correction of such failings would not require drastic change.

(iii) Inadequacies in the role of 'teams' and 'groups'
All too often pastoral care in the secondary school is thought of as being an activity which is almost exclusively carried out by teachers operating as individuals and in isolation from their colleagues. Of course quite often the most effective form of care does take place in a transaction between an individual teacher and an individual pupil, but there are occasions and types of situations where cooperative activity between groups of teachers might well be more appropriate. There are also situations in which the personal and social needs of children can be more effectively met when they are organized in long-standing, mutually supportive groupings. In this kind of analysis the ideal pastoral-care environment is conceived of as being a team of teachers taking a collective responsibility for a defined group of children in such a way that both individual and corporate care is facilitated. The relatively large size and comparatively loosely organized character of most existing house and year systems, whatever their other advantages, are not conducive to such corporate caring. However, it should be admitted that it

is a fine distinction whether the implementation of such schemes would represent an addition to existing practice or a fundamental reworking of it.

Pastoral care as fundamentally misconceived

Some critiques of pastoral-care practice within the secondary school point to the existence of flaws of a more fundamental kind than those considered above. For example, it has been argued that in some schools a number of radically different, sometimes conflicting, activities are lumped together and made the responsibility of the hard-pressed pastoral-care staff; that, furthermore, some of these activities seem to have little to do with care at all except in the most obscure sense and a great deal more to do with control, discipline, containment, and administration. In such a context 'caring' becomes something of a residual activity which 'pastoral-care' staff perform as and when they can find the time. Another criticism, more fashionable if rather less fundamental than the last, suggests that many of the limitations of existing pastoral-care systems in schools can be traced to a misconceived attempt to separate a school's learning from its caring functions – usually referred to as the 'academic/pastoral split'.

Almost everyone shares the view that schools should be primarily concerned with creating opportunities for children to learn worthwhile things in the most effective way possible. If this view is correct it follows that the pastoral endeavour in schools must not be seen in isolation from their essential instructional functions. But in some schools these two endeavours are seen as separate – or worse. For example, elaborate pastoral-care systems which many schools have set up in recent times have absorbed resources which would have been better employed in the creation of more effective teaching strategies, particularly as all too often *the* major function of such systems seems to have been to mask deficiencies in the instructional activities of the school. The logic of such an argument is obvious. Scarce resources of teacher time and energy would be much better employed in improving the learning environment than in swelling the burgeoning bureaucracies of pastoral care which have mushroomed in recent years. In short, the most effective method which schools can use to improve the quality of their care is to devote considerably greater effort to facilitating learning. This account also stresses that the creation of effective learning environments for children is a potent form of caring in itself and one which would diminish the need for other forms of pastoral care.

Other accounts emphasize the learning implications of effective pastoral-care systems. Ideas like 'the pastoral curriculum' (Marland) and 'the social education and careers curriculum' (Watts and Fawcett) draw attention to the demands which various aspects of pastoral care might make on a school's curriculum. Such arguments serve to underline the artificiality of rigid attempts to divorce a school's pastoral from its academic functions. The implications of this kind of analysis are driven home forcefully by Buckley. In the context of a radical critique of 'the pupil-teacher contract' he argues that decisions about the curriculum of schools and their internal organizational structures and processes should be determined by considerations which view 'caring' and 'learning' as two aspects of the same endeavour. This will only be achieved, it is argued, where the same small team of teachers working together ('the teaching team') has the responsibility for making and carrying out both academic and pastoral decisions for and with a particular group of children ('the learning group'). While, on the face of it, such an arrangement bears a superficial resemblance to other kinds of 'team' solution its implementation would entail a change which would be, for most schools, far more radical. Being more radical it would also be more difficult to achieve. However, much less attention is given to the ways in which particular 'solutions' might be successfully implemented than to what changes are necessary, and why. We shall return to this point later. For the present let us consider who has the better of the debate as between those who believe that existing practice is essentially sound and those who advocate more fundamental changes. In the final analysis this is a decision which every reader must make for himself. Our hope is that the reader will have been convinced that the sorts of questions which have been raised in the course of this debate will be relevant to his own situation and that they are worth asking. Can the same be said of the sorts of solutions which have been offered?

Programmes for change

The need for effective evaluation and analysis of existing practice

Teachers are not especially reluctant to reflect critically and carefully on their activities and attitudes. However, what they are being asked to do by a number of contributors is to take seriously the possibility that much of what they do in schools under the guise of pastoral care may, in fact, not be about care at all. Of course schools may well have to discipline, control, administer, and perform many other similar kinds of activity, but are these things really the business of pastoral-care staff? In any case, if these sorts of activity really are the main functions of institutionalized pastoral-care systems, it would be much less confusing if this were made clear. It is hard to see how existing practice can be improved if the reality of that practice is not analysed and acknowledged. If the teachers are to improve what they do they must start from what they really are doing rather than what they say they do or even what they would like to be doing. What is needed is for teachers to undertake an analysis of what pastoral care actually means for them and to assess realistically the existing practices of the schools in which they work. Such an analysis must surely precede any serious attempt to improve upon existing practice. This may not be a solution as such, but it is a necessary condition of any effective solution which does not rely to an inordinate extent on serendipity.

Ending the pastoral/academic split

Many believe that no real improvement can be expected from any solution which assumes or continues to perpetuate this disastrous split in the activities of schools. It would probably be true to conclude that discussions on this issue are less concerned with offering particular, positive, practical solutions to the problems that schools face than with denying the validity of proposals and practices which are seen as being based on an unacceptable premise. However, one elaborate solution based on teacher teams and learning 'groups' has been worked out in some detail (by Buckley), as has a proposal for a 'pastoral curriculum' (by Marland). It has also been suggested that schools should reduce their commitment of resources to 'formal pastoral-care systems' and employ the surpluses so created on improving their 'learning systems' (Williamson).

Pastoral care and the curriculum

If the splitting of a school's academic from its pastoral responsibilities represents an unhealthy development, what are the alternatives? Two seem obvious: firstly, to create structures and develop roles in which teachers combine an academic with a pastoral responsibility; secondly, to keep the pastoral need in mind when making decisions hitherto considered to be essentially academic in character. In particular it is important to be clear about the curriculum implications of effective pastoral care. It is in this context that suggestions about a 'social education and careers curriculum', and rather more radically a 'pastoral curriculum', should be considered.

Both seek to reunite caring and learning, and both do so by stressing the learning implications of effective care as a problem for curriculum planning.

Team and group solutions

The development of new kinds of teams of teachers and team approaches on the one hand (see Buckley, Marland, Craft) and of groups of children and group approaches on the other (see Button, Hamblin) is probably the category of solution that would command the most widespread support. However, the very fact that both those who see a need for dramatic change in the process and organization of pastoral care and those who would be content with more marginal innovations can appeal to what is apparently the same kind of solution suggests that it must be capable of widely differing interpretations. The sheer variety of suggestions and their very different assumptions about the efficacy of existing school practice might make the discussion especially relevant to teachers who wish to reexamine their own corporate activities and who are uncertain as to how they might proceed.

Developing the role of the tutor and of senior pastoral-care staff

That pastoral-care staff are often given far too much to do and too little time and support to do it with is a common enough complaint among such teachers. So, sadly, is the claim that being a tutor seems to mean very little indeed even when a great deal of time is allocated to it. However, limitations of time and resources and lack of adequate guidance as to what is expected of them are not the only problems of role which pastoral-care teachers face. They are too often starved of information and by-passed by more senior staff. They are, too, rarely given the opportunity, still less the encouragement, to develop greater levels of expertise in appropriate skills, for example those of guidance and counselling. Among other things, proposed solutions point to the need to clarify and strengthen the position of pastoral-care staff, the need to encourage such staff to develop necessary skills, and perhaps most of all the need to distinguish clearly and realistically what should and what should not be expected of them. In this context one revealing indication of the lack of seriousness with which the role of pastoral-care staff is taken is the small part which training for 'tutorship' plays in most initial teacher-training courses and the paucity of in-service courses concerned specifically with this aspect of the teacher's role.

Developing the role of the expert

A number of proposals (see Watts and Fawcett, Milner, Craft) are concerned with the role of the expert in the pastoral-care context. The term 'expert' is usually taken to mean someone who is acknowledged as having special skills, knowledge, and experience which have been gained as a result of an appropriate form of professional training. The contribution of a variety of different kinds of 'experts' are canvassed, ranging from school counsellors and home-school liaison officers to be located within the school to social workers and education welfare officers not located in the school but centring upon it. The sort of role envisaged for such experts varies from being an integral part of the pastoral-care system to being an appendage or supplement to it. Perhaps the key problem with regard to the use of the expert within the school lies in his relationship with 'nonexpert' pastoral-care practitioners. Specifically, how does one make the optimum use of the very few experts located in schools when the bulk of pastoral-care activity for the foreseeable future is likely to remain in the hands of a very much larger number of nonexperts? Given this situation, let us consider two possible roles for the expert. The first is widely canvassed and is the basis of much existing practice. In this, the expert is perceived as a resource upon whom teachers may call when they encounter problems which are beyond their abilities to deal with – essentially as a crisis agent of the last resort and as such outside the 'normal' pastoral-care system. The second, though less widely canvassed, is one which many experts find attractive. It is based on an argument about how a few experts can have the maximum possible beneficial effect on a school's pastoral-care system considered as a whole. Given that there are few experts and many nonexpert staff it could be that the greatest contribution the former can make is to assist the latter to raise their level of awareness and skill rather than to exclusively employ their expertise to contain the most intractable of a school's care problems. It is possible that teachers will take a great deal of convincing before they accept this training role as a proper or even necessary activity for the expert.

Pastoral care and the welfare network

The caring activities of schools do not take place in a vacuum. As Craft shows, they are at the focus of a number of welfare networks based in and around the school. To be effective such networks need to be coordinated as a whole and in particular integrated with the pastoral-care systems of schools. In fact it can be argued that many of the limitations of existing pastoral-care systems *within* schools can also be traced to inadequacies of coordination and articulation. Given this specification of 'the problem' a number of possible answers are suggested. Problems of coordination can, at least in part, be overcome by the appointment of a clearly designed coordinator or coordinators. Craft suggests that this would be an appropriate role for school counsellors to perform, though there are indications that this kind of solution has by no means always been all that successful in practice. If articulation of the welfare effort, both in and around the school, is to be improved, suitable teams, involving both internal and external care agents, will need to be set up and clear channels of communication and referral will need to be established between groups responsible for various aspects of the welfare effort.

Up to this point we have attempted to offer a limited analysis of the sorts of issues which can be raised and to summarize the main kinds of improvements which can be suggested. It remains only for us to point to some issues which should perhaps have received rather more attention than they have.

Some grey areas

Pastoral care and the 'needs' of children

Much of the literature on pastoral care is based explicitly or implicitly on ideas about the needs of children. However, considering how crucial the notion of 'need' is to the concept of 'education' in general and to that of 'pastoral care' in particular, it is curious that it has not been analysed at greater length. To some extent this omission can be explained by the hegemony which the 'child-centred' view has established over public accounts of what education should be. We are ourselves broadly sympathetic to that view. However we also feel, along with writers like Bernstein, Dearden, Peters,[1] Sharp and Green,[2] and White,[3] that it might be timely, even essential, to take another and rather more critical look at child-centred ideologies and to clarify what assumptions about 'child development', 'learning', and 'learning processes' they make. It would also be timely to attempt to establish the extent to which 'child-centred' ideologies do actually inform the activities of teachers, as opposed to offering a handy rhetoric with which to justify their practices.

There is one further omission in the general literature of pastoral care. Given that the needs of children are seen as a crucial factor both in justifying the organization for pastoral care and in determining its character, it is curious how little direct attempt has been made to get at the ways in which children perceive their own educational and welfare needs. We do know of people who have begun to look at how children perceive and construct ideas about their welfare needs (for example John Bazalgette of the Grubb Institute[4]), but little has, as yet, been published on this subject. In so far as pastoral care is said to be based on the needs of children it is, as yet, based almost entirely on the ways in which teachers perceive those needs. Perhaps such teacher perception will (even should) always be the determining influence in making decisions about how the needs of children should be met, but surely the views of children should also be considered.

The problem of organizational change

It is the *raison d'être* of this book that existing practices can and should be improved, and as we have seen, numerous solutions to the problem of improving those practices are advanced. Some of these 'solutions' would have far-reaching consequences for the ways in which schools operate – others are rather more modest in scale. Whether modest or fundamental, these would necessitate changes in existing processes, organizational patterns, and, in some cases, even major changes in attitudes among teachers. While the proposals are worked out in some detail, much less attention is devoted to the problem of how the changes which they necessitate can be successfully accomplished. It is possible that the difficulties of achieving successful organizational change have been underestimated. In particular the sort of resistance such solutions may encounter from teachers and others who may have a strong commitment to existing practice must be recognized. To illustrate the problems likely to be encountered let us consider the sort of resistance which the two most widely canvassed 'solutions' might meet.

(i) Team approaches

In advocating new kinds of teams and team strategies, insufficient attention is given to the opposition such proposals are likely to provoke from those who perceive themselves as members of existing 'teams' (e.g., house staff). For the more senior members of such teams the changes may involve a loss of status, and for the more junior they will necessitate changes in work patterns to which they have become accustomed and in which they will suddenly discover virtues they had been unaware of in the past. Furthermore, many team approaches also appear to ignore the essentially hierarchic nature of most schools and the attachment of many teachers to existing patterns of authority and responsibility. Team solutions seem to assume that teachers will easily be able to set aside status considerations and act as groups of equals, even though the bureaucratic and hierarchic patterns in which they normally work ensure and emphasize that they are not equal. Of course, just because labour is stratified and differentiated this does not necessarily mean that cooperation is impossible between individuals at different levels. Neither, however, should it be assumed that to have established the 'need' for such cooperation is to have ensured that it will occur.

(ii) Curriculum approaches

Some of the proposals entail new demands upon, or even whole new ways of looking at, the school curriculum. However logical and plausible are ideas like the 'pastoral' or the 'careers' curriculum, their implementation will involve in many schools difficult negotiations with hostile and well-entrenched groups who (not unreasonably) regard such proposals as damaging to their interests. In short, such curriculum proposals, whatever their other merits, appear to underestimate or even ignore the powers and motives of existing subject and other groups to protect 'their' area of the curriculum. We would not wish to conclude that just because organizational change is difficult to achieve it should not be attempted; rather, we would wish to emphasize that successful innovation has to be carefully prepared and planned for. Too many proposals for change seem to make unwarranted assumptions about the malleability of human beings, or seem to rely to an inordinate extent on the disinterestedness and general goodwill of teachers.

Social reality, the school, and pastoral care

Lastly, it is all too easy to forget or ignore the social reality of the situation in which schools are located. Issues concerned with the hierarchic relationship of teachers to their pupils and of schools to the children in their care have to be seen as a reality. Talk about pastoral care, personal guidance, and the like has to be seen in the context of schools as purveyors of packages of knowledge that lead to particular outcomes in a society which is prestructured and which is very largely beyond the ability of schools to affect. Some things are beyond the powers of schools to control and, as such, represent limitations and constraints on what schools can do. For example, talk of a pastoral curriculum will seem for some people a nonstarter because of the demands of the academic curriculum, buttressed by the imperatives of public examinations, underwritten by the requirements of society for a specified kind of 'acceptable' selection process.

Furthermore, just as too many 'solutions' ignore the realities of power in the individual school, so also do they give too little consideration to similar realities in the society as a whole. In an important sense things happen because they are in the interests of groups and individuals and because such groups have the power to ensure that what they want does come about. We might all be on a fool's errand in trying to improve what happens in schools if at some stage we do not take account of such considerations.

A final thought

Much of what is written in this book is critical of aspects of what goes on under the guise of 'pastoral care' in schools. However, the extent and character of such criticism should not be misunderstood or exaggerated. No one who knows about what schools were like a hundred, or even fifty years ago, can fail to notice the great changes for the better which have taken place. Even in the recent past, rigid discipline backed by the regular resort to punishment (much of it physical) reflected an attitude among teachers in particular and society in general that the personal and welfare needs of children were no part of the responsibility of schools, or if they were, that such needs were seen as those of savages to be civilized. It is, in short, hard to believe that schools have not become more caring, humane, and convivial places than they were. Part, at least, of the credit for such beneficial change must surely be due to the emphasis which schools have given to pastoral care. If the exact meaning of the term continues to be elusive, and if its special contribution to improving the lot of children remains somewhat obscure, there seems little reason to doubt that without pastoral care schools would be grimmer and unhappier places. However, there also seems little reason to doubt that vestiges of those unhappier times continue to exist in some schools, and that even schools with effective pastoral-care systems and practices can be improved.

Our schools have much we can be proud of. But they are by no means perfect. In pastoral care, as in other facets of schooling, the rhetoric of the 'great debate' and the fetish of fashion must be replaced with critical and reasoned analyses of existing strengths and weaknesses.

References

1. In Peters, R.S. (ed), *Perspectives on Plowden*, Routledge & Kegan Paul, London, 1969.
2. op. cit.
3. White, J.P., *Towards a Compulsory Curriculum*, Routledge & Kegan Paul, London, 1973.
4. Bazalgette, J., 'The Pupil, the Tutor and the School', paper presented to Organization in Schools Course on Pastoral Care, Churchill College, Cambridge, July 1978.

All other references in this chapter are to articles which appear in Best, R. et al. (eds), *Perspectives on Pastoral Care*, Heinemann Educational Books, 1980.

CHAPTER 5.5

CROSSING THE BOUNDARY*
Daphne Johnson

The secondary school has boundaries which are both physical and organizational. The place and the function of the school are virtually inseparable, so that 'going to school' means more than turning up at a building; it implies a way of life. Nevertheless no school can be a world to itself. The work which teachers undertake with secondary school pupils both does and must cross the school boundary entailing external relationships and interaction with all who share the task of caring for secondary school pupils. Here, we discuss the secondary schools' boundaries of care and the ways in which those boundaries are managed.

Boundaries of care

The boundaries of care have several dimensions. In the time dimension they stand at the beginning and end of the child's secondary school life – the time of entry, when the school takes on responsibility for his education, and the time when he comes to the end of his school days, whether at the age of sixteen or after further work in the sixth form.

But even during this intervening period, the school is only a part-time environment for the child. Every day he crosses and recrosses the geographical and social boundaries between school and home or one of the other part-time environments which receive him – particular social enclaves in the neighbourhood, whether informal or institutionalized in the form of clubs, or perhaps part-time employment, before or after school or at weekends.

The secondary school pupil may also from time to time cross the school's

* *Secondary Schools and the Welfare Network*, Daphne Johnson (ed), Elizabeth Ransom, Tim Packwood, Katherine Bowden, Maurice Kogan, chapter 5, Allen & Unwin (forthcoming).

professional boundaries, becoming temporarily the client, patient, or detainee of one of the agencies of welfare and control. All these boundaries are potential and sometimes actual boundaries of care, but they are not impermeable. Subject teachers and their pupils make joint forays into the local community or to far-distant geographical areas, for community work, field trips, holidays, and organized 'adventure'. More central to our study, however, are the ways in which pastoral work overflows the school boundary, reaching out to the pupil's home or the available agencies. Agency practitioners, in their turn, cross the school boundary, by communications or visits. So too do parents, if only through notes to the form teacher.

The whole question of the potential and the realities of the home/school relationship was one of the principal areas of our study. Here we shall only briefly discuss the contacts which our study schools had with parents. Our chief concern is with the boundaries of care between professionals, during the school life of the child. We will also look briefly at the chronological boundaries – the moments when the child joins and leaves the school.

Taking pupils on from the primary schools

The boundary between primary and secondary school is a broad one, since what are graphically described as the 'feeder' primary schools pour in their pupils to the secondary school from a number of discrete institutions. Preliminary crossing and recrossing of this boundary by individuals sometimes takes place before children join the school, but institutionalized arrangements for the schools we studied to make contact with their feeder primaries were somewhat sparse.

Several schools were used in this study. Liaison work relating to the continuity of curriculum between primary schools and the first school in the study[1] was the responsibility of heads of department. These and other subject teachers made occasional visits to the primary schools in this connection. However, most feedback to the primary school from the secondary school, for example regarding possible discontinuities in teaching methods, was made through the primary adviser. Information about individual children joining the school was usually forwarded via the education department, on the primary school record card. At the time of the research, new cards had recently been introduced which it was hoped would provide a consistent source of basic information about new pupils, in place of the varying amounts of information previously forwarded by different primary schools.

From the second school, the head of the remedial department, the school counsellor and a tutor visited the contributory primary schools once a year, to inform themselves about the next intake of pupils to the secondary school.[2] Record cards from the primary schools were standardized, and teachers at the second school found them adequate.

Contact between the third school and its feeder schools was more frequent. The head of lower school had particular responsibility for liaison with these schools, which she visited regularly. These visits were chiefly to familiarize the primary schools and their pupils with the work of the third school, but the head of lower school might also glean information about primary pupils' backgrounds which was not included on the record cards subsequently sent to the secondary school. Primary record cards were not always fully completed by the schools in question, but in any case teachers at the third school felt the information on these cards should be treated with caution. There could, they felt, be a tendency to label a child on the basis of a primary record card which referred to a very early age. Subject teachers at this school considered that it would be helpful if they too could visit primary schools, to familiarize themselves with primary teaching methods and content, whilst providing future pupils at the third school with familiar faces and knowledge of the school.[3] Headteachers of local primary schools had an opportunity to find out how their former pupils were getting on at secondary school when they attended an annual lunch at the third school.

The fourth school tried to keep its feeder primary schools informed about new courses and methods, such as the integrated humanities course. Staff were anxious to see primary and secondary education become a more continuous process. This would perhaps mean that certain problems, such as the different approaches to the teaching of French, could be overcome. Work was already being carried out with the borough advisers to unify and modify work in primary schools.

All headteachers of contributory primary schools were invited to the fourth school's open evenings. Once a year, the headmaster, other senior staff, and first- and second-year tutors met these headteachers to talk about prospective pupils. The official record card received from primary schools was felt to be inadequate for secondary school purposes. The fourth school supplemented the information by asking parents to mention relevant medical conditions on the acceptance form when a child joined the school.[4]

Transferring or sharing pupils

Not all the pupils came to secondary schools straight from primary school. Some transferred from other secondary schools, usually because of a change of home address. Occasionally a child with an adverse experience in one secondary school would be transferred to another nearby. This transfer, mediated by the education department, required the concurrence of parents and teachers. Teachers had the impression that some schools were more welcoming than others to such 'problem' pupils. Sometimes, of course, pupils still of secondary school age would cross the boundaries of the researched schools in an outward direction, being transferred either to other mainstream schools or perhaps to other forms of education, for example home tuition, or a school offering some kind of special provision, such as the Unit for Persistent Non-Attenders. Such transfers would usually follow a period of considerable concentration of pastoral resources on the child, and would be negotiated by senior members of staff and possibly the counsellor, as well as by the education department. The child in question then passed beyond his former school's area of responsibility once and for all, but there were other pupils whose departure was only temporary. These might be pupils whom the schools shared with other institutions, whether officially as when a child went to the school psychological service for special help with reading, or unofficially, when a nonattender at school might turn up at a local youth and community centre. It was the policy of one such centre to exclude all truants, but some youth workers took a more flexible line, not always with the approval of headteachers. Teachers' perspectives on these interprofessional boundaries of care are more fully discussed later in this chapter.

Excluding pupils

Another way in which a boundary was sometimes temporarily drawn between secondary school and pupil, delimiting the school's responsibility for the child, was the procedure of exclusion. Seen by most of the schools as an 'end-of-the-line' disciplinary procedure, exclusion might be for several days, perhaps with the proviso that the pupil's parents should accompany him when he returned to school to discuss his future in the school.[5]

School-leaving procedures

When the time came for teachers to see their pupils off to the next stage in life, a distinct set of more institutionalized, if not always very formal, boundary-crossing procedures came into play.

School Four had a well-defined procedure for sifting through pupils who, though eligible to leave at Easter, elected to stay on until the summer. A list of such pupils was circulated to staff by the careers teacher. Individual staff might have comments to make about perhaps ten of the sixty-five or so pupils who were proposing to stay on, and in three or four of these cases a number of staff might comment on the same pupil. A meeting of all concerned with these pupils, whether for teaching or for pastoral purposes, was held under the chairmanship of the deputy head. Where appropriate, the headmaster would write to the parents well before the end of the Christmas term, informing them that if the child were to stay on usefully after Easter, the school would be looking for signs of improvement which should be reflected in the February report. Teachers at this school commented that occasionally staff expressed strong regret that a particular pupil was *not* staying on to take examinations in the summer, but this had never been known to influence a family's decision that the child should leave at Easter.[6]

Whether or not the pupil was sitting for exams, it seemed to be understood that attendance in the final weeks of the fifth year would be only spasmodic. One form teacher commented that all her fifth-year boys and girls would be absent for part of the summer term, coming in only for examinations, then returning for the last fortnight of the term.[7] Valedictory ceremonial appeared to be minimal. The status passage of the pupil leaving school at sixteen was perhaps most formally marked by interaction with the careers service or with the careers teacher at the school, although this would normally precede the pupil's actual departure by at least a term.

School Four, which had a full-time careers teacher, laid considerable emphasis on interaction with the careers service. Teachers pointed out that the careers officer was statutorily required to interview every school-leaver and try to place them in employment.[8] The careers teacher's own interviewing of pupils was structured around these statutory interviews, the time schedule for which was tight, given the size of the pupil year-group. Over 80 Easter-leavers were interviewed by the careers teacher in the first half-term of the final year, and forecasts prepared concerning them, in preparation for the careers officer's interviews during December. The remaining fifth-year school-leavers (about 180 at the time of the research) were interviewed by the school in the second half of the first term, so that the careers officer could conduct his own interviews in January, February, and March.[9]

In addition to School Four, this careers officer serviced three other secondary schools in the locality. If the careers service fell temporarily below strength, obligations to all the borough's 22 secondary schools could not be met.[10]

School Three, in the same borough, had a similar if slightly less structured relationship with the careers service. Teachers at this school added that a careers advisory officer kept in touch with pupils staying on to the sixth form. This officer was felt to have a somewhat difficult borderline role, since it was not clear whether the advisory work was part of the employment placement service or part of the education service.

In the other borough, the careers service provided for the needs of leavers from Schools One and Two on a slightly different basis. Only those pupils who requested it had an individual interview, but the careers office required the schools to supply a record of every child in the fifth year at school. The careers teacher at School One described this record as including 'mock examination results and a forecast of probable future examination achievements; tutors' estimates of various aspects of the pupil's ability (e.g., dexterity); his interests and the type of employment he is likely to seek; the pupil's account of his own interests, subject preference at school, Saturday employment undertaken and type of work wanted in the future'.[11] All this information was available to the careers officer in advance of any interview the pupil might request.

Much of the additional careers work brings outside specialists into the school to talk about their jobs, and takes pupils outside the school for visits to places of employment and, on rare occasions, for work experience. Careers work of varying kinds takes place at intervals during the child's secondary school life, intensifying in fourth and fifth years. However, our chief concern here is with the run up to the child's final departure across the school-leaving boundary.

During the final weeks, the pupil often becomes acutely aware of his impending status passage to the interim state of school-leaver. Any negotiations with regard to employment are often still at a tentative stage. The whole world of work seems an object of some apprehension from which teacher's experience, some pupils felt, was somewhat remote. While the careers work done in school with a view to developing self-analysis and self-realization had been helpful to many of them, some pupils hankered for a more concrete discussion. 'The teacher will talk about working relationships, things like that, but we want to know about the *job*, not what will happen when you get it.' The counsel of teachers who had worked outside teaching was often eagerly sought. But however psychologically alone the pupils felt, at this final stage, most of the schools did to some extent cross the school-leaving boundary with them, either through written references or telephone conversations with potential employers.

Employment agencies were among those who contacted the schools about school-leavers. Senior teachers at School One commented that the careers service was not in favour of the school building up its own employment contacts, and had asked the school not to make the recommendations of pupils requested by the employment agencies. This attempt to restrict the boundary-crossing activities of senior teachers was not felt to be acceptable since, in the opinion of these teachers, the careers service itself had something to learn from the employment agencies' style of dealings with the school-leavers.[12]

All the schools focused on in the research catered for pupils from the ages of eleven to eighteen. In each school the sixth-form pupils, voluntarily staying on after the age of sixteen for a variety of reasons, entered into a slightly different relationship with staff and fellow pupils. Many would leave after only one year in the sixth, having attempted to add to or improve their fifth-year examination results. These pupils, like the sixteen-year-old leavers, usually crossed the boundary of the school for the last time with the intention of going straight into the employment market. But for those who stayed for two or even, very occasionally, three years in the sixth, their next destination was often some form of further or higher education.

Contacts between the comprehensive schools and other educational institutions were not of long standing, nor as routinized as those of more long-established secondary schools. Pupils tended to be active on their own behalf in negotiating their passage to further or higher education, usually with the support of a particular teacher they knew well. While sixth-form tutors were often felt to have been helpful in widening the pupils' approach to the whole subject of future plans, these nominated tutors were not perceived as having any particular expertise with regard either to future employment or to further and higher education, and this was regretted by some pupils. Nevertheless, most sixth-form pupils contacted during the research appeared to identify some teacher with whom they were able to discuss these more specific matters. In one case (at School One) the counsellor was referred to as a provider of full and accurate references. 'He is more accurate than you would believe. He can't really know you, but he seems to find out a lot for the references.'

Pupils who come back

While the pupils referred to above had continued their school life into the sixth form without a break, it was sometimes the case that ex-pupils who had left at sixteen would return to the school, having had second thoughts about leaving their school days behind. One or two pupils not yet of an age to leave school commented frankly that they would try to get a job at sixteen, but if unsuccessful or not happy with the opportunities available would come back to school for a further year or two. This pupil view of education as an available amenity to be taken or left at will, after the official school-leaving age, was understood if not encouraged by teachers. More difficult to understand was the phenomenon, not infrequently encountered, of the pupil who had truanted or been absent during his official time at school but came back to hang around school premises after he had left. A teacher commented that such pupils 'appear to cling to the teachers and classes they once rejected'.[13] Here the attachment would seem to be to the school as a part-time way of life, rather than as a source of specialist help.[14] There was little indication that teachers felt such pupils to be still within the boundaries of school care. Indeed, the concept of the 'old pupil' did not seem to be a highly developed one, in these large and recently reorganized schools.[15] An English teacher commented that school-organized theatre trips at holiday times would sometimes include both former and current pupils, but apart from special activities of this kind the sheer numbers passing through the school hindered the recollection and recognition of former pupils by teachers. A sixth-form pupil claimed that even recent school-leavers were not recognized by teachers when they came back the following year to collect any certificates they had obtained. 'If they didn't come to prominence in some way, people can't remember teaching them.' While this statement would be disputed by many teachers, it can be admitted that the boundaries of care of a school of over a thousand pupils are already widely set, and cannot routinely be widened to perpetuate concern for and involvement with former pupils. These schools, like other more long-established schools, are more likely to see the potential of the school/old pupil relationship as one to which the former pupil, rather than the school, should contribute most, as a response to earlier years of care.

Teachers' perspectives on interprofessional boundaries of care

In all the schools, teachers' attitudes towards the crossing of interprofessional boundaries were ambivalent. Teachers were often eager that children whom they defined as having specialized needs should move out of the mainstream school into a more specialized setting, whether temporarily or permanently. Yet the appropriateness and efficacy of the help available from the specialized agencies was often called into question. And although teachers claimed to have little knowledge of or contact with agency practitioners, generalizations were readily offered about, for example, the youth, personal style, and impermanence of social workers, or the medical profession's obsession with confidentiality.

However, while participating in the research, staff in three of the schools contributed to and debated a more considered analysis of their relationship with outside agencies.[16] The document prepared by School Three[17] spelt out many of the advantages and the difficulties of the school/agency relationship which all the schools were experiencing.

Staff in School Three felt they were building up a knowledge of the roles of outside agencies and of the help such agencies were likely to be able to offer the school. Nevertheless, there were still uncertainties about the role of some agencies and the degree to which the school could look to them for specialized help. Recent cases of child abuse and neglect had alerted welfare agencies to the need for adequate communications and the sharing of information, but teachers found that some outside agencies were not active in approaching the school for information the school had or in informing the school of their involvement in a case. The impression was that some outside agencies undervalued the contribution the schools made towards the welfare of pupils, neither expecting the schools to have relevant information nor thinking it worthwhile to keep the school up to date about the agency's involvement. In situations where the school had built up a relationship with an outside agency, it seemed these bars to communication were being removed. The outside agency had confidence that the school would treat any information that the agency passed on with discretion, and appreciated that the school was likely to be able to contribute insights helpful to the agency. However, these better relationships were often at a person-to-person level, and might be dissipated by a change of personnel.

Teachers at School Three went on to discuss in more detail some factors affecting cooperation between the school and particular agencies. They pointed out that few teachers had actually met social workers in the course of their job. Social workers did not often take the initiative in contacting the school. Teachers did not always know that a case was being dealt with by the social services department. They respected the need for social work confidentiality and stressed they did not expect to be told all the details about a case, but would appreciate being notified of social services involvement in cases concerning children at the school.[18]

Relationships with the social services were made more difficult by the rapid turnover of social workers and the fact that social workers were working with heavy caseloads. Teachers recognized that both they and the social workers might each have an unrealistic view of the other. Learning more about each other's roles might contribute to more effective communication. However, it could be that the two roles, of social worker and teacher, involved differences of approach which, in practice, inhibited full cooperation. The school was an agent of control with certain duties to ensure the attendance of pupils, whilst the social worker might be acting as advocate for the child. These roles might occasionally be reversed with the school being better placed to view the child's behaviour in the light of his other achievements. In this sense the school could sometimes have a more balanced and perhaps more supportive view of the child than the social worker. Even so, the differences of role relationship with the child might prevent successful cooperation between the social services and the school.

Another difficulty was that the teacher had to consider the interests of his colleagues and of the other pupils, whilst the social worker might be more single-minded, with the interests of the particular child as the only factor. School Three had a great concern for the individual pupil, but teachers at the school felt there was a point at which the wider responsibilities of the school affected the possibility of a solution acceptable to both teacher and social worker.

Help available from the education welfare service was also felt to have certain limitations. The school shared the services of an EWO with several other schools in the area, and it was only possible to ask the EWO to follow up the more serious cases of nonattendance. If the school could have commanded more of the EWO's time, he could have acted in a more general welfare capacity on behalf of the school and its pupils.

These teachers felt that the tasks of EWOs and social workers were potentially overlapping. Yet, like the school, the EWO might be unaware that the social services were already involved with a case.

Reservations were also expressed about the role of the child guidance clinic. The issue of medical confidentiality affected the relationship between the school and the child guidance clinic. Psychiatrists were reluctant to divulge information about 'patients'.

There was sometimes considerable delay after referral, and the understaffing of both the psychological service and psychiatric service was deplored.

Teachers felt that the psychiatrists often ignored the points they had made concerning the pupil referred. Sometimes the problem was with a child's behaviour in a group, yet the psychiatrist, dealing with the child in isolation, did not always take notice of the factors which the teachers had mentioned about the child's school behaviour. Psychiatrists rarely gave advice on how to deal with a difficult child. The school would have welcomed advice from psychiatrists, but it seemed that the school and the psychiatric service had differing interpretations of the role of the service.

Relationships with the school health service and the health services generally were on the whole more favourably viewed by these teachers. The school received information about special disabilities from the school health service, and, in general, it was considered the service was adequate, though some staff felt the medicals were too infrequent and not sufficiently comprehensive. Contact with health visitors had been found to be useful, since they were familiar with some pupils' backgrounds. Health visitors sometimes took the initiative in contacting the school after visiting a family and discovering difficult home circumstances.

Many of the views expressed by teachers in School Three were echoed by teachers in the other schools.

Boundary management

Teacher contact across the school boundary with agency practitioners and parents was in all cases closely managed by the headteacher and other senior teachers.

Home and school

Few teachers made home visits, and in most cases it was no part of school policy that they should do so. The school reached out to parents as a whole through circular letters from the headmaster; most telephone calls to parents were made by senior teachers, and letters to individual parents were either written or 'verified' by the headteacher. Parents invited to parents' evenings for their child's year-group could, by appointment, see their child's form tutor and any of his subject teachers. However, if parents came uninvited to the schools to raise a matter with a particular teacher, some barriers might be placed in their way. 'The administrative office would normally use some delaying action, to allow an irate parent to "cool off" before meeting the year tutor or form teacher.'[19] If the parents did find their way directly to the classroom they would be 'politely referred to the headmaster by the teacher or tutor. The head of house, and possibly the tutor, would be asked to join the headmaster in a discussion with the parent concerned.'[20]

Apart from the pupil, who was entrusted with most general communications from the school, the most appropriate go-between between the school and the pupil's home was felt to be the EWO, despite the reservations expressed about the potential size of these officers' caseloads. However, the way in which the EWO was briefed for his task varied considerably between the schools.

In School Four, the work of the EWO was treated as integral to the school's pastoral system. Year tutors were allocated time in which to go through the attendance records of their charges with the EWO, and would in due course receive his report on the outcome of any requested visit. In all the other schools, the EWO contacted a smaller number of more senior pastoral teachers – senior house tutors in School Three, senior tutors or the counsellor in School Two, and, in School One, Counsellor A alone briefed the EWO on pupils' absence.

School and agency

Whilst School One provided the only example of a school where all contacts with outside agencies were channelled through a single role-holder (Counsellor A), the opportunities which pastoral teachers in the other schools had to contact outside agencies were more apparent than real. Schoolteaching is a cloistered occupation. Teachers tend to move from classroom to dining hall to staffroom and back to classroom. A far smaller proportion of teachers than pupils in the schools studied left the premises during the school day. Social workers, health visitors, EWOs all have considerable freedom of movement in pursuit of their work, and many of the more specialized agency practitioners have an explicitly peripatetic mode of working. Teachers, by contrast, are more or less school-bound. Unless on an educational visit with pupils, they were unlikely ever to have visited the office of a social work area team, or a child guidance clinic, or, indeed, the education department of the local authority. Nor did the average teacher have easy telephone access to the outside world. Large schools have far fewer lines than small businesses; the assumption seems to be that most of the work of the school is internal and strictly localized. Telephone switchboards tended to be small and intermittently manned; telephone extensions were few and often inaccessible.

Postal communication was a more practical proposition than using the telephone, but the scarcity of secretarial and administrative resources in the school, and the heavy involvement of most teachers in the classroom, tended to discourage letter-writing about matters for which prompt help was hoped.

Since access to or communication with agencies outside the school was so difficult for the ordinary subject teacher or middle-ranking pastoral teacher, almost the only way in which teachers met their fellow caring professionals was if agency practitioners actually came into the school to undertake work there. From the social services department, an intermediate treatment officer or a social worker might undertake regular work within the school with individuals or groups of pupils. Clinical medical officers came in to conduct routine medical examinations of pupils, educational psychologists occasionally[21] came in to study the school situation of individual pupils referred to them. Police officers and health visitors were more likely to come to the school as contributors to the curriculum (road safety, health education) than à propos of particular children and were thus more likely than other practitioners to meet the full range of pupils and staff in the school. At the time of the research, none of the schools was designated a 'community' school, or had a community warden, who would have represented the youth and community service on school premises.

Most of the visitors coming in to the school were filtered off from contact with the class teachers by the headteacher or one of his deputies. This practice was an amalgam of policy and the location of senior staff in the building – most usually, close to the main entrance of the school. But the headteacher, even if not physically close to the entrance to his school, was spiritually its gatekeeper. He, or the deputy who worked most closely with him, represented the school in almost all its dealings with the outside world, whether on or off school premises. The headteachers in each of the schools personally sanctioned and monitored the research carried out in them.[22] They were accountable for the work of the schools to the governing body and the education department of the local authority.

Notes

1. Brunel University Education Studies Unit Document No. 1/172, paragraph 12.11
2. ESU Doc. No. 2/200, para 16.2.
3. ESU Doc. No. 3/202, para 31.
4. ESU Doc. No. 4/175, paras 13.13 and 14.9.
5. A more detailed study of exclusion from secondary school will be part of the ESU's disaffected pupils project.
6. Uncl. ESU Doc. No. 4/143, appendix.
7. Uncl. ESU Doc. No. 4/147, para 2.
8. ESU Doc. No. 4/175, para 13.4.
9. Uncl. ESU Doc. No. 4/143, appendix.
10. ESU Doc. No. 4/175, para 14.3
11. Uncl. ESU Doc. No. 1/101, para 3.2.5.
12. ESU Doc. No. 1/172, para 13.4.
13. Uncl. ESU Doc. No. 3/131.
14. These concepts will be further explored during the ESU's study of disaffected pupils in outer-London secondary schools.
15. Whilst these comprehensive schools were perhaps too new to have built up a viable interest group of former pupils, the school buildings were in all cases an historical feature of the neighbourhood. Many parents commented that they had themselves been pupils in the schools their children now attended, but 'it's all very different now'.
16. These statements are fully set out in the school documents cleared for wider circulation.
17. ESU Doc. No. 3/203.
18. See also Packwood, T., 'Social Workers in School', in *Health and Social Service Journal*, 3.7.76
19. Uncl. ESU Doc. No. 4/147, para 10.2.
20. Uncl. ESU Doc. No. 1/124, para 9.2.
21. The current ratio of EPs to the school population falls somewhat short even of the target figure of 1:10,000 proposed by the Summerfield Committee in 1968.
22. In Schools One and Two, the counsellors too were members of the local authority steering committee for the research, as were the 'pastoral' deputy heads in Schools Three and Four.

SECTION VI

MANAGEMENT OF STAFF DEVELOPMENT

CHAPTER 6.1

INTERVENTIONS FOR STRENGTHENING THE SCHOOL'S CREATIVITY*
Richard A. Schmuck

Throughout modern history teachers have valued their own continued education for professional development. In addition to these internalized values for professional growth, recent social changes have placed new external pressures on teachers to improve their practices. Research and development have led to new practices in industry; not only in the form of new products and markets, but also new procedures of management. The public sector also depends heavily on basic and applied research by amassing systematic surveys of public opinions and customs, by analysing the consequences of governmental action, and by investing economically in many studies and experimental programmes. No matter what the area of belief, value, behaviour, or tradition, the knowledge-gatherers and researchers of the present often challenge accustomed ways of thinking and behaving with new information. The result is that the modern citizen can take less for granted and must maintain fewer unquestioned and unquestionable assumptions and patterns of behaviour. Thus, the rapid technological and knowledge advances of our modern world have brought new demands on teachers to make the traditional value of continued education a new and challenging reality.

Schools, as organizations, have not been exempt from the effects of this knowledge explosion. Indeed, these changing times also call for less unquestioned tradition and more creative ways of running the school. Among the primary, and most immediate, social pressures on schools which

* *Creativity of The School*, The Centre for Educational Research and Innovation, Organization for Economic Co-operation and Development, Paris, France, 1974, pp. 104–126.

prod them on to change both at the individual level as well as the organizational level are:

a The growing recognition and understanding that individuals learn in different ways and at different rates. I refer to this as the social demand for increased *individualization* in schools.

b The growing view that some required school subjects have little relevance and meaning to the world that students will face after graduation. I think of this as the challenge of *relevance* in education; it is linked at this time to interests in improved *career and vocational education.*

c The increasing demand that teachers and schools be evaluated, and thus financed, on their performance. Increased interest in cost-benefit accounting, programmed-planning-budgeting systems, and writing behavioural objectives highlight this pressure. I refer to this as the social demand for increased *accountability* in schooling.

d The growing recognition that television, movies, audio tapes, and written programmes of instruction can be effective substitutes for the teacher has introduced the social demand for more uses of *educational technology.*

e The increasing interest by experts to change and reorganize the traditional disciplines of knowledge and to make major renovations to combine several different fields can be viewed as a social demand for more *interdisciplinary curricula* and departures from traditional curricula.

f And finally, the criticisms from many citizens that schools are too cold and impersonal and that students are not treated with respect and empathy represents a widespread interest in *humanizing* relationships within the school.

Two interventions to cope with change

Aside from the preservice preparation of future teachers within colleges of education, two intervention strategies stand out today as holding the most potential power for helping teachers to cope with these six social demands. The first is *in-service education* for teachers and administrators and the second is training in *organization development* for entire faculties. In-service education is a strategy for facilitating change in the individual, while organization development is a strategy aimed at dealing with changes within groups of personnel within the school. The former deals with modifications in the information, attitudes, and behaviours of individual educators; the latter aims at modifying the structure, norms, and role-procedure of the faculty that works together.

I have had considerable experience with both of these strategies of change. Both can be effective for helping teachers to work collaboratively and skilfully in improving their teaching. However, because I have recently been more involved in doing research on organization development and because I believe that less is known about it than in-service education, I will present more detailed information about it after first commenting briefly on in-service education.

In-service education

In-service education has been applied primarily to help secondary teachers become more knowledgeable about their subject matter. Recently it also has been used to help teachers individualize instruction, to learn how to write behavioural objectives, to use the current educational technology, to develop their own curricula, and to use new group procedures in their classrooms. Unfortunately, most of these interventions are not documented well, nor have they been carefully evaluated.

The handful of in-service programmes that have been systematically documented and evaluated indicate that the training should involve much more than the presentation of knowledge through lectures and reading. Successful in-service programmes provide opportunities for participants to experience cognitive, attitudinal, and behavioural change. This means that, along with presentations of information, the effective in-service course affords structured opportunities for teachers to communicate with each other about their attitudes and feelings as to the new information and its implications for changes in their role. The effective in-service course also affords opportunities for systematically planning how the new information might be implemented in the classroom and for trying out new behaviours within a 'safe climate' such as can be the case in role-playing and micro-teaching.

The instructors of in-service education programmes might be professors of education, the principal or headmaster of a school, or curriculum specialists in a regional or state office. Whoever the instructor may be, he will be most successful in bringing about teacher's growth in the cognitive, attitudinal, and behavioural realms if he can implement the following principles. The successful instructor:

a encourages the teachers to take an active part in the course, both verbally and physically,
b encourages and facilitates each teacher's discovery of the personal relevance of the course of study,
c emphasizes that individual differences among the teachers are to be expected and are desirable,
d accepts each teacher's natural tendency to make mistakes,
e encourages teachers to be open about themselves rather than to conceal their weaknesses and strengths,
f promotes frank expressions of feelings by freely giving praise and criticism when appropriate,
g models openness by talking about his own concerns and insecurities,
h promotes a climate for attitudinal change by encouraging respect and acceptance for every teacher.

Organization development

However effective an instructor of an in-service course may be in facilitating a teacher's growth in knowledge, attitudes, and new behaviours, many of these new insights and learnings may be difficult to implement within the traditional school organization. My own research and experience have indicated that many educational reforms have collapsed or have been absorbed without effect mainly because of the limited attention given to the organizational context in which the reforms have been attempted.

Any major innovation in curriculum or instructional technique implies a change in the 'culture' of the school. The relationship between teachers and administrators, for example, is apt to change. Often the change affects not only the headmaster and his faculty, but also the relationship between them and the nonprofessional staff and students. Consequently, authority relationships, communication networks, status groupings, and even friendship cliques are forced to change. In this process the innovation itself often fails or is restructured to conform to the 'old ways' of doing things.

The social demands for individualization, career education, accountability, educational technology, interdisciplinary curricula, and humanizing relationships call for new organizational procedures of coordinated and collaborative problem-solving on the part of administrators and their staffs.

Changes on the part of the individual teacher will not be enough to implement new plans and new procedures for the school. They call for new attitudes among administrators as well as new norms between the administrators and the teachers who work together. In other words, adequate adaptability of a school to these six social demands requires both individual and organizational changes.

Although in-service education courses have sought to deal with teachers' attitudes about these six social issues, little emphasis has been placed on how the teacher's new knowledge, attitudes, and skills can be implemented within the social context of the school. Moreover, while in-service education has sometimes successfully brought about changes in the individual teacher, it has not tended to help teachers develop the sorts of communication and problem-solving norms and skills that would increase their adaptability as an organizational unit. This is where organization development comes in.

Organization development (abbreviated as OD) is a planned and sustained effort to apply behavioural science to system improvement, using reflexive, self-analytic methods. Note that the emphasis of OD is on the system, rather than the individual as the target for change. In OD training, group participants are never strangers, as in typical group dynamics workshops; the participants in OD are the interdependent members of the same system or interlocked systems. System may mean either an entire school organization or a subsystem such as an academic department or teams of teachers.

I mean by reflexive, self-analytic methods that involve staff members themselves in the assessment, diagnosis, and transformation of their own school. Rather than simply accepting diagnosis and prescriptions from an outside 'technocratic' expert, organization members themselves, with the aid of OD consultants, examine current difficulties and their causes and participate actively in the reformulation of goals, the development of new group process skills, the redesign of structures and procedures for achieving the goals, the alteration of the working climate of the school, and the assessment of results.

To implement OD on a continuous basis, an organizational subsystem (such as a regional cadre of OD consultants) is created and charged with the specific responsibility for planning, managing, and evaluating the continuous process of organizational creativity. Thus, it should be borne in mind that an organization, such as a school, is never transformed permanently, and institutionalized, built-in OD functions must be continuously involved in facing the dilemmas and vicissitudes of organizational renewal. The essential concept here is that some fraction of a school's resources is devoted to continuous organizational maintenance, rebuilding, and expansion. Such a concept is familiar to administrators in relation to plant and equipment maintenance, but is much less widely known and accepted in the maintenance and growth of the school's human organization.

School organizations as systems

School organizations are complex social systems that gain their stability through role expectations and interpersonal norms. Individuals within a faculty behave predictably largely because of their adherence to shared expectations for what is appropriate in the school. Norms are compelling stabilizers of behaviour because individuals in the school monitor one another's behaviours. It is the strength of this sharedness that makes a school culture so resistent to modification but which, at the same time, offers a tool for planned change. If a school's creativity is to be viable and continuous, changes in interpersonal expectations must be shared so that each staff member knows that his colleagues have changed their expectations in the same way that he has changed his own.

Educational organizations are more than simply the sum total of their individual members and curriculum materials. The total staff has characteristics quite different from those of its individual members. These I refer to as the school's *systemic* characteristics. From the systemic point of view, effective management of schools is evidenced when greater production occurs than would be expected from a simple summing up of individual resources. As an open system, a school's efficiency is measured by how completely resources are used for educating its students. Ultimately a school's efficiency is determined by how effectively it can adopt new ideas and generate internal change to cope with changing times.

These system concepts help to establish a theoretical rationale for OD interventions. First, interventions will be more effective if they deal with subsystems and not just with individuals who lack functional interdependence. Further, since the school takes its shape from the ways the functional subsystems connect their efforts to one another, OD should focus, too, on relationships within and between subsystems. Second, interventions should confront the school with discrepancies between goal-striving and actual goal-achievement. Third, interventions should be aimed at making every subsystem receptive of information from every other subsystem, including the external environment. Finally, interventions should help the school to identify underused resources and to facilitate the creation of new or *ad hoc* systems to mobilize available resources quickly for isolated and nonregular problems. OD interventions quite often lead to formations of problem-solving groups that did not exist in the formal structure of the school before the intervention. If school organizations are to be truly creative, they must be able to form new subsystems, change them or dispose of them as needed.

Research on interventions

Several years ago, Matt Miles and I carefully reviewed the data-based research on OD in schools (Schmuck and Miles, 1971). More recently, Phil Runkel, several assistants, and I reviewed the available research and development on in-service education and OD in schools (Schmuck, Runkel, Saturen, Martell, and Derr, 1972). Although there is not enough space in this chapter to present details on our many discoveries, I do want to summarize some highlights of our findings.

a In-service education of school administrators or of teachers – by itself – is not a powerful enough intervention to bring about sustaining organizational change in schools. (See Miles, 1965; Schmuck, 1968; Lansky, Runkel, Croft, and MacGregor, 1969; and Thomas, 1970.)

b Human relations training which focuses primarily on the individual growth of participants is not an effective strategy for bringing about sustaining organizational change in schools. (See Shaevitz and Barr, 1970; and Schmuck and Miles, 1971.)

c An OD intervention can be an effective means for bringing about sustaining organizational changes in schools, especially when the building administrator is committed to the change efforts. (See Schmuck and Runkel, 1970; Fosmire, Keutzer, and Diller, 1971; Flynn, 1971; and Schmuck, 1972.)

d Finally, an OD intervention can also be an effective means for humanizing the interpersonal relationships between teachers and students. (See Schmuck, 1968; and Bigelow, 1971.)

Goals and instrumental sequences of OD

The following goals constitute some guidelines for a typical OD intervention:

a to increase understanding of how personnel in different school jobs affect one another,

b to develop clear communication networks up and down and laterally,

c to increase understanding of the various educational goals in different functional parts of the school,

d to uncover organizational conflicts for constructive problem-solving,

e to develop new ways of solving problems through creative uses of new roles in groups,

f to develop new ways of assessing progress towards educational goals in the school,

g to involve more people at all levels in decision-making,

h to develop procedures for searching out innovative practices both within and outside the school.

The achievement of objectives such as these naturally depends upon an effective strategy for altering organizational processes in schools. The following seven rubrics of actions constitute the primary ingredients of a prototypic OD strategy for bringing into operation more creative school organizations.

1 *Clarifying communication.* Clarity of communication is essential to all the concepts discussed previously. All school participants must learn to clarify the messages they receive from one another. An aspect of openness is using skill in communication to develop internal networks of higher fidelity and external channels that map the environment more accurately. Ambiguity and conflict about norms and roles can be alleviated by developing more precision in the transmission and reception of information.

2 *Establishing goals.* Educational goals are usually ambiguous and diffuse. Organizational members can learn to clarify and share their objectives and to increase their sense of 'owning' the goals and integrating their efforts.

3 *Uncovering conflict and interdependence.* Clarifying communication processes and objectives will lead to increased awareness of areas of conflict and interdependence. Confronting conflicts and exploring interdependencies will help to establish norms and roles that will aid the school in accomplishing its educational tasks.

4 *Improving group procedures.* Most organizational activity occurs in

meetings of face-to-face groups. Meetings are rarely satisfying or productive for all faculty members and they are often frustrating. Procedures for creating and using new skills for facilitating task productivity and group maintenance can help any meeting to be more satisfactory.

5 *Solving problems*. Adaptability implies active engagement in continuous problem-solving cycles for identifying, analysing, and acting on environmental contingencies. OD can help schools to harness their resources to extract creative solutions that yield a higher rate of success than solutions that merely extrapolate past practice.

6 *Making decisions*. OD almost always disperses influence much more widely throughout the system than is usual in present-day school organizations. Power need not be decreased in one job to be increased in another, although sometimes it is helpful to reduce authority if it is not based on knowledge and competence. Schools must learn alternative styles of making decisions to assure commitment from those who must carry out the decisions.

7 *Assessing change*. Change for its own sake does not necessarily lead to organizational creativity which is also adaptive. Schools must develop criteria for measuring and evaluating progress toward meeting both long-range and short-range goals.

The technology of OD

A typical sequence of OD involves the following seven steps:

(i)   Initial contact with the administrator and the board of education to gain general approval for the intervention.

(ii) Commitment from the entire faculty about the intervention. During discussions with the faculty agreements are made about goals, time, and energy; the consultant makes clear that he is consultant to the entire faculty, not just to one segment of it, such as the administration.

(iii) Data-gathering concerning existent organizational processes of the school.

(iv) Feedback of data to the target school.

(v)   Establishment of the specific goals of the OD intervention for this faculty.

(vi) The training programme is implemented.

(vii) Data are gathered to ascertain effects of the training while it is proceeding. Decisions about termination are guided by these data and made jointly between the consultants and the participants.

The training programme, listed as (vi) above, is made up of certain skills, exercises, and procedures which together form the building blocks of OD technology. The term *skill* signifies a way that certain interactions with others can be executed in a group. Sometimes the skill is one of communication, such as paraphrasing what another has said so that the other can verify whether he has been understood. Sometimes, it is one of the group-convenor, such as guiding a group through a survey of opinion. Sometimes the skill involves writing interview schedules to obtain diagnostic information about a school.

The skills practised during OD interventions are put to work only in reciprocal relations *between* persons; no individual can make use of these skills in isolation. Each skill is actually one person's part of a reciprocal role-relation. Paraphrasing can only be done in conversation with at least one other person and is not a complete act until the other has verified the accuracy of the paraphrase. The skill of a pair or group, consequently, is often surprisingly independent of the presumed skill of the individuals composing it. The convenor can be skilful in conducting a survey only if the members know their parts of the role-relation; an interview schedule can be prepared effectively only if the interviewers using the schedule act with the same goals and values as the writer and only if the respondents join the communicative act in the way the writer and the interviewer anticipate.

A distinction in OD is drawn between *exercises* and *procedures*. An *exercise* is a game that participants are asked to play in order to teach them something very important about group dynamics. Participants are able to understand the important principle about the group processes because they have just experienced the principle through their own behaviours.

A *procedure*, on the other hand, refers to an interpersonal *form* for communication in a group that helps the group to complete a task. A procedure can be used for a variety of tasks or purposes. One example of a procedure would be voting and another would be the 'theatre-in-the-round' procedure for sharing ideas and making observations.

In-service education in relation to OD

Since many schools do not have the resources necessary to enter into an

OD project, I believe it is important to consider the sorts of in-service programmes that might be tried to encourage movement in the direction of OD goals and towards more creativity of the school. I suggest the following ten stages as important aspects of such an in-service training design.

(i)   First, a group dynamics training experience should come to help the participating educators to become more reflective about the effects of their own role behaviours in the school. The major goal would be to help educators to think about their own practices and to increase their readiness to accept new practices. A secondary goal would be to impress upon the educators that their own behaviours, and not thoughts and values, affect the feelings and reactions of those who work with them.

(ii)   Next, knowledge of the behavioural sciences on such topics as clarifying communication, establishing goals, working with conflicts, holding effective meetings, solving problems, and making decisions would be presented. Discussions would be held on how such information relates to the educator's goals and role behaviours. Use of the knowledge, or at least some part of it, would be established as an important objective for each administrator. The group dynamics training, previously set in motion, would support the cognitive explorations of this phase.

(iii) Diagnostic skills related to communication, goals, conflicts, meetings, problems, and decisions would be presented and discussed, and the educator would become acquainted with how to measure the effects of his role behaviours related to each of these. Whenever appropriate, educators would be encouraged to give feedback to one another on these same behaviours. As the educator becomes more aware of his own characteristics, he may make fewer errors in perceiving how others are thinking and feeling.

(iv)   Specific ways in which the knowledge about communication, goals, conflict, meetings, problems, and decisions might be used in practice would be 'brainstormed' and refined. Each educator would be asked to plan various ways of behaviour for implementing this new knowledge. Each might also imagine and discuss the difficulties that he anticipates in using these new practices effectively.

(v)   These new practices would then be tried out through role-playing and immediate reactions would be given by the other educators in the in-service group. At the same time, several different observation schemes might be introduced and some educators would be asked to serve as observers and to give feedback to the role-players.

(vi) Skills in giving, receiving, and using feedback would be discussed and the role-playing vignettes might be repeated again in attempts to use the feedback.

(vii) The educators would be asked next to make commitments to try out some of these practices in the 'real' school setting. Discussions about supportive forces and restraining factors would be encouraged to explore the pros and cons of following through with the plan. Attempts would be made to reduce the restraining forces wherever possible either through revisions of the practice or by helping the educator to gain more confidence by simulating the practice still once more. One effective means for gaining commitment is to have the educator record on a cassette-tape the thoughts he has about the new practices he intends to try.

(viii) At a later session, after the educator has had an opportunity to get started on the new practice, the tape-recording would be played back as a reminder of the details of the practice. If the original commitment was unrealistic, changes can be made at this point in the techniques used to introduce the practice.

(ix) The educator next collects some data about the effects of his practice. He might use questions under certain circumstances, but most often collecting verbal or nonverbal feedback from others will be sufficient.

(x) Finally, during the time when the practices are being tried out, group discussions with fellow educators would be held, perhaps once a week or once every two weeks, to support each educator's efforts and to revise plans further for using knowledge about communication, goals, conflicts, meetings, problems, and decisions. Attention would be given to how the practices should be modified to respond effectively to particular school situations.

For additional detail about how some of the skills associated with OD can be taught in in-service training programmes see Schmuck (1968); Fox, Luszki, and Schmuck (1966); Schmuck, Chesler, and Lippitt (1966); Fox, Schmuck, Jung, van Egmond, and Ritvo (1973); and Schmuck (1972).

Integrating in-service education and OD

Even though I have used up much more space to describe OD in schools than I have for describing in-service education, I have *not* meant to depreciate the latter. Indeed, OD gains strength as it is coupled with special in-service education programmes. So, for example, the teachers of a school are more likely to respond favourably to an OD intervention after they have experienced an in-service course on communication skills, and an OD intervention with a faculty will have greater impact if the administrators and department heads are simultaneously receiving in-service training in leadership skills. Indeed, innovations involving individualization, career education, accountability, educational technology, new curricula, and humanizing relationships between teachers and students all depend on both the individual professionals developing new skills and on changes in organizational arrangements and processes.

Organizational change in schools will not persist if some individual changes do not also occur; and changes in the ways individual professionals think and work will soon dissipate or regress without supportive organizational changes. Increasing the school's creativity depends on interventions that include both training in organization development and in-service education courses.

References

Bigelow, Ronald C., 1971, *Changing Classroom Interaction through Organisation Development*, reprinted by R. Schmuck and M. Miles in *Organisation Development in Schools*, National Press Books, Palo Alto, California, pp. 71–85.

Flynn, Wayne, 1971, *The Principal as an Organisational Consultant to his own School*, Unpublished doctoral dissertation, University of Oregon.

Fosmire, Fred, Keutzer, Caroline, and Diller, Richard, 1971, *Starting up a New Senior High School*, reprinted by R. Schmuck and M. Miles in *Organisation Development in School*, National Press Books, Palo Alto, California, pp. 87–112.

Fox, Robert, Luszki, Margaret, and Schmuck, Richard, 1966, *Diagnosing Classroom Learning Environments*, Science Research Associates, Chicago, Illinois.

Fox, Robert, Schmuck, Richard, Jung, Charles, van Egmond, Elmer, Ritvo, Miriam, 1973, *Diagnosing Professional Climate in the School*, Learning Resources Corporation, Fairfax, Virginia.

Lansky, L., Runkel, Philip, Croft, John, and McGregor, C., 1969, *The Effects of Human Relations Training on Diagnosing Skills and Planning for Change*, Technical Report, CASEA, University of Oregon, Eugene, Oregon.

Miles, Matthew, 1965, 'Changes and Following Laboratory Training: a Clinical Experimental Study', *Journal of Applied Behavioural Science*, 1, (3) pp. 215–242.

Schmuck, Richard, 1968, 'Helping Teachers Improve Classroom Group Processes',

Journal of Applied Behavioural Science, 4, (4) pp. 401–435.

Schmuck, Richard, 1972, 'Developing Collaborative Decision Making: The Importance of Trusting Strong and Skilful Leaders', *Educational Technology*, 12 (10).

Schmuck, Richard, Chesler, Mark, and Lippitt, Ronald, 1966, *Problem-Solving to Improve Classroom Learning*, Science Research Associates, Chicago, Illinois.

Schmuck, Richard, and Runkel, Philip, 1970, *Organisational Training for a School Faculty*, CASEA, University of Oregon, Eugene, Oregon.

Schmuck, Richard and Miles, Matthew, 1971, *Organisation Development in Schools*, National Press Books, Palo Alto, California.

Schmuck, Richard, Runkel, Philip, Saturen, Steven, Martell, Ronald, and Derr, C.B., 1972, *Handbook of Organisation Development in Schools*, National Press Books, Palo Alto, California.

Shaevitz, M.H. and Barr, D.J., 1970, *Encounter Groups in a Small College: a Case Study*, University of California at San Diego, La Jolla, California.

Thomas, Terry, 1970, *Changes in Elementary Principals as a Result of Laboratory Training*, Technical Report No. 5, CASEA, University of Oregon, Eugene, Oregon.

CHAPTER 6.2

IN-SERVICE EDUCATION AND TRAINING: SOME CONSIDERATIONS*
Induction and In-Service Training Subcommittee of the Advisory Committee on the Supply and Training of Teachers

Introduction

The term 'in-service education and training' (INSET) has been used in this chapter in preference to the more common 'in-service training' in the belief that it more adequately describes the wide range of activities which may appropriately be undertaken by teachers as part of their personal and professional development.

INSET has emerged over a long period of time in a variety of forms by a variety of routes. Despite the confidence with which the term is used no firm definition exists of what constitutes INSET for a teacher. Similarly, the objectives of INSET have been assumed rather than defined. The development of this work on the scale envisaged by the White Paper will necessitate some broad agreement on objectives to enable the various contributors to its development to work with some degree of common purpose. INSET should enable teachers

a. to develop their professional competence, confidence, and relevant knowledge;
b. to evaluate their own work and attitudes in conjunction with their professional colleagues in other parts of the education service;
c. to develop criteria which would help them to assess their own teaching roles in relation to a changing society for which the schools must equip their pupils;
d. to advance their careers.

---

* Advisory Committee On Induction and Training of Teachers ACSTT (74), INIST II, Department of Education and Science, September 1974.

In-service training should, in short, enable a teacher to monitor and shape his professional development.

In addition, *local authorities* and other *providing bodies* may use the further education and training of their teachers as a means of meeting specific needs which arise from time to time in the schools and the education service for which they are responsible.

INSET is at present provided by many different agencies and consists of a profusion of activities, ranging from loosely structured discussion groups to the highest levels of formal postgraduate studies. It is difficult to discern in this profusion any relationship of the parts to the whole or any unifying principle other than the fact that serving teachers are participants. The planning of the substantial expansion of INSET proposed in the White Paper will however require the development of a coherent system which will not only comprehend the rich variety of existing in-service activities but will also unify the even greater diversity of provision which is likely to emerge in the future.

INSET needs

The rationale and planning for INSET must start from the needs to be met and for this purpose it is necessary to consider the different but related needs of teachers, schools, and LEAs and how these can best be reconciled within a coherent system which will improve the quality of the education service as a whole.

The needs of teachers

While it is accepted that specific needs will vary widely from one individual to another, there would seem to be general needs related to different stages in a teacher's career which must be met if his potential is to be fully developed and utilized. The career profile suggested below will not precisely fit the professional development of every teacher, nor will teachers advance along it at a uniform pace. It does however provide a framework which would offer teachers a variety of opportunities within a programme of professional development.

A teacher first needs to be initiated successfully into his professional career in a specific school. The *induction year* will include a teacher's first INSET experience.

After induction there follows a period of perhaps some four to six years when the young teacher needs to consolidate his professional confidence by adding to his knowledge and developing his skills. This is probably best achieved by a series of relatively short courses which are specific in their content and application. Since teachers would wish to relate INSET undertaken to the work they are immediately involved with, a lengthy period of absence from school would be unhelpful and these specifically focused courses would perhaps best be dealt with by a combination of short periods of full-time study and more extended periods of part-time study rather along the lines of existing ATO/DES courses. There might, however, have to be a degree of flexibility to permit some teachers to take longer courses.

After some five to eight years in the profession, there is the need for a teacher to reflect on his work to date and in the light of this evaluation to consider the direction of his career over the next few years. If this *orientation* and refreshment is to be successful, a teacher will need to distance himself to some extent from the immediate situation in which he has been involved and this would seem an appropriate time for secondment for at least one term to a centre where advanced studies would be taken. This period of study could initiate a change in career direction or confirm and enhance the direction to which a teacher was already committed.

Following this period of secondment and the more clearly defined career commitment which should result from it, there would seem to be the need for further studies on a part-time/full-time basis, somewhat similar in length to the specific courses outlined above but different in character and higher in standard. These *advanced seminars* should give teachers the opportunity to develop specialist expertise and knowledge and should also provide means by which they would become more aware of the totality of the curriculum and the limitations of specialism. It should also be a means through which teachers could meet the ablest minds working in their particular fields and thus prepare themselves for more sustained advanced studies.

Before the mid-point in a teacher's career, say, after twelve to fifteen years in the profession, a number of teachers will need to reequip themselves in a major way for new and substantial responsibilities which will require of them leadership and management in various forms within the education service. It would be an appropriate time for *advanced studies* which could take a variety of forms, requiring a substantial period of release – at least one term and in some cases a year. Some teachers will not be undertaking more responsibilities but will need a period of secondment at this point in their careers to reassess their existing ones.

While it is more difficult after the mid-career point to discern broad requirements it is possible to identify two groups of teachers with distinct needs. A relatively small number of 'middle managers' and administrators will need to be prepared for what one might term *top management* within the education service and specific provision for them could be made at a relatively small number of centres. There is also a more substantial group of teachers with long service, perhaps in one school, who may not have, and possibly have never sought, prospects of advancement in the profession. The major need of this group is for *refreshment*, not necessarily within the setting of a formal course. They need the opportunity to get away from school in order to replenish their intellectual and cultural reserves so that to the qualities of experience and stability which they bring to their teaching there may be added some new interest or renewed enthusiasm as they enter the latter part of their careers.

The framework outlined above could be adapted to meet the needs of teachers returning to service after a period of absence. The varying length of such absences, the various kinds of previous experience and qualifications, and the various kinds of teaching to which the teachers will return produce a variety of needs which defies simple prescriptions. It can be said however that whereas the serving teacher has some need to 'distance' himself from the classroom, the returning teacher needs the reverse. Where the absence from teaching has been of some length a period of supported reinduction would be helpful, affording a gradual reintroduction to teaching duties with some retraining during the first term or two in school. If the returning teacher is taking up duties with an age-group of which he has had no previous experience, the need for a period of retraining will be particularly apparent. A returner whose absence from teaching has been short could logically enter the INSET sequence at the point he had reached in his career profile before leaving the service. Similarly teachers returning from service abroad who have been adding to their professional experience but in another educational setting should be enabled to avail themselves of those in-service activities which they feel are most appropriate for the range of duties which they are taking up.

The needs of schools

Educational and social change makes new demands upon schools, as upon local education authorities, and leads heads and teachers to reconsider the existing curricular and organizational patterns to make them more appropriate to the new situation. This in turn creates a need for a programme of staff development so that the staff may acquire the skills necessary to achieve the educational objectives they have formulated to serve the children they teach.

Whilst some of these in-service training needs result from changes originating externally, such as the reorganization of secondary education in an area, others arise from innovation within the school itself. Examples of the latter might be the adoption of vertical grouping in a primary school, and in a secondary school the introduction of some form of integrated studies or more substantial careers education provision.

A staff development programme will be no less necessary for a school in a relatively 'steady state' situation to provide for such needs as the induction of new entrants to the profession and of experienced teachers new to the school; refreshment and up-dating for long-serving teachers; training or further study in preparation for promotion or new responsibilities in the school.

There is increasing interest in basing some INSET activities more directly upon the concerns of functioning groups in the school (a departmental team, the heads of house, the whole staff) or on focusing upon a specific innovation or problem and for some purposes this method may be more effective than the traditional course attended by individual teachers. The fact that such INSET is school-focused does not mean it has to be school-based: it can take place either on or off the job and can be provided either by outside agencies (e.g., a college or LEA advisers) or by the school itself (e.g., a staff conference). Neither does this school-focused perspective mean that all the normal processes of staff discussion within the school should be labelled as INSET. The latter usually implies some external stimulus, a deliberate intention to become trained or to train or educate, and also some standing back from, and analysis of, the teaching task. This last element is important and it may be missing in some school-based activities which familiarize newcomers with existing procedures in the school, or introduce existing staff to new procedures, but do not provide or encourage any scrutiny of the educational justification for those procedures and so do not really forward the professional development of the teachers concerned.

The needs of LEAs

The LEA's concern arises from its statutory duty to make adequate educational provision for the area for which it is responsible. Some exam-

ples of needs identified by LEAs for which they may have to make provision
include preparing staff to deal with:

    a. new school structures arising from reorganization (e.g., introduction
       of eleven–sixteen schools and sixth-form colleges);
    b. less fundamental modifications of existing systems, such as increasing
       collaboration among schools at sixth-form level;
    c. demands for greater attention to particular aspects of teaching (e.g.,
       improving competence in the teaching of reading; developing new
       techniques for dealing with mixed-ability groups in, say, science or
       modern languages);
    d. new methods of assessment and evaluation.

Procedures and machinery

Planning for a systematic expansion for INSET to meet the variety of
needs discussed in the preceding section will require the close cooperation
of the local education authorities, the teaching profession, and the providing agencies. The new Regional Committees for the Education and Training of Teachers will have an important role in the coordination of plans at
regional level but there are a number of issues on which national agreement
and guidance would seem desirable. These are discussed in the paragraphs
which follow.

An agreed basis for release

The determination of an agreed basis for the release of teachers will
require agreement on a rate of progress towards the target of 3% release, on
the scope of activities which will count towards the target, and on methods
and criteria for deciding between the competing claims of individual
teachers.

Many of the in-service activities which have been mentioned earlier do
not fall within the definition of substantial courses (i.e., those of one month
or longer full-time equivalent) which was suggested by the James Report
and should not therefore count against the 3% target. On the other hand it
would be inconsistent with the James Committee's recommendation that
release might be used for purposes other than attendance at formal courses to
attempt to define closely the kinds of activity for which release might be
granted.

Release may be sought by a teacher in order to equip himself for a specific task in his present school, to improve his qualifications and so his career prospects, or to further his personal education. All are entirely legitimate grounds for release and in practice an activity, though chosen for one purpose, may effectively meet others; the professionally relevant course may – and indeed should – further a teacher's personal education just as an activity found personally educative and rewarding should enrich the teacher's professional work.

Selection for release will involve decisions between the competing claims of individual teachers and between courses or studies in different subject areas and at different levels, taking into account local needs and circumstances. It is important that the profession should be closely associated with the selection process which must be seen to be fair to all concerned. This could be achieved by including teachers in the group within a local education authority which has responsibility for deciding upon applications for release. It would seem desirable that the criteria for selection should include:

a. the degree of the teacher's commitment to in-service education;
b. the extent to which the proposed study could contribute to the needs of the individual teacher, the school, and the authority;
c. length of service and of any previous release.

In making their decisions the committee or panel concerned with selection will no doubt take into account any previous unsuccessful applications for release.

Incentives

In addition to establishing criteria for the selection of teachers who seek release it will be equally necessary to create a climate which encourages all teachers to undertake in-service education. It is possible to identify three aspects:

a. the removal of disincentives;
b. the use of positive incentives;
c. the acceptance that a commitment to further training is part of a teacher's job.

Greater opportunity to obtain release and the provision of adequate replacement staff would remove two present disincentives to further training. Positive incentives might include improved opportunities to obtain academic and professional qualifications and support and encouragement for teachers in implementing new ideas in their schools. As to the third aspect, we should recognize those motivational factors which relate to the teacher's sense of the development of his own career and of his personal competence in the exercise of his professional role.

Local consultation

There will be a need for consultative machinery at local level to ensure that the development of an expanded programme of INSET reflects not only the needs of teachers, schools, and LEAs, but also the experience and advice of the providing agencies.

Although the ultimate responsibility for decisions about a teacher's INSET needs and the best way of meeting them rests with the teacher himself, it is no easy task to identify one's own professional and personal educational needs, to relate these to the needs of the school and the LEA, and, finally, to locate the INSET provision that will best serve to meet these needs. Most teachers would probably welcome assistance with this task. Each school should ensure that facilities for advice, both from inside and outside the school, are available and are made known to teachers. Counsel of this kind would be among the duties of an appropriate member of staff who, in a large school, might be secretary of an INSET committee within the school. In addition to giving advice himself, he would also put members of staff in touch with the external help available from local authority advisers and tutors in colleges and universities.

The school too is faced with a complex task in seeking to identify and arrange provision for its own needs and those of individual teachers and the LEA. It is desirable that each school should formulate by staff discussion a policy for INSET in support of the general policy objectives of the school.

A local education authority will not only have responsibility for making decisions on the release of teachers, but will also have the task of considering INSET needs, provisions, and policy for its area. It is desirable that an advisory committee should be established for the area of each authority, which should include representatives of the authority, the teachers, and the providing agencies, to identify needs and priorities, to suggest ways in which they might be met, and to advise the authority on general policy for INSET. Such an advisory committee could appropriately deal with the induction year as well as with INSET.

CHAPTER 6.3

MAKING INSET WORK*
Induction and In-Service Training Subcommittee
of the Advisory Committee on the
Supply and Training of Teachers

This discussion is about the in-service education and training (INSET) of teachers. It is intended for consideration by every teacher and every school. It is an open invitation to you and your colleagues to comment upon some key issues and practical suggestions.

INSET is particularly important at the present time. Society is changing faster than ever and is making increasingly complex demands upon schools. Teachers are having to introduce changes in school structures and curricula. Falling school rolls are causing new problems, including reduced promotion possibilities for teachers. If they are to respond positively to these and similar pressures, teachers will need access to good facilities.

INSET is a voluntary professional activity which depends for its success upon the goodwill of teachers. It is therefore vital that it should be relevant to staff needs and of high quality. Too often in the past it has been thought of only in terms of individual teachers attending courses which are designed and provided by outside agencies. This discussion, while recognizing the extremely valuable contribution made by such courses, sets them in the context of a wider approach in which teachers and schools also plan their own INSET programmes in the light of needs which they have identified.

Naturally this approach raises many questions and some of these are asked in the following pages. But the fact that many schools are already moving in this direction indicates that these questions can be answered. As a first step to sharing ideas about this approach this discussion suggests four practical steps that any school can take to plan its own programme:

---

* Department of Education and Science and the Welsh Office, November, 1978.

1 Identify the main needs
2 Decide on and implement the general programme
3 Evaluate the effectiveness of this general programme
4 Follow-up the ideas gained

Of course, these steps will not necessarily take place in sequence: they will overlap with each other in any real-life situation but they should provide useful guidelines.

Step 1: Identify INSET needs

The first step is to identify the various needs which there are in any school. Identifying INSET needs is just as difficult as identifying other educational needs. It will require discussions and negotiations and the definitions arrived at will have to be acceptable to the staff concerned. It must also be remembered that no definition is ever likely to be final: thus needs will have to be reconsidered in the light of changing circumstances. In view of all this, most teachers will probably welcome the opportunity to consult with colleagues about their needs. In this way, and by doing some background reading, they can widen and deepen their understanding of the problem and thus begin the INSET process itself.

INSET needs can usefully be considered at three main levels:

the needs of individual teachers;
the needs of functional groups within the school;
the needs of the school as a whole.

Two main aspects of an individual teacher's needs have to be considered. First, those problems occurring in the teacher's everyday classroom and school work can generate needs of a concrete and immediate kind; the need to keep up-to-date with the latest developments in a subject, like geography, or teaching area, like reading, are obvious examples but the deputy head who feels the need for some training in management skills comes into this category, too. Second, teachers will, from time to time, want to take stock of their careers and decide what form of INSET, for example an advanced course involving secondment, would best help them to develop further. It is worth remembering, in this context, that the professional needs of those teachers in the latter part of their careers have to be considered alongside those of younger colleagues.

Teachers often belong to several different working or functional groups whose members face common problems and therefore have similar needs. In the larger primary schools they could be the reception class teachers. In the secondary school they could be in the same subject department or pastoral team. They could be a group of probationers with induction needs or a group of senior staff facing new and difficult management problems. In some schools, for certain purposes, these functional groups will be large enough to meet within the school but often, for example in small primary schools, it might be more advantageous for groups to be formed with similarly placed teachers from nearby schools.

The school as a whole will also have needs which can, partly at least, be met through some form of INSET activity. These needs will frequently arise from an innovation like the adoption of a policy on language across the curriculum or in response to falling schools rolls.

Schools and functional groups that have set out to identify needs have usually soon found themselves considering their fundamental aims and methods. With this in mind, it is, perhaps, worth asking some fairly general questions at the outset:

How can you and your colleagues define the distinctive needs of particular groups: departments, year groups, those at different levels of responsibility, those charged with carrying through a particular innovation, those about to change their role?

How often should you and your colleagues review your needs and how can this best be done?

Can you review your own needs unassisted?

What advice or guidelines would be helpful?

How can your head best fulfil the responsibility for identifying and meeting the needs of the school and the staff development needs of you and your colleagues?

How open should be the appraisal of needs in your school?

Are the review arrangements likely to be the same if the possibility of promotion is involved?

Step 2: Decide on and implement the general programme

The next step is to decide which needs should be given priority in any one term or year. An underlying problem is to be clear what exactly is meant by INSET. This discussion concentrates on activities which have it as their main aim, while recognizing that many normal school activities – like working parties and team-teaching – have considerable INSET spin-off. A second problem is to decide just how much to tackle without outside assistance. Some activities, particularly those that are school-based, can be planned and implemented internally. Others, particularly longer courses, will be suggested or requested in broad outline only, the detailed planning being left to someone like an LEA adviser or college lecturer.

Before any programme or activity can be planned or requested the staff need information about the range of providing agencies available. Although universities, teachers' centres, colleges, and advisers will usually be well known, it is easy to forget that other agencies, for instance, reading centres, radio and television, may have something valuable to offer: a place for teachers from several schools to hold a joint conference; reprographic equipment and technical expertise to assist a group making reading games for older infants; a large collection of children's literature and someone who knows what is available; an Open University series which could be used in a staff discussion group. Perhaps most important of all, are not teachers in the same and other schools themselves valuable 'providing agencies'?

Staff also need information about the type of INSET available. Outside courses, short and long, award-bearing or not, will probably be uppermost in their minds and the great value of such INSET should certainly not be underestimated. However the wide variety of options, both in terms of courses and other approaches, is worth stressing, as the following examples indicate:

A home economics teacher spends a day in another school to find out about a new child-care course.

Two deputy heads in very different primary schools exchange jobs for one week to broaden their experience.

A large comprehensive school timetable frees staff for one week each year to work on materials preparation with the resource centre coordinator.

Two colleagues in the same school systematically observe each other teaching over a term and discuss their observations after each session.

A group of comprehensive school staff developing a new integrated-studies curriculum invite a teachers' centre warden to coordinate a term-long school-based course involving outside speakers.

A college of education offers a week-long course for primary schools for four weeks in succession. Each of four members of staff attend in turn thus having a similar experience. College staff follow-up by visiting the schools.

Two LEA advisers offer a school-based course of eight weekly sessions on primary maths. They spend from 3.00 to 3.45 working with teachers in their classrooms and from 4.00 to 5.30 in follow-up workshop/discussion sessions.

A university award-bearing course for a group of staff from the same school includes a substantial school-based component.

A school runs a conference on 'Going Comprehensive' which begins on Friday morning, in school time, and ends on Saturday afternoon. Outside speakers include a chief adviser, a comprehensive head, and a university lecturer. As a result, several working parties run throughout the following year.

Where staff meetings are to be used for INSET it is wise to have separate meetings for this purpose which are quite distinct from routine meetings concerned with general administration and the communication of information. Special meetings are variously labelled, e.g., staff seminars, staff conferences. If this technique is to be used it is important to choose issues which are relevant to the whole staff, to make sufficient time available for a thorough discussion, and to ensure, by means of either an introductory talk or a paper distributed beforehand, that the discussion is informed. Such principles apply equally to departmental meetings and those which are interdepartmental. Keeping a record of major points made and decisions arrived at for circulation and action is helpful.

The setting-up of working parties can be a useful device for examining issues and providing information and views upon which decisions can be based. The composition of a working party needs careful consideration; usually it needs precise terms of reference and a fixed date on which to present its findings. Given good leadership, a suitable input of papers and reading matter, and sometimes outside consultants, the experience of serving on a working party can be valuable. Working parties need not be drawn from a single school. Teachers from a secondary school and its associated primaries may well meet to discuss continuity in pastoral care and in different parts of the curriculum, staff from the science departments of several secondary schools might form a working party to discuss the content of a common science course for pupils in the first three years at secondary school.

Thus, in planning a programme to meet the identified INSET needs, several questions arise:

Which needs should have priority and what kind of criteria should be used to decide?
– those of individual teachers
– those of functional groups
– those of the school as a whole.

Are regular reviews of priorities feasible in your school?
– to meet short-term needs
– to meet medium-term needs
– to meet longer-term needs.

How do you think these priority needs can best be met? e.g., a longer, external course for individual staff
– courses, workshops, seminars, conferences for functional groups or the whole staff based either in school or elsewhere
– a staff working party
– visits to other schools
– collaborative teaching, e.g., team-teaching and observation of colleagues' classroom teaching.
– school or classroom-based external advice/consultancy for an individual or group for, say, a term.

What can the providing agencies in your area offer?
– courses – nonaward-bearing or award-bearing
– resources and facilities

– consultancy
– acceptable and relevant help
– a flexible response to requests for help.

Your LEA advisory service will have expertise which can help you in considering the answers to these questions.

Step 3: Evaluate the programme

Everybody agrees that INSET should be evaluated: the problem is to know how best to do it. School staffs may well want outside help with this important and difficult task, but the following questions and suggested answers should help to clarify some of the options.

Who wants to know and why?
– the teachers who participated in the activity
– the school
– the providing agency staff, e.g., college of education lecturers, LEA advisers, staff in the school with in-service training roles
– the providing agency itself
– those to whom the teachers or providing agency staff are accountable, e.g., the head, governors, parents, or LEA.

Who will carry out the evaluation?
– a teacher or group of teachers
– the head or senior staff
– the providing agency staff
– an LEA adviser
– an independent evaluator
– a working party representing different interests.

What will be evaluated?
e.g., – the achievement and worthwhileness of the providing agency's aims
– the achievement and worthwhileness of the participating teachers' aims
– the extent to which the experience aids the teacher's professional development
– the extent to which the event has given value for money.

How will the information be collected?

e.g., – document analysis of reports, records, minutes, etc.
– questionnaires designed for a specific INSET activity
– standardized achievement and attitude tests
– interviews: structured or unstructured
– observation: structured or unstructured
– reports of informal discussions and conversations
– written reports by participating teachers or providing agency staff
– audio or video-tape recordings.

Are the proposed evaluation methods feasible?
– in terms of the time available
– in terms of their acceptability to those involved.

What procedures, if any, will govern the collection and release of information about the activities and views of those involved?

e.g., – will they have any control over what is collected and reported and
     how it is used?
– will they have the right to reply to reports of their activities and views?
  will their replies be incorporated into the final report?
– will the acceptability of methods of collecting data and reporting the
  results be negotiated with those involved?

What back-up resources are necessary for the efficient conduct of the evaluation?
– equipment, paper, postage
– secretarial assistance
– working space
– special time allocation to those carrying out the evaluation.

How can you feed-back your views to the organizers so they can make any necessary improvements?

Step 4: Follow-up the ideas gained

It is important for teachers and schools to make practical use of the knowledge and skills gained. Some teachers may be ready to accept new responsibilities, for example, by acting as consultant to other teachers after attending a course on primary science. Their experience may be shared through staff seminars or departmental meetings, thus informing colleagues, arousing interest, and provoking discussion about the application of ideas and principles. Teachers' evaluations of particular courses are also helpful to others who are about to decide what training they wish to undertake.

If teachers are to develop and put into practice what they have learned, they require encouragement and support, especially from the head, but interest shown by other colleagues can be a great help and, for this reason, it may be profitable for two or more teachers to attend courses together. Support may also involve expenditure on equipment and materials.

Key questions about follow-up include:

What procedures are necessary to ensure that the school is made aware of the results of INSET undertaken by you and your colleagues?

How can serious consideration be given to changes in practice in your school when an INSET activity is ended?

Are there adequate resources – e.g., staff and time – to put the good ideas into practice?

If you came back from a course with much wider professional horizons, what kind of 'reorientation' arrangements would you like?

Ways and means

If INSET is to be effective it will require adequate resources. First and foremost, careful thought has to be given to ways of organizing the release of teachers. At one end of the scale individuals may be pursuing academic or specialist studies at universities or training institutions which require full-time or part-time release for a term, a year, or longer; at the other end of the scale a teacher may require half a day to visit a neighbouring school. Such varied demands require a flexible approach to the release and replacement of teachers.

All needs cannot, and should not, be met in teachers' own time. There is now widespread recognition that, at any one time, a proportion of the teaching force should be released for INSET, including induction. Indeed, there is a national commitment to the figure of 3% release by 1981 and ways must be found of translating this into local action, for example, to ensure the replacement of participating teachers. Teachers can do a great deal to convince local education decision-makers of the value and importance of INSET in maintaining and improving teaching standards through the development of the teaching force.

Of course, not all activities require release. In-school programmes include a variety of activities such as staff seminars, working parties, conferences, courses, school visits, and exchanges. Some of these may be held during lunch hours, after school, in the evenings, or on the day before a new term begins; some schools have used occasional closures; block timetabling and team-teaching may release all members of a department for meetings during school time; one teacher may take a class for a colleague or two classes may be put together for singing or story.

But time has also to be found for planning and coordinating a school's INSET policy. At the most basic level, there is a need for someone to coordinate information. Simply to display course lists on the staff notice-board is not enough; a member of staff should be asked to take responsibility for collecting, displaying, and disseminating information about courses to colleagues in the light of their known interests and responsibilities. Schools which have professional tutors usually see this as part of their role. In secondary schools this may be taken on by a deputy head in association with heads of departments while in primary schools it is most often managed by the head dealing directly with individual teachers.

The same person can take active steps to seek information and advice from outside. Few schools have enough expertise among the staff to cover adequately all aspects of their work. It is therefore very helpful if you and your colleagues can call on a knowledgeable outsider to observe what you are doing and discuss it in a sympathetic and constructive way. Having identified what is needed, this 'consultant' may then be used in staff training or may suggest how such training might be done and who could do it. LEA advisers are an important source of such advice and help. Numerous other people can and do fulfil this role: teachers' centre leaders, teachers from other schools, college and university staff.

In some schools the 'professional tutor' also chairs the committee or working party which plans the programme and is responsible for informing all staff about its aims, content, timing, and costs. Similarly, such people may represent the school on teachers' centre steering committees or on the LEA's INSET Advisory Committee.

Some underlying questions about ways and means include the following:

What arrangements are needed to plan and review priorities and programmes in your school?

Should there be a separate INSET staff committee?

Who is responsible on a day-to-day basis? e.g., for information provision, timetabling, and monitoring.

Are you assumed to be self-sufficient in determining your needs, or is there systematic provision for you to discuss your needs with a colleague?

What arrangements are needed to make the best use of outside help and advice?

What are the implications of 3% release for the school?

What are the costs of INSET in a school and how can they be calculated?

How can you get started on devising and implementing a policy in the school?

What do you think?

The ultimate outcome of INSET must be the improved education of children. It can help to achieve this by constantly improving the quality of the nation's teachers, but it can only do so if it is judged to be relevant by the teachers themselves.

This discussion has looked at tasks and opportunities from the viewpoint of the school and the individual teacher. It has argued that effective INSET will involve a variety of activities and that it can be initiated and planned by teachers and schools. The activities themselves may take place in the school or at an outside centre and may be provided by teachers or outsiders. Their focus may be upon the school, groups of staff, or individual teachers. This latter point deserves special emphasis. It is vital that individual teachers continue to be able to pursue their own professional and career development and to have the opportunity to attend longer award-bearing courses.

INSET is currently at a take-off point in this country. If it is to achieve its full potential then every teacher in every school needs to be involved in an ongoing discussion about it. This discussion has tried to offer some practical guidelines and questions. It doesn't contain all the answers, nor even all the questions.

CHAPTER 6.4

ANALYTICAL SKILLS AND THE UNIVERSITY TRAINING OF EDUCATIONAL ADMINISTRATORS*
James G. March

The context of training

I take a training perspective. What are the kinds of things that a university programme in educational administration should attempt to teach? The viewpoint is not heroic. I assume the educational apparatus will change over time, but that educational institutions approximately as we know them will persist. There will be schools, school districts, and colleges. I assume that the activities of administrators will be modified in the future, but that recognizably administrative roles will continue to exist in recognizably bureaucratic organizations. I assume that university schools of education will continue to develop and change, but that the fundamental role of the university in the training of administrators will not disappear.[1]

A professional training programme should provide opportunities for intellectual growth along several dimensions that are only loosely tied to immediately usable administrative skills. A university-trained educational administrator should be an educated person, capable of interpreting and elaborating ideas from the culture of intelligence. He should have an elegant appreciation of society, its problems, its heterogeneity, and its heritage.

This graceful wisdom of an educated person, however, is not enough. An administrator needs to be competent both in the fundamental skills of administration and in the basic technology of the institution he administers; and universities need to provide education in those competences if they are able to do so efficiently. Administration is a job, and it calls for talents. Some of those talents are learnable.

* The Journal of Educational Administration, Vol. XII, No. 1, May 1974, pp. 17–44.

The kinds of basic skills that a university programme in educational administration should attempt to teach are the skills that are useful, will be used, and can be taught. The trilogy is not redundant. We need to examine the problems of educational administration, and to be attentive to those problems. But we also need to be concerned with what educational organizations are, what educational administrators do, and what universities are good at.

Schools as organized anarchies

Educational institutions are organized anarchies.[2] By this I mean that they frequently exhibit three important, and troubling, features:

First, their goals are problematic. It is difficult to specify a consistent set of goals. Instead, goals seem to shift over time; they seem to vary from one part of the organization to another; they seem to be stated in terms that are hard to translate into action. There is conflict over goals, and the conflict is not resolved easily. Although it is sometimes possible to impute goals to the organization by observing behaviour, such imputations appear often to be unstable or to define goals that are not acceptable to all participants in the organization. The decision process seems to reflect more a series of actions by which goals are discovered than a process by which they are acted upon. Speeches on goals express platitudes that are not useful administratively.

Second, their technologies are unclear. Although we know how to create an educational institution, to staff it, and to specify an educational programme for it, we do not know much about the process by which it works. It does work, at least in some senses. Students seem to change. Moreover, we can duplicate our results. If we recreate the procedures in a new school, they will often have approximately the same outcomes. But we have remarkably little capability for designed change in the system. We do not, in general, know what will happen if we make changes; we do not, in general, know how to adapt the standard system to nonstandard students or situations. New occasions require a new set of trial-and-error procedures, either in the school or in an experimental laboratory.

Third, participation in the organization is fluid. Participants come and go. Students, teachers, and administrators move in and out. There is even more turnover in other participants or potential participants. Parents, individually and collectively, are erratic in their involvement; community leaders sometimes ignore the schools, sometimes devote considerable time to them; governmental agencies are active, then passive. All of the potential actors in the organization have other concerns that compete with the school for their attention. Thus, whether they participate in the school depends as much on the changing characteristics of their alternatives as it does on the characteristics of the educational organization involved.

Organized anarchies are not bad organizations. They are not unusual. Indeed, they are quite common. Decision situations involving problematic goals, unclear technology, and fluid participation are familiar to all types of organizations. They do, however, pose some problems for administrators, and particularly for our standard theories of administrative action.

The manager of an organized anarchy requires a modified theory of decision. Almost all of our current ideas about intelligent decision-making relate actions to preexistent goals that are clear and widely shared. A manager is directed first to determine his goals and then to act. Such behaviour is often possible and useful, but it is not always so. When he wanders into the domain of coalition decision-making or goal-free problem-solving, the administrator is little aided by our current ideas about problem-solving.[3]

The manager of an organized anarchy requires a normative theory for the allocation of attention. In a system in which participants wander in and out, outcomes frequently depend on the timing of involvement. Time and attention are key resources that need to be managed.[4]

The manager of an organized anarchy requires a new set of ideas about management. The fundamental postulates of management emphasize control and coordination of the organization with respect to a set of well-specified objectives. Where goals and technology are unclear and participation is fluid, it is not clear what to make of the usual managerial precepts.

What do managers do?

One of the persistent difficulties with programmes for reform in the training of administrators is the tendency to try to improve managerial behaviour in ways that are far removed from the ordinary organization of managerial life. Unless we start from an awareness of what administrators do and some idea of why they organize their lives in the way that they do, we are likely to generate recommendations that are naïve.

Henry Mintzberg has recently taken a careful look at the literature on managerial time-allocation and attempted to identify how managerial time is organized and what roles a manager plays within an organization.[5] The studies he reviews do not significantly involve educational administrators, but attempts to make similar studies of executives in educational institutions show similar patterns.[6]

With respect to the organization of time, these studies indicate that executives work long hours. The exact number of hours per week varies, but it is substantially greater than the number of hours worked by most nonexecutives in most organizations. Much executive work is brief, disconnected, incomplete, and initiated by others. Most time is spent in verbal interaction with others. Executives tend to move to problems and information that are specific rather than general, concrete rather than vague, solvable rather than impossible, and currently pressing and local rather than distant in time and place. Relations with subordinates and with individuals who are not in a direct line relationship within the organization occupy substantially more time than do relations with superiors. A considerable amount of time is spent in scheduled meetings.

Mintzberg also tries to identify the roles that a manager performs. His breakdown is based on data that are more difficult to interpret and, therefore, subject to greater doubt than the data on the allocation of time; but his categories are more carefully based on empirical observations than others in the literature and have some substantial implications for management training. From his analysis, Mintzberg deduces eight basic sets of managerial skills that would improve managerial performance in doing better what they now do.

1 Peer skills: The ability to establish and maintain a network of contacts with equals.
2 Leadership skills: The ability to deal with subordinates and the complications of authority, power, and dependence.
3 Conflict-resolution skills: The ability to mediate conflict, handle disturbances, and work under psychological stress.
4 Information-processing skills. The ability to build networks, extract and validate information, and disseminate information effectively.
5 Skills in unstructured decision-making. The ability to find problems and solutions when alternatives, information, and objectives are ambiguous.
6 Resource-allocation skills. The ability to decide among alternative uses of time and other organizational resources.
7 Entrepreneurial skills. The ability to take sensible risks and implement innovations.

8 Skills of introspection. The ability to understand the position of manager and its impact on the organization.

Although the process of deduction is not always clear, Mintzberg's judgements are informed by as good an understanding of what executives actually do as we are likely to obtain. If we are going to consider ways of improving the effectiveness of managers in their behaviour, as opposed to their 'function' or 'purpose' deduced from 'needs' or 'problems', we might intelligently start from here. In particular, if we wish to identify tools of analysis that will be used, they will need to be tools that match the pattern of managerial activities.

Five critical skills of analysis

If we are going to use universities effectively in the development and dissemination of critical administrative skills, we need to attend to the problems posed by the context of decline and by the nature of educational organizations, managerial work, and university comparative advantage. Not all problems can be solved, and certainly not by university programmes in administration. But there are some things that are relevant, appropriate to the things managers do, consistent with kinds of organizations in which they do them, and intellectually demanding.

I will mention five different analytical skills that seem to me to satisfy the criteria. They include:

1 The analysis of *expertise*. The management of knowledge.
2 The analysis of *coalitions*. The management of conflict.
3 The analysis of *ambiguity*. The management of goals.
4 The analysis of *time*. The management of attention.
5 The analysis of *information*. The management of inference.

Each of these skills is important to the problems facing the administrator; each is consistent with organized anarchies; each can be adapted to the things that managers do; each is appropriate to academe. Others might identify a different list. Mine has no necessary uniqueness. It is one person's view of some important problems and skills in administration and administrative theory.

Each of the skills is linked closely to the everyday requirements of managerial life, but each is clearly an intellective skill. Each involves a technology of analysis and thought. Each is based on the intellectual development of a scheme of analysis. Each is a tough problem, incompletely understood. Each demands a programme of research as well as a programme of training and testing. For each we have a start.

The analysis of expertise

Much administration involves managing the taking and giving of advice. Administrators deal with experts, and are experts. They give advice, and they take it. Both aspects are important. Indeed, both are important in a single relationship.

Consider the problem of dealing with individuals who have greater knowledge in an area than the administrator does but to whom he is not willing (or permitted) to delegate full responsibility for action. The situation is a daily one. Educational administrators confront experts on teaching, curriculum, finance, management science, research, construction, bus schedules, and the rest of the technical knowledge necessary to schooling. The level of expert sophistication often considerably exceeds that of the administrator.

Our problem is to specify a set of procedures for coping with differentials in technical knowledge. Imagine the following experiment:

> An administrator is presented with two individuals, each claiming to be certified as an expert on computer-assisted instruction. In fact, neither of them, one of them, or both of them may be expert. The false experts are all as highly educated as the real experts, have all had the same general kind of training, and have all been given a short time to familiarize themselves with the literature on computer-assisted instruction. The administrator is faced with a series of decisions on whether to buy equipment for a computer-assisted programme, if so, which equipment, which programme, and which organization for instruction. His problem is to solicit advice from the 'experts' in order to reach a decision.

Although such an experiment, or some variation on it, is quite feasible, we have not conducted it. We should.

We do not have a clear picture of how to analyse expert advice, but we do have a start. It comes, for the most part, from work on evidence and testimony in the law. The techniques are the techniques of interrogation and confrontation.

Interrogation is the skill of asking questions that solicit information on two critical issues. First, what can the expert say that is relevant to the decision problem? Second, what degree of confidence can be placed in what he says? These are the classic problems of testimony. They are, it should be noted, joint problems of the expert and the administrator. The expert, as well as the administrator, is uncertain about what information might be relevant and what degree of confidence to place in the statements he makes. This does not mean that the expert and administrator share the same perspective; they may be quite different. The expert may, in effect, be a salesman peddling a solution. The jointness of the problem is not destroyed by the conflicts of interest.

Skills in interrogation are learnable. The rules of interrogation that are taught in legal training have some difficulties as a model for administrators, and their basis in serious data is a little obscure; but they are a good start. They summarize a long history of concern by individuals of considerable intelligence and institutions of impressive durability.

Confrontation is a procedure of observation. We confront one expert with another and observe the interaction. Where do they agree? Why do they agree? Where do they disagree? What inference can be made from the disagreement? The main point to confrontation, however, is procedural; we wish to improve the quality of questioning. We proceed from an assumption that the quality of answers can be assessed if the right questions are asked. It is an interesting assumption, with substantial administrative significance.

In fact, both interrogation and confrontation require inferences to be made. The logic of those inferences is not well articulated or understood in the literature, but it seems to depend on several simple analytical assumptions:

1 *The homogeneity assumption*. We attempt to assess the competence of an expert by sampling from his knowledge. Since we have no independent way of knowing whether he speaks correctly in most areas of his expertise, we check his knowledge in some areas we have in common. If he knows what he is talking about there, we assume he probably knows what he is talking about elsewhere. We assume that the level of competence in the areas we cannot judge is approximately the same as the level of competence in the areas we can.

2 *The density-precision assumption*. It is harder to tell whether an expert's knowledge is correct than it is to assess the density of his knowledge. Does he know a lot of things that appear to be related? If he can recite facts, studies, theories, documents, reports, and obser-

vations, we are inclined to suspect that the precision of his knowledge may be greater than if he reports only a sparsely occupied memory. If he reports conclusions without a richness of detail in support, he is subject to more doubt.

3 *The independence of errors assumption.* We assess each expert's expertise by comparing his observations with the observations of other experts. In effect, we assume that the errors made by different experts are independent. Thus, we infer that if several experts say the same thing, it is likely to be true. An expert who says many things that other experts do not say is less likely to be reliable than is an expert who usually agrees with other experts.

4 *The distribution of confidence assumption.* In any body of knowledge, there is variation in the degree of confidence in which different beliefs are held. Individual experts who do not exhibit such variation are likely to be less well informed than those who do; the relative confidence an expert has in different statements is likely to be more reliable across experts than any absolute level of confidence he may express.

5 *The interconnectedness assumption.* Expert knowledge tends to be interconnected rather than discrete. There are theoretical interconnections and contextual interconnections. We infer that experts who report knowledge in terms of a series of independent bits of knowledge are either experts in a domain in which the knowledge is less reliable than others, or are themselves less reliable experts.

Clarification and elaboration of such assumptions would be of substantial significance to improving the way in which managers receive advice from experts. They would also help in the giving of advice. I have suggested that the relationship requires an assessment of what the expert can say that is relevant to the decision problem and an assessment of the degree of confidence that can be placed in what he says. Although there are frequently some elements of conflict between expert and nonexpert, the relation is nevertheless an interactive one. The expert needs to have the right questions posed in order to provide the right answers; he needs to solicit help in understanding his own confidence in his beliefs, particularly since the terms of confidence relevant to the manager may be quite different from the terms of confidence familiar to the expert in his other activities.

The expert and the manager also need to be wary of situations in which the assumptions by which the manager forms inferences may be quite incorrect. Knowledge is not necessarily homogeneous; density of knowledge is not necessarily correlated with precision; the errors of experts may not be independent at all; the variations in confidence across experts may be quite meaningful; knowledge may be quite unconnected.

Finally, the analysis of expert testimony (giving or taking) requires an awareness of the expert and the manager as actors. The taking and giving of advice are performances with certain rules that simplify the process at the cost of sometimes confounding it. So long as the rules of the performances are satisfied, we are inclined to certify the 'expert' as expert and the 'manager' as manager. Since socialization into the performances is a part of the training to become one or the other (or both), most experts know how to play expert and choose to do so; most managers know how to play manager and choose to do so. An expert or manager who does not know how to play the role, or chooses not to, will sometimes confuse the process. This is particularly a problem with an expert who, though entirely competent as an authority in his field, is inexperienced in the role of giving advice; or with a manager who, similarly, is inexperienced in taking advice. Expertise in the relation is an important aspect of success.

The analysis of coalitions

An educational manager is a builder of political coalitions. The process is not identical to the process in governmental affairs, but key elements are the same. Different individuals and groups bring different interests and objectives to the organization. The interests vary in their mutual compatibility partly as a consequence of the form they take, but also partly as a consequence of the alternative combinations of policies and options that are provided. Administrative skills at coalition-building and assessment are the skills of developing and exploiting nonuniqueness in coalition solutions.

The technology of coalition-building can be moved from a relatively pure art form practised with various levels of success by different managers to a learnable skill. The technology requires more development, but the rudiments are there. The rudimentary base for the techniques lies in a simple perspective on decision-making:

> We assume that any decision can be made *if* there is enough support for it within the constituencies of the organization. In order to secure support, various trades are undertaken. A policy proposal is modified to include (or exclude) items of concern to key potential supporters; agreements are made to trade support on future issues for trade on current issues; arrangements are

made to encourage third party intervention. A market in political horse-trading is established; an omnibus policy is developed.

This perspective on decision-making has been developed over many years of research into political negotiation. Although most of the ideas were originally spawned within political science for the analysis of governmental politics, they extend easily to other organizations.[7] What makes them interesting from the point of view of educational management is not only that they appear to capture some significant truth about organizations, but also that they have been specified with enough precision to allow some efforts at simple skill development.

The analysis of ambiguity

Educational administrators are involved in decision-making under ambiguity. That is, not only are they uncertain about the consequences of alternatives. They are also unclear about their goals, uncertain of their technology, and unaware of their alternatives. They need help in defining how decisions are made under such situations.

Our usual management recommendations are classic: If you do not know what your objectives are, take the time to identify them. If you do not know what your alternatives are, search until you find them. If you do not understand your technology, undertake research (or hire consultants) to establish the cause-and-effect connections in your activities.

Such recommendations are not wrong; but they are frequently inadequate. Experience with efforts to establish goals is often positive. It generates attention and interaction. As a side-effect, people worry about the organization and each other; they talk to one another. But the process is slow and the output rarely precise enough or stable enough to be of much decision help. The idea of establishing goals first and then acting has some limitations as a model of behaviour.

The search for alternatives is often important, but it is rarely improved by the simple injunction to search. What are the techniques of search? Where do alternatives lurk? How do you invent new alternatives? How do you find alternatives that have been invented? How do you avoid the creation of pseudo-alternatives as ways of making a preferred alternative look good?

Recently, there have been some efforts to invent some ideas for goal-free problem-solving. They occupy some of the current literature in psychotherapy, problem-solving, and leadership. The techniques are not well established, but they are close enough to imagine that something is already known and further analytical tools are likely to be possible.

Probably the most difficult domain of analysis is developing some ideas of how we can act without knowing the objectives of our action. In terms of our standard theories of intelligence, such a conception is nonsensical. We are deeply committed to the idea that goals come first and actions should be related to those preexisting objectives. Elsewhere[8] I have tried to suggest some reasons why such a conception is overly limiting and some ideas about the possibility of acting without a good reason and the possibility of discovering goals through behaviour. A major concern in any such effort is how managers might plausibly relax the requirements of consistency in order to experiment with doing things for which they have no good reason and with alternative conceptions of themselves.

I think an analysis of the problems of decision-making under ambiguity suggests some things that a manager can reasonably do:

1 He can treat goals as hypotheses. He can experiment with imagining that he wants something other than what he now believes he wants in order to test his beliefs.
2 He can treat intuition as real. It is not obvious that intuition is any one thing, or anything. It is, however, an excuse for acting differently and an alternative way of consulting our intelligence.
3 He can treat tradition as meaningful. In our efforts to glorify the ability of an individual to comprehend his world, we sometimes overlook the attractive coercion of traditional rules as a device for discovering goals.
4 He can treat memory as an enemy. Rationality and consistency require a memory, and for most purposes good memories make good decisions. But the ability to overlook, or forget, is also useful.
5 He can treat experience as a theory. He needs to revise what he has learned yesterday on the basis of his interpretations of today, and to try alternative rewritings of history.

All of these are adaptations of devices more familiar to discussions of behavioural pathology than they are to our usual understanding of managerial behaviour, but I believe they provide some clues on how to introduce a more inductive version of managerial goals.

The general ideas extend easily to the problems of educational organizations:

1 We need to reexamine the functions of management decision. One of the primary ways in which the goals of an organization are developed is by interpreting the decisions it makes, and one feature of good managerial decisions is that they lead to the development of more interesting value premises for the organization. As a result, decisions should not be seen as flowing directly or strictly from a preexistent set of objectives. Managers who make decisions might well view that function somewhat less as a process of deduction or a process of political negotiation, and somewhat more as an opportunity for upsetting preconceptions of what the organization is doing.

2 We need a modified view of planning. Planning in organizations has many virtues, but a plan can often be more effective as an interpretation of past decisions than as a programme for future ones. It can be used as a part of the efforts of the organization to develop a new identity that incorporates the mix of recent actions into a moderately comprehensive structure of goals. Procedures for interpreting the meaning of most past events are familiar to the memoirs of retired generals, prime ministers, business leaders, and movie stars. They suffer from the company they keep. In an organization that wants to continue to develop new objectives, a manager needs to be relatively tolerant of the idea that he will discover the meaning of yesterday's action in the experiences and interpretations of today.

3 We need to reconsider evaluation. As nearly as I can determine, there is nothing in a formal theory of evaluation that requires that the criteria for evaluation be specified in advance. In particular, the evaluation of social experiments need not be in terms of the degree to which they have fulfilled our *a priori* expectations. Rather we can examine what they did in terms of what we now believe to be important. The prior specification of criteria and the prior specification of evaluation procedures that depend on such criteria are common presumptions that restrict the serendipitous discovery of new criteria. Experience should be used explicitly as an occasion for evaluating our values as well as our actions.

4 We need a reconsideration of social accountability. Individual preferences and social action need to be consistent in some way. But the process of pursuing consistency is one in which both the preferences and the actions change over time. Imagination in social policy-formation involves systematically adapting to and influencing preferences. It would be unfortunate if our theories of social action encouraged leaders to

ignore their responsibilities for anticipating public preferences through action and for providing social experiences that modify individual expectations.

5 We need to recognize the role of duty and obligation. Recent work on organizations has emphasized theories in which individual action is intentional and self-interested. Such theories account for important aspects of behaviour in organizations; but they ignore the significant ways in which action follows a logic of obligation rather than a logic of choice. By developing systematic systems of duty we introduce a strain between current conceptions of self-interest and the claims of duty. As a result, we can encourage the reconciliation of the two through creative elaboration of goals.

6 We need to accept playfulness in social organizations. The design of organizations should attend to the problems of maintaining both playfulness and reason as aspects of intelligent choice. Since much of the literature on social design is concerned with strengthening the rationality of decision, managers are likely to overlook the importance of play. This is partly a matter of making the individuals within an organization more playful by encouraging the attitudes and skills of inconsistency. It is also a matter of making organizational structure and organizational procedures more playful. The managerial devices for maintaining consistency can be varied. We encourage organizational play by permitting (and insisting on) some temporary relief from control, coordination, and communication.

I am not sure where we go from here. Clearly, we need a better idea of how we should decide which among all of the possible foolish things we might do is most likely to lead to attractive new conceptions of ourselves and our organizations. We need better notions of the costs and benefits of playfulness. The problems of decision-making under ambiguity, however, are conspicuous problems for educational administrators. They are not a residual category; they are a major category. They require the development and use of new kinds of techniques.

The analysis of time

Educational administrators, like other managers, operate under time constraints. Time is a scarce good. As a result, the procedures by which time is allocated are of some significance to the management of an enterprise. Recent research has indicated that many administrators (including those in education) have the subjective sense that their time is badly allocated.

As I noted earlier, Mintzberg has described management time allocation as it appears in a series of recent studies:

> The manager feels compelled to perform a great quantity of work in an unrelenting pace. . . . [His activities] are characterized by brevity, variety, and fragmentation. . . . Interruptions are commonplace. . . . [He] gravitates to the more active elements of his work – the current, the specific, the well-defined, the nonroutine activities. . . . [He spends] most of his time in verbal contact. . . . [Nonline] contacts generally consume one-third to one-half of the manager's contact time. . . . Subordinates generally consume one-third to one-half of the manager's contact time. . . . On the order of 10 percent . . . of his time [is spent] with his superior.[9]

Students of executive behaviour have noted the extent to which the allocation of time is dictated, out of the control of the executive.

> A President's priorities are set not by the relative importance of a task, but by the relative necessity for him to do it. He deals first with the things that are required of *him* next. Deadlines rule his personal agenda.[10]

> The latent absurdity of being the executive leader of an organization that does not know what it is doing haunts the presidential role. That sense of absurdity is somewhat ameliorated by a pattern of attention that reinforces a feeling of reality for the role. This means a busy schedule, the press of work, the frequent reminders of the fact that one *is* the president, the attention to minor things one *can* do.[11]

At the same time, there have been efforts to develop techniques for the management of time. In effect, these efforts start with an economizing view of time-allocation. The manager considers alternative uses of his time in terms of the return each provides. The cost of attending to one problem is not attending to another. The broad implications of such a view of a 'rational' allocation of time are contrasted with a broad view of the allocation of time generated by the behavioural process within an organization. On the basis of that comparison, some areas of over- and under-allocation of time are identified; and some techniques for introducing shifts in the allocation are proposed.

The analysis is close enough to being useful to warrant more development even though we may have some doubts about the kinds of recommendations that are usually generated now. If we take a conventional view of a manager's role, we would expect his high leverage activities (i.e., those with a relatively large return per unit of time spent) would include long-run planning, nonprogrammed tasks, general consideration of overall objectives, systematic surveys of the organization for potential problem areas, and the establishment of major strategies. Despite the widespread acceptance of a view of executive leadership that lists such matters as being of first concern, most studies of actual management indicate that such activities represent relatively minor claims on the total time in a manager's day.

The usual analysis then proceeds to suggest some ways in which the activities that are apparently overallocated (e.g., ceremonial activities, short-run decisions, idle chatter, interpersonal interaction, deadlined commitments, minor actions, etc.) can be reduced in favour of the underallocated activities. The methods are ordinarily some mixture of conscious rationing by the manager to replace the reactive pattern of much of his life, and the development of staff to perform some of the functions to which the manager currently attends.

The problem is probably more subtle than current solutions suggest. The solutions seem significantly to misunderstand what a manager does with his time and why he does it. For example, conventional enthusiasm for time spent on long-run planning and overall objective-setting seems to me excessive. I think a case can be made for the proposition that activities normally used to accomplish such goals are rarely worth significant amounts of administrative time. Similarly, I suspect that many current advocates of time-management overestimate the importance of thinking time as something distinct from sequential action to crises. The model of thinking as an activity that is inconsistent with acting seems unlikely to capture very much of the real process of management.

These potential quarrels with the details of some current recommendations, however, should not discredit the effort to develop a good analysis of how time is used and how it might be used better. We need to develop routine procedures for reporting time-allocation. We need to understand the rough character of the return to time-investments. Most managers, for example, seem to operate on the implicit assumption that managerial time on a problem or in a single contact has a strongly negative first derivative with respect to time. Such a conception seems to be quite possibly correct and to have considerable implication for time management. It suggests that managers should try to encourage many brief contacts rather than a few long ones.

At the same time, we should be able to move from an improved understanding of the decision process to a clearer idea of how an educational administrator might spend his time if he wants to accomplish a programme. For example, one analysis[12] of college administration lists the following key attributes of decision-making in organized anarchies:

1 Most issues most of the time have *low salience* for most people. A major share of the importance an issue gains is related to its symbolic significance.

2 The total system has *high inertia*. It is hard to start and hard to stop.

3 Any decision can become a *garbage can* for almost any problem. What problems are attached to which choice is heavily dependent on timing.

4 The decision process is easily subject to overload.

5 The system has a *weak information base*. Histories and current statuses are obscure.

Time analysis points to the two-sided nature of time as a scarce resource. On the one hand, since time is scarce, it needs to be rationed. On the other hand, since time is scarce, the willingness to provide time places one in a strong position. Thus, when a set of simple tactical rules is derived, many of them become rules for managing one's own time, exchanging time and energy for acquiescence, or managing the time of others.

Specifically, the analysis leads to eight tactical rules, of which four are connected directly with time-management:

1 Spend time. Since time is scarce, the willingness to provide time considerably increases the likelihood of being present when things happen and provides a resource that permits exchanges.

2 Persist. Do not assume that the mix of individuals and interests that decided things yesterday will return today. If defeated today, return tomorrow. If victorious today, beware of a new combination of people tomorrow.

3 Overload the system. When time is scarce, an overload on the system produces decisions that are more in the control of relatively full-time participants.

4 Provide garbage cans. Manage the time of others. Provide opportunities for them to exercise problems away from your concerns.

Although such recommendations are clearly subject to qualifications, they indicate some of the possibilities for the systematic management of time based on an analysis of the role of time in the organization.

Finally, it should be possible to develop some clearer ideas about the impact of deadlines on time-utilization and techniques for using deadlines. Weiner has shown how deadlines affect the organization of time in a public school decision.[13] Particularly where there is a conflict of interest, he has suggested some strategies for the use of deadlines that operate to aid allies and confound opponents.

Managers not only impose deadlines; they also react to them. The description of managerial time-allocation makes it clear that deadlines are an important factor in the time-pacing of managerial life. This opens up the possibility that a manager might be provided a strategy for creating and responding to deadlines on his own behaviour. Such a strategy would build on some notion of the time distribution of response to deadlines of various sorts, an area of research that is quite feasible but barely begun.

The analysis of information

Decision-making in education involves data. There are data on student performance, exposure, background, and capability. There are data on teacher training, assignment, reputation, and cost. There are data on facility utilization, cost, expected life, and design. There are data on administrator experience, training, responsibilities, and performance. There are data on birth and mobility rates; on experience with alternative programmes; on aspects of other school districts; on the relation between educational output and the weather, social structure, cultural tradition, physical surroundings, diet, and investment. There are data; the data are often relevant to some decision; they are usually incomplete or subject to some error or indecisive; as a result, they require some kind of inferential judgement.

The obvious answer is an understanding of statistics. It is a correct answer. Statistics, and particularly management statistics, are well-developed domains of analysis. They do not qualify as 'new developing' techniques in the same sense as the other cases. However, educational administrators are notoriously undertrained in statistics; in so far as they are trained in statistics, they tend to be trained in the wrong kind of statistics.

It is difficult to defend the present ideology or practice of quantitative training for educational administrators. The dominant ideology is that administrators should (as a part of their doctoral training) learn the quantitative techniques of the research scientist – most commonly those of the educational psychologist. The secondary ideology is that, as future chief executives, they do not need any serious exposure to formal skills in quantitative analysis. They can always hire a statistician.

Neither ideology seems defendable to me. To suggest that senior administrators should not have the professional skills to deal with data is to handicap them in any serious effort they might want to make to manage or lead the organization. I have argued elsewhere some of the reasons why the technology of decision-analysis is not, in itself, adequate for a manager. I will repeat that assertion here. But an ability to make inferences from data is certainly necessary.

At the same time, however, it seems to me inefficient, and often quite misleading, to base the statistical training of managers on the statistics of behavioural science. If the student goes far enough and achieves a high enough degree of sophistication, he can see that the logic of decision and the logic of research are similar; but the recognition of that fact is not trivial. It is almost never a part of the elementary training in statistics provided the administrator and reinforced by reading he may do in the professional educational literature.

In so far as statistics is taught to educational administrators, the teaching tends to emphasize description, experimental design, and hypothesis-testing at an elementary level. Despite the fact that such a focus has been built into the sacred beliefs of the profession, various departments of education, and inumerable schools of education, they are usually the wrong kind of statistics for the problem faced by an administrator.

What underlies this failure in analysis for administrators is the curious relation between administration and research in the social system of education. The educational administrator is supposed to be certified as an educational researcher. This makes him vulnerable to the methodology of the research establishment; he accepts it. On the other hand, he doesn't ordinarily use it. The research is often not relevant to his problems and the results are often stated in a form he cannot use. For example, relatively few administrators (or students of administration) appear to be aware that the statement that there is 'no significant difference' between two treatments (or groups) is notably different from the statement that the two treatments are probably equal.

The research/administration relation needs to be strengthened by the development of genuine decision-analysis skills among administrators; we need first-class analysts of decision data. The technology of decision statistics exists. It needs to become a part of the basic administrative repertoire and of the research concerns of programmes in educational administration.

Conclusion

I have tried to identify five critical analytical skills. They are, I believe, central to the job of most high-level educational administrators. The management of expert knowledge, the management of conflict and coalitions, the management of ambiguity, the management of time, and the management of inference from incomplete information are all consistent with the criteria I suggested earlier. They are relevant to the problems an administrator faces; they are appropriate to educational organizations; they are attentive to the way an administrator defines his own job through his behaviour; and they are consistent with the comparative advantage of the university.

References

1. Mayhew, L.B. *Changing Practices in Education for the Professions*, Atlanta, Southern Regional Education Board, 1971.
2. Cohen, M.D., March, J.G., and Olsen, J.P., 'A Garbage Can Model of Organizational Choice' *Administrative Science Quarterly*, XVII, 1, March, 1972, pp. 1–25.
3. March, J.G., 'Model of Bias in Social Action', *Review of Educational Research*, XLII, 4, March, 1973. pp. 413–429.
4. Cohen, M.D. and March, J.G., *Leadership and Ambiguity: The American College President*, New York, McGraw-Hill, 1973.
5. Mintzberg, H., *The Nature of Management Work*, New York, Harper & Row, 1973.
6. Hemphill, J.K. and Walberg, H.J., *An Empirical Study of the College and University Presidents in the State of New York*, Albany, Regents Advisory Committee on Educational Leadership, 1966, Cohen, M.D. and March, J.G. op. cit.
7. Baldridge, J.V., *Power and Conflict in the University*, New York, John Wiley, 1971; March, J.G., 'The Business Firm as a Political Coalition', *Journal of Politics*, XXIV, 4, October, 1962. pp. 662–678; Wirt, F.M. and Kirst, M.W., *The Political Web of American Schools*, Boston, Little, Brown and Company, 1972.
8. March, J.G., 'Model of Bias in Social Action'. op cit.
9. Mintzberg, H., op. cit., p. 171.
10. Neustadt, R.E., *Presidential Power: The Politics of Leadership*, New York, John Wiley, 1960, p. 155.

11. Cohen, M.D. and March, J.G., op. cit., p. 150.
12. Cohen, M.D. and March, J.G., op. cit., pp. 206–216.
13. Weiner, S.S., *Educational Decisions in an Organized Anarchy*, Stanford, Stanford University Doctoral Dissertation, 1972.

SECTION VII

THE MANAGEMENT OF CONTRACTION

CHAPTER 7.1

CONTRACTING SCHOOLS: PROBLEMS AND OPPORTUNITIES
Tony Bush

The inevitability of contraction

Demographic trends make a contraction of the schools' service inevitable, perhaps even desirable. The cold figures show just how much the market for schools has declined. The number of births in the UK fell from a peak of 1,013,000 in 1964 to only 657,000 in 1977, a drop of 35%. The figures for the same years for England and Wales are 886,000 and 569,000 – a similar percentage fall. No organization or service can be unaffected by such a dramatic drop in demand. In any language, fewer clients means a reduced service. It is inevitable and the full acceptance of this inevitability by all concerned with education is an important first step if the problems of decline are to be tackled and the opportunities of contraction grasped.

There will be geographical variations in the rate of decline and a very few areas may avoid falling numbers as immigration compensates for the reducing birth rate. By contrast, some areas are experiencing a greater than average rate of decline, and this is particularly the case for England's big cities. Live births in Manchester, for example, fell from 13,600 in 1964 to 5,600 in 1977, a drop of some 60%. The implications for cities like Manchester are stark. The schools are emptying at an alarming rate. The problems posed by falling numbers would be minimal if central and local government decided to maintain current levels of spending in education despite the fall. Some teachers and teacher unions cling to this view. Fred Jarvis spoke for many on this issue at the 1979 NUT Conference. 'The question of educational expenditure and resources is absolutely central to what the schools can achieve. . . . We must insist that far from there being further cuts in expenditure, cuts which have been made should be restored.'[1]

Such a policy may well be desirable but it is not realistic and it tends to divert attention from the real issue of coping with contraction. A few economic considerations expose the fallacy of such optimistic thoughts. There is no economic growth and we may well be entering a period of absolute decline. Within this static or falling national product the Conservative Government of 1979 has indicated a preference for private spending rather than public spending by its policy of tax and expenditure cuts.

Public expenditure is set for stagnation or absolute decline and within the total education will not receive a high priority. The government has an ideological commitment to higher spending on defence and law and order. Moreover, demography will tend to determine increased spending on health and possibly social services. How can education, with a sharp fall in the number of its clients, compete effectively with services whose clients are the rapidly increasing elderly population? Demographic and economic considerations combine to ensure contraction for Britain's schools.

The problems of contraction

There are four issues which appear likely to pose serious problems during the period of contraction.

The curriculum

The number of teachers employed in any school is determined almost universally by the device of the pupil/teacher ratio. This ratio is determined individually by local education authorities (LEAs). This local discretion gives rise to wide variations in levels of provision. In primary schools the January 1977 ratios were 18.9 in ILEA and 27.5 in Stockport while secondary ratios ranged from 15.6 in ILEA to 18.8 in Somerset.

The significance of the pupil/teacher ratio is that no policy changes are required to effect a reduction in staffing levels. Maintaining existing ratios in a period of falling rolls inevitably reduces staff numbers. Dudley Fiske, Manchester's Chief Education Officer, has predicted that the average eleven–eighteen comprehensive school will decline from some 900 to 1000 at the peak to a norm of some 600 to 700 pupils.[2] If the pupil/teacher ratio is 17 to 1, staff levels in this 'typical' school will fall from 53 or 59 to 35 or 41. Such dramatic falls in staffing levels have very serious curriculum implications and heads and senior staffs will face some harsh decisions. Some subject specialisms may well become luxuries that few schools can afford.

Eric Briault's research provides evidence of 'schools where only one foreign language was offered, where sciences could no longer be taught as separate subjects and where music had disappeared from the timetable'.[3] It is perhaps just as well (indeed suspiciously convenient!) that HM Inspectorate and others are advocating a core curriculum. 'It may be timely, therefore, to seek a new rationale of the secondary school curriculum and a simpler structure, with fewer options, in which all pupils carry forward a broader programme of studies until the age of 16.'[4] Staffing levels may make such proposals very timely indeed.

Teacher redeployment

In some schools pupil numbers may fall at a faster rate than teacher resignations. LEAs often respond to this by moving staff from one school to another. This has occurred to a significant extent in primary schools and will occur with increasing frequency in the secondary sector despite the inflexibility of teacher specialization. Redeployment is often unsatisfactory for the teachers concerned but it creates serious problems too for the head receiving redeployed staff. Traditionally the head has enjoyed a substantial measure of freedom in staff selection. That freedom is eroded if the LEA insists on the appointment of redeployed staff. Moreover, the quality of redeployed teachers is variable. Heads required to release staff will tend to retain the better teachers and allow indifferent people to go. Receiving heads thus not only lose the freedom to select staff but may have rather poor teachers imposed upon them.

Career progression

Promotion prospects in schools depend to a considerable extent on the Burnham group numbers and points score ranges. A six-form entry eleven–eighteen school with a sixth form of 100 is in group 11, with points in the range of 54–74. If this 'typical' school declines, as Fiske suggests, to four-form entry with a sixth form of 70, it will be in group 9 with a points score range of 35–49. Reviews of group numbers and points are triennial so this dramatic reduction would be achieved in two sharp stages.

The effect of falling points score ranges is to reduce the number of posts available above scale 1. Existing staff are protected at their present scale but promotion from scale 1 or through the higher scales will become more and more difficult. Robert Spooner sees declining promotion prospects 'as the largest fly in what I regard as a very beneficent ointment'.[5] In a graphic passage he outlines some of the implications of limited promotion opportunities.

> Now teachers are obliged to adjust themselves, sometimes as a result of harsh experience, to a slower and more uncertain climb, with fewer jobs to apply for, greater competition and a much more static situation in which long stints will be served in the same school without the fillip of promotion to counter a sense of stagnation and bleak moments of despair. It is not even a question of waiting for dead men's shoes as there is some risk that, with novel obsequies these will be buried with him.[6]

Staff frustration and demoralization are the inevitable consequences when career progression is determined, not by the ability of individual teachers, but as a result of a decline in school numbers. The situation is in direct contrast to that prevailing in the 1960s and early 1970s when demography determined rising school rolls and each triennial review produced a rich crop of extra posts at scales 2, 3, and 4. Then teachers gained promotion relatively easily, perhaps too easily, often before they were ready for the responsibility which accompanied it. As in biblical times, the rich years have been followed by the lean years. Now very able young teachers, more than ready for promotion, must kick their heels as staff only marginally older, and often less able, hold the promoted posts to which they aspire. Fifty percent of teachers aged twenty-five to thirty are on scale 2 and they and somewhat older colleagues block the way for the 84% of teachers under twenty-five who remain on scale 1.[7]

Closure – the ultimate consequence

One option which may become increasingly attractive to hard-pressed LEAs is to close some schools as numbers fall. Barely viable village primary schools become less viable and small secondary schools may find it more and more difficult to provide adequate curriculum cover, even with the newly fashionable 'core' curriculum. Falling rolls raise in stark form the once academic issue of the viable size for comprehensive schools. It seems that only yesterday educationalists were advocating six-form entry as a minimum for the all-through school. Now four-form entry is commonplace and there are many 3 F.E. and even some 2 F.E. comprehensives. Even with cooperation at sixth-form level and the establishment of more sixth-form or tertiary colleges, this cannot be the right response to falling numbers. Some schools must close to allow the rest to survive. I will return to this issue later in the chapter.

The opportunities of contraction

The issues discussed so far show a gloomy picture of the impact of falling numbers but fortunately there are some benefits to set against the problems.

Staff quality and stability

The period of rapid expansion for schools had an undeniable impact on the quality of staff teaching our children in both the primary and secondary sectors. Students were admitted to colleges with the minimum qualifications. That minimum of five 'O'-levels was abandoned long ago by all other groups with a claim to professional status. Many of those admitted to colleges were not sufficiently good intellectually for the demanding task ahead of them. The problem of quality was compounded by the colleges whose pass rate was consistently high.[8] The paternalism of many colleges led to marginally suitable students being deemed adequate teachers. This issue was glossed over by the DES and LEAs who were far more concerned with the problem of supply than the question of quality. Many heads and LEA officers (including the author) were forced into appointing poor quality teachers simply because the alternative was no teacher at all. A crude and unsatisfactory criterion, but in August in the early 1970s there was no other choice.

The prospect for the 1980s is substantially more attractive. New entrants to the profession will be better qualified than before. From 1981 the minimum entrance requirement will be two 'A'-levels with at least 'O'-level standard in both English and maths. The greater flexibility offered by incorporating much of teacher training in polytechnics and colleges of higher education is also to be welcomed. When the student, or his tutor, recognizes that the wrong career has been chosen it is far easier to switch to an alternative course when it is readily available within the same institution. Finally, it is far easier for individual schools, which now have several suitable candidates for each vacancy except in a few specialist areas, to ensure that only good new teachers are appointed.

The long-term impact of these developments will be a significantly better qualified and more able teaching force. In the short term there is far greater stability in the teaching staff of any one school. The corollary of reduced staffing levels and limited promotion prospects is that teachers will remain in one school for longer periods. A recent survey by the Assistant Masters and Mistresses Association shows that all 21 LEAs in Greater London had a lower rate of teacher turnover in 1977–1978 than in 1973–1974. The most dramatic improvements were recorded by Brent, where turnover dropped from 32.7% to 12.1%, and ILEA where the figures were 25.8% and 9.1% respectively.[9] It is acknowledged that continuity is of considerable benefit to young people. Higher quality and a substantial measure of continuity offer a better prospect for the 1980s than that offered to the children of the 1970s.

Accommodation

One of the problems of rising school numbers was that accommodation rarely seemed to increase in pace with the numbers. As a result, various unsatisfactory areas were pressed into service as classrooms. Most teachers have experienced teaching in canteens, cloakrooms, and corridors. This will not be necessary as pupil numbers fall. Many teachers have taught in 'temporary' huts that have a depressing air of permanence. The school building surveys showed that 1710 primary and 110 secondary schools had more than 40% of their capacity in temporary accommodation while a further 3160 primary and 510 secondary schools had more than 20% of their capacity in this form.[10] Soon many schools will not need temporary classrooms and teachers and pupils alike can work in more suitable permanent accommodation. In the days of rising rolls there were rarely enough laboratories, workshops, and other specialist areas. LEAs responded, if at all, by giving schools more and more of the ubiquitous 'mobiles'. The curriculum was often determined by the availability of specialist accommodation rather than by more fundamental educational considerations. As numbers fall the prospect is of classes being taught in that permanent accommodation appropriate to the subjects required to give a balanced curriculum.

Split-site schools

Schools on two or more sites have been an unwelcome by-product of amalgamated comprehensive schools. The impact of split-site working on the welfare of pupils and staff alike has been harmful. Moreover, the management problems for the head and his senior colleagues have been greatly underestimated by the politicians who arranged these 'shotgun marriages'. Declining rolls offer a good opportunity to reduce, and perhaps even eliminate, the split-site phenomenon.

Parental choice

All political parties pay lip-service to the idea of parental choice of schools, and the present government embraces the 'choice' philosophy more eagerly than its predecessors. The practice, rather than the principle, of choice is severely limited if the number of school places is equalled or exceeded by the number of pupils requiring a place. As numbers fall, however, it becomes easier to meet parental preference at both primary and secondary levels. This is to be welcomed because parents are more likely to support and cooperate with the school of their choice than one which has been foisted on them unwillingly. It is arrogant of educationalists to seek to limit parental choice in order to achieve a 'rational' solution to the issue of falling numbers.

Contraction – the way forward

The question of falling rolls is now well established as a major educational issue for the 1980s. Yet, as is so often the case in our diffuse educational system, response to this phenomenon is patchy. Action is needed urgently at all levels if the era of falling numbers is to be remembered as one of 'opportunity' rather than an era of problems.

Burnham points score ranges

A major overhaul of the Burnham points score ranges is needed urgently to improve promotion prospects for the able new teachers entering the schools. This can be achieved either by increasing the points available at each review average range or by increasing the unit value for pupils at each age. Action on this should be a major objective of the annual Burnham salary negotiations. The local authority associations may well argue that improvements here would be an expense difficult to justify at a time of tightening cash limits. I would suggest that a slightly smaller annual salary increase would be an appropriate sacrifice for teachers as a whole in order to minimize the frustration of those trapped on scale 1.

In addition, it is desirable for LEAs to be flexible in applying points in some ranges as the review average falls. They might decide to implement any reduction over a period of years or, more positively, to apply a greater proportion of the points available within a range. Some LEAs apply the minimum of a range while a few apply the maximum with most falling somewhere in between. In large secondary schools the difference between the minimum and the maximum would be some 20 promoted posts. The improvement in teacher morale and performance may fully justify improvements in this area.

Pupil-teacher ratios

There is widespread recognition that the pupil-teacher ratio cannot be applied rigidly as numbers fall. It must remain possible for specialist staff to be replaced, particularly in the smaller departments. Whereas it might be reasonable not to replace one of 6 or 7 staff teaching English, maths, or French it is not possible to maintain adequate curriculum cover if one of two German or music teachers is not replaced.

Nevertheless, it is unrealistic to expect LEAs to maintain anything like existing staffing levels as pupil numbers fall. The medium-term answer is a much more versatile teaching force. Staff capable of teaching two or more subjects, at least to 'O'-level, offer the head and his curriculum planners far greater flexibility than a staff composed entirely of single-subject specialists. An in-service training programme to promote versatility would be a very good investment even on crude economic criteria and would certainly enable schools to ride the bumps of falling pupil and staff numbers rather more easily than at present.

School closures

I suggested earlier that closure of some schools was necessary, even desirable, if the system as a whole is to remain viable and individual schools to stay healthy. This option is especially attractive in urban areas where the problem of travel is less acute. In any case it is the most densely populated urban areas which are experiencing the sharpest falls in pupil numbers.

The fundamental issue is that of determining the criteria to be applied in proposing schools for closure. One factor might be the age and quality of buildings. Another might be related to a policy of phasing out split-site schools. Or geographical considerations might suggest one school rather than another. All these factors, and others, might be relevant but it is naïve to believe that any of them can be the major determinant of a school closures policy. The overriding consideration must be the popularity of the schools. If parents believe that school A rather than school B will provide a better education for their children, then let officials and politicians alike recognize the reality of demand. To close school A and retain school B because it has better buildings or a better location is to deny parental preference and to reduce the level of satisfaction with the system as a whole.

Marketing – a task for the 1980s

Marketing is a major element in private sector management and is relevant to some parts of the education service, for example, public sector higher education. It has never played any significant part in school management because schools have not had to compete for pupils. Demand for school places has exceeded supply for so long that schools have felt able to concentrate on educating their pupils while largely ignoring the outside world.

In a period of falling demand, marketing must become an essential component of a school's management strategy. Schools must project themselves to their community and particularly to employers and feeder schools. Above all, they must explain curriculum change and seek, and respond to, parental opinion. If schools don't respond to their views, parents may vote with their feet and send their children elsewhere. In this respect, William Tyndale Junior School has a message for other schools. It is simple and stark – 'respond or die'.

Notes

1. Quoted in *Education*, 20.4.79, p. 451.
2. North of England education conference, 1979.
3. Quoted in *Times Educational Supplement*, 11.1.80.
4. Department of Education and Science, 1979, 'Aspects of Secondary Education in England', HMSO.
5. Spooner, R., 1979, 'The end of the ladder', *Education*, 4.5.79, p. 513.
6. ibid.
7. Figures derived from Wright, D., 1979, 'Management and motivation in a contrasting secondary schools system', BEAS Annual Conference, September 1979.
8. In 1976–1977, for example, 36,986 students passed an initial teaching training course while only 1674 failed, a pass rate in excess of 95%.
   Source: *Statistics of Education 1977*, Volume 4.
9. Quoted in *Education*, 23.2.79.
10. *Education*, 27.4.79.

CHAPTER 7.2

LIVERPOOL COPES WITH CONTRACTION AND YOUTH UNEMPLOYMENT*
Kenneth Antcliffe

In Liverpool, the education service has had perhaps three main preoccupations: falling rolls and their consequences, financial constraints, and youth unemployment. The problems, of course, are not unique to this authority but they do in this city loom larger than in many and create a background against which other activity has paler shades of significance.

In 1966 the number of live births was in excess of 16,000; in 1976 the figure was barely 6,000. The effect on school rolls has been even more dramatic than those figures would lead one to suspect because, in the same period, families were being rehoused outside the city boundaries with the result that there is now a vast surplus of school accommodation. The problems this sort of situation creates have been well rehearsed and are generally recognized but the change comes as a shock to those who worked in the service through the years of rapid expansion and one senses more alarm than relief at its implications.

But the contraction can be seen as an opportunity rather than a disaster and the authority has, despite the financial constraints, tried in a number of ways to take positive decisions to turn the situation to advantage. Recognizing that the age-structure of its teacher force and the declining mobility of its teacher force generally would make it impossible to effect reductions in teacher numbers proportionate to the annual reductions in pupil numbers (which will continue until the mid-1980s), the authority decided to use this opportunity to move to the progressive achievement of the pupil-teacher

* *Education*, 21 September 1979, pp. 308–309.

ratios set out in 1965 in the ninth report of the National Advisory Council on the Training and Supply of Teachers. Those ratios seemed, in the context of the still expanding numbers of 1965, unattainable – even unrealistic – and one seldom sees reference to them today so that it may be helpful to quote them:

	Ratio
Primary schools	19.7:1
Secondary schools:	
11 to 16 year olds	16.3:1
16-plus	10.6:1

In Liverpool they have not yet been achieved but they are in sight and it is almost impossible to overstate the value this will bring to the schools and their children compared with the ratios which existed when the advisory committee made its recommendations in 1965.

The decline in the number of live births seems to have been arrested in Liverpool and has remained steady at the 1976 figure for the past three years. Some optimistically believe the trend of the 1966–1976 decade may be reversed at least to some extent but, even if that optimism proves unfounded, there is enough hard evidence to conclude that the period of contraction in school rolls will end in the mid-1980s and the schools will enter a phase of much needed stability. Until that happens anxieties are bound to remain.

One startling effect of these changes over the past five years can be seen through the induction scheme for probationer teachers. When the pilot induction scheme began in 1974 it was dealing with 750 probationers; in 1975, 450; in 1976, 280; in 1977, 170; in 1978, 110; and this year a mere 70. It is difficult to see that figure rising in the next six years. Quite apart from the regret that this brings that fewer opportunities can be offered to newly qualified young people, it has important implications for the future age-structure of our teacher force and, as soon as we can, we must try to get the balance right. Years ago we scarcely gave this problem a thought. We were only desperate to reach our 'quota' of teachers in the days when the quota system operated. Today we have redeployment schemes and, more recently, early retirement schemes in our attempts to even out our distribution of teacher resources and achieve a balance in our age-structures. It is a very difficult task as any other authority experiencing or facing the same realities will recognize. There is no simple solution in the short term and it requires the most understanding relationships between the teacher associations and the authority to work towards a longer-term solution.

As everyone else, we have gone through a rough period and may well face more. The authority's view on teacher staffing has already been explained. Not so very long ago the now defunct Association of Education Committees used to give guidance to local education authorities in conjunction with the National Book League as to what might be the 'good' levels of allowances to schools and otherwise. Long ago, Liverpool elected to provide the Association of Education Committees' 'good' levels of allowance and, in all the pressures of the past few years, the authority has sought to maintain this level in spite of the effects of inflation. Though we seem to face greater financial problems next year and in the years immediately ahead, this is one sacred cow which will not be sacrificed without bloodshed. Schools need teachers and the teachers need the tools. Simplistically that might be taken as a view of the authority's priorities though, of course, they are much more complex than that.

Liverpool has a long-standing problem of unemployment to which there is no simple or speedy solution. Whatever the national level of unemployment that in Liverpool is twice as bad and so it has been for some years. Perhaps for the education service the most alarming aspect of this problem is that of unemployment among young people. The number of young people registered as unemployed has peaked above the 10,000 mark each August for the past five years and this bleak prospect has had a noticeable effect on the motivation in the classroom.

Such a problem cannot but be of concern to those in the education service. But how to help, given all the constraints, presents a challenge to which we have not been accustomed and which our traditional patterns of provision do not meet. Of course the abler and more strongly motivated will find their way into appropriate training in our colleges of further education. But the greatest problem lies with those who left school with minimum levels of attainment – those whom the system failed and who failed in the system. There is little previous experience of dealing with this group in postschool years. They have shunned a system which appeared to shun them and, in the further education field, there was always good reason to devote resources to other purposes.

Nevertheless, there was a need for the education service to respond in some way to this problem alongside the Manpower Services Commission provision for Job Creation Schemes and its later Youth Opportunities Programme. The colleges of further education could make a limited contribution constrained by lack of space and by their geographical location. But there was surplus capacity in schools and, not unexpectedly, the surplus was greatest where the unemployment levels were highest. Could this resource then be used to alleviate the problem? If it could, then how could the courses be staffed?

The answers to these questions depended very much upon the flexibility of the service. Of course there was, at the very least, some suspicion about the suggested use of surplus capacity in schools for young people no longer of school age. The department of Health and Social Security were prepared to pay unemployment benefit only if the courses offered were less than full-time. That was defined as not more than 21 hours of tuition per week. But might not this concession dissuade potential sixth-form students from continuing at school full-time when they could leave but return part-time and draw unemployment benefit? Would not this element of part-time low-achieving students who might well be reluctant to accept the norms of school régime disrupt the normal functioning of the school? If the only way for the authority to staff these courses was by recruiting unemployed teachers funded under the Job Creation and later the STEP scheme, what guarantee could there be that these inexperienced teachers could make the scheme work? All these and more were legitimate questions which gave rise to suspicion and doubt.

Nevertheless, when the proposition was put to the schools there was in some a ready, in some a cautious, response which ended in 17 schools eventually participating. Perhaps surprisingly there was a more varied response to this development than we most optimistically anticipated. The target group was the sixteen- to nineteen-year-old but others beyond this age-range and into the thirties were attracted. We were thinking mainly of those who were of lower attainment than GCE or CSE examinations provide for. In the event, the teachers found themselves dealing with a range of need from the barely literate to the potential Ordinary and Advanced level. It proved to be very much a case of devising courses for individuals drawing, wherever practicable, on the specialist skills of the permanent teacher force of the school.

The scheme, advertised locally under the heading 'Return and £earn', is still continuing and we hope will do so at least as long as present problems of unemployment persist. It has taught a number of lessons and, as experience grows, may well teach more. Firstly, it has shown that many who were thought of as having rejected the system are ready to respond if the system can be reshaped to suit them. Secondly, it is evident that learning motivation, not particularly strong in school years, can strengthen with maturity and when the lack of it is seen to place barriers to prospects. Thirdly, it has revealed the extent of the gaps in our school-based preparation of young people for the needs of working life which suggests the need for a close examination of what we do. The list could become tedious but one more should be included and that is the evidence now revealed that, in our provision for further and adult education, there is an enormous area of unmet need which stretches far beyond the very proper aims of the adult literacy schemes.

This is, of course, a mere glimpse of some of the aspects of the education service in Liverpool chosen to show how the authority has tried to respond to circumstance by making opportunity. If there had been no fall in school rolls we should not have been able to house the Return and £earn schemes. If there had been no Return and £earn schemes many young teachers employed in them would have had no teaching appointments in this city. Without the schemes, many young people would have had no opportunity to retrieve past failures. Significantly, most of them have left the schemes for work or other training. Equally, most of the teachers have found permanent jobs.

CHAPTER 7.3

MORALE, MOTIVATION, AND MANAGEMENT IN MIDDLE SCHOOLS
Colin Hunter and Peter Heighway[1]

Introduction

The current education scene is dominated by the problems caused by contraction and constraint in comparison to the expansionist period of the 1960s and early 1970s. These problems are focused on economic cuts and falling rolls in schools. Both are independent variables but they have become linked within political and administrative contexts. This chapter attempts to identify these trends at a national, structural level and to connect these with their perceived effects on the morale, motivation, and management of heads and teachers in the middle schools studied.[2] Alternative strategies for coping with these problems are discussed at personal, institutional, and structural levels involving concepts of career, participation, and 'creative turbulence'.

Trends and problems outlined

The first trend is economic. The rise of oil prices and the growth of earnings were two basic reasons the Labour Government in the mid-seventies defined the controlling of inflation and the regeneration of industry as their main priorities. Accordingly, there was a reduction in real terms in public expenditure which led to stringent cuts in education spending. These affected such basic requirements as school equipment and materials, maintenance of buildings, and numbers of nonteaching staff. The enthusiastic official campaign for the continued reduction of class numbers suddenly became quite muted. After a relative relaxation of cuts in the preelection year of 1978, the incoming Conservative Government has effectively spread 'moral panics' throughout the education service with one of its major priorities of cutting public spending. Already schools are trying to absorb short-term crisis measures, with promises of more substantial long-term cuts in the rate support grant.

The other trend is demographic, involving a real and projected falling birth rate with a corresponding fall in school rolls. There have been cut-backs defined largely by political rather than educational criteria in school buildings and resources, and a drastic reappraisal of teacher training which has involved halving the yearly output of newly trained teachers in the eight years between 1973 and 1981 (i.e., 40,000 to 20,000 (DES, 1977, p. 24)). The demographic predictions used are that the primary school population is likely to fall from the 1979 figure of 4.6 million, to 3.4 million in 1986 (=26%), and the secondary school population from 4.1 million (1979) to 2.8 million in 1991 (=32%) (DES Report, 1978).[3]

There is a third trend involved, however. As the economic and demo-graphic trends have validated a quantitative contraction in resources and manpower in schools, the qualitative expectations have risen. The recent 'great debate' and much subsequent public discussion have highlighted the criticism that schools are not providing suitable recruits for 'the needs of industry'. A common theme is that schools and teachers need to be more 'accountable' to the wider society and so curriculum reform, testing, and assessment (and more 'adequate' discipline) are said to be required to raise the 'standards' which many believe have fallen in recent years.

It is argued here that the effects of these trends are the basis of a recent lowering of morale in schools in that teachers are faced with consequences of falling rolls and higher expectations of others in a nonexpanding service where there is a rapid decrease of teacher mobility between and within schools. While it is acknowledged that elements of these trends include positive aspects such as experienced teachers and greater stability, the consequences for the management of schools are potentially critical in that a 'career' in teaching, based on an expanding service, is being eroded. The continuance of such a career structure crucially negates the development of alternative, and perhaps more relevant, organizational arrangements which may enhance the morale and motivation (and hence effectiveness) of many teachers.

The traditional concept of career

Becker has used the concept of career as referring to 'the patterned series of adjustments made by the individual to the network of institutions, formal organizations, and informal relationships in which the work of the occupation is performed' (1976, p. 75). In teaching this corresponds closely to his 'vertical aspect' of career in that the Burnham scales of salaries related to positions of responsibility are connected with the numbers and the age of pupils in schools. Falling rolls therefore decrease the possible posts for promotion, and particularly for the newer entrants to the profession.

Not only are the numbers of opportunities for promotion contracting, but fewer people are leaving the profession. In 1972, for example, 9.5% of teachers left teaching and a further 11% changed schools. In 1976 wastage was only between $6\frac{1}{2}\%$ – $7\frac{1}{2}\%$ and in many urban authorities turnover was less than half the 1974 figure. The effects of these trends at a national and structural level were clearly mirrored in the schools visited in the first part of our ongoing study.[4]

A problem most clearly and frequently mentioned in our inquiry was the lack of mobility between schools. As one probationer put it – 'People are just stuck here, they can't move.' One head and another school's deputy head pointed out that movement through promotion, now that the middle schools are established, had tended to slow down almost to a standstill, and that increasingly change is often based on either female members of staff leaving because they are pregnant, moving away because of a change in husband's job, or through 'natural wastage'. One respondent had been teaching since 1964. In seven years he had taught at three schools and gained a scale 3 post. After eight years at his present school he felt that:

> I am beginning to get a bit frustrated. In normal circumstances I would have had a good chance of a deputy headship a couple of years' ago. I'm beginning to wonder what I will do now. Mind you, I don't want the other staff to know that.

It may well be that the last remark infers a more realistic expectation of promotion in that, what in previous years would be publicly accepted aspirations, now remain private hopes hidden from colleagues who may remain his associates for many more years. One head at a 'commuter school' thought that this lack of movement of staff was a disadvantage with staff likely to stay 'five, ten, or even till they finish'.

It was mostly heads and deputy heads who talked of another danger of little staff movement – that of teachers getting 'stale' or 'falling into a rut'. One other head talked at great length of the dangers that such stability could bring with it the tendency for frustrated teachers to 'satisfice' rather than 'optimize' their opportunities. (See Perrow, 1973, p. 284.) That is, some would take the easy way out, and get by in their teaching with as little effort as is required.

One of the conclusions he drew was that such teachers may have a more powerful influence in the school than in the past because they will remain on the staff with their growing disenchantment, rather than having moved elsewhere and possibly gained some rejuvenation from a new situation. Such an ethos could begin to percolate through the staff, so that a uniform approach to teaching could be adopted by the staff as a whole. One probationer saw the dangers inherent in this:

> Without any new blood entering from the outside, or without any exchange of ideas, I could see a particular style of teaching developing.

In further studies of other middle schools by the teacher group (see note 1) this last point has clearly been illustrated. Among other points which are emerging consistently is the frustration of some teachers with some of their colleagues who seem to fulfil the minimum requirements ('the nine to four brigade') while receiving similar financial rewards to those who are involved in extracurricular activities, though these sentiments were rarely openly expressed. At two schools in particular there has emerged a clear division between the younger staff who are involved with the children in field studies, trips, camping, drama, and music activities, while the older staff with higher responsibility allowances for administrative duties involving a lower timetable commitment are seemingly able to fulfil their obligations without much effort. A newly appointed head to one of these schools which is severely affected by falling roles, in answering the question 'Can you identify any effects on your school of having a number of staff for a long period of time?' wrote, 'They become a very tight group, and become complacent and isolated.' To the question 'Can you give examples of the effect on the curriculum of low staff turnover?', he answered, 'The curriculum becomes fossilized, long-term aims become lost. People pursue their own interests.' With regard to the last point the 'teacher group' has been struck by the growing evidence of 'moonlighting' jobs undertaken by colleagues. This seems to be linked to the degree of commitment to the job of teaching itself, and to the growing disenchantment caused by the erosion of the Houghton relativities since 1975.

These points can be related to Beckers' further ideas on career (1977, p. 57) where he introduces the notion of 'situational adjustment' in which individuals take on the characteristics required by the situation they participate in. This notion can be closely connected to his other notion of commitment, for if the actor has developed a secure and nonthreatening situational adjustment, then the commitment will be directed to preserving the status quo (see ibid, p. 62). This has been illustrated in three ways in the study so far:

1 Some teachers prefer the maintenance of the status quo in that they have positions of seniority and prestige defined within the terms of the prevailing structure.
2 They have become committed to their situation because of the routine they have developed to suit the school's requirements, and the relationships they have built up with others in the school organization make the present situation a comfortable one.
3 The present situation may be so demotivating 'because it denies them the means, the chips, with which to make side-bids of any importance' (ibid, p. 62), that commitments for personal fulfillment are focused elsewhere than in the classroom or school towards which a purely instrumental attitude is formulated.

The strategy that all have in common is a resistance to change in the basic structure and organization of the schools so that issues such as economic cuts and falling rolls are seen as threats. Both 'commuter school' heads of the initial study saw an answer to motivation based on the professional career structure as it is constituted at present. Crucial to this is that there should be schools big enough to carry enough scaled-posts to make a structure viable 'which will keep the teachers happy'. The head described the optimum structure, in his opinion, in detail:

> I would have head, deputy heads in the plural, talking now in terms of Group 7 school, scale 4 posts for year heads, scale 3 posts for senior subject departments, scale 2 posts for more minor responsibilities, and scale 1 posts. Then you've got a career structure in a middle school which is meaningful, which promises the prospects of promotion to the groups on the lower scale, and which creates an organization which ensures that everybody gets some kind of attention.

It could be significant that this approach was linked to a philosophy of the middle school which clearly maintained the dichotomy of primary and secondary schools within it, with a bias towards the secondary approach – 'after all we're a ten to thirteen school with two-thirds of children in the secondary group anyway, so certainly I would say that the school is secondary oriented anyway' (head). This orientation is consistent with the career structure outlined above in that it is based on specialization. Although the West Riding middle school philosophy is identified by the head and deputy at the level of rhetoric – they were definitely of the opinion that 'a middle school *ought* to be an extension of a *good* primary school' (head) – in practice they felt that the buildings and resources that such a philosophy requires were unsuitable for the *raison d'être* of middle schools – that of making an easier and smoother progression from general to specialist teaching to meet the requirements of the secondary school.

The argument is that this goal can only be achieved if there are a majority of specialist teachers defined as 'somebody who is trained as a specialist', and you can only get them if you pay them, and you can only pay them if you've got a career structure, 'which in turn is dependent on the size of the school'.

This is a consistent argument which is fundamentally based on a hierarchical system with motivational 'carrots' consisting of higher positions in the organizational structure. Departmental and year-group meetings are spoken of in terms of the opportunities given for the direction of others by heads of departments or year tutors, and falling rolls are seen in terms of making specialist building and curriculum areas available to pupils earlier than at present to meet the secondary school academic requirements. This approach has its advantages in that it is based on the traditional system in which most teachers are at present socialized.[5] This point was illustrated by four nonadministrative teachers who connected lack of motivation with the necessity of teaching curriculum areas in which they felt incompetent. One probationer argued:

> The lack of motivation may come from having to teach in areas where we are unsure. I think this is happening here to some extent. At fourth-year level I teach my class for several subjects. In a secondary school there was a clearly defined sphere of competence that does not happen so much in a middle school, and it is difficult too . . . well, for instance, I am English trained and I don't always feel safe in class subjects in the same way that I do in English.

The in-service coordinator at one of the urban schools felt similarly that:

> I am English trained – and don't like having to teach maths. God, some days
> I'm only just in front of the twelve-year-olds – that makes me feel bad.

Another probationer, a specialist craft teacher, found that he could go to in-service training sessions during the day, but that in-service courses for general class teachers were held after school, which could mirror differing levels of status within in-service priorities. This 'traditional' approach then could be the most practical answer to future organization of schools in that it takes into account the present system, and mirrors the identified requirements of even recently trained teachers. There are other points, however, to be taken into consideration. Firstly, this approach enhances the process towards the teacher becoming more isolated. As one teacher put it, 'We used to work in a very open situation, but the doors are closing. I've seen that happen gradually over the last two years.' A deputy head thought that he detected the classrooms becoming like 'little boxes' and 'private units' and the increased specialization advocated in middle schools in this approach would accelerate this process.

The second point concerns the attitude towards power that this approach engenders.

The higher up the hierarchy people go, the greater their power and the resources and opportunities at their disposal to keep themselves motivated, and, crucially, the opposite is the case. In this type of situation the possibilities of 'silting up' or 'falling into a rut' or being 'content to plod along', for those who are restricted in terms of resources and opportunities, become understandable coping or survival strategies.

Thirdly, such an approach is necessarily based on contingencies which lie outside the control of the school in the political, economic, and demographic spheres. The head with the 'traditional' approach was asked what he would do to keep the teachers motivated if the optimum numbers required for the career structure outlined fell, due to a lowering of school population: 'I hope there is a terrific influx of people into this area, and a massive building programme,' or, more seriously, he hoped that the boundaries of the catchment area would be changed. Otherwise the total number of pupils would drop 'to the region of 450 which I think will be too small – neither one thing nor the other'.

It could be argued that this 'traditional' approach is really offering old answers to new problems, and, by being based on hierarchical and static notions of organizational structure and power distribution, is ultimately incapable of coming to terms with the problems that staff stability, motivation, and morale of teachers and falling pupil rolls present.

An alternative 'progressive' concept of career

There is, however, evidence to suggest that many schools and teachers are making positive 'situational adjustments' to the economic and demographic trends outlined at the beginning of the chapter. Firstly, not all consequences of the changing trends were viewed negatively. One deputy head especially looked forward to the effect of falling rolls in that there would be more space available in the school; lower forms could have greater access to specialist facilities; and timetabling would be made easier. One head thought that there may be more generous staffing ratios available, and also space to develop 'resource banks' if there were fewer classes. From a different organizational viewpoint another head welcomed stability because, 'on the whole I do not want to develop and train staff simply for them to go and get a job elsewhere'. In some ways this more parochial view will be better suited to the newer stable situation than the 'bargaining' strategy of another head whose approach was – 'If they [the staff] can give me three good years and I can help them to climb the ladder I'll be very happy.' The nonadministrative teachers were more likely to point to the advantages stability gave to the pupils – especially with regard to better systems of pastoral care – 'The kids get to know the teachers and the teachers get to know the children,' as one probationer put it. The same teacher also pointed out that one advantage to her of limited possibilities for promotion was that it eased the pressure of having to conform to the expectations of the hierarchy in order to gain good references for other jobs and that she felt more free 'to do what you like in the classroom'.

Secondly, what also emerged was broad agreement on some of the requirements that were needed in the present contracting situation – especially as it affected middle schools. The first point was that smaller schools will necessitate teachers covering larger areas of the curriculum, and fewer opportunities for specialization. One head saw his school changing 'to being more general subject-oriented over the next five years simply through the decline in numbers'. Another head agreed in that he said he was increasingly looking for very versatile people, and this seemed to describe an efficient 'jack of all trades'.

This is close to the thinking of yet another head who regarded falling rolls as requiring 'tremendous improvisations' from the staff. It is at this point that a basic paradox emerges with regard to the development of middle schools. When they were opened and developing in the last ten years or so there was a great deal of turbulence caused, in that new organizational forms, age-groups, educational philosophies, and curriculum innovations were being carried out in a volatile teachers' market with a good deal of movement between schools – exactly at the time when such schools needed more stable staffs. Now that middle schools have become more established and the need for fresh ideas from new people has become more important, there is a slowing down of movement between schools. One head alluded to this when he said:

> Stability is obviously great so long as it does not mean repeating the same thing year in, year out. You want people, I think, who are willing to tackle more areas of work and this is more readily obtained if you have a steady input into the schools of people with fresh ideas who are willing to try things.

This movement of staff is less likely to happen in that there seems a general agreement that promotion when it occurs should be given internally. As one head put it, 'I'm not going to advertise for a scale 3 post, I can tell you from the start.'

The position therefore presented is one in which the staffing is more stable so that the development of the school can be viewed from a more long-term perspective; but at the same time there has to be interest and motivation engendered which cannot necessarily be implemented through rewarding staff with promotions of scale posts, as defined at the present time.

An alternative strategy has emerged which involves a more open interpretation of participation and the notion of 'creative turbulence', as opposed to the static nature of a 'silted up' situation, or to strategies which simply react to the vicissitudes of constantly changing external constraints, or to use Becker's terms, situational adjustments without a stabilizing long-term commitment. This alternative strategy for situational adjustment (labelled here 'progressive') involves a *long-term* commitment to the educational requirements of pupils and a professional basis of teacher involvement within a view of participation which includes a notion of power that is not regarded as a limited 'commodity', but which is defined as expandable participation. If it cannot be shared *explicitly* through appointments to hierarchical positions, then it can be done *implicitly* by the involvement and opportunities for initiative given to the whole staff regardless of organizational status. One head sees his role as facilitating and developing this process:

> One of the things we must do is give people status . . . they must be made to feel important. . . . As far as possible we must create situations from peoples' interests . . . it is a question of developing skills . . . and in any case to make sure leadership roles are not static.

A number of examples were given in the schools as to how this might work in practice. They included the 'young chap who is keen on rural studies' who, when he organizes weekends for pupils, 'takes charge in every sense'; the young English teacher who was able to use her specific skills and take over the leadership of a teachers' meeting to inaugurate an interclass project; and the art teacher who was willing and able to extend art into other areas of the curriculum.

Three of the four heads emphasized that all the staff should be able to have their say, to have a hand in the planning of aspects of the school, and that opportunities for control and involvement should be widely distributed. In such a flexible, open situation the problems of staleness or silting up could become less acute, for by generating turbulence, it is argued that freshness and interest is maintained. This was previously attained by the movement of staff between schools. One head in particular now tries to produce the same effect by moving staff, with their cooperation, within the school.

> After two years in a particular year-group I would like to think I could move a teacher out into another year-group. I think if we are effective as teachers we are far more effective if we are in a learning situation, and once we pass that learning situation I don't think we are as effective as we were.

Another way in which motivation was encouraged through the generation of 'turbulence' was by giving opportunities to all staff to be 'involved' in curriculum development – either through formal discussion or through negotiating the timetable. With regard to planning, one head believed that:

> If they have personal interest in some particular aspect, in something they have agreed is worthwhile, they are going to push it. They are going to be more motivated than if they had just taken someone's edict to put into practice. . . . So, I've tried here to involve people in curriculum planning, not just in their participant area, or their interest area, but in the whole lot. So if

you have a staff meeting on some area, say maths or . . . what . . . home economics, I would expect all members of staff to chip in – even though perhaps they wouldn't be involved in teaching it.

The extent to which this actually happens in practice is of course open to empirical study (see for example Hunter, 1979a) as are the effects of the 'negotiated' timetable in which participation is built into the organizational structure. In this the year heads are in charge of a year group's timetable, and they have to consult with heads of departments and/or individual staff for their time; or departments and/or individual teachers offer 'packages' to negotiate with year heads their preferred timetable. The necessary coopera- tive spirit between teachers to make this open form of organization viable is constantly alluded to by most of the staff interviewed, usually in a positive manner, in particular at three schools. As the in-service coordinator com- ments:

> The things that have kept me going are two people in the classroom. It makes a big difference when you know there is going to be someone working with you. It affects your preparation – there is a pride thing involved.

One deputy head felt that there must be a positive feedback coming out of this cooperation, to the individuals involved. The point often made in educational theory that the teacher's colleagues are the most influential role-set[6] was constantly underlined and, interestingly, often in terms of referring to the reactions of those at the top of the hierarchy. A deputy head put it this way:

> One of the important things is the attitude of the hierarchy to what a teacher is doing. They must make teachers realize that they understand what the teacher is doing is good.

Another connection with the staff motivation often repeated is the rela- tionship with pupils: 'to feel that you are getting through', 'you're picked up by the children', 'the job satisfaction comes from the kids', 'getting the children on our side', etc. are representative examples.

Although it could be argued that the 'progressive' answer confronts the evolving problems of staff stability, motivation, and falling rolls to a greater extent than the 'traditionalist' answer, there are also dangers and weaknes- ses inherent in this approach. It is possible, for example, that too much 'turbulence' could become disfunctional. As the deputy head of one school suggested after explaining the open system, in which there was an intense, pressurized atmosphere 'constantly revitalizing and rethinking what we are trying to do', he yearned for a period to 'reassess what we're doing, to recharge the batteries. I think I'm arriving at the point where you wouldn't mind a settling down period and a routine situation.'

There seems to be an optimum level of turbulence which needs to be grounded on a secure base for it to be creative rather than destructive. There is also a possible tension between the ability and the willingness for teachers to cooperate and teach with other staff, and the need – expressed particularly by the probationer in the 'traditionalist' school – for personal autonomy and freedom in the job situation. It may well be that this delicate balance between cooperation and autonomy should be met at individual teacher level rather than at a wholesale school policy level. If the socialization of the teacher is oriented to reinforcing separate, rather than cooperative, teaching activities, it could well be that this more open approach in solving some problems could generate others.

Another possible weakness in the approach is identified in a comment in parenthesis of a head who, while making the point that low status, 'junior' positions in a hierarchy demotivated teachers, then went on to say: 'Poor teachers need direction; good teachers need choice.'

An open system, as advocated above, presumably needs to take into account that some teachers might not be able or willing to take on the duties and responsibilities that such freedom entails. As one head, in another situation, wrote in a memorandum to his deputy, 'Unless you go with Mrs. X and Mr. Y, on their school trip, it is off. There is no way I'm letting them loose with children.' Any 'open' structure would need to take into consideration the capabilities of individual teachers in order to incorporate safeguards, as there are many constraints involved in preventing the fulfilment of an ideal type of open or 'progressive' answer.

Some exploratory conclusions

It seems that there could be a need in situations where morale and motivation is low and where there is a stable staff for 'creative turbulence' to be engendered or facilitated, while recognizing that it is possible for too much turbulence to be demotivating. Given the resulting constraints and possibilities of falling rolls and economic cuts it is postulated as a hypothesis that the prime (but not only) source of higher morale and motivation lies initially within the school itself rather than central government or local authority centres.

Such aspects as school-based or school-focused in-service training[7] and development of staff could become an integral part of the ongoing structure of the school. Greater participation in curriculum planning, assessment procedures, and organizational decision-making could be elements which generate wider accountability and responsibility-sharing in a more open organistic school structure, rather than in the closed mechanistic management structures which still exist. Such changes give cause to review fundamentally the roles of teacher, head, head of year/department, etc. in the light of the potentially changing career structure in the teaching profession due to decreasing mobility between and within schools. Questions which could arise from such an agenda may include the following:

Is the position of head too central and dominating on the running of schools? Why are ongoing training schemes for heads not part of their contract? (as they are in Sweden – see Mats Eckholm 1977). Might short-term contracts be a possibility? Might it be possible to move a proportion of teachers and heads around different schools to try and engender turbulence and alleviate the possible silting up effects of static staffs?

Might the whole concept of 'career' in the teaching profession be reviewed? Instead of the Burnham System, which is basically geared to expansion, might a more flexible arrangement be formulated which could simplify the often elaborate structures of school management and give greater recognition to those who retain a full teaching timetable? Dudley Fiske (1979) suggests that a possible way is to give a basic career grade for a teacher which is adequately renumerated, and then the posts of responsibility, at present given extra payments, could be recognized instead by a reduction of timetable and teaching loads. Might such a system offer greater possibilities for posts of responsibility to be rotated round the staff, thereby offering greater involvement and participation for a greater number of teachers?

To what extent should local authorities help? By making available staff developmental tutors? By encouraging developmental curriculum teams from a number of schools? By motivating schools in the planning to meet the needs of falling rolls?[8] What should the function of the local advisers, or HMIs, be? What should their relation be to elected members?

Such basic questions need to be reviewed in a changing situation, and the situational analyses should take into consideration the structural basis of many of the constraints. The present situation of contracting resources and falling rolls in schools offers tremendous problems with regard to morale, motivation, and management while based on outmoded premises of career, success, and involvement. It offers opportunities, however, if the premises of decision-making and management change to meet new requirements. The basis of identifying, planning, and executing the accomplishment of these opportunities could lie in transcending the dichotomies of turbulence and stability, direction and choice, cooperation and autonomy within schools by a negotiated, shared commitment of LEA officials, political representatives, and teachers in the school levels controlling the situational adjustment, rather than reacting in an atomized and fragmented way.

Notes

1. This study originated in the spring of 1979 as a cooperative venture between Colin Hunter and Peter Heighway, the latter being seconded for one term to Bingley College. Since then a group of West Yorkshire (mostly middle school) teachers have joined together to share experiences and case study material and explore possible avenues of research. Some of this latter work is included here, though a full report is to be published later this year. This study is therefore based on early preparatory work and does not seek to provide answers but to clarify some pertinent questions.

2. A recent trend in the sociology of education has been the attempt to link the phenomenological and structural approaches by connecting the experiences of teachers and pupils in everyday classroom and school life with wider societal processes. (See Bernstein, 1975; Banks, 1978; A. Hargreaves, 1978; Hunter, 1979b). In C. Wright Mills' terms this involves clarifying the interpretations of personal troubles with public issues, for the 'sociological imagination' is to him, 'the capacity to range from the most impersonal and remote transformations to the most intimate features of the human self – and to see the relationship between the two' '1970, p. 11). It is perhaps in this area regarding economic and demographic structural trends as public issues, and their effect on the personal troubles of administrators, politicians, heads, teachers, and pupils that this synthesis can be illustrated clearly.

3. The distribution of the national and intralocal authority falling rolls will vary according to geographical area, building programmes, etc. In Leeds, for example, the projected decline in middle schools is 25% between 1979 to 1986 though this is concentrated in the inner-city rather than the outlying areas in which, in some schools, the rolls are rising. (See Cracknell, 1979.) Alternatively, in Bradford, it is in some inner-city schools that rolls are rising due to the concentration of new Commonwealth ethnic minorities.

4. Most of the material used here is taken from the pilot study of four middle schools. One in South Yorkshire and one in a large metropolitan district were in urban situations (the former an EPA school). Both had been opened, for ten years, and had to some extent pioneered the ethos of middle schools as distinctive and new educational establishments. They had in the region of 450 pupils and

had purpose-built facilities. The other two schools were in a rural/commuter area in West Yorkshire. The largest (650 pupils) was housed in an adapted secondary school and had been functioning for eight years, while the smallest (400 pupils) was purpose-built and had a shorter history of four years. Five people were interviewed in each school, including the heads and deputy heads, and the designations of the other teachers are given where appropriate. Interviews were open-ended and tape-recorded.

5. For a fuller discussion of this point see Bartholomew (1976) and Wardle and Walker (1979).

6. See, for example, D. Hargreaves (1972, p. 402).

7. See Henderson (1977) and Sayer (1977) for a discussion on the difference between and efficiency of school-based and school-*focused* in-service training. The latter is preferred as being less parochial and more outward-looking. It is 'a synthesis of the course-based and school-based models, but emphasising the direction of INSET towards the immediate and specific needs of one school and its teachers' (Henderson, p. 6). Conference paper – unpublished.

8. 'It was not the case of the Authority finding the answers and simply applying them, but of each school, in close association with the Authority, facing up to the implications and shaping its own future' (Cracknell, 1979, p. 266).

References

Banks, O., 1978, *School and Society in Sociological Interpretations of Schooling and Classrooms: A Reappraisal*, Barton, Len and Meighan, Roland (eds), Nafferton Books.

Bartholomew, J., 1976, 'Schooling Teachers: The myth of the liberal college', in *Explorations in the Politics of School Knowledge*, Whitty, Geoff and Young, Michael (eds), Nafferton Books.

Becker, H., 1976, 'The career of the Chicago public schoolteacher' in *The Process of Schooling*, Hammersley, Martyn and Woods, Peter (eds), Routledge & Kegan Paul.

Becker, H., 1977, 'Personal Change in Adult Life' in *School and Society*, Cosin, Ben et al. (eds), Routledge & Kegan Paul.

Bernstein, B., 1975, 'The Sociology of Education: A brief account' in *Class, Codes and Control*, Volume 3, Routledge & Kegan Paul.

Cracknell, D., 1979, 'Consultation and Planning in Leeds', in *Education*, 14 September 1979.

DES, 1977, *Education in Schools, A Consultative Document*, HMSO.

DES, 1978, Report on Education, 'School Population in the 1980s', No. 92, HMSO.

Ekholm, M., 1977, *School Header Education in Sweden*, School Header Education, Box 249, 581 02 Linkofing, Sweden.

Fiske, D., 1979, *Falling Numbers in Secondary Schools – Problems and Possibilities*, North of England Education Conference, 1979.

Hargreaves, A., 1978, 'The Significance of Classroom Coping Strategies', in

Sociological Interpretations of Schooling and Classrooms: A Reappraisal, Barton, Len and Meighan, Roland (eds), Nafferton Books.

Hargreaves, D., 1972, *Interpersonal Relations and Education*, Routledge & Kegan Paul.

Henderson, E.J., 1977, *School-Focussed Inset: Another Perspective*, Advisory Committee on the Supply and Training of Teachers. Conference paper – unpublished.

Hunter, C., 1979a, 'Control in the Comprehensive System', in *Decision Making in the Classroom*, Eggleston, John (ed), Routledge & Kegan Paul.

Hunter, C., 1979b, 'The Policies of Participation; with specific reference to teacher-pupil relationships', in *Teacher Strategies*, Woods, Peter (ed), Croom Helm.

Mills, C. Wright, 1970, *The Sociological Imagination*, Penguin.

Perrow, C., 1973, 'The neo-Weberian model: decision making, conflict and technology', in *People and Organisations*, Salaman, Graeme and Thompson, Kenneth (eds), Longman.

Sayer, J., 1977, *The School as a Focus for In-Service Training*, Advisory Committee on the Supply and Training of Teachers. Conference paper – unpublished.

Wardle, G. and Walker, M., 1979, 'Strategies and Structures: some critical notes on teacher socialisation', in *Teacher Strategies*, Woods, Peter, (ed), Croom Helm.

SUBJECT INDEX

References followed by n are to footnotes and chapter endnotes

AUTHOR INDEX

References in italics are to bibliographic details